3/22

A lovely present to myself!

$\frac{1}{10}$

URAL OWL.
SYRNIUM URALENSE.

EX LIBRIS

Gina Petermann Sidransky
Dec. 3rd, 1991

FOURTEEN NINETY TWO

By the same author

Ben-Gurion of Israel
To the House of Their Fathers
A Peculiar People: Inside the Jewish World Today
Weizmann: Last of the Patriarchs
A Woman's Way (with Flora Solomon)
The Letters and Papers of Chaim Weizmann (ed.)
The Essential Chaim Weizmann (ed.)
The Burning Bush: Antisemitism and World History

Fiction
Another Time, Another Voice

FOURTEEN NINETY TWO

The Decline of Medievalism
and the Rise of the Modern Age

BARNET LITVINOFF

CHARLES SCRIBNER'S SONS

New York

MAXWELL MACMILLAN INTERNATIONAL

New York   Oxford   Singapore   Sydney

Charles Scribner's Sons
Macmillan Publishing Company
866 Third Avenue
New York, NY 10022

Macmillan Publishing Company is part of the Maxwell Macmillan Communication
Group of Companies.

Library of Congress Cataloging-in-Publication Data
Litvinoff, Barnet.
    Fourteen ninety-two : the decline of medievalism and the rise of the modern age /
Barnet Litvinoff.
        p.   cm.
    Includes bibliographical references and index.
    ISBN 0–684–19210–1
    1. Europe—History—1492–1517. 2. Fifteenth century. I. Title.
D203.L58   1991
940.2′1—dc20   91–12428   CIP

Macmillan books are available at special discounts for bulk
purchases for sales promotions, premiums, fund-raising, or
educational use. For details, contact:

Special Sales Director
Macmillan Publishing Company
866 Third Avenue
New York, NY 10022

10 9 8 7 6 5 4 3 2 1

Designed by Nancy Sugihara
Printed in the United States of America

For Sylvia

. . . Si mi caccia il lungo tema,
che molte volte al fatto il dir vien meno.
Dante, *Inferno*, Canto IV

. . . Such is the theme, driving me forward by its extent,
that the telling often fails to convey the full reality.

CONTENTS

Illustrations   XI

Principal Personalities   XIII

Introduction   XVII

1   The World in Transition   1

2   Spain Returns to Europe   21

3   Christians, Muslims, Jews   41

4   Commerce Intrudes on Politics   63

5   Medici, Borgia and the Italian Paradox   83

6   The Voyage   105

7   Dreams and Realities of Empire   127

8   Leaders in the Hands of Fate   151

9   Dishonour Abounding   171

10   Twilight of the Lesser Gods   197

11   Habsburg over Europe   213

12   The Iberian Zenith   231

Select Bibliography   251

Index   257

ILLUSTRATIONS

Between pages 140 and 141

Ferdinand and Isabella of Spain, with their two eldest children *(Museo del Prado, Madrid)*

Alfonso of Portugal, with his heir Prince John and Henry the Navigator *(Museu Nacional de Arte Antiga, Lisbon)*

Christopher Columbus *(Metropolitan Museum of Art, New York)*

Pope Alexander VI

Columbus taking leave of Ferdinand and Isabella *(National Maritime Museum, Greenwich)*

The papal bull *Inter cetera* dividing the world

Maximilian I, Holy Roman Emperor *(Kunsthistorisches Museum, Vienna)*

Michelangelo's David , Florence Italy , Uffizi Galerie

Lorenzo the Magnificent *(Verrocchio—Samuel H. Kress Collection, National Gallery of Art, Washington; Anonymous—Medici-Riccardi Palace)*

Cesare Borgia

Lucrezia Borgia *(Berlin Museum)*

Execution of Savonarola *(San Marco Museum)*

Burning of Aztecs in Mexico *(Bildarchiv, Österreichische Nationalbibliothek, Vienna)*

Charles V, Holy Roman Emperor *(Museo del Prado, Madrid)*

Pope Sixtus IV with his nephew, later Julius II *(Vatican—Pinacoteca)*

Maps

The four voyages of Christopher Columbus   118-119

Portuguese domination of Africa and the East   122-123

(drawn by John Mitchell)

PRINCIPAL PERSONALITIES

The Monarchs

John II, King of Aragon 1458–79
Isabella the Catholic, Queen of Castile 1474–1504
Ferdinand the Catholic, King of Aragon 1479–1516
father Frederick III, Habsburg, Holy Roman Emperor 1440–93 *painting in Siena cathedral*
& son Maximilian I, Habsburg, Holy Roman Emperor 1493–1519 *painted by Dürer*
Charles V, Habsburg, Charles I of Spain 1516–56, Holy Roman Emperor
brothers 1519–56 (abdicated) *(grandson of Maximilian I & Mary of Burgundy)*
Ferdinand I, Habsburg, Holy Roman Emperor 1556–64
Ivan the Great, Grand Prince of Moscow 1462–1505
Alfonso V, King of Portugal 1438–81
John II, King of Portugal 1481–95
Manuel I, King of Portugal 1495–1521
Louis XI, King of France 1461–83 *, son of Charles VII (Agnès Sorel) mistress*
Charles VIII, King of France 1483–98 ⎫ *Anne of Brittany*
Louix XII, King of France 1498–1515 ⎭
Francis I, King of France 1515–1547 *, Margaret of Navarre his sister*
Henry VII, King of England 1485–1509
Henry VIII, King of England 1509–47
Muhammad II, Sultan of Turkey 1451–81 *the Conqueror, 1453 fall of Constantinople*
Bayezid II, Sultan of Turkey 1481–1512
Selim I, Sultan of Turkey 1512–20
Suleiman I 'The Magnificent', Sultan of Turkey 1520–66
Charles the Bold, Duke of Burgundy, Ruler of Netherlands, d. 1477
Mary of Burgundy, Ruler of Netherlands 1477–82
Philip of Burgundy, Ruler of Netherlands 1482–1506 *& Joanna the Mad (1555)*
Matthias Corvinus, King of Hungary 1458–90
Ladislaus II, King of Hungary and Bohemia 1490–1516
Louis II, King of Hungary and Bohemia 1516–26
Casimir IV, King of Poland—Lithuania 1446–92
Ferrante, King of Naples 1458–94
Alfonso, Ferrantino, Federico, Kings of Naples 1494–1501

The Popes

Alfonso Borgia, Calixtus III 1455–58
Aeneas Piccolomini, Pius II 1458–64
Pietro Barbo, Paul II 1464–71
Francesco della Rovere, Sixtus IV 1471–84
Giambattista Cibo, Innocent VIII 1484–92
Rodrigo Borgia, Alexander VI 1492–1503
Francesco Piccolomini, Pius III 1503
Giuliano della Rovere, Julius II 1503–13
Giovanni de'Medici, Leo X 1513–21
Adrian of Utrecht, Adrian VI 1522–23
Giulio de'Medici, Clement VII 1523–34

The Blood Royal

Henry the Navigator, Son of John I of Portugal
Anne of Beaujeu, Sister of Charles VIII
Jeanne de France, Sister of Charles VIII, 1st wife of Louix XII
Anne of Brittany, m. 1) Charles VIII, 2) Louis XII
Anne of Hungary, m. Ferdinand, Holy Roman Emperor
Margaret of York, m. Charles the Bold, Duke of Burgundy
Margaret of Austria, m. 1) Juan of Spain, 2) Duke of Savoy; Regent of Netherlands
Boabdil, Moorish Prince of Granada
Germaine de Foix, Princess of Navarre, 2nd wife of Ferdinand of Aragon
Charlotte d'Albret, Princess of Navarre, m. Cesare Borgia

Issue of Ferdinand and Isabella

Juan, m. Margaret of Austria, d. 1497
Isabella, m. 1) Alfonso, Crown Prince of Portugal, 2) Manuel of Portugal, d. 1498
Joanna ('The Mad'), m. Philip of Burgundy, d. 1555 *(son of Maximilian I & Mary of Burgundy)*
Maria, m. Manuel of Portugal, d. 1517
Catherine, m. 1) Arthur Prince of Wales,
      2) Henry VIII of England, d. 1536 *(daughter Bloody Mary)*

Issue of Philip and Joanna (The Habsburg–Spanish Union)

Eleanor, m. 1) Manuel of Portugal, 2) Francis I of France
Charles V, Holy Roman Emperor, m. Isabella of Portugal *, son Philip II of Spain*
Isabella, m. Christian II of Denmark
Ferdinand, Holy Roman Emperor, m. Anne of Hungary

Mary, m. Louis II of Hungary; Regent of Netherlands
Catherine, m. John III of Portugal

Columbus Family

Christopher, The Discoverer, m. Felipa Perestrello
Diego, Son, succeeded to titles
Ferdinand, Son, illegitimate, by Beatriz de Harana
Bartholomew, Brother, with Christopher on 3rd and 4th voyages
Diego, Brother, Christopher's deputy governor on Hispaniola

Amerindian Chiefs

Guacanagari, Cacique in N.W. Hispaniola
Caonobó, Cacique in central Hispaniola
Montezuma, 'Emperor' of the Aztecs
Atahuallpa, 'Emperor' of the Incas

Spanish Courtiers

Count of Medinaceli
Hernando de Talavera
Abraham Senior
Luis de Santangel

Isaac Abrabanel
Pedro de la Caballeria
Juan de Fonseca

Writers, Artists, Scientists

Paolo Toscanelli
Abraham Zacuto
Marsilio Ficino
Angelo da Poliziano
Pico della Mirandola
Michelangelo

Leonardo da Vinci
Raphael
Sandro Botticelli
Pinturicchio
Niccolò Machiavelli
Desiderius Erasmus

Mariners, Explorers, Conquistadors

Martin Alonso Pinzón
Vicente Yañez Pinzón
Bartholomew Dias
Alonso de Hojeda
Amerigo Vespucci

Ferdinand Magellan
John Cabot
Vasco Nuñez de Balboa
Juan Ponce de León
Juan Sebastian de Elcano

Vasco da Gama   Hernando Cortés
Pedro Alvarez Cabral   Francisco Pizarro
Bernal Días   Diego de Almagro

Overseas Administrators

Francisco de Bobadilla   Francisco de Almeida
Nicolás de Ovando   Alfonso de Albuquerque
Diego Columbus

The Clerics

Tomás de Torquemada   Francisco Jiménez de Cisneros
Bartholomew de Las Casas   Martin Luther
Girolamo Savonarola   Francis Xavier
Georges d'Amboise

The Medici

Cosimo, 'Pater Patriae', d. 1464   Piero, d. 1503
Lorenzo, 'The Magnificent', d. 1492 Giovanni, Pope Leo X, d. 1521
Giuliano, d. 1478

Issue of Pope Alexander VI (Borgia)

Pedro Luis, 1st Duke of Gandia
Juan, 2nd Duke of Gandia
Cesare, m. Charlotte d'Albret
Lucrezia, m. 1) Giovanni Sforza, Lord of Pesaro
          2) Alfonso, Duke of Bisceglie
          3) Alfonso d'Este, Duke of Ferrara
Jofrè, Prince of Squillace
(four other known children)

The Sforzas

Francesco, Duke of Milan, m. Bianca-Maria Visconti, d. 1466
Ludovico, Duke of Milan, m. Beatrice d'Este, d. 1508
Ascanio, Cardinal, d. 1505
Giovanni, Lord of Pesaro, m. Lucrezia Borgia
Bianca-Maria, 2nd wife of Maximilian, Holy Roman Emperor
Caterina, Ruler of Imola and Forli, three marriages

INTRODUCTION

No survey of the last ten centuries can avoid the conclusion that the year emerging as history's turning-point divides the millennium in half. The time when Christopher Columbus brought America into European perceptions and gave birth to the race for possession of unexplored territories coincided with lasting change within Europe itself. Of equal significance to the transatlantic navigational accomplishment was the supremacy of Italy in the realm of the mind, with the Renaissance spreading to infect all other streams of thought.

Moreover, Spain rose to the station of a European great power (the only other being France) in 1492. The country unified itself and initiated the retreat of Islam from the white man's soil through liquidation of the Moorish kingdom of Granada. In that same year, Spain introduced a new ideology, one of purity of blood, to the old continent when it expelled its ancient Jewish community. The doctrine fathered successive agonies enduring almost to the present day.

As a consequence of these developments, what was previously a mere fragmented promontory of the Eurasian landmass drew away to add a transoceanic dimension to trade and to project capitalism on its path. There resulted a spectacular growth of economic strength and soaring technological achievement. Thus Europe was enabled to resist fierce Turkish expansionism and remain a Christian continent. Islam confronted Christendom as a formidable rival. Now it could be compressed within the Old World, allowing Christendom to dictate the nature of the society to be imposed upon the New. History rejects absolutes of assertion but it is by no means too facile to suggest that the events of 1492, taken together, obviated the possibility of America's conquest by the warriors of Muhammad rather than the warriors of Christ.

As this narrative opens, the Turks had already swallowed what remained of the Byzantine Empire. Their onward march appeared irreversible. What Columbus's dogged persistence brought to Spain could surely have been encompassed by a Turkish or Arab mariner but for the Spanish conquest of Granada. This locked the Straits of Gibraltar against exit by any other Mediterranean fleet. Turkish advance continued to menace the heart of Europe itself. But the Sublime Porte had lost out in the search for the Atlantic's second shore.

In 1492 our globe was still calculated by the savants as being a fixed, motionless mass at the centre of the universe. The maps charted its geography as a single continental unit bordered by unknown watery demons. Periodic upheavals within the East and from the East produced mighty land-bound empires: Chinese, Mongol, Turkic, all accompanied by great migrations. Classical Greece and Rome had in their turn inserted themselves in the Near East and North Africa though without major transplantation of peoples. And while Columbus was not alone in his conviction that the Atlantic could be navigated to reach the frontiers of Asia by a westward route, he was the first to succeed and return to tell the tale. (The sagas of the Norsemen were unknown to Europe as a whole.)

Fanciful ideas of what might be encountered on such a voyage to Cipangu (Japan) abounded—a mighty Christian king, monsters without heads, fabulous riches—but never the possibility of a civilization, the one we now know as comprising Olmec, Maya, Aztec and Inca peoples on a different continent with another history. Columbus initiated the latest migration—Spanish at first and then by Europeans generally. To be sure, their baggage soon included black Africans as breathing merchandise. This transfer of white populations occupied the second half of the millenium, carrying non-Europeans in its train, and remains in progress still.

What was Europe? Amazingly, even as Columbus embarked upon his adventure and the Turks bestrode the Danube, Europe constituted a jigsaw of precarious statelets lacking the slightest element of cohesion. Perennially engaged in mutually destructive conflict, these little countries, where crowns were easily won and quickly lost, hovering beneath the threat of an Islamic deluge, were taking their leap across the frontiers of the mind. The Renaissance might be described as a cultural rebirth, or an intellectual mutation, or perhaps a reaction against hard ecclesiastical formalism. Definitions carry their limitations and to apply any one of them to the Renaissance would leave too many questions unanswered and many ambiguities unresolved.

Certainly, the common denominator in the various aspects of the change that penetrated Europe invested the continent with a dazzling artistic vitality. This both grew out of and challenged the religious orthodoxy of the Middle Ages. Philosophers and scientists had been preparing the ground for an era of 'humanism'; that is, a questioning of the belief that our existence entire was controlled by divine regulation, with God's design working through his appointed agents. It was no longer so readily accepted that the Pope and his bishops alone comprehended all the mysteries of life.

According to the humanists, the Church Universal did not command every aspiration towards piety as preached by the Saviour and exemplified by the saints. Man, within the limits of his endowed powers, could strive for another, spiritual perfection by personal exertion and through a more adventurous engagement with literature, science and the visual arts.

To a substantial degree, these endeavours gained their inspiration from a renewed acquaintance with the ancient thinkers of Greece and Rome. Of course, a superstitious reverence for matters and phenomena unseen still survived—would it ever die?—and the Bible, employed by Columbus as guidebook, would long be universally accepted as literally true. Yet the Bible too was subjected to textual revision. Humanist scholars insisted upon a ruthless analysis of the original sources of the scriptural canon—Hebrew, Aramaic and Greek. What did holy writ genuinely say, they asked, before successive generations of copyists added new inaccuracies and embellishments?

The Renaissance might also be described as a rediscovery by man of his own emotional creativity. The wonderment of this lay in the restricted geographical area of the cultural movement's emergence: the soil of Tuscany and the atmosphere of Florence. Buried there were the medieval roots out of which the Renaissance blossomed. The timespan from Dante to Michelangelo (a century and a half) gave the Renaissance its Florentine stamp and placed the Medici imprint on history. Such an insignificant city-state—even by Italian standards—and so great a destiny!

Yet there existed a parallel: tiny Portugal. That narrow strip of Iberian coastline, barely detectable at Europe's western extremity, contained a population of perhaps a million. One of these was Prince Henry, called 'the Navigator'. It was his dedication to oceanic exploration that first carried Europe into regions far beyond itself. Stage by stage the Portuguese assumed command of the high seas, reaching the Cape of Good Hope even before Columbus sailed. Then, much more so than Venice in Wordsworth's poem, Portugal 'held the gorgeous East in fee', planting Christianity and stealing riches along the way.

Now add to these horizons the invention of printing, 1446–50, in the cooler climate of Germany. At a stroke the elect few—scholars, prelates, statesmen—were deprived of their monopoly of literacy. In the year 1492 some 15,000 book titles were in circulation and the transition from medievalism to modernity could be said to have passed through all its preliminary processes.

However, we are left at a point of painful speculation: with European ascendancy presiding over the world's communications, its virgin lands, its trade and industry, its intellectual and artistic destiny, might history have evolved differently? Should society have learned a lesson in 1492 to apply a moral in 1592, and yes, 1992? Was war, piracy and slavery, bequeathed by previous ages, an inevitable reflex of Europe's primacy? Simply put, are we today what we were 500 years earlier? In the course of a savage annexation we had made of the New World a *tabula rasa*, then imported all the ills of the Old—injustice, rapacity, overweening racial pride. Sir Thomas More, in his *Utopia* (published 1516), postulated freedom in benevolence, equality of opportunity, rights for women, religious tolerance. Was this a pointless cry in a continuum of wilderness or a manifesto of practical reform? And are we too late to change?

Chapter One

THE WORLD
IN TRANSITION

thousand years ago, following the previous thousand years of stumbling progress, Christianity prevailed throughout Europe. To be sure, paganism continued to survive on its fringes, but most of Scandinavia, the Balkans and the eastward limits of the continent had accepted the Bible. At the crest of the Middle Ages it seemed as though the competing ambitions of just a few monarchs alone were delaying the inevitable march of Catholic Europe towards union under a single crowned head, a ruler standing in secular authority beside the Bishop of Rome who, as Pope, expressed that unity in terms of the spirit. Within this ideal the stranger could at best serve, if at all, in the role of helot.

Yet Christendom was far from secure. Turn back 500 years and European concerns were already directed to the possibility of losing that ethnic absolutism which excluded all others. For another military power, bearer of an impressive culture and blazoning the religion of Islam, threatened to swallow the continent. Ottoman Turkey, spearhead of a thrusting ideology, had already organized itself into an empire. At its rear loomed the shadow of a land-mass embracing practically the totality of the known world.

Nor were the Ottomans the first invaders to penetrate deep into Europe and challenge the white man's hegemony over his destiny since the assimilation of Goth, Hun and Vandal barbarians during the so-called Dark Ages and the Christianization of the continent. Earlier, the Mongol cavalry stood supreme near Europe's heart, having subdued most of the habitable space in the eastern hemisphere within a span of twenty years and established the largest empire ever to exist. Kublai Khan, grandson of the ferocious Genghis, controlled a realm in 1291 extending from Hungary to the China Seas, with a magnificent capital at Pekin.

Originally nomads, the Mongols obliterated great cities, slaughtered captive armies and enslaved entire populations. In the Far East they had been halted before independent Japan and were foiled by the obstructive Javanese. The Mongols, who detested Islam, never effected a conquest of the Muslims entrenched in northern India. To the west they harried Poland and crushed the Slav principates to make all of Russia their vassal, through the independent kingdoms, themselves owing allegiance to the Great Khan, of the Tatar Golden Horde. Indeed, long into the fifteenth century the Horde still remained nominal overlords of the steppes, though the Mongol Empire had declined almost to oblivion and the Tatars were now Islamicized and tamed.

Dynastic problems had stopped Mongol progress in Europe before their horses, so fleet of hoof, could raise new dust beyond the Danube. Retreating into their infinite homeland beyond the Urals, they left eastern Europe to make itself in its own fashion. But no such difficulties deterred the Turks, for Islam, in its appetite for conquest and conversion, admitted of no obstacle. Islam was an empire of religion, not citizenship. It offered a continuity from this world to the next. The Prophet died in AD 632, and it required just a hundred years for the faith to extend from Arabia along the coast of Africa to the Sahara, then over to Spain, through Central Asia and into India. Commerce worked hand in glove with Allah; ascetic Sufi missionaries, joined by Arab traders, spread the creed in the ebb of Mongol power. Skirting the periphery of China, they reached further still, to Indonesia and the South Pacific.

All this did not occur as an unbroken succession of triumphs, however. Muslim rulers arose, quarrelled and declined like all others. Their triumphs had turned to ignominious defeat in the Iberian peninsula. Could Christendom wholly defeat the scourge? Christendom was convinced of it, and tried often. But when the Ottoman Turks secured domination over their Asian neighbours and assumed what they could only regard as a sacred mission in Europe, crowned heads trembled on their Christian thrones. In the year 1453 the Sultan Muhammad II brought up a huge force 250,000 strong to take the city of Constantine, with its last ruler, also named Constantine, falling in its defence. The 1000-year long epic of the Eastern Byzantine Empire, which regarded itself, not Rome, as the guardian of the true Cross, came to an end, its threnody pealing from the bells of Santa Sophia, Justinian's cathedral due for conversion into a mosque.

Like Christianity, Islam had surged forward in the assurance that it alone was chosen by Providence to announce the truth to the infidel, to rule the world and perform God's works. Despite the emergence of many different versions of the faith, each with a passionate belief in its own path, Islam postulated the inevitability of its ultimate triumph. As with Christendom again, internal rivalries and weak-willed rulers periodically stalled the Turks' progress. Such was ever the penalty of indolence, or corruption, or indecision. Still, what the Sublime Porte knew of Europe persuaded it of the limitations of Christendom as a concerted military machine. Europe would succumb one day as others had succumbed.

Islam owed its spread into the uttermost Orient primarily because of the prowess of its mariners in navigating the waterways. The Turks now shared the Mediterranean with the Christians, so they had to dominate that inland sea, then force a passage through the Pillars of Hercules. The Moors had lost the occasion. But their successors planned ahead. Having cleared the Mediterranean, they would assuredly bring their fleets northward along the western perimeter of Europe and thereby engulf, if not convert, the entire known world.

A question remains: had they achieved their objective, could the Ottoman Turks have been the first to cross the Atlantic and gain dominion over another continent? Their skills in seamanship equalled such a challenge. Decidedly a race would have ensued to uncover the mystery of where those seemingly endless waters lapped their second shore. A century before the fall of Constantinople in 1453 the Turks had sprung from Anatolia to capture Adrianople and win for themselves a European in preference to an Asian capital. Adrianople proved a springboard of enormous import from which to leap across the Balkans. In 1382 they brought Bulgaria to submission. Now, with Constantinople as their base, they saw themselves as the continuation of the ruined Byzantine Empire. It took no great effort to sweep Genoa from its lucrative trading posts in the Aegean and on the Black Sea (except the island of Chios), held since the days when the Genoese, with their rivals the Venetians, transformed the Crusades into Christendom's biggest business. The Venetian Republic struggled with the Turks to retain its command of the Adriatic. And no wonder, since Venice lived with the seas as though in hereditary ownership, and regarded the eastern Mediterranean as the life-line of its commerce with the Indies. Playing its customary lone hand (except, that is, when danger approached) Venice boasted a navy not one whit inferior to the Turks'.

Strange indeed did Europe appear through Ottoman eyes: no prince so powerful he could not be supplanted by an insolent rival, no knight so feeble he did not aspire to a throne. Then this region's perplexing fragmentation! The Muslim invaders observed a hundred statelets in kaleidoscope, some no larger than a township, others with pretensions continent-wide, and few of them existing in harmony with their neighbours. Left alone, Europe might well collapse beneath the accumulation of its unrelenting discords. The response of some Turkish sultans was to bide their time, though others could not wait to grasp the Christian nettle. Intelligence services kept rumour abuzz. The Porte's ears received a stream of confidences inviting alliance from one Christian prince to defeat another, or for a Mediterranean pact to frustrate the corsair predators intercepting precious cargoes like a plague of ravenous sea-monsters. European princes spoke eternally of Crusade, but they were self-seeking at the heart, and the enemy of one's enemy could be reckoned, if only momentarily, a friend. The Turks despised them for it. Even popes played the cynical game.

Physically, Europe was less a continent in its own right than an indented promontory hanging from the ledge of Asia, eight times its magnitude. Yet until the arrival of the Turks, western rulers knew so little of the world that they failed to recognize Christendom's chronic, perilous debility. Theology taught of their situation in terms of Christendom as the centre of the universe, and the only significant part of it. Chroniclers unfolded history as a succession of great happenings personalized through selected individuals, royal or martial or perhaps combining the two. As they recorded its past, Europe since the Dark Ages constituted a form of theatre, its grand characters enacting scenes that appeared to cast in the balance and seal the destinies of the humbler millions: the crowning of Charlemagne, the campaigns fought by Normandy, St Stephen's conversion of the Magyars, the German King-Emperor Henry IV grovelling before a pope at Canossa, the Crusades, Magna Carta, the schisms in the Church, Henry of Lancaster at Agincourt, Joan of Arc.

The records that have survived from those times, and they are meagre, do not do justice to medievalism, which at its thirteenth-century zenith produced St Francis of Assisi, abolition of the worst aspects of feudalism and savants of great originality. That medieval figure St Catherine of Siena merits regard as early Renaissance woman. Furthermore, from that age date European cathedrals that stand to this day unsurpassed as monuments of architecture and art, testifying not simply to the extraordinary skill of those sculptor-builder-masons but to the heights of imagination to which the mind could soar in conceiving the human soul as bridging heaven and earth.

The chroniclers also related how good men and women of lesser station served the poor and tended the sick. They described the activities of mendicant orders, and gave due significance to the preservation of the pure Christian legacy with accounts of scholastic foundations and the transcribing of sacred books. Natural visitations such as famine and pestilence received their place too, written into the records as catastrophes requiring explanation and interpretation by the wisest ecclesiastics, for these events could only be messages from God or interventions in human affairs by Satan. But such matters were proportionately allocated to a minor significance in the evolution of the world as it was then understood—rightly so, because warfare featured as the dominant activity of the age. To fuel their ambitions, rulers secured loans by pledging territories complete with their inhabitants, and as a consequence, wealth accumulated in just a few hands. Jews could be expelled or sold to other rulers for their taxation potential. Captured prisoners had their uses as a commodity of trade, while engineers were recruited (as now!) to perfect new methods of destruction.

Between 1450 and 1660 only four years were completely free from organized warfare. So how much attention could this European chequerboard of constantly shifting relationships give to its vulnerability from beyond? Precious little in the early part of the fifteenth century. The continent had still not recovered its enormous human losses from the Black Death; London contained only 60,000 people, hardly greater than Ferrara in northern Italy and one third the population of Paris.

Unlike their Turkish successors, the Mongol conquerors had arrived and departed after only the barest personal and intellectual contact with Europe. They evinced little curiosity in its civilization and brought nothing enduring of their own. True, European merchants in the spice and silk trades, journeying the land route to China and beyond for camphor and precious stones, would report the circulation of paper money. They told of printing presses, fire-proof materials and other marvels of invention. Missionaries, despatched from France, returned with instances of baptism, vaunted as Christendom on the march, and this was demonstrated in the flesh when a Mongol pietist, raised in the Nestorian heresy, received communion from the Pope. Still, an insurmountable barrier, composed of space, time and deities, separated western and eastern societies.

Not so in the case of Islam. The faith derived its theology from Judaism and Christianity, gaining converts from both. Muslim contact with the Iberian peninsula and Sicily had left monuments in profusion. Most of all, Islam had snatched something of classical Greek thought during the Hellenistic flight into obscurity in the Dark Ages, so little of Muslim philosophy could be properly termed alien to the Christian mentality.

Where then did the hiatus between the two Oriental invasions leave the Christian Middle Ages? They flourished as an insulated European epoch. From our vantage point it appears as though, for some three centuries at least, Europe had been locked into time to play out its conflicts in the intimacy of its own dimension—almost until the fall of Constantinople, which coincided with what might be termed, for lack of an exact phrase, the end of the Middle Ages. Till then, everything not directly pertaining to Europe's parochial outlook had dropped out of the West's perception, except as a remote repository of superstition and legend.

Now, it will not do to date the changed horizon from an isolated occurrence, no matter how significant. Dividing history into precisely defined eras has its perils, that we know. Certainly, the disappearance of Constantinople from the map of Christendom shattered Europe's self-esteem and sent a charge through the corridors of the intellect to clear a path for new ideas. But the Middle Ages were already due to expire in the Renaissance anyway. However, the Renaissance required an extended preparation, like all revolutions. It was no collective brainstorm, but rather a rediscovery of man's capacities on the humanistic, artistic and intellectual plane. And for this reason we focus on the year 1492, when a new world entered into calculation to give the Renaissance its clearest benchmark, that defined by geography. For an explanation, we might describe 1492 as the hinge of a door not completely closing upon one epoch nor completely opening upon another, but allowing for a replacement of the atmosphere that people breathed.

Until the Renaissance, our civilization had largely lost contact with its classical sources in the culture of Rome and Greece. The cataclysm wrought by the barbarians in their usurpation of the Roman world around the fifth century AD had broken everything up, including the chain of European thought. As a consequence, the process by which Europe arrived at its fifteenth-century situation—a mosaic of peoples diversified by custom and language, and at unequal stages of advancement—fell into a distorted mental picture, submerged beneath superstitious accretions attired and sanctified in religious forms. The limbs of what had been coalescing into a civilized, centralized society became atrophied.

Ancient Rome's empire of immense tribal variegation had emerged, to be sure, as a perquisite of conquest. Yet it simultaneously nurtured political sophistication, freedom of thought, splendid architecture and administrative genius. This foreshadowed a smooth progression to a more gracious way of life for all, a promise that embraced also legal emancipation of the slaves. With Rome's collapse each population grouping was set adrift, to flourish or decay according to its individual qualities of survival.

Having endured approximately until the Pope crowned Charlemagne with the auspicious title of Holy Roman Emperor in the year 800, the Dark Ages, if one might dare a generalization, bequeathed to medieval man a kind of amnesiac void. He neglected to investigate his roots. He failed to address the evidence of the pre-Christian antiquities, in stone and manuscript, that still survived—not much in manuscript, given that St Gregory alone, the eighth-century Pope, is said to have destroyed entire libraries lest they undermined Catholic faith. Slavery regained justification in Christian society as being ordained by God, while marble relics of the Eternal City itself, much to Dante's disgust, were crushed to powder for use as building material. However, thanks to the continuance of the eastern empire of Byzantium (outliving proud Rome by a millennium) and despite the decrepitude to which that Christian realm ultimately sank, all was not lost. Though crippled as a political force, and blinded by age, Byzantium nevertheless preserved memories of the extinct classical world. Furthermore, Muslim societies earlier than the Turks, in supplanting the Hellenistic civilization, themselves drew nourishment from it and carried Arabized vestiges with them to western Europe. Slender shoots, not necessarily recognized for what they were, thus gathered strength, notably in Italy, France and Spain.

To the medieval mind, most of knowledge, all of history and destiny, was discernible in the Bible. It only required the correct interpretation, and this reached down to the common man from the Vicar of Christ in St Peter's. Mythology retained household gods in the daily order of things: the noble families of Europe truly imagined their descent, by divine preference, from the ancients—those heroes whose dramas had materialized Troy and Rome out of the mists. The pretension refused to die. Even in Renaissance times the Borgia Pope Alexander VI, who ascended to St Peter's in 1492, affected a pedigree dating from Apis, the sacred bull of Egypt, as illustrated by Alexander's favourite artist Pinturicchio in his Vatican frescoes. In the absence of information to the contrary, Italians deemed their lineage to stem directly from the Romans of yore, the Paduans adopting the historian Livy as their collective ancestor. Rulers in the colder climes of the Norsemen preferred Woden.

In an age when astrology enjoyed equal authority with astronomy, this planet could not be other than the source of all cosmic force, with the sun and heavens rotating around it. Few educated men doubted that God created the world as a sphere. The Greeks had known it since before Aristotle, and medieval savants, notably Roger Bacon, the thirteenth-century Oxford scholar, considered Asia to be within navigable distance westward from Europe. Nevertheless geographers of the Middle Ages, resorting to the Scriptures whenever engaged in controversy, drew their charts on a flat earth projection: a disc surrounded by water. Such, at least, was the accepted principle in map-making almost until the dawn of the fifteenth century. Yet an infinitely more accurate description of the physical world survived from classical times, in the eight-volume work compiled by the mathematician and astronomer Ptolemy, who lived in the second century after Christ. Ptolemy had calculated a measurement for the circumference of the globe and its distance from the moon. By his computation Eurasia extended continuously half-way round the whole, and he described the southern hemisphere as water and land intermingled, so that the Indian Ocean appeared as a huge lake. His lines of latitude and longitude fell short of the true width between each degree of space. As a consequence, the entire mass became roughly a quarter less than its actual size. Christopher Columbus, in estimating the width of the Atlantic, miscalculated by the same proportion.

Ptolemy's learning was lost to western scholarship for many centuries. His ideas might indeed have disappeared for all eternity in the Dark Ages, along with so much else of man's creativity never recovered, had his work not been preserved by the Byzantine monks, who then neglected it. Ptolemy was salvaged by the Arab astronomers, successors to the scientists of Hellenistic Alexandria. An Arab traveller, Al-Idrisi, devised a Ptolemaic map of the world for Roger II, Norman ruler of the half-Islamicized kingdom of Sicily in the twelfth century. His source remained a secret until about the year 1400, when a Byzantine brought Ptolemy's eight volumes to Florence, for their translation and reproduction in Latin.

It thus transpired that Ptolemy's cosmography, in which the world stood fixed at the core of eight crystalline spheres reaching into infinity, as expressed by the Sienese painter Giovanni di Paolo in his 1445 work 'The Creation', remained the accepted wisdom until—when? Certainly it was undisputed still in 1492, the year in which Rodrigo Borgia bribed his unworthy way to the papal throne and Christopher Columbus sailed the Atlantic into the unknown, to tread what he insisted were the islands of offshore Asia.

Explorers had preceded Columbus to plough uncharted seas and make landfall in remote parts. The Norse sagas told of Leif Erikson, of a family in exile in Greenland, adrift off the Labrador coast of Canada. Conceivably Leif (incidentally, he was not the first) also reached a warm haven in Newfoundland about the year 1000, though nothing of this was known to southern Europe. Indeed, others might well have attained America without returning to tell the tale. A little before Columbus sailed, Portuguese explorers had peeped into the Indian Ocean from the tip of Africa, without venturing further. So much still remained to beckon the curiosity of man. Ptolemy's spheres, and the heavenly bodies affixed to them, could not be confounded by holy writ; nor his location of the Equator, marked too far to the north and extending for 22,500 Roman miles instead of its true length, 26,410 Roman miles. Columbus had little more to guide him. Yet after taking his dramatic step in global navigation, the world would need to regard itself afresh.

Survey the century in which he lived and Columbus emerges by no means as an exceptional human being with qualities extraordinary for the age. He was not in advance of his time, nor did he rank as an inspired thinker, nor yet as an original one. This son of a Genoese weaver linked his fortunes to the sea during an epoch noted for daring maritime expeditions, for in the fifteenth century Renaissance man challenged conventional wisdom in all directions. Leaving aside for the present the perennial savagery of humankind once its skin was torn away, this period brought Christian civilization to an efflorescence. Every idea suggesting enlarged frontiers was seized and subjected to intense debate. First among the many casualties was the priestly dogmatism which had demanded too much and tarried too long. As already indicated, all this was accompanied by a rediscovery of those classical masters of the Graeco-Roman world—especially the Greeks, who had diagnosed rationalism in the universe and perceived a harmony in the workings of the human spirit.

Scholars, artists, poets and even prelates placed their indelible stamp upon the fifteenth century as they embarked upon these new paths; hesitantly at first, for they trod close to the limits of religious belief and, guided only by the compass of instinct, they ventured towards destinations unknown. Columbus had his prototype in those explorers of the spirit. They strained to extend human perceptions, just as he tested his physical and mental endurance in crossing the ocean.

It was to be the century which gave birth to so much creativity in

Europe as to surpass Asia altogether, and inaugurate this continent's long domination over the human race. Paradoxically, Europe was also grievously sick, politically and socially. The ravages of earlier catastrophes were as yet unhealed, and Europe's mood wavered unpredictably. Columbus was born in 1451, in a city that embodied much that was promising in Europe, and much that was chronically wrong. As the capital of a small northern republic, Genoa epitomized that side of disunited Italy incapable of rescuing itself from intrigues, feuds and greed. Individual rulers of the petty states in the peninsula could descend, for cruelty and ignorance, to the nadir of personal morality. Dante had written of his native land as a slave and a brothel combined. He was of course condemning its condition well before the Renaissance, of which he might be termed the earliest precursor. But the description would just as exactly apply for the next three centuries. Yet how frequently do we encounter those same rulers redeemed, the generous patrons of other Italians in touch with the sublime!

If artistically Genoa in the fifteenth century never truly sparkled as a Renaissance city, it certainly contributed the fruit of its mercantile enterprise which permeated through the towns and communes of the entire Italian motherland—and this since the early Middle Ages. Exploiting its superb location on the Ligurian Sea and the finest natural harbour on the Mediterranean, blessed with a spectacular amphitheatre of fertile hinterland reaching to the mountains on its perimeter, Genoa was the most ingenious of Italian city-states when it came to amassing wealth. Its agents were ubiquitous. Until losing its Black Sea colonies to the Turks, inevitable on the fall of Constantinople, Genoa virtually monopolized the importation of slaves bought from the Tatar chiefs controlling southern Russia. Its vessels, and the seafarers its environment bred, sailed for no matter whom, on purposes of war or peace. Whether the commerce was clean or squalid troubled the Genoese not at all. Only following Byzantium's demise did its towering brokerage house of San Giorgio surrender omnipotence to a banker mightier still, the Fugger dynasty of Augsburg, and then only temporarily. Successive doges, elected, if rarely ruling, for life, slept on a bed of nails to retain the republic's independence. Having lost out in the eastern Mediterranean, they intrigued relentlessly to steal Sardinia from the Kings of Aragon, though without success. But they still clung to Corsica, so Genoa managed to keep the western roadsteads clear of Venetian competition while relegating the docks of Barcelona to lesser traffic. Genoese ships carried the Black Death to Europe, laying as it were a curse of instability upon a city given entirely to the worship of gold. Ever at the mercy of rival families disrupting civic peace, annexed in turn by France and Milan, envious of Florence's cultural glory, Genoa exploited its theoretical allegiance to the Holy Roman Emperor as a convenience. Its identity remained undefined, so it compensated by emphasizing its international role. The French had captured Genoa in 1396, only to lose it shortly afterwards. Nevertheless France added this claim to other of its ambitions in the peninsula to justify intervention in Italian affairs time and time again.

Italy would be the highest prize whenever the dice were thrown by European monarchs clashing in the hunger for power, the Pope included. With its city-states (so described because they were more than a city, less than a state), Italy was like an opulent orphan, chased by competing foster-parents, each of whom pretended to love it the most. As fifteenth century conflicts flowed into the sixteenth, the battlefield for Italy's possession emptied of all contenders except the House of Valois (French) against the House of Habsburg (part Spanish, part German). In the process, a tangle of tactical dynastic alliances drew others into the web: bargains struck by offering royal daughters in marriage, their handsome territorial dowries as bait, thinned the blood of many a reigning family till the present century.

The Italian peninsula suffered the worst of all political fates—regular invasion, periodic civil war, Vatican machination and, not least, the rapacity of Venice. The 'Most Serene Republic', as it liked to vaunt itself, concealed a claw behind its gracious Levantine exterior. How then explain the existence of another Italy, evolving as the most advanced nation in Europe amidst such a catalogue of travails?

It was no enigma. Italy's unique redolence derived from the country's inheritance as the central burial-ground of the old Roman Empire. Even those who came to ravish the land departed entranced by its spell. We have spoken of the ignorance, since the Dark Ages, of the true character of Rome's defunct empire. Nevertheless reminders of its grandeur lay in the decaying ruins exposed to the sunlight everywhere in southern Europe, and particularly so in Italy. A specific magic hung over that country, made almost tangible by the mystique inspired by the city of Rome itself. Rome was a sad place, neglected and provincial, at the dawn of the fifteenth century, its settled population a bare 20,000. It had only lately been restored, after the 'Babylonian captivity' in Avignon, as the seat of the Pontiff, and its cavernous streets concealed nests of murderous robber bands. Yet special pilgrimages could bring a million visitors in a single year, so much did believers venerate the European cradle of their faith.

Just as history, in the European understanding of the term, terminated its apostolic phase in the Bible, so it restarted politically in Italy. Medievalism confronted its earliest challenges in that country, despite the stubborn feudalism of its south, which clung to traditional ways favouring baronial despotism and serf labour while western Europe as a whole began grinding the system into the dust. The Calabrian St Thomas Aquinas— a cousin of the Holy Roman Emperor, who chose the ascetic life at the monastery of Monte Cassino—had already in the thirteenth century placed Aristotle within the context of Christian theology. Most probably, he had detected the Athenian's influence on the philosophers of Arabized Spain, particularly Maimonides of Córdoba. Aquinas developed a theory of constitutional government, with an upper and a lower house, that could have worked for eighteenth-century England.

The Italian landscape had produced Giotto, father of all naturalist painting, as a wondrous gift to Europe in the thirteenth century. Soon Dante, Petrarch and Boccaccio arrived, all within the space of fifty years. They pointed literature in directions expressing a novel range of humanist impulses that reached to the matrix of congealed Christendom. Written in Italian dialect rather than Latin, their poetry, sagas and satire arched over the ecclesiastical elite to touch a lay populace. A few decades on and their works won appreciation in foreign translations, inspiring emulation from Chaucer and François Villon among others throughout the continent. Stronger western countries might be developing as nations in the modern sense, under a single crown. They could trample over Italy and frequently did so. They could defy the Pope and make a tool of his spiritual authority. But in taking Christian ritualism by the hand and bringing it into relation with the secular world, in reviving Platonist thought and breaching the traditional cultural frontiers, Italy created the Renaissance and dominated Europe. The necessary primal force was born in Florence, for Giotto, Dante, Petrarch and Boccaccio all came out of Tuscany. Florence led Italy as Italy was to lead the world.

A dynasty of merchants whose wealth and power gave them the lustre of kings—in fact several European monarchs and four popes would carry their blood—turned Florence into a fifteenth-century Athens. Such were the Medici. Cloth manufacturers and international bankers in an age which saw the earliest manipulation of capital for political ends, they also produced poets, statesmen and patrons of the arts. While they won admiration for their magnificent endowments, the Medici also roused the animosity of fellow-Florentines for their vindictiveness and seemingly unassailable authority.

The greatest of them all, Lorenzo, called the Magnificent, was born in 1449. He was sharing control of Florence with his brother Giuliano when, in 1478, the latter fell to an assassin at Mass in the cathedral. Lorenzo just managed to escape, saved, it is said, by his friend the humanist writer Poliziano. This occurred during a conspiracy engineered by the rival Pazzi family, with the Archbishop of Pisa and Pope Sixtus IV in the plot. There were consequences, among them a torrential rainfall so continuous as to ruin the Tuscan harvest. People gave as its cause the execution of the archbishop fully robed, on Lorenzo's order, with Giacomo de Pazzi in his turn offering his soul to Satan as he expired. Sixtus then excommunicated Lorenzo, Pazzi's body was dug up, paraded through the streets of Florence and thrown into the Arno. Only then would the sun shine again. A fifteenth-century Athens? Yes, though a leaden gullibility still dragged on the mind, as in the conviction that everything significant for Florentines, good or evil, took place on a Saturday.

When Christopher Columbus was born Lorenzo, an ugly Tuscan child of two, could already recite lines from Dante by heart, for the poet wrote in the local speech. In 1449 the long struggle between France and England was at its last gasp, but still had four more disastrous years to run. The exchequers of both countries had by this time reached exhaustion. The Hundred Years War began in 1346 with skirmishes where the English archers wrought havoc upon the stolid French, immobile in their heavy armour. Now Henry VI's army faced artillery, and gunpowder was turning the scales for its skilled users. By 1453 the English, no less than the Byzantines in Constantinople, were ready to admit defeat. They had anxieties at home in the dispute between York and Lancaster for the succession, soon to burst into the Wars of the Roses, an episode that decimated the noble families of England and, incidentally, cost the Medici bank a fortune in unpaid debts. Yet the English king still coveted the crown of France. His successors would intervene on the continent whenever this might stir the pot of French troubles, and they retained their hold on Calais in evidence of their intention. By a similar calculation, France meddled in the affairs of Scotland.

The long Anglo-French war had originated in one of those medieval dynastic stupidities, but then forgot the passage of time. The countryside of France lay waste, its northern farmlands uninhabited except for wolves, its villages made derelict by banditry and disease. Its king as yet lacked a truly functional Mediterranean outlet, for Marseilles belonged to his

Angevin cousins, rulers of Provence, where people spoke another language and obeyed a different law. The feckless Charles VII yearned to punish Burgundy, which had expanded northward into a disjointed confederation, though the richest state in the West. Burgundy was an empire in miniature, embracing the Netherlands entire and a strip of northeastern France dividing Flanders, besides its original lands deep in the body of the fractured kingdom. The Duke of Burgundy, doubtless for reasons valid in his own eyes, had betrayed allegiance to the House of Valois in a treacherous compact with England. He was another cousin of the king and premier peer of the realm, but had delivered Joan of Arc to the English within the terms of an alliance that had kept the hated foreigner in the *patrie*.

To be sure, France was not yet capable of direct intervention in the affairs of Europe as a whole, but the inclination was always there. France aspired to overrun Flanders in the north-east and capture the Netherlands, thus crippling Burgundy at a stroke. Next, down into Italy as far as its troops could march, if not in association with others then alone. Lorenzo de'Medici grew to manhood in the conviction that unless the Italian city-states learnt to live in peace with each other they would succumb to any determined invader, be he Turk or Frenchman or Spaniard. He refused to admit that internecine conflict was an affliction endemic to Italy. Noble as the argument sounded, it ignored the factor of Venice. Here was power indeed, and opulence, and a narrow pride, the rock against which Italian peace would always founder. A republican empire in its own right, Venice still controlled Cyprus and Crete, so it would sup with the devil himself to deter Turkish progress in the eastern Mediterranean. Now Venice was encroaching upon the smaller 'principates' of the north Italian mainland, raising the ire especially of Milan, dominant in the region. So the two found themselves at war. Milan, ruled for nearly two centuries by the ruthless Visconti dukes, fell during Lorenzo's infancy to Francesco Sforza, a brilliant mercenary captain risen in status to marry a Visconti wife. This unhappy lady (given cheaply because of her illegitimacy) restored herself to the marital bed by murdering Sforza's mistress. Jealousies driving men and women to such acts of vengeance were by no means rare among the oligarchs of divided Italy, though generally the stakes were worthier—not *amour propre* but a territorial possession.

In the Old Testament, God is recorded as a partisan in the wars of the tribes of Israel. Christendom therefore took armed conflict as within the natural order of existence. Calixtus III, the first Borgia Pope, con-

structed a fleet in 1457 on the banks of the Tiber, largely at papal expense
and with a cardinal as its admiral, for the reconquest of Constantinople.
Everything went wrong with the sacred expedition and the ships became
a fleet of lost souls stranded in the Mediterranean. Calixtus did not
survive long enough to learn the extent of the disaster. It was in no
small measure due to a failure of support. His successor, Pius II, who
before his elevation served the Holy Roman Emperor as secretary and
produced a significant body of humanist literature, tried in his turn to
rally Christendom for a crusade, with even smaller result. An exceptional
man even for a fifteenth-century Pontiff, Pius intended to captain his
armada in person. Generally in their *alter ego* as ambitious sovereign
princes, the popes schemed to increase their secular power, lusting after
possessions for themselves, their families or their favourites. Church lands
cut a broad swathe across Italy from shore to shore, with everything to
the south embracing the kingdoms of Naples and Sicily, now in the
hands of separate branches of the House of Aragon. Naples marked its
allegiance to the Pope by the annual gift of a white palfrey. Not so Sicily
which, with Sardinia, belonged wholly to Aragon itself.

Some might have judged the ruler of Aragon to be none too secure
on his own throne: his Spanish base amalgamated from three individual
states, Catalonia, Valencia and Aragon proper, all harbouring grievances
sporadically erupting in rebellion against their monarch. While Columbus hovered at court with his proposal to find the Indies by sailing west,
King Ferdinand of Aragon, the Castilian Queen Isabella's consort, cherished a dream of his own. This envisioned his house standing supreme
among the monarchies of Europe, its authority universally accepted, its
head an emperor in the classical, Augustan meaning of the term. Many
who were already old in 1492 would live to see the dream's realization.

Before long the Renaissance of course ceased to be specifically a man-
ifestation of the Italian genius for extending human capacities. It crossed
the Alps and spread over western Europe as a whole, though some of
those fortresses of the old theology, the universities (Italy had twenty in
the fifteenth century, England two) strained to keep humanism at bay.
Still, God's world was not yet ready for remaking. Science remained a
subject awaiting its turn, for at the middle of the century no one had as
yet seen a printed book. Reading was the prerogative of the few with
access to manuscripts. Nevertheless western Europe was quick to sense
the impending challenge to the Age of Faith.

Not so in the Europe east of a line drawn north to south from Hamburg
to Venice. The two halves of the continent constituted widely unequal

regions. The east lagged far behind. The Middle Ages survived here for a complexity of reasons: among them a later adherence to Christianity, the subsequent decay of the Byzantine Empire as a modernizing influence, and direct exposure to the scourge of successive Oriental predators.

We cannot speak, however, of an absolute divide. This was prevented by the Holy Roman Empire, a Central European political sealing wax whose continued existence defied progress (and, frequently, common sense) but which periodically awoke to its historic role in keeping Europe as a unit. More than a fiction, the empire was less than a fact. Several European kings fancied themselves as emperor at one time or another in the fifteenth and sixteenth centuries, including Henry VIII of England. He would be an emperor unable to raise taxes or organize an imperial army. Neither could he take his succession for granted or retain within the realm any part of it which declined the privilege of membership. The Holy Roman Empire was long deprived of real constitutional authority or basic territorial sentiment. Sovereign in his own state and suzerain over the rest, its nominal ruler for life was decided by seven electors, six of whom were German: the Margrave of Brandenburg, glorying as the emperor's Chamberlain; the Duke of Saxony, his Marshal; the Elector Palatine of the Rhineland, his Steward; the King of once-powerful Bohemia, his Cup-bearer; and the Archbishops of Mainz, Cologne and Trier in their dignities as Arch-Chancellors for Germany, Italy and Burgundy. In earlier times the office of Holy Roman Emperor alternated between the Habsburgs and French-speaking Luxemburgers, but the title passed now almost automatically, though frequently lubricated by bribery, to a Habsburg in his persona as Archduke of Austria. Towards the end of the fifteenth century the Germans themselves regarded the term Holy Roman Empire as embracing their country, in all its parts, alone. Nevertheless the emperor counted much of northern Italy within his domain, the Burgundian Netherlands beyond the actual dukedom (in vassalage to France) and, despite its vocal and physical protests to the contrary, Switzerland. Bohemia formed its Slav extremity, bordering on Magyar Hungary in the east. In fact the emperor claimed Hungary as his fief too. That the Holy Roman Empire survived at all since its collapse as a political force after a thirteenth-century struggle with the pope could be ascribed to its primary function as a linguistic German Reich. Germany as such did not exist. Its fragmentation was greater even than Italy's, so this imperial concept substituted for a fatherland. On its fringes subjects of the Holy Roman Empire spoke French, Italian, Danish, Flemish, Czech, Serbo-Croat and, for a time, Polish and Magyar.

This unwieldy combination, dating back to Charlemagne, would theoretically hang its banner over Christendom, despite defections, until Napoleon demolished the shadow in 1806. It was by no means regarded by the emperors as a nullity. They felt naked until anointed by the pope, though this lustrous ceremonial disappeared in the tideways of the Reformation. They sought to defend its irregular frontiers against all threats. To the emperors, a crusade against Islam remained the supreme Christian obligation. They pledged themselves to crush the Turks, revive the secular dignity of old Rome and restore Jerusalem to Christ. Germany played along with the illusion but it turned a deaf ear on the troubled affairs of the rest of the continent; nor did the German people accord respect to every utterance of the pope.

A new Habsburg, Frederick III, had succeeded in 1440. The man detested war, had no money with which to conduct it, and was of indolent disposition into the bargain. The eastern flank of his empire was dangerously exposed. The Tatar Golden Horde stayed out of neighbouring Muscovy only on the payment of a regular Danegeld, while Bohemia lay prostrate as the result of the long, debilitating Hussite rebellion, that tragic Czech Reformation antedating Luther. Austria itself, Frederick's homeland, was coveted by the Hungarian regent, Janos Hunyadi, an outstanding military leader who was to grant his country its moment of greatness. He organized a grand army with which he repulsed the Turks, drove them south from his capital Buda, captured Belgrade in 1456 and advanced to the Black Sea, where he destroyed an Ottoman fleet. As it came so soon after the fall of Constantinople, the Hungarians called their campaign the last, victorious crusade. But the sultan returned, regaining Serbia and Bosnia. Suddenly quiet reigned again in the Balkans while a Hungarian-Polish union kept guard over the security of Europe. Left alone, Poland would have preferred to concentrate on the elimination of the Teutonic Knights, those German soldier-missionaries ostensibly in the service of the emperor. Having carried Christianity to this part of the world they remained as alien colonizers pure and simple. The Knights, now constituted into an independent principality in the Baltic region, were governed by their Grand Master and shamelessly exploited the native peasantry.

A large span of the fifteenth century therefore passed for eastern Europe as an epoch of successive local insurrections interspersed with wars of defence. The land was soaked in blood. A battle lost against the sultan implied massacre, deportation and slavery; a victory could never be celebrated as decisive. The Turks appeared to favour a strategy of cat and mouse, particularly as they felt menace enough of their own along their untamed Persian border. Turkey would not fight willingly on two fronts. Worryingly too for Christendom, the old Bosnian aristocracy distrusted the Hungarians and Austrians in about equal measure. The Bosnians proved impervious to Catholic Christianity (they were Bogomils, for whom the world and all things visible belonged to Satan, the soul alone being created by God) and had converted to Islam.

Now Magyar Hungary, floating on the glory of its 'victorious crusade', made its bid to be a power of consequence in Europe. Hunyadi's son Matthias Corvinus, a king and a general, saw himself as the future head of the Holy Roman Empire, which had grown in desperate need of a life-preserver. During a respite from the Turkish janissaries Corvinus annexed the eastern portion of Bohemia, including Moravia, and in 1485 fulfilled his father's dream of entering the Hofburg in Vienna to proclaim large Austrian territories as his own. Hungary had four million people, but with the two millions in its conquered territory could boast a population equal to England's.

Enter the Polish question. The Poles had lost a king in battle against the Turks—it was at Varna in 1444, and for two years this people, convinced their king was in hiding, prayed for his return. If a prisoner, they would ransom him. Poland, like Hungary, was an elective monarchy.

Alas, King Ladislaus failed to reappear, and his younger brother Casimir, Grand Prince of Lithuania, accepted an invitation to join the vacant throne to his own. Strategic marriages had meanwhile brought Poland, Lithuania and Hungary into a fair harmony of interests, only slightly complicated by other aspirants to one or more of the three crowns. The Emperor Frederick, as a Habsburg, was himself a token claimant, though too passive except to lodge a right on behalf of his future heirs.

Now Casimir decided that Polish freedom depended less on removing the Turkish threat from the south than in toppling the Teutonic Knights controlling the Baltic north of his territory, with its Prussian landowners and Prussianized towns within their grip. Further, in his capacity as ruler of a vast Lithuanian duchy—it stretched beyond Kiev in the Ukraine— Casimir did not refrain from treating with the Tatar Khans who maintained a vassalage over the Duchy of Moscow and other huge tracts of Russia. Blessed with a long reign, Casimir subdued the Knights and so gave to Poland a shore facing the northern seas. Suppression of the Order was not greeted as wholly good news in Moscow, whatever the inspiration it gave to Polish cultural endeavour in the centuries to come. More would be heard of the Teutonic Knights, for their home base, Pomerania, would transform into the Hohenzollern dukedom of Prussia.

What of Matthias Corvinus, and his loud ambition for a Hungarian Empire? He died prematurely and without an heir, leaving the future to decide the destinies of his conquests in Bohemia and Austria. We need pursue the labyrinth no further here than to report its outcome: in the year 1492 three members of a single family, the tolerant Jagiellos, were conveniently arranged on the three thrones. One of them ruled Bohemia and Hungary, the second was King of Poland, the third Grand Prince of Lithuania—all achieved via an interchange of desirable princesses and the failure of the Holy Roman Emperor to intervene. It could not matter less to their serf populations, owned by the nobility and forbidden to leave their tiny portions of tillage, except when required to fill the armies of a liege. These were backward regions, a century at least behind the West. However, a great European dynasty seemed in the making, its Lithuanian branch anxiously watching not only the Turks and not only the Habsburgs, but the Muscovite dukes too. For here a giant was awakening from its long Asiatic servitude.

The Duchy of Moscow was ruled from 1462 by Ivan the Great, who gained his place among the creators of Imperial Russia by open defiance of the Tatars. That was in 1480, and he refused to pay them further tribute. Ivan had decided on this moment to declare himself sovereign of all Russia, which was his way of warning Lithuania off any part of it. Ivan had married the niece of the last Byzantine emperor, Sophia Palaeologue, she of 'the haughty mind'—Milton's phrase in his *Brief History of Moscovia*. Sophia apparently encouraged her husband to regard himself as the heir to the defunct glories of Kiev and Byzantium, perhaps also Rome—in fact gathering within his person every previous Christian greatness stretching back to Jerusalem. Lithuania shrank from Ivan's challenge. Poland reconciled itself to a less exalted role, and was ultimately fated to extinction. Such were the dreams of princes.

It was all too much for Emperor Frederick III, now in his dotage. The old man had invented a family tree making him a direct descendant of King Priam of Troy, but he survived long enough to be informed of the discovery of America. He died in 1493, to be succeeded by his flamboyant son Maximilian, and the contrast persuaded the Germans that now they had an emperor indeed. Maximilian was the incarnation of a medieval knight, chivalrous, not too shrewd, a man of letters, and withal a political architect with a grand design for Europe. While the father secluded himself in Linz to await death, the son could report the ejection of the Hungarians from Vienna and recovery of the stolen Austrian lands. Later he would secure a lease on Hungary itself by betrothing an infant grand-daughter to a child yet unborn, trusting God to make it male. But God had not so far accorded Europe safety from the Turks: Hungary and much of Austria would yet crack between the jaws of Islam.

Such was the century which was to reach its end amidst the flowering of the Renaissance: torn by jealousies, constantly at war, obsessed by maladies it was unqualified to cure. Battles were not infrequently fought out by mercenary armies, provided in the main by the Swiss. The Alpine peasantry made superb European infantry, though sometimes their price could be too high. In that case other volunteers lacking peaceable em-ployment became available for hire, usually from Germany. They enrolled no matter for whom. An army was a motley formation. Soldiers brought their wives and children along, to forage and to cook, while entrepreneurs stood by at a respectable distance, awaiting the outcome of a battle. They knew how to secure the best payment for prisoners, and where appropriate could negotiate an exemplary ransom. Wars ran up tremen-dous bills which princes discharged by repairing to the bankers of Genoa and Florence, or to the great Augsburg houses, the Fuggers notably. These latter ended the fifteenth century as concessionaires for Central Europe's mineral deposits, silver and copper, and the great pasturelands of Spain; later, a substantial portion of the wealth of the New World with much else besides.

Mercenaries also fought for booty as legitimate reward. They made unpredictable armies, as that penetrating student of the human element in politics, Machiavelli, warned. The Turks would not trust their fate to hired soldiery; their troops fought for the greater glory of Allah. More, none of his subjects could defy the wishes of a sultan: all of them, including his Grand Vizier, were his personal slaves. As such this people entrenched themselves on the European mainland and harried Italy from the sea. The sultan told himself he could afford to play a waiting game while the West lay dying. Islam had work enough pacifying its eastern frontierlands before delivering the *coup de grâce* upon Europe.

But Christopher Columbus, the Genoese who studied his Bible and trusted it to bring him to another hemisphere, would be taking this continent beyond itself. Because of Columbus, and the stimulus he gave to rivalries in oceanic exploration, Christendom would leave the Oriental competition standing still. The global destiny fell into the ready hands of Europe.

Chapter Two

SPAIN RETURNS TO EUROPE

ings and princes, cardinals and captains—they might all pursue their grandiose schemes in Spain and Portugal, building castles in the air as well as on the ground, yet virtually until the dawn of the fifteenth century it could not be said for certain whether the Iberian peninsula constituted the south-western extremity of Europe or the northernmost outpost of Africa. It was on the wrong side of the Pyrenees. The Moors had been implanted there too long. So had the Jews. This latter people fell into a situation by which they would be recognized throughout subsequent history. They identified with both the others, and with neither. On the Iberian Peninsula the Jews could as happily reside in an Islamic as in a Christian civilization; or as unhappily, which was sometimes the case.

The critical moment for Spain had been the abandonment of Toledo by the old Visigoth kings to the Moorish Emirate of Córdoba early in the eighth century. Worse than a defeat, this appeared to the Christians as though God had lost a struggle with Satan, the beginning of the end of the world. Rising tall on a granite tableland in the heart of Castile, selected by the Visigoths as their capital for its supposed immunity from attack, Toledo now proclaimed the Arab ascendancy at its proudest. After conquest it flourished in religious and social tolerance, a golden city watered by the swift Tagus to take the golden Arab age to its zenith; not exactly the end of the world, only a local change of civilization.

Thenceforward the Arabs, leading their vassal tribesmen of the Atlas mountains, would not be denied. Ignoring only the north-western corner of Spain fronting the Bay of Biscay, they swarmed over the peninsula and traversed the Pyrenees. Would they subjugate France too? It was to be touch and go. Under the command of their governor of Spain the

Charles Martell

Muslims advanced beyond Poitiers on one flank and to the mouth of the
Rhône on the other. There, in the year 732, the invaders could at last

song of Roland

be arrested. Still they would not leave France unmolested. Charlemagne
himself led an army over the mountains, determined to thwart Arab
designs upon Europe. In 778 he reached Saragossa. But Charlemagne's
campaign, hampered by the undisciplined Basques, ended in disaster
with the Moors hot on his heels. The great ruler had to leave them in
possession of Narbonne. Only after a sustained counter-attack some years
later was that city cleared and France could breathe free of Islam.

On the other hand, Iberia consolidated into a powerful Muslim realm,
self-confident enough to break contact with the Arabian Orient whence
the conquerors had sprung. Defiantly, it declared itself an independent
Caliphate in 929, divorced from far-away Baghdad. In no capital city of
Europe did Christendom equal the civilization of Muslim Córdoba, either
in its architecture and scholarship or in the humanity of its administration—half a million population, 300 public baths, paved streets policed
night and day; except that internal divisions had already thrown up
factions in other parts of Spain at odds with Córdoba. These were recognized by the Christians as signs of decay, and therefore their opportunity.

Just two years had been required for the Moors to subjugate this barren,
mountainous land. Its recovery for Christendom became a crusade enduring, with stops and starts, for eight centuries. Nothing was gained
without its price. In the process Portugal separated from the rest, while
the entire peninsula assumed its character of two hybrid Christian nations
embracing various tribes of extraordinary intensity and passion. The unity
eventually achieved under the Church disguised only weakly their many
conflicting loyalties. The Moors had arrived as conquerors but they stayed
as colonists, demonstrating a skill hitherto unfamiliar in these parts:
agriculture by irrigation. The Jews beside them—some arrived with the
invasion, others had been among the conquered—adopted Spain as a
substitute Holy Land. Christian, Muslim and Jew intermingled confidently. They might have ultimately melded into one had not Christendom, suffering the shock of its narrow escape, decided, upon regaining
its own destiny, that its preservation here demanded a purity of blood.
Thus the doctrine of racialism was born.

By an irony, the Spanish secured less of a purity than probably any
other European nation. Yet some new consistency entered into their
character: an introspective readiness for sacrifice in the service of a cause,
be it ever so uncertain, and evident still in the twentieth century. When,

in 1936, ideology combined with regional peculiarities to incite a civil war, a million people had to die before one side would surrender to the other. No doubt men and women in both camps drew their inspiration from the memory, ever latent, of Spain's epic Reconquista.

Centuries though this would ultimately entail, the Reconquista began almost immediately. Little more than a twelve-month of subjugation had elapsed before Spaniards arose to challenge their alien masters and seek to reverse their terrible fate as an appendage of Islam. The germ of revolt was born in the Asturian north-west, where a certain Don Pelayo, a man claiming descent from the Visigoth kings, successfully defied a Muslim force at Covadonga. It was merely a skirmish, but a torch had been lit, registering to the continuance of a living Christendom. To the Spaniards this small victory was as if the Star of Bethlehem had appeared in their sky. Legend gave to Pelayo the glory of the foundation of the royal house of Castile.

However, the recapture of Toledo had to await another 350 years. In the mean time Castile and Aragon emerged as the two monarchies upon which Christian vitality in the Iberian peninsula rested. They had already liberated Portugal, achieved after some reverses with the help of crusaders from abroad, mainly England and Burgundy. The latter's leader intended to assert his own independent rule, while an English priest became the first Bishop of Lisbon. The Pope recognized Portugal as an independent kingdom under a Burgundian dynasty in 1179.

Slowly the Castilian monarchy, having absorbed all the north-west of the country with its centre at León, added the craggy heartlands to its role. It fell to the Aragonese to liquidate the smaller emirates that dotted Catalonia and Valencia. As it transpired, traditional Moorish structure within North Africa had itself declined and Spaniards now confronted Muslims of a fanatical Berber breed who placed in their vanguard African slaves chained together to form a wall of flesh. It was a fight to the death on both sides. The recovery of Toledo and Valencia featured the exploits, promptly mythologized, of the famous Christian captain Rodrigo Díaz, called El Cid. He bore an Arab title as the ruler of a Muslim kingdom himself, but had then changed sides. To such a degree had Catholic and infidel grown together. The process would engage Catholic and Jew similarly.

Thus we reach the end of the thirteenth century, by which time even the great city of Córdoba had been recaptured. Still, the Reconquista was brought almost to a halt. A territorial rump of the once mighty Caliphate clung to its sovereignty as the shrunken kingdom of Granada, where the passion for conquest was replaced by a struggle for survival. Slowly but surely the Moors, caught in a downward spiral of impotence, lost their possessions and their pride. Throughout the peninsula the warriors of Islam found themselves transmuted into a subordinate class, craftsmen and shepherds most of them, though some of such ingenuity they were the first people in Europe to discover the science of paper-making. It had occurred at Jativa, in Valencia, about the year 1150. The little hillside town would one day earn another kind of fame as the place that produced the Borgia family. For the majority of Moors and Berbers, now leaderless, Spain was the only homeland they desired. Some reinforced the embrace to the point of Catholic conversion, and in the composition of epic poetry written in the Castilian tongue.

The Islamic faithful could take heart in a pilgrimage to Granada. As the centre of the only Islamic statelet left on the European continent, the city served almost for a western Mecca. Their ancestral civilization continued to flower there, its Alhambra unrivalled in splendour by any Christian edifice, a little dominion at the foot of Spain where Arabic literature could be studied and where a mosque escaped desecration as a church. Catholic Spain nibbled away at the kingdom's edges, appropriating tracts where convenient. It allowed Granada to survive as a docile tributary of Castile, though for how long Allah alone knew.

It goes almost without saying that Portugal, Castile and Aragon fell short of harmonious coexistence, for the peninsula was an unmade bed. So many problems ensued from the centuries of struggle and the bitter recollections of frustrated hopes, that the victorious parts, added together, refused to form into a whole. Each portion nurtured a dynasty with ambitions of expansion. They went their separate ways, forged alliances, clashed, made temporary peace, intermarried and bred descendants persuaded of their right to occupy one another's thrones. Furthermore, no monarch enjoyed undisputed authority within his territory, yet he indulged in dreams beyond his own frontiers. In the Hundred Years War Portugal found itself enmeshed as the ally of England, Castile as the ally of France, while Lisbon suffered a sacking by Castile in 1373. This was chastisement inflicted upon Fernando of Portugal for seeking to annex his neighbour, an inspiration that also put him at odds with another claimant, his treacherous friend John of Gaunt, Duke of Lancaster. Fernando and the Englishman were in fact related. As elsewhere in Europe, whenever a daughter was sacrificed in marriage to assuage an enemy or seal a treaty, one quarrel ended only to create more for another time.

(John never gained a desired Kingdom but his son did, Henry IV of England. His daughter became the mother of Henry the Navigator of Portugal.)

It had taken much blood to secure the future of Christendom in Spain and Portugal, and their peoples understandably preferred to turn away when, in the fifteenth century, the menace of Islam approached Europe from the Orient. There, a crusade meant exactly what it said: redemption of Jerusalem for the Cross. But crusading in the East had met with successive failure, except for a brief spell long ago when for eighty-seven years a Christian king ruled in the Holy City. Since then talk of its resumption flowed continuously, with little achieved. Here in Iberia, however, they had not given up. Except in Granada, now just a puppet, Islam was vanquished. More, there was good prospect of a crusade in reverse, with Islam itself coming under threat on its Moroccan shore. The Muslim rulers in Africa were in disarray, destroying each other in pursuit of conquest. Portugal leapt to exploit the situation by stealing Ceuta, opposite Gibraltar, from the King of Granada in 1415.

Portugal felt the wash of the ocean, and sought a destiny there. Aragon looked more naturally towards the Mediterranean; its perspectives came to rest in Italy on the European shore and Tunis, long regarded as a Catalan protectorate, in Africa. Castile seemed stronger than either of its neighbours, in population and area, but its dominance was only in theory: much of the land, though cleared of infidel rule, lay in the grasp of the military and ecclesiastical orders, which had so valiantly fought for it. And, as in the case of the Teutonic Knights of the Baltic, these resourceful soldier-priests intended to retain those lands, and the wealth therefrom, practically independent of their feudal master the king. Castile knew it had to absorb Granada one day, but this was now of lesser concern to Aragon. And what of Navarre, strongly Basque but partly French-speaking, and wedged between Castile and Aragon astride the Pyrenees? Was it Spanish or French? Perhaps neither. Aragon fastened greedy eyes upon it.

We are speaking of a period when Catholicism sharpened its religiosity at the point of a spear. A priest could just as easily be a politician in another garb, while a king of course, in seizing another's realm, manifested the will of God on earth. Royal violence against persons high and low found sanctification in an *auto-da-fé*, as the Portuguese called it. In truth, religion could justify any amount of deceit, forgery, persecution, rapine, and therefore a ruling house dropped its guard at its peril. Hence the Burgundians failed, late in the fourteenth century, to keep the crown of Portugal. They lost it to the House of Avis, linked to Fernando's family through a bastard half-brother of the king.

The transfer of power in Portugal, necessitating a baronial civil war, would hardly concern us here, for such regal substitutions affected the common people but little, except that John I of Avis produced, in a younger son Henry, the architect of Portugal's maritime greatness. Henry, apotheosized as the Navigator, was a cousin of Henry V of England (they shared a grandfather in John of Gaunt). He stood apart from the usual dynastic preoccupations of princes. What obsessed him was the continent of Africa. What was its extent? Where did it lead to? How much of it had the Muslims explored and plundered and enslaved? Henry had participated in the campaign that won Ceuta for Portugal. This was the furthest he ever travelled on water, but the difficulties experienced by the Portuguese sailors in navigating through the currents in the Straits of Gibraltar drove his thoughts to the challenge of the sea. His country's long coastline demanded marriage with it. The prince pondered the splendours of Genoa and Venice. The greatness of these maritime republics grew from their mastery of the Mediterranean, virtually navigable in sight of land at all times. But Portugal possessed a wilder shore on the Atlantic, an ocean infested with terror unknown.

Henry decided to enlist the Genoese—numerous in Lisbon, where they conducted good business—in uncovering the secrets of the Atlantic. The prince was born in 1394, of a generation straining towards the humanist thought peeping over the mental frontier, when traditional beliefs about the world, the form God had given it, indeed man's significance in Creation, were already coming under searching examination. The Arabs, in their occupation of his country, had brought the astrolabe from the Near East, to guide a vessel's position latitude at night by the stars, while learned men at Amalfi had built on the Chinese contribution to navigation, the magnetic compass.

Henry's designers increased safety at sea by making noteworthy improvements in the caravel. It now had a stouter forecastle than had previously shaped the craft, three masts and a lateen sail, so that adverse headwinds were no longer a mariner's nightmare. A still more significant advance produced the carrack, a larger vessel of two or more decks, enabling the ample storage of provisions for an extended voyage. Sailing in any case needed no longer to be a matter of navigation between visible headlands. Portolan charts, to assist a pilot more surely through an estuary into port, were also in common use. Fishermen regularly visited Iceland, which was regarded as *ultima Thule*, though no European merchantman had as yet sailed into the Indian Ocean. Even Venetian traders waited at Alexandria and the Black Sea ports for their Oriental merchandise.

Henry the Navigator occupied a position of high Christian authority as head of the Order of Christ (formerly the Templars crusading order, abolished by the Pope allegedly for blasphemy and sodomy in its initiation rites but now re-established under royal supervision). The office carried a resolve to bring the Gospel to the heathen. This imperative was all the stronger now, in view of Islam's deep penetration of Africa. The prince proclaimed the crusade as his intended motive, but few doubted his deeper concern, the riches which, by all accounts, lay spread for the taking in distant continents. Travellers' tales spoke of mountains of gold dust and pearls no less than of habitations of giants, creatures half-man, half-beast, others headless, in places remote from Europe. No one had as yet been able to separate fact from fantasy. And among all these wonders did there not reign, somewhere in the East, a mighty Christian king, possibly immortal, Prester John?

This intelligence had been brought to Europe by Marco Polo, the Venetian explorer who died in 1323. He had travelled with his father and uncle over the Mongol Empire, among other adventures winning the confidence of Kublai Khan. Marco Polo's return, after a period of twenty-four years, led to the birth of a legend, culled from his dictated memoirs, of Prester John's rule over a powerful, God-fearing nation amidst the lands of the pagan. Christendom wished to believe that all Marco Polo's reports were true, and other travellers worked the legend into assortments of their own, usually by the device of westernizing the title of a reputed Khan (never actually encountered) into a kind of anagram of 'Priest King'. Henry the Navigator certainly gave the legend of Prester John credence, as did Christopher Columbus many years later. But whereas Henry, to assist his cause, located the Christian monarch somewhere in Africa, perhaps Ethiopia, Columbus preferred to believe he would be found in the 'Indies'.

Pointedly, Henry established his base at the furthermost south-western extremity of his country, Cape St Vincent. He gathered his cartographers, astronomers and skilled mariners there, where he remained until his death in 1460. The location seemed to announce that all the seas to the west and south of Portugal, and all the islands of the sea, fell within that country's patrimony. Employing the immense wealth enjoyed by the Order of Christ, Henry despatched his well-remunerated crews along the African coast, and seaward to find the terra firma on which to plant the national flag. And as there would be no land anywhere that did not come under the ultimate ownership of God, their baggage also included the blessing of the Pope.

In 1419 Henry's expeditions made landfall at Madeira, in 1425 the

Canaries. Then, in 1427, they dared a voyage deep in the Atlantic as far as the Azores. The year 1457 brought the Portuguese as far as the volcanic Cape Verde group west from Senegal. These islands, all except the Canaries hitherto uninhabited, were soon colonized and planted with olives, vines and sugar cane. Portugal was on its way to creating the first extra-European empire. Gold and ivory came home from the African mainland by way of trade—exchanged not only for baubles of the cheapest glass, but also for horses and cloth. In 1444 the first human cargo, Negro slaves from the Guinea coast, was brought to market in Lisbon, inaugurating the shameful commerce that would corrupt the white man's contact with the black for centuries, and their mutual relations long after that. Hitherto Europe's slaves had been, for the most part, the discharge of wars fought by Tatar and Turk against Serbia, South Russia and Central Asia, to be transported by the traditional entrepreneurs from Genoa and Venice.

Insignificant Portugal, whose population numbered well below a million, suddenly burst from its bonds as the poor man of Iberia. Wealth flowed into Lisbon. The busy port echoed with the cacophony of a dozen tongues as fortune-hunters from all corners hastened there, lured by the prospect of easy riches. Turning its back upon Europe, the kingdom took to expansion as if by instinct. From Ceuta it spread itself over the whole Moroccan coast, Tangier to Casablanca, besides establishing trading stations (they were fortresses) down the shore of Africa tucking into the Gulf of Guinea. And however vague their comprehension of land's disposition about the globe, the Portuguese understood that every new day of exploration wrote them another page of glory and took them closer to the fabled wealth of the Indies. To be sure, there were disasters enough, when 'the ship it was their coffin, their grave it was the sea'.

How could Castile view Portugal's dramatic aggrandizement? Did not Castile, seven times greater in population, four times in area, regard its western neighbour as virtually a subordinate principality of its own? And did it not expect Portugal one day to follow its historical logic and join a wider Hispanic union? Anxieties in fact sharpened in Castile, where a new monarch, Queen Isabella, succeeded to the throne in 1474. She was joined there with a consort by no means universally admired—the deeply calculating and ambitious young prince of Aragon, Ferdinand.

Isabella's accession had not occurred without controversy, nor without heartache on the part of another princess of uncertain parentage (daughter of the previous queen's favourite?) who had strong grounds for asserting that the Castilian crown was rightfully hers. This latter princess was intended for marriage to the King of Portugal, Alfonso V, who aspired to be the mouse swallowing the Castilian cat. The consequence—yet another war—was rendered even more complicated by an internal Castilian battle of loyalties, since important elements there rebelled against Queen Isabella's union with Ferdinand of Aragon.

While dynastic conflict furnished ground enough for war, the true root of enmity in this case lay elsewhere. Undisguised, the inter-Iberian hostility resulted from a struggle for dominance over the lucrative West African trade, and placing in the scale ownership of all those offshore islands. By what right did Portugal claim them? Others had reached the Madeiras before the Portuguese without declaring occupation. And the Canaries, the only ones inhabited, had once been visited by French seamen in the service of Castile, though as nothing proceeded from that expedition sovereignty had been left in abeyance.

Alfonso of Portugal, candidate for the hand of that disconsolate young princess reputed to be a bastard, enlisted French support and marched into Castile, proposing to take the kingdom there and then. But Alfonso had overreached himself, proving no match in battle against his neighbour. Notoriously anarchic in its past, Castile now enjoyed a more ordered, centralized administration and was drawing benefits of strong monarchy, wise counsellors and an efficient army. Four disastrous years for Portugal therefore ended with its king's recognition of Isabella as lawful Queen of Castile. He refrained from marrying her rival, still in her teens, who thereupon entered a convent. Additionally, Alfonso surrendered claim to the Canaries, islands so called because the Romans, who knew them, had discovered this archipelago to be overrun by wild hounds. In fact the fifteenth-century natives, Guanche cave-dwellers living in the Stone Age, worshipped their dogs.

Castile in its turn recognized Portuguese rights in the other islands and in those portions of Africa to which they had brought the doubtful privileges of their civilization. The parties signed the treaty of Alcaçovas in 1479, but as far as Castile was concerned this left a large question unresolved. Which of them would possess territories still to be discovered in the future? Undoubtedly they would belong to one or the other. The Pope decreed so.

Sixtus IV, a Franciscan, had been involved in negotiation of the treaty of Alcaçovas. He recognized the Iberian nations as his most faithful allies, and wished to reward them accordingly. He needed them for his own devious purposes in Italy, and to strengthen his hand against his disagreeable flock in Germany, where Rome was called the Unholy See.

Sixtus brought nepotism to a fine art, and in return for future favours he issued in 1481 the bull *Aeterna regis*, by which all discoveries south of the Canaries and west of Africa would belong to Portugal. Castile saved its displeasure for the moment at the paltry gift of the Canaries, although it had no intention of honouring all the ambiguities implied in the papal bull. Ferdinand would have something to say about that on a more appropriate occasion. He did not equal his wife's reverence of the Holy Father.

The Castilian-Portuguese war was, in May 1476, beginning to generate tedious complications, customary in Hispanic conflicts, when Christopher Columbus signed in Genoa with the *Bechalla*, a Flemish vessel bearing cargo from the Mediterranean to northern Europe. He had turned twenty-five, and whether Columbus, by this age, was a seafarer in constant employ has never been firmly established. Certainly he had already been on several voyages, one of them to the island of Chios, which was all that remained of the extensive Genoese trading empire in the eastern Mediterranean. In his youth Columbus had also shipped with a fleet chartered by Duke René of Anjou, and found himself involved in a minor naval engagement against Aragon. Nevertheless, as the eldest of five offspring of the master weaver Domenico Colombo and his wife Susanna, he was destined apparently for a landlubber's existence never too far from the loom. Christopher—named as it happened after the patron saint of travellers—had been given little education and spoke only the Genoese dialect, which was hardly understood outside that corner of Italy. Still, which young man would not seize the opportunity, always available in Genoa, for an occasional voyage with a handsome bounty at the end? So here he was, in what capacity we know not, sailing through the Straits of Gibraltar on a merchantman bound for Flanders. Now fate intervened to change Christopher's life and alter the course of history.

For safety's sake ships travelled in convoy in those days, as a protection against pirates. Suddenly this one came under fire from an armed Frenchman plying those waters on purposes hard to discover, and the *Bechalla* was one of three ships sent to the bottom. Columbus thereupon exhibited that capacity for commanding the waters that would one day make him the most famous of all sea-captains. He grabbed an oar, swam and floated and rested till washed up on the nearest shore. It transpired to be near Lagos, just a few miles from Cape St Vincent and the headquarters established by Henry the Navigator, long dead.

Surely Columbus was born under the luckiest of stars, for as it happened his brother Bartholomew lived in Lisbon, a member of the sea-port's substantial Genoese colony. Bartholomew was employed by a chart-making company there and, indeed, contemplated opening such a business on his own independent account. The brothers ultimately went into partnership, spending all their time in what was then the most adventurous of maritime environments. Christopher, with his surname transliterated to Colón to suit the local atmosphere, learnt Latin and Portuguese. He took off on occasional voyages, certainly to Ireland and possibly also (he could be a story-teller) to Iceland. The brothers prospered. Christopher married a local girl, Doña Felipa Perestrello, whose father and grandfather had served as Portugal's hereditary governor on Porto Santo, one of the smaller Madeiras. He studied his Bible, he scrutinized the charts, he dreamed. The spell of the Atlantic and conversation with those who ventured on it became part of his daily diet. Genoa ceased to figure in his mental map of the world. Columbus returned on occasion, and had dealings with the San Giorgio bank. True, he remained a Genoese all his life, though Italians, then as now, took to expatriation as to a new coat.

He would shortly become enslaved to an idea whose consummation would set the principal courts of Europe against each other in a rash of new ambitions and extra jealousies. Kings would give voice to their shrill pretensions. Consequent upon their actions, armour would clang against armour in places remote from Europe, ships would interlock in battle on the high seas, and the repercussions would multiply across time. But these events come within the category of power-politics; none of it would affect Christian civilization at its root so much as a silent revolution already in progress. The art of printing had arrived. Various North Europeans were working on its perfection before the middle of the fifteenth century, though three cities, Bruges, Strasbourg and Mainz, all noted for their piety, craftsmanship and ingenuity, competed for the honour of being the first.

The secret of writing a page by the mechanical process of movable type, centuries-old in China, seems to have been effectively concealed in the West till about 1451. Or perhaps the idea of producing a book without employing a scribe of the utmost saintliness was held to be unnatural, almost a blasphemy. Books were not intended for a general readership, and in earlier times many were withheld from vulgarian eyes by deliberate destruction. However, the era of humanism brushed some of those old shibboleths from the mind in the fifteenth century, as we have seen. Pope Nicholas V, before he died in 1455, collected many thousands of manuscript volumes, having spent a fortune in searching them out, to start the Vatican library. The very uniqueness of a book made it all the more precious. Copyists (Lorenzo the Magnificent's grandfather Cosimo employed forty-five) enjoyed the highest trust, which they repaid by including artistic embellishments of their own. To some scholars printing debased learning, and many priests saw the invention as endangering the prerogatives of the Church. One highly cultivated prince, the Renaissance patron Federigo da Montefeltro, Duke of Urbino, declared he 'would be ashamed to own a printed book'. Indeed!

This was a revolution that could not be stayed. The earliest printed document extant is dated 1454. It was an 'indulgence', a grant of papal absolution for all sins in exchange for a contribution towards the cost of a crusade. Johann Gutenberg, a Mainz silversmith, printed it, along with his Bible about the same time. Henceforward the Renaissance, from its Florentine breeding-ground, took wing. In 1492 some 15,000 book titles were in circulation embracing all the world's accumulation of learning, with Venice as the publishing capital of civilization. At a stroke, an elect few, deprived of their monopoly of literacy, ceased to be the elect. However, while the new humanism bred the Renaissance, it did nothing to raise standards of humanity.

Once printing was commonly established as a medium of communication, language itself came under intense scrutiny. Latin had its fixed rules, but what of vernacular writing? Italy once again led the way. Its poets and philosophers gave attention to the joys of elegance in their language. Soon others followed, through the long process of standardizing grammar and spelling. Printing had the effect of reducing the importance of Latin and stimulating national cultures, which in their turn gave birth to national pride. This could carry destructive elements in its baggage, self-pride and hatred often travelling together.

Thus the easier availability of books, and the growth of a reading public, increased the dissemination not only of knowledge but also of religious intolerance, which fostered persecution. Printing, that most civilizing of man's inventions, also gave wider expression to the less generous aspects of his nature. And now that so many more people became closely familiar with the Gospel story, they could more easily recognize the villains of the piece: those ubiquitous people of ancient stock, the Jews. The Church, from the time of its Founding Fathers to its latest teachers, had long prepared the ground. St Thomas Aquinas among others spread animosity against the Jews, perpetuating as doctrine the myth that, in crucifying Jesus, they dwelt with Satan and were destined for eternal damnation unless redeemed by recantation and baptism.

Because the circumstances of the Iberian peninsula's national evolution had brought into cohabitation three disparate peoples, Christian, Islamic and Jewish, to a degree unknown elsewhere, this region created particularly fertile soil for racial hostility. By a paradox constant in human society, harmony and discord among racial groups have always existed side-by-side; hate and love make common bed-fellows (Germany in our own time emulated the Spanish example absolutely). Each of those three sects performed a role periodically rendering the other two incompatible. The Muslims, during their Iberian supremacy, tolerated unbelievers in Muhammad, but this had to be on the basis of a defined inferiority. The Christians, once victorious, reasserted their religious dogma by force and punishment. After all, did not the struggle to recover their soil constitute a holy war? The Jews, being without territorial claims, endeavoured in all vicissitudes to serve whichever of the other two assumed dominance. Their ancestors had opened the gateways of Toledo to the Moors early in the eighth century. They were a substantial community of 12,000 in that city, when, switching sides, they assisted the Christians to recapture it in 1085. Jews flourished under both regimes, in culture, wealth and privilege. Not surprisingly, they were also distrusted by both. The appearance of the printed book and the spread of literacy coincided with Christendom restored, or all but restored, throughout the peninsula. Thereupon alienation of the other two turned into persecution.

Such persecution was bound to take different forms; or rather, attain unequal intensities. The Muslim population, because its aristocracy fled before the reconquering Christian armies, found themselves reduced in the main to countrymen stripped of privileges. They congregated chiefly among their own. From a state of grandeur, they had descended the scale to the despised lowest strata of this society, albeit as small holders working on their own land, whereas Jews had long forgotten peasantry. They dwelt in towns and cities. Their craftsmen favoured the dyeing and tanning trades, their rich could be counsellors to royalty, tax-farmers, merchants and money-lenders. Multilingual, their scribes worked in Arabic, Castilian, Catalan, Hebrew, Latin and Greek.

Unlike the Muslims, Jews in the main—their men anyway—were literate and sought education as the path to adjustment. Both tribes rejected Christianity, but in the case of the less isolated Jews the penalties arising from their exclusion from general society could be too high,

resulting in a progressive movement towards baptism. The more numerous Muslim produced fewer apostates and therefore less heartache in
their closed, patriarchal system. Jewish converts developed almost into
a specific class of 'New Christians' as they were termed, separated from
the Mosaic faithful. Such was the situation of a minority population
following residence in this outpost of their diaspora for a thousand years
at least. Intermarriage, as already indicated, mingled the blood of all
groups, not excluding royalty. Ferdinand of Aragon was unpopular with
some sections of the Castilian nobility for, among other reasons, his
known descent from the Jewess Paloma of Toledo. She was remote by
any measure, a great-grandmother. Ferdinand was tarnished nevertheless.

We require to fold history back a hundred years. In 1391 the tide rose
against all heretics, Moorish and Jewish, throughout Castile. Owing their
origin to the crusading eloquence of a Dominican friar, Ferrand Martinez,
confessor to the then queen, the persecutions assumed catastrophic proportions. Martinez roused envy and resentment against the Jews particularly, by citing the contrast between their aristocratic style and the
general population's wretchedness. Little wonder then that the Juderias,
their residential quarters, were penetrated and pillaged in a hundred
towns, to the degree that the instigator of it all is said to have been
shocked at the carnage wrought by the fury he had unleashed. The
Muslims, by the nature of their dispersed settlements, were given time
to organize armed resistance in the hills against their oppressors and were
able to demonstrate, if briefly, the fire that had made their ancestors
superb warriors. It will be recalled that this was still a lawless Spain,
uncontrolled by feeble crowns in both Castile and Aragon.

It would never have dawned upon the Jews to rise against this land:
was it not their surrogate Jerusalem? The persecutions spread from Castile
into Catalonia, province of Aragon. Synagogues were seized and converted into churches. To the Jews of Barcelona, important shipowners
among them, fearful alternatives were offered: destruction, or baptism,
or flight. Some died, some converted, some fled. In the process, economic
crisis struck at Barcelona. That city, capital of the kingdom of Aragon,
lost its place as a major entrepôt and ceased to challenge Genoa for the
prized Mediterranean traffic. By the worst of ironies, the fiercest perse-
cutors were themselves Christian apostates from the Jewish faith, or
descended from converts—Fr. Martinez among them

The sorrowing Jews, formerly so integrated, were left in a peculiar
limbo. So many hurried conversions occurred that the description 'New
Christian' came in many cases to imply a coverage of deceit, a masquerade

by heretics for personal advancement or gain, a badge of the untrust-
worthy. Their detractors labelled them 'Marranos' (the word could mean
pigs') and the name stuck. Those Jews remaining loyal to the religion
of their fathers were suspected of suborning the others, seeking to return
them to the fold—in a measure undeniable. Thus devout New Christians
not infrequently taking to the cloth and rising high in the Catholic
hierarchy, themselves kept the animosity alive. As a notorious example,
the early fifteenth century saw Bishop Pablo de Santa Maria, who had
formerly occupied a synagogue pulpit as Rabbi Solomon Halevi and now
claimed descent from the Holy family—hence his adopted name—raged
at the continued exalted status of some Jews. He inspired new regulations
(the Laws of Valladolid) forbidding Jewish physicians to treat Christian
patients, or employ Christian servants, or reside elsewhere than in the
Juderias. Bishop Pablo served the royal household as guardian to the boy
King John II of Castile, future father of Queen Isabella.

The mood now led to a clamour for a radical solution to the problem
of the Jews before the race contaminated Catholic blood beyond cure.
If a Jew remained identifiable as such well and good, he would receive
punishment in the next world. But should crypto-Jews give cause for
suspicion of deviating from the true faith they should be arraigned for
trial and torture and, if necessary, burned at the stake. New Christians
and orthodox Jews fought each other in the streets of Toledo in 1449.
It was time to revive the Inquisition, that papal tribunal established in
medieval times to hunt out heretics throughout Christendom.

Ferdinand's father (also a John II) died in 1479 and the kingdoms of
Aragon and Castile thereupon federated under the joint rule of Ferdinand
and Isabella. The Portuguese war was done, ending victoriously; the
Castilian civil war likewise. The joint monarchy could now survey its
unfinished business: most immediately, the liquidation of independent
Granada, an objective requiring monies for a campaign beyond the capacities of the exhausted royal exchequer; that, and the Jewish question.
To the second another urgent issue was connected. This concerned
relations between Spain and the Vatican. From the beginning of their
reign Ferdinand and Isabella insisted upon personal rule, free of interference by the bishops. Agreeable though the monarchs might be to hear
their advice, and to acknowledge their spiritual role, they understood
well how the bishops could double as the Pope's secret agents, jealously
intriguing to extend Rome's authority beyond matters ecclesiastical. Religion of course overlapped politics, limiting a monarch's freedom to an
oppressive degree in the past. In the humanist fifteenth century this was

no longer tolerable. We are speaking of a period during which the Vatican exploited the rivalry of Spain and France for domination in Italy, a rivalry successive popes manipulated to further their own interests as temporal rulers. In matters Inquisitorial, the Pope's servants alone could erect tribunals, pass judgment and administer punishments.

As the Curia itself admitted, the Vatican was in dire need of reform. A victim of its own grandiosity and venality, it had degenerated into a party to the quarrels of nations. Italian cardinals were given to Mammon and could not be trusted; French cardinals served their country first and then God, while regarding the Pontificate as their own preserve. Germany's prelates were irregular clerics, territorial barons in fact, rarely to be discovered inside a church. France flattered itself as 'the eldest daughter of the Church', though it was the Christian nation most liberated from papal influence. England gave Rome little trouble for the moment— that would come—while Spain was in the process of that centralization which, as already stated, required royal control over all institutions, even those professing first allegiance to the Pontiff.

This did not imply that Christian monarchs dared dispense with papal sanction for their conduct. They required Vatican authorization in questions of marriage and divorce, of course. A coronation did not bestow divine right to rule without the Pope's recognition of its legality. When reluctant, he had to be pressed, by *force majeure* or simple bribery. The Pope could be a nuisance, but he was always necessary to those in the grip of earthly ambition.

The sovereigns of quasi-united Spain (each kingdom of the partnership kept its separate administration) determined to make their stand by installing the Inquisition strictly under their own rather than Rome's auspices. Ferdinand, less of a pietist than his spouse, made this his particular concern. He refused to tolerate Roman interference in a matter of such national significance. Sixtus IV demurred from granting the privilege. Truthfully, the Pope did not favour the Inquisition's establishment in Spain. But if he could not prevent it, he must take it under the authority of Rome: it had to be the 'Holy Inquisition', not the 'Royal Inquisition'. Ferdinand refused to give way. He charged Rodrigo Borgia, Bishop of Valencia, a Spanish cardinal of unbounded aspiration, to intercede. Through his uncle, Pope Calixtus III, Borgia had been appointed cardinal at twenty-five. Several youthful Borgias received the hat in the undisguised nepotism of those times, whether or not their murky careers intended a whole life in the Church. This one anticipated his eventual enthronement in St Peter's. He would need Spain's support then, as he needed it now for the advancement of other members of his family to his own sumptuous life-style. Dutifully, Cardinal Borgia worked his charms upon Sixtus, offering inducements. The Pope relented.

It began in Seville, this cruellest of all tribunals, and was conducted with such ferocity—hands chopped from the 'guilty' preceded the consignment of living men and women to the pyre—that a general flight of Jews from that city ensued, their property going forfeit to the crown. In the mean time the Aragonese provinces, which recalled their drastic economic decline resulting from the anti-Jewish persecutions of 1391, determined to defy the king. The regional Cortes or parliament of Catalonia would not admit the Inquisition to Barcelona. Assassination of the appointed Inquisitor in Saragossa Cathedral, organized by a group of New Christians, told of their strength of feeling. Still, nothing deterred the king.

Repenting of his decision to sanction the Inquisition in Castile, Sixtus absolutely forbade its extension to the kingdom of Aragon. Angry Ferdinand threatened reprisals against the Pope. Short of funds though he might be, he held a strong hand in Italy as King of Sicily (a patrimony of Aragon) and Sixtus was ever in need of allies. The Pope therefore cringed before the show of force, to the extent of withdrawing his allegation that the tribunal's primary motive was expropriation—greed for the Jews' property. The Spanish Inquisition received papal blessing as a royal institution. Ferdinand could therefore count himself somewhat compensated for the bull *Aeterni regis* of 1481, which favoured Portugal in rights of overseas discovery. More, the Pope's successor, Innocent VIII, went further in making an unholy virtue out of necessity. He ordered all Christian rulers to extradite to Spain any suspected heretics seeking refuge abroad. Those untraced were to be burnt in effigy.

It had taken five years before Ferdinand could install the tribunal, with all the melodrama involved in its ghoulish ceremonial, throughout the kingdom. It made a mockery of judgment. A man or woman could be condemned purely on the verbal testimony of blasphemy by a single witness whose motives could well be remote from religious. Some denunciations for heresy arose from ordinary family quarrels.

How many died or spent long years in the dungeons cannot be exactly established, though a reasonable estimate, during the fifteen years while Tomás de Torquemada held the office of Grand Inquisitor, gave four to eight thousand secret Jews and suspects burnt alive, besides many fewer Moorish New Christians, called Moriscos, and other presumed heretics. All was meticulously registered, as if some heavenly accountant was keeping check on Christendom's gains and Satanism's losses, though only in part have the records survived. Among those suffering incarceration were several relatives of the Archbishop of Granada, a former confessor to Queen Isabella. Established in all territories under the Spanish crown, the Inquisition in due course travelled across the Atlantic to follow Christopher Columbus to the New World. Before its final abolition in 1820, some 32,000 heretics were consigned to the flames. Spain will ever be haunted by its criminal history even though, in the matter of the incineration of human beings, it has in our twentieth century found its master. The Portuguese Inquisition would likewise sully the history of Spain's Iberian neighbour.

As he sat with all Catholic eminence on his throne beside Isabella, Ferdinand's thoughts were not restricted to the issues troubling Spain alone. The marriage had so advanced his prestige and authority, he visualized a role for himself in the first rank of European statesmen. The next move must precede all others: completion of the Reconquista, too long delayed. By 1480 occasions in abundance presented themselves for the amputation of that last enclave of Muslim rule from Granada. This had to wait yet again, however, for an urgent call arrived from Pope Sixtus. The call might be regarded as coming within the arrangement whereby His Holiness permitted establishment of the Royal Inquisition.

The year 1480 found Italy in a state of panic, Venice particularly. The Turks had arrived dangerously close in another of their periodic conquering moods, and Ferdinand's help alone could seal the cracks in divided Italy long enough to repel an invasion. To be sure, nothing pleased him more than to come to Italy's aid. Usually a *pourboire* was available for services rendered that country. Louis XI of France knew as much. He had Italy's city-republics in the north at his beck and call in return for his benign interest in their affairs. Louis was enjoying new-found strength as a Mediterranean potentate, for Provence, granting deep-water harbourage at Marseilles, was at last absorbed in his kingdom. That brought France nearer to Italy by more than just a step. The French king placed little faith in annexation through military action unless absolutely necessary. So much was commonly known. But why tempt him? Frederick III, Holy Roman Emperor, could be nobody's champion, not even the Pope's. He had no army. It had to be Ferdinand of Aragon.

Before the fall of Constantinople, Venice, sometimes assisted, sometimes impeded by the Genoese, had taken on the Turks in the Mediterranean and inflicted a resounding defeat upon them. The 'Most Serene Republic' now sheltered its vessels the length of the Adriatic as unchallenged queen of that busy seaway, and no one dared molest their entry into the open Mediterranean. Venice doubled as Italy's champion and its scourge. The grandest and most stable of the city-republics, it had started as an island. Now it could trespass at will on the squabbling mainland and anticipate the creeping annexation of Lombardy entire.

However, times were changing for Venice. War of punishing duration against the Turks from 1463 to 1479 stripped the confident Venetians of much of their serenity and left their traditional enemy in possession of Greece and its islands. But Venice, it will be recalled, still ruled Crete and was consolidating ownership of Cyprus. To bring back their produce—sugar, salt, olive oil—its argosies, unless they wished to end up as floating wrecks, were compelled to seek Ottoman permission of transit and pay heavily in excise and docking rights. Worse now, the hated infidel came overland and by waterway to encamp in Albania, so passage through the Adriatic was no longer a cruise. The great Venetian fleets gazed disconsolately on a prospect of inglorious imprisonment in their lagoon close to home.

All Italy trembled while France, its spies everywhere, observed the situation as perhaps a blessing in deep disguise. Then came the heaviest blow of all. In August 1480 the sultan disembarked several thousand janissaries in the little port of Otranto, on the heel of Italy adjacent to Brindisi, allowing his force its customary three days of pillage. Long familiar with the rules whenever enemy sails appeared over the horizon, Otranto's local inhabitants collected their women together with all movable possessions and fled to the hills. A moralist saw it as retribution for the excesses, almost a dissolute paganism, prevalent in Italian life: 'We must not be amazed if God is now punishing the Christians through the Turks as he once punished the Jews when they forsook their faith. The Turks are today the Assyrians and Babylonians of the Christians, the rod and scourge and fury of God.' Old Sultan Muhammad, victor of Constantinople, showed every intention of taking his loaded mules overland to Italy's western shore and making an assault upon Naples. Where would that leave Rome?

Hence the appeal to Ferdinand. The latter despatched a fleet of seventy ships. The Turks, not yet a full year in Otranto, melted away. Naturally, Ferdinand boasted of an historic triumph for the faith. Perhaps so, but the Turks were preparing to leave anyway, as Muhammad, for thirty years the sultan, died unexpectedly in his Albanian tent. Here was one more instance of the Ottoman's military characteristic: advance, destroy, withdraw. In this case his retreat was induced also by a dispute over the succession, arising from a flaw in the sultanate's creed of power. That creed dictated that every ruler, on his enthronement, must have all his brothers executed together with their sons, thus avoiding debilitating family rivalries. To be sure, Muhammad had in his day performed that drastic duty, but his sudden demise far from home left the Seraglio undecided as to which of his own two sons, Bayezid or Jem, should succeed. The janissaries supported Bayezid; the Grand Vizier, Jem. The Grand Vizier was thereupon put to death, Jem took up arms, and the army was summoned home to suppress the revolt.

Jem's ultimate fate cast illumination on European attitudes to the Turkish menace. The defeated brother fled to Rhodes and sought asylum among the Knights of St John. What to do with him? Bayezid solved the problem by making the Knights an annual payment provided they kept Jem in captivity. They took the prisoner to France, but soon passed him into the charge of the Pope. The satisfactory financial arrangement transferred too, like a noose tied to Jem's neck. It proved a handsome pension—40,000 ducats a year for successive popes, though the detention was of the gentlest kind. Jem adjusted. He became a familiar *habitué* of Roman society, often in the company of Cardinal Rodrigo Borgia's tear-away son Cesare. But until he died, in 1495, Jem constituted a valuable hostage for papal blackmail, with messages of dire consequences if money was not forthcoming.

Mystery surrounds Jem's death. Was he poisoned at the order of Rodrigo Borgia, now Pope? Jem died one month after being handed over to the new French king, Charles VIII, following an ill-advised invasion by the latter of Italy. The allegation of poison suited the French cardinals, but it was based on a captured letter that may well have been a forgery. Bayezid hesitated from committing his troops overseas in large detachments while his brother lived.

Spain had justified itself to Europe by the Otranto expedition, but Ferdinand of Aragon most needed to justify himself at home. He dearly wished for universal popularity there, yet it still eluded him. His administration irritated important people among the privileged by its harassing determination to rectify outworn practices. Once his fleet returned from Otranto he would complete the process of rendering his domain a fortress of Christendom, by whatever surgery necessary. If only he realized it, Spain was at a turning-point and already approaching the threshold of world supremacy. That obscure mariner, Christopher Columbus, was possessed of his great obsession and was seeking a sponsor, offering in return empires beyond any previous monarch's most imaginative dreams.

Chapter Three

CHRISTIANS, MUSLIMS, JEWS

The marriage of Ferdinand, prince of Aragon, to Isabella, princess of Castile, which took place in 1469, possessed an ingredient rare in the days when statecraft resorted to royal wedlock for purposes close to the manipulation of power: romance. They were of an age, Isabella eighteen, Ferdinand seventeen. Mutual attraction could only be fostered from a distance. Their prospects for a long and happy partnership were clouded by fierce opposition, and neither had the certainty of retaining a throne. By the standards of fifteenth-century royalty both were as poor as church mice. Yet this pairing could not be willed by politics alone. It needed the extra propulsion of their higher instincts. True, Ferdinand later followed royal usage, much to Isabella's distress, of indulging in casual adventures with other women. For the present Isabella saw only a handsome young knight who would surrender his heart.

It is customary today to diminish monarchy as a function of historical change, substituting instead economic and social factors. These, we now insist, fomented revolutions, sent countries to war, forced them to make peace and conditioned inequalities of national growth. Justifiable as this argument might frequently be, it did not so surely apply in earlier times. A king's personality, and the circumstances of his accession, were, after geography, paramount in guiding the organization and policing of nations, not to mention their destiny in the ever-changing constellation of international relationships. So it was in the case of Ferdinand and Isabella. The union of the two Spanish cousins must be seen, from any perspective, as the first link in a chain whereby the course of European history, and the world's, altered direction. Spain defined itself as a new European power by their marriage.

As already related, Isabella's presumed right as heir to the Castilian crown was vigorously disputed by another young girl more directly in line, her niece. This contender found important champions among the nobility, strong suspicion of her illegitimacy notwithstanding. Her supporters would one day prompt the invasion from Portugal discussed earlier. And Ferdinand of Aragon was an unfavourable candidate for Isabella's hand, on several counts. His father King John floundered in a protracted, costly Catalonian rebellion, causing him to pawn a strip of land to France against a loan of 300,000 crowns which he was unable to repay. Aragon, despite possessions in the Mediterranean (the Balearics, Sardinia and Sicily) was a declining force, insignificant in European affairs. Unpopular as a king, avaricious too, John laboured under a variety of complex grievances. Himself a Castilian prince through a cadet branch of its royal house, he could trace a genealogy proving that the succession to Castile rightly belonged to his descendants alone. Doubtless other royal houses in western Europe could do as much, but here it worked to his son Ferdinand's disadvantage rather than the reverse. Cousinhood with Isabella represented a degree of consanguinity that to many churchmen prohibited a union. King John schemed for its achievement regardless.

Isabella's need for a consort began stirring rival ambitions from the moment her half-brother succeeded in Castile as King Henry IV and reluctantly recognized her as his heir against the girl he called his daughter (mockers derided *him* as Henry the Impotent). Now, in his kingdom's interest, he did not intend wasting so strong a bargaining counter as his sister's marriage on cheap goodwill. Henry proposed Charles of Valois, brother of Louis XI of France, as her husband. The match would rekindle an old alliance dating from the time Castile gave succour to France in the Hundred Years War. More, it would stave off potential animosity from the French side of the Pyrenees, where King Louis had signalled his opposition to any move towards further unification of the Iberian peninsula. Louis naturally preferred that region to remain weak and divided. But Isabella would not have Charles of Valois. Then how about King Alfonso of Portugal?

Alfonso was more than eager. Had the gods willed it, this would have proved a match indeed. Just an early dawn away and the two nations would transform themselves into empires. United they would bridge the Atlantic and Indian Oceans, circling also the continent of Africa: no mutual conflict to arrest their development, time enough to forge the inner cohesion and structural resilience required to keep the English, the French and the Dutch out of the race, the whole world within their reach. Arguably the proposition ranks as the biggest 'if' in modern history. However, immature though she might be, and alive to the cruel reality of her destiny as a human vessel for the carriage of someone's heirs, Isabella obstinately kept the King of Portugal at bay. That old widower did not want the wife but her patrimony. He was spreading his chances, with his eyes simultaneously fastened on the other claimant, Isabella's niece, still a child at this time, should the crown fall to her. As we know, when it did not, he went to war on her behalf, suffered defeat, then discarded the maid. While holding out on Alfonso Isabella secretly negotiated with representatives of that infinitely more attractive specimen of manhood waiting in the wings, Ferdinand.

Despite the obstacles, John of Aragon proved a formidable protagonist of his son's cause. He had inherited vast estates in Castile and hungered for the rest. John's friends in that country were as numerous as his enemies. He seemed to be related to every monarch within sight: uncle of Henry of Castile; uncle by marriage to the King of Portugal; brother of the King of Naples; a kinsman of the King of France through his first marriage, which had given him temporary lordship over Navarre. Other members of John's Castilian family enjoyed power as princes of the Church. Such a man felt belittled by his domestic troubles. He planned to emerge from them via his son. Envoys were soon travelling to and fro in a courtship by proxy unobserved by Isabella's brother, King John's own nephew the King of Castile. Who would be his most effective intermediaries? Whom could he trust to keep the confidences, and possess the means to deal out the required inducements at court, and share his interest in the outcome? No question about that, it was a group of important Jews, *conversos* among them, variously described as New Christians or Marranos.

Since the massacres of 1391 the Jews in both Castile and Aragon had been anxiously watching over their situation. Fear of another explosion of anti-Jewish sentiment was never remote from their thoughts. The Inquisition had not yet been established, nor by this time was it actively mooted. Still, they searched with a degree of desperation to strengthen their position, believing that Ferdinand as Isabella's consort would be their most likely protector: their blood ran, albeit thinly, in his veins. The long tradition of Jewish service to the kings of Aragon had not ceased despite the abandonment of Barcelona by many of them following the 1391 persecutions. A Jew, Abiathar Crescas, advised King John in the capacity of court astrologer. In his capacity of court physician he was reported to have saved the king from blindness.

The funding of Ferdinand's suit, quite beyond the parental purse, was provided by Jewish financiers in the king's employ. Their contacts reached to the centre of power at Valladolid, then Castile's capital. Success necessitated enlistment of the Archbishop of Toledo, Don Alfonso Carrillo, later elevated as Primate of all Spain. The crucial errand of persuasion fell to Pedro de la Caballeria, a Marrano belonging to a Saragossa clan exalted in wealth and honours, and himself a Catholic cleric. The prestige of the Caballerias spread far and wide. One of Pedro's brothers occupied high office in the Aragonese parliament, the Cortes. Another was the assistant curator of Saragossa University, a third, chief treasurer of Navarre with a son admiral of the Balearic fleet, while a fourth, on his conversion to Christianity, earned notoriety as an anti-Jewish propagandist. Scions of this house would, some years later, participate in the plot, described in the previous chapter, that brought the assassination of the Inquisitor selected for Aragon. Sadly, when the Royal Inquisition finally came to be instituted, and while some members of the Caballeria family extended their influence with further appointments, others were sentenced to burning at the stake for heresy, or made to humiliate themselves in public penance. In the mean time their blessings multiplied. For a wedding present Pedro brought Isabella a necklace said to equal a king's ransom.

Pedro de la Caballeria's contact with Isabella personally lay through Abraham Senior, tax-farmer to the King of Castile. Still a professing Jew, this man's lack of theological training did not impede his appointment simultaneously as Crown Rabbi, as it were Judaism's own Castilian archbishop. Caballeria despatched young Ferdinand to Abraham Senior's mansion in Segovia. The journey was secret, the prince in disguise. Senior then accompanied the prince to Toledo, for his introduction to the Castilian dignitaries privy to the arrangement It was now October, 1469, and only then did King Henry receive intelligence of the deceit in progress. In a fury, he sent men-at-arms to arrest his sister the princess. Too late. Archbishop Carrillo had hurried her off to Valladolid where the couple set eyes on each other for the first time, and where, on 19 October, they were secretly joined in matrimony. The modest ceremony took place in a private house. It required a further year before Abraham Senior could effect a reconciliation between the king and Isabella. The necessary instrument of dispensation allowing the marriage between cousins would not pass close Vatican scrutiny: it was a forgery uttered by the Archbishop of Toledo in conspiracy with King John of Aragon. An authentic instrument arrived from Rome in due course, brought in person by Cardinal Rodrigo Borgia, the so-called 'Spanish Bull'.

Isabella, it will be recalled, succeeded her brother in 1474, Ferdinand his father five years later. Perhaps the fusion of their two thrones would have arrived eventually, and inevitably. Common sense might have impelled it as geography demanded. Nevertheless its achievement at this critical juncture constituted an act of statesmanship producing a new regime and at once placing Spain in the forefront of European power. The country progressed swiftly, from a largely medieval closer to a Renaissance society, alert to its importance and strong enough to cure a host of inherited ills attending its archaic administration. The monarchs began abolition of the economic prerogatives vested in the Church, in the feudal orders of knighthood and in the agricultural monopolies. Aragon was not the same as Castile and could never be so, but Ferdinand and Isabella formed as equal a partnership as any dynastic alliance would permit. This was mainly due to Ferdinand's pragmatic character. He accepted what to another man would have seemed a humiliating arrangement granting the queen precedence in the realm. Originally this was not the case, to the degree that Ferdinand actually put in his claim as rightful sole heir when the Castilian throne became vacant on the death of Henry—a hopeless claim, readily abandoned.

Isabella revealed a strength of purpose in no way inferior to her husband's. She insisted on Ferdinand's permanent residence in Castile and, whatever the complications arising in Aragon, he was to give priority to the protection of her national interests. Each remained monarch in his own kingdom, the laws of one did not automatically apply to the other and they retained separate exchequers, Cortes and customs regulations. Castile enjoyed more substance and was far more populous than Aragon, but together they became a nation within the peninsula of some six millions (excluding Aragon's Mediterranean possessions), still much smaller than France but greater than England.

Ferdinand's capabilities went far beyond his years. During the early troubles of the reign he eliminated the Portuguese threat, suppressed the Castilian civil war and broke the Pope's resistance against the Inquisition. Now the moment had at last arrived for realization of the nation's dearest wish, completion of the Reconquista. The Muslim kingdom of Granada had survived long enough, a painful reminder of Spain's long obscurity within Christendom. To obtain the finance for the military campaign

Ferdinand first resorted to loans from his favourite Jews, principally Luis de Santangel, about whom more will emerge later. This enabled Ferdinand to hire a strong infantry of Swiss mercenaries. But, he declared, Spain was embarked on a crusade, not a war of aggrandizement. It warranted papal sanctification of the project. Sixtus readily concurred. He granted indulgences assuring absolution of sins and a place in the heavenly hereafter to all who contributed their services and funds. Gifts of money poured in. Even after retaining his papal commission much remained for prosecution of the war. To mark the piety of the enterprise the Pope also sent a great silver cross, which was borne aloft by troops in the vanguard. But the grace of God could prove a capricious ally in military affairs, and for the Christians this war was to be a test of the force of artillery, in which the Muslims were unskilled. They could only offer stubborn devotion to their soil as defence against heavy bronze cannon, and yet did well. Ferdinand summoned reinforcements from every part of the realm. As the exchequer was running dry a huge community tax was imposed upon the Jewish population.

According to the military doctrine enamoured of the Swiss, a successful campaign demanded ruthlessness above all, and ruthlessness accompanied their tactics in the conquest of the kingdom of Granada—the Moors still called it Al-Andaluz, the name applied to most of Spain while they held it in their power. Hitherto, an easy relationship had prevailed between Christian and Muslim in these parts, guided by the mutual respect of rights and susceptibilities. Now no longer. The Swiss took no prisoners and ignored the wounded. Their infantry formed into compact squares of pikemen behind a thin line of arquebusiers, but in this hilly terrain advance proved painfully laborious. In a gesture of comradeship with the regiments of the line, the Catholic Monarchs established their headquarters in the massive Alcazar at Córdoba. This was in 1482, and they intended to participate personally in the final triumph. Could it be long delayed? Indeed it could. The first considerable victory was not achieved for another two years, to be followed by a respite in the fire while Ferdinand sought to undermine resistance by diplomacy. Treachery in the Muslim camp facilitated the king's efforts, for the ruling family was rent by feud. Ferdinand kept this alive by deceptions of his own invention. He treated with Boabdil, son of the aged King of Granada, who clung to the hope of continuing in his father's stead as a vassal.

Boabdil played a double game. The Muslim kingdom fragmented into mutually hostile segments with Boabdil first surrendering his portion, then again resorting to arms. Ferdinand's commander, Gonsalvo de Córdoba, ordered a piecemeal conquest. Malaga lay under siege for three gruelling years before its ultimate capitulation. Meanwhile an importunate visitor had arrived in Córdoba, Christopher Columbus.

He had already placed his scheme for an expedition westward to the Indies before King John of Portugal, son of Isabella's old suitor Alfonso and nephew of Henry the Navigator. Columbus had been living for a period with his Portuguese wife Doña Felipa in her family's hereditary concession at Porto Santo in the Madeiras, later at Funchal where she bore him a son, Diego. Christopher was then thirty-three years of age, a master mariner well connected in Lisbon. Life had nevertheless been strenuous for a man too easily frustrated, and this one cherished aspirations to great wealth and high honours. During his Lisbon audience he informed King John of his certainty that in sailing west he would reach Cipangu, Marco Polo's designation for Japan, with its limitless riches so far untapped. He had convinced himself after studying a printed edition of research, translated from the Latin into Castilian, that had been produced by one of the leading astronomers of the day, Abraham Zacuto. This man, a Jewish scholar at the University of Salamanca, won fame among seafarers for his achievement in making the first astrolabe in copper, so much more accurate than in wood. Columbus possessed Zacuto's calculations of solar and lunar eclipses, indicating the exact position of the stars. The work was decorated with fanciful illustrations, astrological symbols and signs.

Columbus had long pored over the writings of Ptolemy and was in touch by correspondence with other scholars, notably the Florentine mathematician and astronomer Paolo Toscanelli. The latter had once prepared a navigational chart for the King of Portugal calculating the direction and distance across the Atlantic to the Asian land mass. Everything seemed to confirm Columbus's own belief that a voyage westward of 2,400 nautical miles from the Canaries (modern measure) would carry him to Cipangu. This was woefully inaccurate (Japan is five times that distance as the crow flies) but contemporary scientific knowledge, together with his absolute faith in the meaning to be extracted from the literal texts of the Bible, gave him confidence in this first crucial interview. Columbus requested a squadron of fully equipped ships to undertake his expedition under the patronage of Portugal and thus bring the message of Christ to the pagan world.

John is reported to have been completely unimpressed. A conscientious ruler unaccustomed to hasty decisions, he referred Columbus's proposition to his counsellors nevertheless. And they took no great time to dismiss the project of a westward route to the Indies as the stuff of a sailor's fantasies. However, another factor might well have contributed to their curt rebuff: the man's arrogance. Columbus appeared before the king not as a humble petitioner, but with demands for a reward that would have astounded any ruler. Columbus's terms included his appointment, on his successful return, as Grand Admiral of the Ocean Sea, entitling him to the arms and golden spurs of knighthood. He was to be recognized as hereditary viceroy and governor of all lands discovered by himself or any person under his command. One tenth of the income received by the king from the precious metals, pearls, spices and all other valuables realized from the trade generated within his admiralty would be his lawful right. Evidently, this mission for the sake of Christ promised Columbus the income of a Medici, for he further demanded the right to finance any future expedition to the proportion of one eighth, in return for which he would earn a corresponding entail. For an Italian of humble origin to address their king as though this was virtually a negotiation between equals must surely have struck the Portuguese counsellors as too preposterous for the slightest consideration.

It was then that Columbus received a blow even more grievous. His wife Doña Felipa died. Now he could see no purpose in tarrying one more barren day in Portugal. Bidding farewell to his brother Bartholomew, he took his five-year-old son Diego and left for Spain, to seek sponsorship from Ferdinand and Isabella. Subsequent reports indicated that he was also fleeing his creditors. The situation seemed hopeless, and it was a depressed Columbus who boarded ship for the port of Palos de la Frontera, on the Huelva coast. How long the prospect before he climbed this new arduous hill to an audience with the Spanish rulers?

Hitherto a tranquil haven where sailors might recuperate while their ships were refitted, Palos was at this time caught in a fever of activity: bustling volunteers disembarking for the crusade, stores funnelling through ready hands from ship to shore, no human emotion but it was directed towards the defeat of infidel Granada. It was now 1485, and while that struggle proceeded with ever-increasing savagery on this southernmost strip of the European mainland, the Inquisition conducted its remorseless tribunals and gruesome executions, open to the public gaze, elsewhere in the realm. Perhaps the two activities formed part of the same intention, to drive Satan out of this precious land. So it appeared at least to Isabella and Ferdinand in the Alcazar at Córdoba. The Inquisition brought them much property sequestrated from condemned heretics, but still they called for more money, more troops, heavier artillery. There never was enough. Christendom, they might have sensed, required constant reminders of their mission. It failed to comprehend the saintliness of their formidable task on its behalf.

But Spanish preoccupations could hardly be expected to trouble other rulers. Their own affairs spawned anxieties in plenty. Having withdrawn from Otranto, the Turks, in a renewed burst of martial vitality, extended Ottoman control to the Romanian coast on the Black Sea, thus closing off the Slav river traffic on the Dniester from its only outlet and bringing Islam a stage closer to the heart of Europe. This occurred while the intrepid but accident-prone Maximilian, heir to the Holy Roman Emperor Frederick III, was engaged against France for possession of Flanders and the Low Countries; and as King Richard III, England slipping from his grasp, prepared for his encounter (it would end in his death) with Henry Tudor at Bosworth Field. Soil was turning in Christian dispute throughout Europe. Could the sultan doubt that such leaders had no God-given right to possess this continent? And to cite a further example, who in these western battlegrounds would spare a thought for the agitated neighbours of Ivan, Grand Prince of Moscow? At that precise moment Ivan was snatching territory on all sides in his bid to create a second Byzantium and nominate himself ruler of all the Russians.

Certainly not Columbus, whose own concerns included one dearest to a father's heart: a home for his little Diego. Now his lucky star reappeared. He not only found a warm shelter for the boy, but also a turn in his own fortunes no further than at a Franciscan priory, La Rabida, overlooking the Rio Tinto almost within sight of Palos harbour. Yes, they would gladly take Diego, and educate him, said the prior, Juan Perez de Marchena. What business brought the father to Palos? It all spilled out—the dream, the method, the apathy encountered—when Columbus discovered that the prior was himself a student of astronomy. The project fascinated Fr. Perez to the degree that he offered to introduce his visitor to a friend, a rich shipowner of Cadiz. Wouldn't that be the logical next step? After all, it was ships Columbus needed to sail the ocean.

The man contacted by the prior gloried in the title Count de Medinaceli. (His descendants would feature prominently in the affairs of Spain for the next two centuries.) The count was of a Marrano family long converted, one of the group of New Christian courtiers unrestrained by their Jewish roots from occupying important roles in the commerce and administration of both Castile and Aragon. Such was the case even while the Inquisition dealt ferociously with many of their people, sometimes their own close kin. We may assume that the possible expulsion of the Jews, given over as the entire realm was to a nigh-hysterical mood of crusade, already circulated. How then should this people, both its converted grandees as well as those still following the Mosaic code, respond except to strain every effort in proclamation of their devotion to the monarchs? Their counsel was not repudiated, nor their services rejected, nor their loans made to the state, with or without interest. Eagerly, they offered their all in the hope of closing the ears of Isabella and Ferdinand against the anti-Jewish tirades of the Church, which threatened a climax of catastrophe.

Medinaceli, once won over to Columbus's plan, expressed a wish to finance the entire expedition from his own pocket. What greater service could a member of his tribe perform than to sponsor the discovery of worlds unknown for presentation to his motherland! The gratitude this would merit! On the other hand would not such a venture demonstrate the truth of the allegation that this people, a tribe accursed of God, had risen in their arrogance to an intolerable degree of influence? Surely the charges brought against them by Tomás de Torquemada, Inquisitor-General since 1483, would be granted justification?

Medinaceli thought the better of it. This was a project to be pursued only by command of his royal mistress Queen Isabella. He wrote a warm recommendation for Columbus to carry to Córdoba. Medinaceli had a dear friend in the royal circle there, or he may have been a kinsman. Luis de Santangel held office as Comptroller of the Household in Aragon and enjoyed Ferdinand's fullest confidence. His name alone betokened his origin, in the way that many Jews, on their baptism, somewhat overstated their identification with Christianity: 'Santangel' indicated 'Holy Angel'. The letter of recommendation reached Santangel and was duly conveyed to the queen. Columbus arrived in Córdoba in December 1485, and on delivery of his letter was requested to await the queen's pleasure for an audience. He settled down to wait, and he waited. Months expired. His expectations ebbed.

For so impulsive a man it proved an agony. Had Columbus been forewarned of the delay, his impetuosity would surely have triumphed and turned him away from the Catholic Monarchs there and then. In his calculation the scheme brooked no temporizing, and he sought an immediate sponsor. Weren't there rulers enough in Europe to whom he could plead his case for an enterprise of such moment? What about the successor to Louis of France, the boy king Charles VIII, or the victorious new King of England, Henry VII? But he had little choice now except to sit it out in Córdoba, and so took lodgings among the Genoese fraternity, in strong evidence here as anywhere on the continent where business prospered. In his loneliness the widower became smitten with a young peasant girl of Genoese stock, Beatriz Enriquez de Harana. She was to bear him a second son, Ferdinand, who would one day leave to posterity the first biography of his father.

One suspects that Christopher's failure to marry the humble Beatriz was born of his profound faith in his ultimate elevation to high rank. His first wife came from a Portuguese family highly placed through service with Henry the Navigator; it would not have been appropriate to descend the social scale for her successor. Mistresses of any class were however publicly accepted, even peasant girls, even Jewesses. At length Columbus's long awaited invitation to present himself at court arrived. This was in May 1486. Five precious months wasted, and his funds, no less than his patience, were virtually exhausted.

From all that we know of it, this proved a brief interview indeed, doubtless squeezed into a busy day when thoughts paramount in the royal minds concerned the slow progress of their war. One contemporary report stated that Columbus requested no more than 'three or four caravels', without specifying his further terms. And King Ferdinand apparently dismissed the project out of hand. Isabella alone took it seriously. The difference would have immense implications after 1492. In the event, Ferdinand and Isabella reserved their final decision pending advice to be tendered by an expert commission.

Chroniclers have alluded to the threadbare appearance of the would-be explorer as he laid his scheme before their majesties. The very sight of him may have moved Isabella to compassion, for she awarded Columbus a pension, pending the commission's report, of 12,000 *maravedis* for a year, something in the region of twelve pounds—a not insignificant amount for those days, though the man's financial situation must have sunk low indeed. As to the expert commission, it chose to convene at Salamanca, whose renowned university included among its academics the Jew Abraham Zacuto, author of those astronomical tables in Columbus's possession.

Shortly after the royal audience Ferdinand and Isabella left their headquarters in Córdoba to visit the shrine of St James the Great at Compostela, in the extreme north-west of the peninsula, and the locality most distant from the scene of battle. According to legend Compostela was the landing place of the apostle when he arrived to convert pagan Spain, and his remains were believed to be buried there. Santiago de

Compostela, cherished as the holiest Christian shrine after Jerusalem and Rome, attracted many thousands of pilgrims annually, particularly those seeking divine guidance and intercession in their good works. Manifestly the royal couple sorely needed spiritual renewal, for the war seemed unending, as though casting doubt upon their religious passion. They travelled in leisurely state, granting interviews to their subjects in many towns *en route*. It was not until October that they reached their sacred destination.

The commission charged to study Columbus's proposal eventually convened at Salamanca near Christmas-time in 1486. It was presided over by the queen's confessor, the Dominican friar and New Christian Hernando de Talavera. Zacuto himself gave expert evidence, but hesitantly and with a negative emphasis. The illustrious astronomer failed to confirm the likelihood of a voyage westward attaining the Indies. This may well have reflected a majority verdict of scholars at the university, disputed though it was by several of the royal advisers, notably the large Marrano element. These included Santangel, Diego de Deza (a later Inquisitor-General despite his descent from an old Jewish family) and Alfonso de la Caballería, brother of that Pedro de la Caballería who had been among the intermediaries concerned in Ferdinand's marriage to Isabella, as well as Talavera himself. The indecisive judgment held Talavera back, in the way of lawyers throughout time, from offering concrete advice. Adjourning the commission until some future date, he recommended that the queen retain Columbus in her service in the mean while by renewing his allowance for a further year.

Isabella could hardly be described as being in suspense. The siege of Malaga, long in progress, was taking its fearful toll. At last, in 1487, the Christian forces broke through. When its two fortresses fell all was over for the lovely Moorish town and Gonsalvo de Córdoba claimed his first major victory. He sold the entire population of Malaga and its surroundings, 15,000 men, women and children, into slavery, bringing 36 million much-needed *maravedis* to the royal treasury. Boabdil, holding the eastern sector of the area for the Moors, now wavered between submission and continued resistance. He recognized the situation as hopeless. He held in his hand an instrument of surrender. In the end he determined to fight it out.

The year passed for Columbus without an indication of a yea or nay. But there was a letter from his brother Bartholomew still the industrious chartmaker in Lisbon. Bartholomew informed him f King John's continued interest in the search for a sea route to the Indies. In fact Portugal had entered a new epoch of exploration reminiscent of the times of Henry the Navigator. Travellers' tales spoke of ships exploring the western approaches in quest of islands hitherto unknown, so perhaps the king had come round to the view that a way to the Indies truly existed in that direction. Not all the stories circulating in the port of Lisbon merited credence, but there was no doubt at all concerning the object of an expedition fitted out in that year of 1488 and led by the daring Portuguese seafarer Bartholomew Dias. He was navigating along the coast of Africa well beyond the limits so far attained. His intention could only be to discover whether that land mass continued unbroken all round the globe, Ptolemy's projection, or whether it had an eastern shore fringing another sea. If this was the case, such a sea must indeed join the ocean covered by Arab mariners out of Egypt, which was known to lead to the Indies. Merchants arriving from those parts traded with Europeans based at Alexandria. In conceiving the Indian Ocean as a huge lake Ptolemy may well have erred.

Dias however was gone several months and all was silence. Perhaps he would never be heard of again, devoured by African barbarians or resting in a watery grave. For Columbus this was intelligence enough to warrant a second appeal to the King of Portugal. Of course, he assured himself, Portugal was the obvious answer! No other nation enjoyed so splendid a maritime tradition. He wrote to King John imploring another interview, though a safe-conduct ensuring his protection from imprisonment for unpaid debts would be required.

The surmise proved correct. The king invited the Columbus brothers to his court. The enterprise certainly merited further investigation, and the tone of the king's reply was evidence enough that Christopher would be received with honour, healing the wounded dignity he nursed from his earlier abrupt dismissal. His spirits soaring once more, Columbus returned to the familiar territory of Lisbon.

Alas, the visit transpired as a bitter anticlimax for the brothers. Here they were in Lisbon preparing for their audience when there, on the horizon, they could descry three caravels sailing towards the mouth of the Tagus. The harbourside was preparing a great welcome to Dias, home after a seven-month voyage with dramatic news. No, Africa did not extend without end beyond man's compass. Dias had sailed round the edge of the continent and explored a long stretch of its eastern shore. He would have sailed further but for a mutiny threatened by his homesick crews. One thing was clear: a sea route from Europe to the Indies really existed, and had been discovered. The news so delighted King John he named that tip of Africa the Cape of Good Hope. Portugal had shown once again that she was queen of the oceans. Columbus was once again ignored. Even if a route to the Indies really lay there across the Atlantic, and assuming the distance were as navigable as Columbus calculated, why need anyone now trouble himself with the problem?

Surprisingly perhaps, it was clearly the case that no ruler felt so inclined. Christopher took himself wearily back to Spain while Bartholomew travelled on to England in the hope of interesting the island kingdom's new master. It is nowhere stated that Bartholomew was accorded so much as an interview with Henry VII, nor again could he report the slightest interest by Anne of Beaujeu, the 'least foolish woman in the world', who acted as regent of France on behalf of her brother, the immature King Charles, not yet allowed to make his own blunders. Before the century ended, a decade hence, both these powers would be trailing in the wake of Columbus's path. Others soon pressed after them. The scramble for empires would have begun, inaugurating 400 years of competition not absolutely concluded until the Second World War. Yet at this time none but the King of Portugal evinced the least curiosity concerning any portion of the globe except Europe, and the lands closely abutting. Power obsessed them all, but they visualized nothing of significance beyond their own doorsteps. Anne of Beaujeu apparently retained Bartholomew in Fontainebleau, commissioning him to prepare navigational charts. This was all. The brothers would not meet again for six years, and then on the other side of the world.

The Talavera Commission dallied until December 1490, before delivering a final verdict. Its conclusions added up to a definite refusal, and that might have been the end of it. However, Luis de Santangel, possibly the monarchs' most influential adviser, had been personally impressed with the character of Columbus, his tenacity of purpose, perhaps also his religious zeal. He urged Isabella to offer Columbus some little hope. Shortly Granada would fall, there could be no question about that, and she might feel disposed then to give Columbus her authorization and blessing. Santangel himself undertook, should she grant consent to the expedition, to advance a substantial sum towards its cost.

If history requires a parallel to the biblical Joseph at Pharaoh's court, Santangel is surely that man. From an obscure origin he had risen to statesman's rank, a Hispanic Jew endowed with great wealth, as devout a Catholic as any, yet acknowledging to his conscience an obligation towards the Israelite connection. The sentence hanging over the Jews weighed heavily upon him as he tendered his counsel to the royal couple.

Since returning from their pilgrimage to Compostela an extreme religiosity characterized their conduct, fuelled not only by this war against heathen Granada but also by the anger generating from that reigning psychodrama the Inquisition. Doubtless Ferdinand's intensity was not equal to his wife's, but then, her wishes reached him as directives in Castile, if not in Aragon.

As Santangel viewed the situation, Christopher Columbus allowed the possibility of diverting the fanatical rhetoric of Torquemada. The latter preached an apocalyptic cause: the destruction of the Muslim state was not enough, nor the rigorous exposure of Jews secretly performing Satan's work while masquerading as Christians. This nation would be Catholic or it would be nothing. And so, in the course of the year 1491, the banishment of the Jews grew from a mood to a proposal, then to a divine injunction. If they wished to remain, said Torquemada, let them do as the good and faithful Santangel had done, abandon the synagogue and their devilish faith for the baptismal font. Many Jews had already taken the step, and honestly, to serve as virtuous Catholic citizens. The rest must not be tolerated in this land.

An uncle of Santangel had died at the stake for his part in the assassination of the appointed Inquisitor for Aragon. Another relative, escaping to Bordeaux, was burnt in effigy. Luis himself had nothing to fear because of his closeness to Ferdinand, who protected him and his children. But the Jews' situation continued to hang on a thread, simultaneously with the fate of Columbus. Several orthodox Hebrews, like Abraham Senior of Segovia openly loyal to their ancient *Torah*, continued to hold important offices of state, all the while praying that the worst would never arrive. How could it, when their roots in this soil extended back into antiquity, preceding Moorish rule? Frequently as the question was posed in the final weeks of 1491, the answer never changed. Yes, the Jews would have to go.

Ferdinand and Isabella moved closer to the rump of territory still remaining to the Muslims during that year. The Christian forces established their headquarters at Santa Fe, and the king, who readily shared the fire with his troops by riding through the most advanced ranks, ordered the construction of a city there. The enemy saw this activity as marking the end of their cause. Boabdil sought terms. If honourable, he would personally surrender the city of Granada to the king and queen. Gonsalvo de Córdoba, a cautious general, now had 40,000 soldiers in the field preparing for the final onslaught, though to cover these last few miles and take possession of the Alhambra by force would demand heavy casualties in combat hand against hand. Better, honourable terms for a bloodless surrender. Consequently Ferdinand sent a conciliatory message to Boabdil. He undertook to respect the autonomy of the Muslim region after surrender. Its inhabitants could retain their property and their arms. Spain would allow them to keep their religion and customs, and would impose no punitive taxes.

Boabdil, persuaded by these conditions, rode out to Santa Fé. His surrender would enable Muslim life to continue in Andalusia, as had happened elsewhere on the peninsula, where a doctrine of live and let live prevailed following Christian conquest. And there would be no repeat of the catastrophe that had befallen the defenders of Malaga. Boabdil dismounted, knelt before Ferdinand on 2 January 1492 and handed over the keys to the city of Granada. For the first time in almost 800 years no Arab ruled in any part of Spain. Boabdil's mother, already rejected by her husband for a Christian beauty, is quoted as reproaching her son: 'You weep like a woman for what you could not hold as a man.'

And as Ferdinand and Isabella, four days later, led their cavalry up the Sabika hill to the Alhambra and placed the Pope's crucifix together with their standard upon the highest tower of the rose-red fortress, Christian fervour enveloped all Spain. It spread, be it said, throughout Europe, though Cesare Borgia, son of Rodrigo and soon to become a cardinal himself, found it appropriate to celebrate the event in Rome with a bull fight. Yet the moment had its sacred mystery, as if the Catholic Inquisition was being laid upon the Moorish nation in its totality. Words could not fully express the emotion. Ferdinand's solemn undertaking to the stubborn enemy now brought low proved in the event to be a light promise blandly made. However, in the excitement of the historic occasion he gave every indication of keeping his word.

Much as Queen Isabella relished the triumph, her vows as a Christian monarch could not as yet be described by some of her advisers as fulfilled. They compelled her to turn her attention directly upon those professing the Hebrew faith. In this country every noble family had its favourite Jews, as did every bishop, every merchant, and citizens down to the meanest occupation. But none more than the king and queen themselves. What in truth were this people? They might worship in their churches, or their synagogues. They might eat pork and still not be immune from suspicion. In making its fearful selection of heretics the Inquisition was known to convict on the evidence of witnesses whose testimony was born in spite and nourished in the imagination. None other than Talavera, head of the Columbus enquiry, who had served as the queen's confessor and was to be nominated the first Archbishop of Granada, would in later years be arraigned. A 'prophetess', while under torture, alleged he had conducted a kind of black Mass where the early arrival of the 'Jewish Messiah' was invoked. Talavera managed to clear his name, and survive the ordeal, though not before he was made to walk bare-headed and barefoot through the streets of Granada for what was deemed a light penance.

Spain could count itself fortunate in the extreme that Santangel was not among those New Christians falling victim to the national hysteria. By that lucky accident his sovereigns, shortly to be elevated by Pope Alexander VI to a condition almost of living apotheosis with conferment of the title Los Reyes Católicos, the Catholic Kings, gained their empire. For Santangel reminded them of the man waiting at the gate, Christopher Columbus. His endurance had vanished absolutely late in 1491. The queen had fobbed him off with a vague and temporizing reply: the times were inappropriate for an expedition, the royal treasury was depleted, let him make a fresh approach later. It was the last straw, this audience at Santa Fé, and Columbus determined there and then to shake the Spanish dust from his feet forever. Within hours he was on the road again, to gather up his family and join Bartholomew in Fontainebleau, where his brother had at least earned some modest standing. At this critical moment Santangel begged the queen to have second thoughts. As Comptroller of the Treasury he stressed how little was at stake should the contemplated expedition fail. After all, Columbus had only requested three or four caravels, a bare minimum. Medinaceli, who had been participating in the war at the head of his own detachment of troops, vigorously supported Santangel. They were heavy of heart. Perhaps the queen detected the mingling of sentiments driving the two New Christians. She gave her assent.

Now there was not a moment to lose. The impatient Genoese was just a few miles out of Santa Fé when Santangel's messenger overtook him, with the royal summons. A positive reply at last! The queen accepted his terms, not altered by so much as a syllable since that first meeting eight years earlier with John of Portugal, though now all in the name of the Spanish crown. Should Columbus return successfully from a voyage across the Atlantic to the Indies, he would be Admiral of the Ocean Sea, hereditary viceroy and governor of all lands discovered, a knight with golden spurs granting nobility for his descendants in perpetuity. He would carry three letters of introduction to the monarchs he encountered proclaiming his journey as a royal errand of friendship and brotherhood in the name of Christendom. So far he had no ships, no money, no contract of agreement. But he felt like David about to take possession of Jerusalem.

The financing of the hazardous expedition: it was left to Santangel to fulfil his undertaking to produce the necessary means. Those most willing to contribute, eager rather, emerged from the ranks of his tribal confrères, whether following Christianity or Judaism, and each branch haunted by its separate dread—if not the Inquisition then exile. Santangel started the fund with a loan of more than a million *maravedis*. Medinaceli matched him coin for coin. From the other side of the theological divide came Abraham Senior, Crown Rabbi of Castile, a go-between in the royal marriage and now chief treasurer of the Hermandad, the powerful organization of 'brotherhoods' which originated as a militia policing the various provinces but now served the state as a great tax-collecting agency. The rabbi's support of the project made it certain that Columbus would put to sea. Senior was joined by Don Isaac Abrabanel, Lisbon-born but now of the Castilian élite as principal tax-farmer and army contractor. Abrabanel, distinguished as a philosopher, unshakeably faithful to Judaism, was the scion of a once New Christian family that subsequently recanted, and was universally recognized as the official spokesman of Spanish Jewry.

In the excited days while Ferdinand savoured the capitulation of Boabdil, a charge was levelled against the Jews with the murder of a Christian child in the course of a Judaizing ritual. Such monstrous allegations had long been current in Europe, despite a bull of Pope Innocent IV as early as 1247 condemning the stories as evil falsehoods. The Pope had stated: 'Wherever a corpse is found somewhere the murder is wickedly imputed to the Jews. In mockery of all justice they are stripped of their belongings, stoned, imprisoned and tortured, so that their fate is perhaps worse than that of their fathers in Egypt.' In this case it was alleged to have occurred at La Guardia in the north, bringing some dozen Jews, a baptized few among them, to the Inquisition and death. Now the king and queen dared not ignore the clamour for a general retribution. So much pressure lay upon their emotions in the course of the long war, aggravated by the advice of conflicting counsellors, that finally they could only adopt the easiest course. On 28 March 1492 they signed the royal contract with Columbus. Three days later they issued an edict of expulsion. With the voyage of Columbus Spain gained a continent: with the expulsion of the Jews it lost a limb.

Allowing the Jews four months to liquidate their property, the edict applied also to the Aragonese possessions of the Balearics, Sardinia and Sicily. Both Senior and Abrabanel refused at first to accept it as the last word. They are reported to have offered the queen a huge sum to rescind the order, upon which her Inquisitor-General is said to have taunted Senior as a second Judas bearing another thirty pieces of silver. 'Baptize and remain!' the Jews were urged to the end. A minority did so, but the mass could not. More, they were joined by thousands of New Christians openly declaring their true faith at last, tired with living a lie which, if discovered, could exact the penalty of the pyre.

Amid anguished separations of parents from children, brothers from sisters, and with tearful farewells to their Christian friends and neighbours, the Jews uprooted themselves from the soil to which they had clung through every vicissitude. They were some 150,000 altogether, everyone attached to some portion of Iberia he would never forget, as to this day their descendants have not forsaken its language. Beyond Spain there could be only one homeland. They departed in the conviction of ultimate transplantation, following another symbolic wandering through some symbolic Sinai, to a resting place in the Promised Land.

The Jews were led away by Abrabanel, to whose pain was added the unthinkable: Senior himself accepting conversion. Saving his own skin, or a vain attempt to reprieve his people? No one knows. The sovereigns themselves stood as godparents for his baptism, a public event which took place at Guadaloupe, sacred to a miraculous appearance of the Virgin in 1300. For the rest, they would meanwhile seek asylum wherever Providence allowed. About 60,000 sought refuge across the frontier into Portugal, where they were admitted at the price of eight *cruzados* on every head—Abraham Zacuto of Salamanca among them, but to be honoured in Lisbon with an appointment as royal astronomer. Others found their way into the Low Countries, many more to the welcoming gates of the Ottoman Empire. 'Spain is impoverished, the Sublime Porte enriched!' declared Sultan Bayezid. Most of those Jews seeking refuge in Portugal fell to a further wave of persecution, when those not escaping suffered enslavement or enforced baptism. The Borgia Pope Alexander VI, a humanist by instinct, offered sanctuary to those reaching Rome, much to the displeasure of the Spanish rulers. England waited a further 150 years before officially admitting them, thanks to Oliver Cromwell.

Refugees have at all times divided into rich and poor. The former could elude misery through their contacts overseas, and the bribery which secured them easy escape and smooth travel. Such was the case in the Jewish expulsion. Those with modest means found the heart to rebuild their lives elsewhere, but the poor were rendered destitute. Thousands of the latter perished from sickness or starvation as they sought new shelters. Others begged for readmission to Spain early in their tribulation, on the grounds of having discovered Christ and been reborn. Shipmasters sold their human cargoes to slave-dealers; truthfully, slavery was often accepted as the least merciless fate. Wealthy Jews survived for another day, to be observed in distant cities, entrenched in their old professions, trading in the international markets, even leaving their traces on history. These were the fortunate few. Records do not survive of the inarticulate, helpless mass, for they died as they had lived, in obscurity.

If the conquered Moors believed in the promise of King Ferdinand, solemnly made, to safeguard their rights and practices, they were doomed to early disappointment. Talavera, in his role as first Archbishop of Granada, proved a friend, desiring to protect them from further hardships. He hoped to entice their baptism by kindness rather than compulsion. It was not to be. In the first place, too many of the Moors, particularly their aristocracy, maintained close ties with their North African brethren and thereby constituted a dissident force prone to enlisting overseas allies. Cunningly, Ferdinand proceeded to remove that top layer of Muslim society by bribing its departure. In fact Boabdil himself accepted substantial payment and, accompanied by several thousand of his followers, crossed the straits to Africa.

The leaderless residue, their stubborn pride evaporated, soon came under the pressure of an ecclesiarch superior to Talavera and more rigorous: Archbishop Jiménez de Cisneros of Toledo. He ordered the Muslims throughout Spain to baptize or depart. Most of them defected to the Cross, for they too acknowledged Spain as their only homeland, and cherished it as had their forefathers since the early Middle Ages. However, the Moorish problem hung over the land for a further century. This people, coerced into baptism, thwarted every effort to enforce their assimilation with Christian Spain—retaining their customs, resorting to rebellion, while ominously intriguing with the Turks. Moreover, they committed that most unforgivable of all sins—they multiplied. The Inquisition laboured to eradicate Muslim survivalism, but without success. So they too went into exile, in 1609. Their miseries exceeded those of the Jews, even though the Inquisition laid a lighter hand upon them. The Marrano attracted envy, while the Morisco was exploited and despised.

A neurosis had attacked the balance of the nation, its pathology identifying Judaism and Islam as the scars upon the body politic. By the standards of the fifteenth century this country could not hope for acceptance as truly European and Catholic until the two were removed. Geography had exposed the peninsula to deep penetration by the people and ideas of Africa. Surgery, that desperate remedy, was enlisted as the only cure.

Spain thus surrendered itself to the chimera of racial purity. Perhaps it spent itself thereby. This country was the first in our modern age to demonstrate how religious despotism cannot serve as a formula for national greatness. While the splendour of its sixteenth-century preeminence, made possible by Christopher Columbus, radiated into the early seventeenth century, Spanish potency as a world power was already on the wane.

Chapter Four

COMMERCE INTRUDES ON POLITICS

f this we may be sure: the late fifteenth-century Staffordshire wife seated at her spinning wheel gave hardly a thought to whether England would fall to the House of York or the House of Lancaster. As she deftly spooled her threads ready for the weaver she was certainly aware that the raw, washed wool reaching her from Bristol would be of the fine Spanish kind, while the coarser fibres most probably came from home-reared sheep. Her stake in England ended with her job done. Others could take over for the weaving, fulling and dyeing of the cloth, and they in their turn would know little of the further processes that kept impatient wheels of industry and distribution turning in London. In a good year cloth provided a living for a multitude of workers in town and country—labourers in the warehouses, clerks preparing invoices, insurance and excise declarations.

Higher up the ladder merchants or their agents negotiated loans with the bankers so that factors at Bruges and Lyons could despatch the fruits of English enterprise far and wide. In slack seasons the women would help their men in the landowners' fields, while the weavers and fullers would be laid off, perhaps to wander the countryside in search of casual work. The first victims of a merchant's economies had always to be the lowest paid.

And of what concern to the Bavarian miner settled with his family among the Slavs in Bohemia, hacking the silver ore out of its dripping seam (and unlikely ever to see his native turf again because this work often paid with premature death) were relations between his emperor and his pope? He would certainly be oblivious of the ultimate ownership of the precious metal he recovered, though as likely as not the concessionaires were either the Hochstetters or the Fuggers, two of the great family concerns which avoided competition by manipulating the market between them. Their loans enabled the Holy Roman Empire to wage war. Central European silver boomed at that time, in a last explosion of profit before sinking beneath the torrent of New World riches.

So with the Sicilian peasant. He tended his vineyard unconscious of any force except nature's rain and sun, fiercer masters than the barons who possessed him in this surviving relic of western serfdom. Sicilian laws were made by Barcelona in faraway Catalonia, and the headaches they caused on this Mediterranean island were the lord's, not the peasant's. Some historical accident had united the latter's destiny to that of the Spanish shepherd, though in fact the two were worlds apart. The *contadino* was confined to his patch while the *pastor* lived a nomadic existence, for the hot summers required the shepherd to drive his flocks hundreds of miles north in search of grazing, and every winter bring them south again. The drover followed a well-marked route exactly determined by the Mesta, the powerful Spanish syndicate which owned the flocks and regulated the migration.

Perhaps all this is a truism, but it is well stated. The closing decades of the fifteenth century saw Europe torn as ever by the discontents of a violent age. Territories were won and lost, knights trumpeted over battlefields while the continent suffered the depredations of lawless bands. Pestilence attacked cities as frequently as human enemies. Yet Europe had another life whose pulse was trade. This never ceased. On the contrary, it flourished.

As we know, Leonardo da Vinci was an Italian realist endowed with a caustic blend of humour. In the year 1492 he designed his airborne machine, patterned on the eagle's flight, and he may well have been making a fanciful comment on mankind's incapacity to dissolve distance; there had been no progress in mobility since the invention of the wheel. Trade demanded swift decisions but proceeded at a crawl, involving the transportation of goods and materials over wearying unmade roads, those built by the Romans having mostly fallen into decay. Heavily loaded pack animals had to be escorted through numerous land frontiers marked by tolls that involved transactions in a perplexity of different currencies. Long stretches of road lay deserted, mountain paths concealed unexpected perils. River traffic, easier to police, was least expensive and by far the safest, though north-western Europe offered smoothest transit, through its well-preserved canals.

Luxury goods such as perfumes, spices, camphor and silks predominated in the commerce connecting the East to Europe. This merchandise carried heavy premiums levied by the many intermediaries through whose hands it arrived from the Orient. Almost all direct land contact with China (the old 'silk route') had ceased since the decline of the Mongol khanates and the establishment of the Ming dynasty in 1368. Produce originating in distant Asia was therefore transported round India by Muslim traders under sail. Venetian entrepreneurs, having disposed of most of the Genoese competition in the eastern Mediterranean, took over at Alexandria and the Black Sea ports. They offered furs, hides, metal articles in exchange, but wool particularly, finished as cloth and even raw. Then—Ottoman tensions reduced, pirates evaded, the stars read for omens—the imported cargoes would leave in galleys, oar-driven for the short Mediterranean passage or wind-propelled on the long haul from the Levant through the Straits of Gibraltar and up the Atlantic coast. The best markets converged in the prosperous Low Countries and northern Germany. All this could consume months. Nevertheless, while politics divided Europe, trade unified it.

Such of course had been the pattern for centuries. Climate, location, geology and enterprise all played their part, though we are now speaking of trade too highly organized for simple transactions directly sealed between merchants as under the closer rules of feudalism. Almost all labour at the base of Europe's economic pyramid was now performed for agreed wages, with consequences for society as a whole. A thrifty peasant might rise to landownership, an artisan could qualify as a guild member, though a baron might find himself stuck with unsaleable crops and go bankrupt. The year 1492 is as accurate as any to mark the birth of an infant who would grow into a colossus—capitalism. Commerce now required elaborate servicing conducted in cities where all the knots were tied. Capitalism granted respectability to moneylending where previously loans had to be camouflaged, since lending for interest was condemned by the Church as usurious and immoral, a practice better left to the Jews, who were condemned to perdition anyway. Christian morality now allowed men to accumulate wealth, speculate in it, use money to make money, compete to preserve their monopolies and to advertise their riches by patronizing the arts. Their women dressed like princesses as capitalism began making decisions affecting the daily lives of anonymous millions. It could decree which agricultural activities should be encouraged, which left to decay. While English wool developed as a major industry, cheap to manufacture and expertly marketed, Spanish weaving declined, giving way to greater concentration on sheep-rearing.

In the way nature chooses of spreading mischief with its favours, the country inherited by Ferdinand and Isabella was covered with barren rock. Rain fell sparsely and rivers were few, so the land defied regular cultivation. The Moors had introduced the merino sheep together with irrigation from North Africa. These herds now numbered in millions, their fleeces supplying the textiles that clothed half Europe. Hence those annual north-south migrations. The end of the road? It was at Medina del Campo and Burgos in Old Castile, where great agricultural fairs had existed since time immemorial. Here the supervisors of the Mesta organization (Jews before their 1492 exile) concluded their deals with foreign agents, after which the fleeces would be loaded on to the mule trains for San Sebastian, partly for shipment, partly for the onward land journey to Lyons, where credit from a branch of the Medici bank was available, and subsequent distribution. Certainly the Iberian peninsula still retained its share of those staples of the Mediterranean lands, wine and olive oil, though little corn. Some meagre iron and silver deposits were mined in the hills, and salt dredged from the coastal marshlands. The country was among the largest importers of grain, much of it coming from North Africa, with quantities also from England and Sicily.

In return for the produce travelling north, England sent back textiles, Scandinavia and the Netherlands herring, furs too, pitch and potash. Organization was everything, taking precedence over national sentiment among the merchants. However, in some countries over-manned bureaucracies hampered commerce more than in others. In this regard the Netherlands possessed all the advantages of an easy-going, laissez-faire tradition—but only when left undisturbed politically.

We can thus understand the intensity with which Ferdinand nurtured his plans for expansion. He observed how France had pulled itself up, after the twin visitations of the Black Death and the Hundred Years War, to subdue the conflicting pretensions of royal princes and utilize its size and natural resources in a bid for European domination. No country could match its dedication to greatness. Nor, Ferdinand was thinking, its arrogance.

Ferdinand brooded over the future of his line. He too had defeated internal enemies and enjoyed more loyalty than his father had been vouchsafed in Aragon, and Isabella was now absolutely secure. But they needed alliances for their dynasty to survive—alliances sanctified by tactical marriages whereby their descendants reaped the benefits of wealth located elsewhere in Europe than in their own harsh terrain. What that adventurer Columbus offered in his years of pleading could not be a serious proposition to a realist like Ferdinand. Wasn't it exasperating how those European countries weakest constitutionally had locked up the most lucrative commerce and contained the most prosperous cities?

The paradox directed Ferdinand's thoughts towards those Burgundian Low Countries, equable on the surface but concealing a hornet's nest of simmering rivalries comprising fractious, semi-autonomous provinces. Bruges, from whose belfry the captivated Longfellow would sense all medieval history, had long been a metaphor for easy gold. It was now a metropolis in decline, grudgingly ceding its eminence to nearby Antwerp. Ferdinand furthermore anticipated a stake in the glittering prize that was Italy (his own Sicily and Sardinia hardly rated as Italian). Drawn together and harnessed to a single crown, Italy and the Netherlands could clamp western Europe between their economic teeth. As it happened, France coveted ownership of those same two fragmented countries.

Bruges and Antwerp, the one within the County of Flanders, the other in the Duchy of Brabant, held dominance over the greater entity of the Netherlands—those Low Countries combining present-day Belgium with Holland. In those days they formed the richest portion of the domain inherited in 1467 by Charles the Bold, Duke of Burgundy. He was of the blood royal, a Valois kinsman of the King of France. Their traditional enmity, we recall, dated from the Hundred Years War. Burgundy constituted a realm yielding nothing in chivalric splendour to the mythic kingdom of Arthur and the Knights of the Round Table. Charles's forbears had fought against the Moors and given Portugal its first royal family. He now recognized the Holy Roman Emperor as his liege-lord in respect of two thirds of his territory, but knelt to the French king in respect of the rest. The duke, who embodied mystical essences ranking him among the gods of yore, could buy and sell them both. Needless to say, he yearned for more—everything between Rhone and Rhine, then to be a king like his cousin of France and eventually his place in Christendom as the next emperor. He vowed he would then lead a European army to destroy the Turks. This dream suddenly vanished in 1477, when Charles fell in battle against the Swiss at Nancy (he claimed the cantons). Lying undiscovered in the snows for two days, the man who aspired to the ultimate diadem of European sovereignty was half devoured by wolves. He was forty- four.

Charles the Bold's stunned subjects in his capital Dijon accepted the inevitable—integration of the original duchy (from which the rest had grown) within France. An old French law of succession, source of much disputation, could justify the annexation. But King Louis XI saw no reason to stop there. Burgundian rulers had never warranted French trust.

Total absorption of all lands called Burgundian at last lay within his grasp. He marched into Flanders, taking its western half (Picardy, Artois) and, further south, threatened a Burgundy fief within the Holy Roman Empire, Franche Comté. At once, the hornets in their Netherlands nest became agitated, stinging everything within reach. And while each of the score of Netherlands provinces, Luxembourg included, argued in their ornate Gothic council chambers on their attitude to France, and the temperature rose with French-speakers denouncing the Flemish and many wavering, Charles the Bold's daughter and successor, the half-English Mary (her mother was Margaret of York) seized the day. She married Maximilian, Archduke of Austria and heir to the Emperor Frederick III. Thus the nearly irresistible Valois force met the almost immovable Habsburg object. We scent the beginnings of a conflict with many twists and turns that would trickle down to the twentieth century.

Mary, having lost Burgundy proper, could not take her succession to the Burgundian Netherlands for granted. She had to be formally ratified by the components of the confederation individually, each jealous of its separate prerogatives. What a meal they made of it! Her father's wars, they complained, had obstructed their commerce and drained their wealth, although those wars derived solely from personal disputes with his French kin. They now insisted upon freedom of trade, including therein trade with Mary's enemies in times of trouble. In fact pro-Gallic sentiment, fostered by bribery, was strong in the Low Countries. Some local leaders had been hoping for the betrothal of Mary to Louis XI's Dauphin, the nine-year-old already encountered as Charles VIII earlier in this narrative.

Hence Mary, coaxed by her widowed mother Margaret of York, had acted with understandable despatch when, eight months after her father's death at Nancy in 1477, she solemnized her marriage with that knight Maximilian in shining German armour at Ghent, capital of Flanders, in whose Benedictine abbey her ancestor John of Gaunt had been born. Mary made her vows to Maximilian in the Prinsenhof nearby. It was a wondrous glass-towered edifice of 300 huge chambers, in one of which their grandson, destined to wear the greatest crown ever to be achieved in Christendom, would first see the light.

Not that the marriage was actively opposed, even in Flanders. Certainly the burghers of Ghent had wished for Mary's husband to be one of their own, not a foreigner, not even the Dauphin. They had gone so far as to contrive the release of their chosen candidate from prison, accord him a high civic honour and advance his suit just as his death intervened. The man most angered by the match was King Louis of France. As an eighteen-year-old Habsburg prince in possession of all his faculties (the Valois, on the other hand, suffered regularly from a con-genital degeneracy) Maximilian could prove a neighbour too close for comfort. Louis embarked on a strategy combining war with diplomacy to bring the Netherlands into French possession.

Ferdinand of Aragon was not yet a king in his own right at that time, but he judged the situation otherwise. This was 1478, and the Spanish prince, while awaiting his own succession to Aragon, ruled in Castile beside Isabella. Ferdinand, preoccupied though he might be with internal reforms, his dispute with Pope Sixtus and the pressure to introduce the Inquisition, had detected a personal vista in the marriage. He likened the union of Mary and Maximilian to his own with Isabella: two families joining youth with ability, soon no doubt to produce children available for dynastic alliance of the first importance. Mary in fact gave birth to a son that very year. The child Philip, described as Duke of Burgundy like the dead Charles the Bold, would on maturity rank as a most desirable catch for any woman in Europe. As it happened, Ferdinand had looked to his loins to furnish dynastic capital, with auspicious results. His eldest daughter he had reserved for marriage to the heir of the Portuguese king, in the interests of harmony in all Iberia. Three more would be available for distribution as the pursuit of power required. When the one christened Joanna was born in November 1479, she seemed intended by God for a Burgundian alliance. It all struck the Spaniard as obvious. He would obtain by nuptials what Louis of France sought by force of arms.

Ferdinand took the long view. Quick to realize how the Low Countries held their little prince Philip close to their money-making hearts for being Flanders-born, he saw how they refused to excuse the child's father Maximilian for what *he* was—a hero perhaps to his own Austrian people, but a German among the Germans. See how he surrounded himself with German counsellors! With no money of his own he would no doubt be expending Netherlands wealth to pay German mercenaries to fight his wars. In resisting Louis XI it was less the interests of the Low Countries that he sought to protect than the concerns of the Habsburgs in Central Europe. Or so it appeared in Flemish eyes.

To be sure, Maximilian came up against a populace in the Low Coun-tries almost impossible of centralized government. This most significant portion of Charles the Bold's dukedom, vibrant, industrious, cosmopol-itan, could in no sense be described as an extension of agrarian Burgundy proper, where Charles had not so much been served by his subjects as worshipped by them. The Low Countries felt no awe for the man flaunting his glorious ancestry and constantly promising a new crusade against the Turks. They on the other hand drew their pride elsewhere: in their manufacturing centres, those fine Flemish cities that bade fair to dictate the marketing of the continent, and their coal exports, which ranked with Newcastle's. Now, in the late fifteenth century, Dutch shipping had all but taken the Baltic trade away from its monopolists of feudal times, the Germanic Hanseatic League. Bruges still retained its prestige as the jewel in the Burgundian coronet. It was nearly twice the size of Brussels, even though the silting up of its river mouth was already sending the English cloth trade to Antwerp. Dijon harked back to its medieval chivalric past; Antwerp in Brabant looked to a future of dazzling economic promise. A burgher's patronage could enrich Ghent's cathedral with the Van Eyck masterpiece 'The Adoration of the Mystic Lamb' and allow Hans Memling to fill a palace in Bruges with paintings which gave that city its air of a northern Florence. Where else in Europe could a princess dream of such an inheritance?

Mary and Maximilian soon produced a second child, their daughter named Margaret like her grandmother, born in 1480. The couple intended to enjoy every moment of their fortunate lives. But it was not to be. They were out falconing one day in 1482 when Mary, just twenty-five, was thrown from her horse. Courtiers rushed to her aid, only to find their duchess mortally injured.

A grief-stricken Maximilian—he would of course marry again but always thought of Mary as his true wife—returned to Ghent, where he and his mother-in-law Margaret of York consoled each other in the knowledge that Mary had bequeathed a son to continue the Burgundian line in the Low Countries. This was arguing without the peculiarly intense nationalisms that divided province from province, city from city, in that region. They were prepared to recognize little Philip, a four-year-old boy, and repeat all the constitutional procedures that had made his mother their ruler. As for Maximilian, in no circumstances would they have the man as regent during the child's minority.

Ghent and Bruges went so far as to intrigue with King Louis of France, stimulating rebellion. They secreted the infant Margaret away, then traded the princess where they could never have used her mother, by surrendering her in betrothal to the Dauphin, the future Charles VIII. For her dowry, they sanctioned French ownership of the lands Louis had already occupied. Maximilian, ostensibly the guardian of national independence in the Burgundian Netherlands, found himself instead wrestling with a national insurrection led by Flanders. He would need one day to protect his son Philip from elevation as the figure-head of the dissidents by sending him out of Ghent and into the care of grandmother Margaret of York in her castle at Malines. Such was the humiliation forced upon the Habsburg son due for an emperor's crown. Louis of France had chopped the loyalties of the Netherlands half a dozen different ways—not by any means exhausted by the account described here. Louis gloated. He was half-way into Europe's richest spoils. And having won the Netherlands he intended to complete the double by making France paramount also in Italy.

These developments were bound to give Ferdinand of Aragon cause for acute anxiety. He was particularly displeased by the rough treatment accorded Maximilian by the insolent Flemings. It was no part of his scheme that France fish profitably in the turbulent waters of the Netherlands. In this respect he differed from the detached attitude of his wife's Castilian advisers. They thought of France as a traditional friend. He saw it as a menace, recalling how Louis XI had foreclosed on two Catalonian provinces (Cerdagne and Rousillon) when his father John II had been unable to repay a loan. He wanted them back—Navarre too, where John had worn a crown for twenty-two years by right of his first marriage. Ferdinand would combine with anyone—England, the emperor, disaffected Flemish princelings—to restrain that incurable Gallic resentment of others' progress. He professed complete disinterest as he courted the various leaders of the sensitive Netherlands provinces. This Spaniard was a natural ally for any European monarch with a secret longing to squeeze the French. He could, in regard to the Netherlands, exploit a special relationship by virtue of his country's role as an essential customer in the continued prosperity of the northern wool trade—which did not imply, be it said, that Ferdinand would not switch his preferences should the occasion serve him.

Thus he and Maximilian were guided by a mutuality of interest. Imperious the latter might have been, erratic as a military commander and too fond of the good life. Furthermore, he struggled against complicated responsibilities made manifold because they stretched across the continent to threaten his person whenever his back was turned. Maximilian's mind and body seemed never to be in the same place. But he recognized potential friends as well as actual enemies. He calculated that Ferdinand would not waver. He knew he could count when desired also on the English. So here were three countries sharing common cause in their baleful observation of France, which in consequence felt surrounded by a hostile force whose weakest point was located in the Netherlands. King Louis had striven for the marriage of his heir to Mary of Burgundy specifically to keep the Habsburgs away from his north-eastern frontier, and when Maximilian won her he accepted their child Margaret as a poor second-best. Margaret was now undergoing spiritual preparation at Amboise consistent with her anticipated role as the future Queen of France.

Maximilian took steps to reverse his ridiculous situation as a cold-shouldered interloper in the Netherlands. He exploited such local rivalries as that between Bruges and Antwerp and won the loyalty of the latter together with Brussels. He found supporters in Holland. With their help he reinstated himself in Flanders and by 1486 he felt ready to engage the French in a decisive clash of arms. Propitiously for him, Louis XI had died in 1483, after a long reign of superior if capricious diplomacy and considerable achievement. Now infantilism succeeded craftiness in Paris (we have it on the evidence of that most authoritative of royal chroniclers, Philippe de Commynes) when the Dauphin, betrothed to Maximilian's child, assumed the crown as Charles VIII. However, the law of averages came to the aid of France, for a while at least. As we know, the reins of government were taken into the hands of Charles's brilliant sister, Anne of Beaujeu, pending the king's majority.

Louis XI had been a king with a talent for skilled persuasion, and only after this failed did he resort to the blunt instrument. His campaign of war had been conducted with the utmost ruthlessness. His strategy in the first place relied on picking off the provinces of the Netherlands confederation one by one, each being jealous for its traditions, its language, its trade—particularly its trade, which, like flowing water, seeped through the obstacles as if the region were at peace. Netherlands citizens were none too keen to leave their counting-houses and well-stocked emporia to chance themselves in battle for this conglomerate homeland's independence (did it really matter to them?), especially not at the call of a Habsburg prince. Maximilian shrugged their lack of enthusiasm off and brought up his German mercenaries. He had no funds for the expense and was already up to his ears in debt to the Fuggers of Augsburg. Earlier, he had approached the Florentine bankers, principally the Medici. On Louis's instructions (France and Florence were closely linked) they had turned him down. The tough German infantrymen thereupon found their wages in plunder.

Louis had furthermore sent his ships to blockade the English commerce with Bruges and Antwerp, frustrating also the Baltic herring fleets, which were henceforth easy prey to another nuisance—Dutch pirates. Violent scenes of banditry, burning of crops, intrigues with the enemy, the local population disaffected, all these had contributed before Louis XI's death to isolate Maximilian in a quicksand.

The prince's problems accumulated through Habsburg concerns elsewhere. His father, the ageing Frederick III, persuaded him in 1485 to return to Germany so as to ensure his election as King of the Romans, the misnomer signifying king of the Germans and expressly designed for an heir to the Holy Roman Emperor. Other aspirants to the crown were never in short supply. Death had interrupted both Charles the Bold and Louis of France from its pursuit. The newest candidate was Matthias Corvinus, King of Hungary and a warrior who had claimed victories against the Turks.

Frederick was now seventy, his handsome son only twenty-six, and they had not set eyes on each other since that happy day, eight years earlier, when Maximilian was married to Mary of Burgundy. In the interlude Frederick had been reduced in the estimation of his subjects to an incapacitated weakling. For proof of it, Matthias Corvinus had just snatched some provinces of Austria, the Habsburg heritage, evicting the lack-lustre emperor from Vienna (see p. 18). Could this mark the end of the grand dynasty? It had already lost territory in Italy to Venice. Only Maximilian could expunge the ignominy. He travelled to Frankfurt and confronted the Diet of the Reich. What a contrast in his reception here to the one accorded him on entry into the Netherlands! In Frankfurt French agents, their purses full of gold, had a gift for every Elector denying the Habsburg prince. But Germany wanted him—oh, how it wanted him! If any man offered a prospect of making something out of the constitutional raggle-taggle that was Germany it could only be Maximilian. In assuming his crown in the ancient imperial capital of Aachen as King of the Romans, he pledged to himself that his father would live to see Austria restored, that he would unite Europe, that he would lead a crusade and vanquish Islam. We shall see.

In the mean time, however, the Netherlands beckoned. He must grasp that nettle and put the French to flight. This was optimism prevailing over discretion. Maximilian suddenly appeared in Bruges declaring his intention of summoning the Estates General, a full council of all the Netherlands, and appealing to their sense of urgency. Bruges had other ideas. It locked him up, together with his German hangers-on, pending

his acquiescence to the earlier arrangement: betrothal of his little daughter Margaret to the boy king Charles. This in truth would leave the
country open to the French for further penetration at their leisure.

The humiliating situation was too much for Maximilian's father. Suf-
fused with unexpected vitality, the old man surprised everybody. He
arrived in Bruges at the head of an army intended against the French
and liberated an embarrassed King of the Romans from the shopkeepers
of Flanders. It was now May, 1488.

Time passed. Maximilian's presence was required in other latitudes.
Understandably, he was a much chastened man. His little daughter
Margaret remained inaccessible within the care of the French bishops.
His son Philip, inheritor of the title Duke of Burgundy and reared by his
grandmother at Malines, came into the guardianship of a Council of
Regency composed of the Habsburg's opponents. Maximilian had sworn
an oath accepting the situation, but few believed he would be bound by
an arrangement forced upon him under duress. As for that grandmother,
ever faithful to her name and still fighting the Wars of the Roses, she
was herself to stir the pot of troubles. Margaret of York would soon be
persuaded that one of her nephews, the boy Duke of York presumed
murdered in the Tower of London, was in fact very much alive, in the
improbable person of a certain Perkin Warbeck. Not long, and she would
be encouraging the pretender's claim to the English crown against Henry
VII, Maximilian's English ally. Where would all this double-dealing end?

Perhaps a period of retreat in Germany, following the stress of dealing
with the obstreperous Low Countries, would be welcomed as a well-
merited respite. Not by Maximilian. He decided at this juncture to cross
the continent and retrieve the historic seat of his own authority. He had
to expel Matthias Corvinus from Vienna and reestablish Habsburg rule
in those portions of Austria obtained by Corvinus while Maximilian was
otherwise engaged. Thankfully, the task was easily achieved. Corvinus,
though still young, was not the man he had only recently appeared, a
powerful monarch with his eyes upon the Holy Roman Empire. He now
offered to surrender the Austrian provinces if only Maximilian would
stay within those bounds and recognize his bastard son John Corvinus
as King of Hungary. Maximilian was now in possession of Vienna anyway
and made ready to seize Hungary too. But he could not keep his German
army together (lack of money for its pay again) and hence made his
peace with a dying Matthias. He lost nothing thereby, since various
channels of circumstance brought Hungary into Habsburg rule within
another generation.

While this still lay in the future, the present demanded the unravelling of other frustrating knots. Maximilian sped back westward with another plan of attack against France, a plan that secured the armed support of his two friends, Henry VII of England and Ferdinand of Spain. A back door had opened: Brittany. This duchy, since the annexation of Burgundy following Charles the Bold's death at Nancy, constituted the last independent royal province, *apanage*, within the kingdom of France. The Duke of Brittany had died in September 1488, leaving a daughter, Anne, as its new ruler. An old anxiety passed through the quick mind of Anne of Beaujeu as she contemplated the dangers and possibilities this other Anne posed for France. Anne of Brittany was twelve years old. The man she married would possess the duchy. Could Anne of Beaujeu, stewardess of the kingdom during her brother's minority, break her trust to their father Louis XI by allowing Brittany to fall to a foreign prince? It must remain French and emerge from its vassalage to return unreservedly to the kingdom proper.

Maximilian decided otherwise. Brittany was not truly French to the marrow. Its people cherished their separate status and enjoyed a centuries-long association with England—indeed they hugged their Celtic ancestry. This was a stepping-stone for successive English invasions, and Henry VII, formerly an exile in Brittany, had not absolutely relinquished the English right to the French throne. In December 1490, Maximilian, by an arrangement with Henry that the English would prefer to forget, sent emissaries to Rennes, capital of the duchy, to stand in for his proxy marriage to the young duchess Anne. He actually intended to plant the Habsburg banner in this north-western corner of France! Anne of Beaujeu, horrified, perceived that her country was thanklessly frittering away energies in the Low Countries while a mortal threat was essaying a stab through its backbone. She settled the matter at a stroke.

The young Anne became a pawn in the older Anne's plan. The proxy marriage to Maximilian was annulled, along with the betrothal of King Charles VIII to Maximilian's daughter Margaret, who was nevertheless retained as a hostage at Amboise in France and her dowry (principally Artois and Franche Comté) retained in forfeit. This was adding insult to a host of injuries. Charles then travelled personally to Rennes and demanded—yes demanded—the hand of the Duchess of Brittany. She submitted, first extracting a condition that the autonomy of her land be respected. Their union took place with appropriate ceremony just as Ferdinand and Isabella were preparing their triumphant entry into Granada, in December 1491. But the marriage had a curse laid upon it: the

Queen of France could not give this husband (there would be another) an heir. All their children were born abnormal and died in infancy. Artois, disgusted by the conduct of the French king towards its princess Margaret, declared independence and rejoined the Netherlands. Franche Comté then allowed Maximilian to return and reclaim the county on behalf of his son Philip of Burgundy.

At the heart of Charles's failure to put up a struggle for these territories was a recurrence of the French obsession with Italy. Had he been a more rational individual, and listened more attentively to the wise advice of Anne of Beaujeu (jogged by her husband Pierre), Charles might have consolidated his realm at this stage, when it could fairly lay claim to being the arbiter of western Europe. By marrying Anne of Brittany he threw into disarray Henry VII's plan to come to Maximilian's aid in the duchy. The English king made an undignified exit in 1492 and by the treaty of Etaples with Charles renounced all further claims to France (except for Calais) on payment of a sum in gold crowns as reimbursement for the expenses of a pointless expedition. Henry had little heart in any case for a military operation to help Maximilian in the Low Countries, since Margaret of York had chosen that precise moment to recognize the Flemish youth Perkin Warbeck as Richard IV, true king of England. Spain would shortly follow England's lead, and more happily. Ferdinand patched a peace with France restoring to Aragon the lost Catalan provinces of Cerdagne and Rousillon. Maximilian's turn for assuagement came next, when his daughter Margaret was returned home, amid universal relief.

Charles was clearing the stage for his conqueror's entry into Italy. Determined to be master in his own house, he summarily deprived Anne of Beaujeu of her influence at court. She died in 1492. When Charles moved, in a series of blundering adventures, France was started on a course which was to embroil his country in perverse Mediterranean politics for a long time to come. A later king would then disembarrass himself from Italy in the sober realization that Charles's gamble, to be repeated by his immediate successor, had cost the *patrie* fifty years of progress towards territorial integration.

Of all the actors in the inglorious denouement unfolded by the death of the Duke of Burgundy in 1477, who could claim to have reaped the greatest benefit? It could only be Ferdinand of Aragon. He had reached the year 1492 sharing a common distrust of France with Maximilian, still not yet an emperor. All the preceding events had brought their interests into conjuncture, not least because each had also his war against

Islam to disturb whatever calm existed, the Moors on one side of the continent, the Turks on the other. We shall shortly observe the fusion of their blood, with a Francophone man of Ghent, their grandson yet unborn, bestriding the world.

One little-advertised moment, on the dawn of 3 August 1492, carried more significance for Spain than all the tumult of that discordant age. Christopher Columbus departed from Palos armed with a document in triplicate, to serve both as his passport and as a letter of introduction to the rulers of whatever territories the explorer would discover during his voyage to places unknown. One of those rulers would doubtless be the Great Khan, another the mighty Priest King of a Christian realm. The document, in Latin, was appropriate to them all:

> Ferdinand and Isabella, King and Queen of Castile, Aragon and Leon, etc., to the Great King: We have heard with pleasure of the great esteem and love that you and your subjects have for us and our nation. We are also informed that you wish to have news of our country. We therefore send you our Admiral Christopher Columbus bearing the news that we are in good health and excellent prosperity—I the King; I the Queen. Granada, 30 April 1492.

Columbus had command of two caravels and a larger, wider flagship, this being the *Santa Maria*, cargo capacity of about 100 tons and doomed never to return from the Indies. We only know it from second-hand description. *Santa Maria* lifted a tall mast carrying a broad square sail surmounted by a small topsail. Two further sails fore and aft with a lateen rigged to the mizzen would help to take the wind. Trembling against the tide with the flagship were the *Niña* and the *Pinta*, neither carrying more than 70 tons. They were locally built, whereas the *Santa Maria*, chartered by Columbus at short notice, was a visitor from a yard up north. All three vessels flew the banner of the expedition, a crowned cross of green on a white field. The *Santa Maria* alone hoisted the royal ensign, and it marked this expedition as a Castilian enterprise, not of the combined thrones. Isabella had ordered it. If it carried any august blessing it was hers; if it brought back any profit it would be Castile's.

The *Santa Maria* shipped thirty-nine men, the *Pinta* twenty-six, the *Niña* twenty-two, all of whose names are recorded. Doubtless the complement numbered a few more hands, commonly found around the docks, who had obtained their release from jail by enlisting. And there was a representative of the queen, Rodrigo Sanchez of Segovia, to ensure that the crown received its agreed share of the spoils. Columbus had prophesied abundant treasure. Ordinary seamen would receive 1,000 *maravedis* (about ten grams of gold) per month, officers twice as much. But extra rewards would await their successful return. One man was delegated to make an official record of the voyage, another cared for the light gunnery carried, while a third, Luis de Torres, was appointed, because of his knowledge of Arabic, as official interpreter in the belief that he could understand the native languages spoken under distant skies.

Torres, the only crew member known to be a Jew, went through a ceremony of baptism before sailing, whereupon they all made their confessions and received absolution for their sins. Columbus was now forty-one. He had been rehearsing this moment of truth in his imagination for a decade, yet it now appeared as though all was improvised, haphazard, with hardly any suggestion of a major expedition. He was no Bartholomew Dias.

Little, moreover, helped to give the impression that this was a national event. The occasion was localized at Palos. Columbus had found the *Santa Maria* there, and three brothers of the Pinzón family, prominent in the commerce of the place, sailed with him. Two of the brothers, Martin Alonso and Vicente Yañez, commanded the *Pinta* and *Niña*, which were government-owned, having gone forfeit to the crown to purge the town of some municipal offence—in all probability arrears of excise. The armourer, Diego de Harana, belonged to the family of Columbus's mistress Beatriz and was a personal friend.

It was a Friday when the little fleet slipped gently down the Rio Tinto, passing La Rabida and then into the Saltés. The day would live in the memory of the Jews for a different reason: in sailing through the Saltés Columbus overtook another vessel, a barque packed with the last of this sad people scattering to their exile. Noting the sight, the Genoese made a vow that none of that infidel race would ever be permitted in the lands he discovered. Christ voyaged with him, of that he was convinced. Close to his person he carried the Jews' Book, by which he felt guided to the undiscovered world, together with a copy of *The Travels of Marco Polo*.

A slight miscalculation? Much more. 'One civilization against the rest,' Fernand Braudel, the French historian, has described the Jews, but immensely adaptable. It would not be long before they would be observed in the New World. Many Christians had warned that driving them out would cost Spain dear. And so it transpired at once, evidenced in the first autumnal migration of the sheep population from north to south. The Mesta organization had in the past largely relied on Jewish proficiency in animal husbandry to select the sheep for the long journey, and such business as arranging the herdsmen's shelter, as well as the Mesta's financing and the keeping of records. The Jews' departure left a gap requiring years to replace.

Already many of them had joined their fraternity in the Low Countries, where they were not opposed, so that Castilian Spanish circulated among the languages most commonly employed in the commerce of Bruges, and was heard also in the handling of multifarious chores at Antwerp. Larger numbers had made their way east to receive a welcome in the Ottoman cities of Constantinople and Salonika, introducing such skills as printing, but the Netherlands suited them best because of their expertise in European commerce and its ancillary pursuits of money-lending and credit finance. Their settlement in Antwerp coincided with the city's ascent to the pinnacle of early capitalism, for nothing helped Antwerp's accelerated progress to world leadership, already destined, so much as the Jews' acquaintance with the trading rules of the Iberian peninsula. It gave little cause for surprise that the next century saw them established in the New World too, as commodity dealers in Spanish America, while in Brazil they even had their explorers licensed to navigate the South Atlantic shoreline on behalf of the Portuguese. Capitalism implied the capacity to think internationally, and here was the world's most international people at capitalism's service. Along with their savants, paupers and itinerant pedlars they spread over Europe, to lend immense contrast to the Jews' economic pattern and social tapestry.

Once those three little ships disappeared down the Rio Tinto, Ferdinand and Isabella most certainly put Columbus out of their minds. In their plans for the future his expedition intruded hardly at all. They had fulfilled a sacred trust in uniting Granada to Spain. They now satisfied their people (or most of them) that each monarch spoke for the other, and for both. But they shared the common preoccupation of all rulers: the uncontested continuation of their house. This responded to their vanity, it forestalled civil war, it safeguarded the patrimony against foreign invasion and it testified to the dynasty's rule by divine right of succession. Anxieties there had to be. Royal families, by their incessant interbreeding, frequently produced sickly children. Despite the best physicians deformities and premature death dogged the genetic strain.

The Catholic Monarchs had been blessed with a son, Juan, who in 1492 reached the age of fourteen, so their assurance of a smooth continuation could be reasonably anticipated. It was on their daughters, all four of them, that their further hopes hung, first to harmonize the relations of Spain with Portugal, then to expand their influence in other directions. Already, they had suffered one grievous disappointment. Their eldest daughter, named Isabella like her mother, had in 1490 been married to Alfonso, heir to the Portuguese king. It was intended as the act of reconciliation that would bring peace to Iberia, bygone quarrels forgotten, and at some time, if not in the early future, forge a union of the entire peninsula. However, Isabella's husband died after one year of marriage. The young widow was now, in the brutal dynastic calculations of those days, provisionally 'non-functional' as an instrument of diplomacy. The succession in Portugal fell to another line, allowing Isabella to return to Lisbon as bride of its King Manuel. But not yet, and not for long, for she died in 1498, when a second daughter was made available—Maria—to take the place of her sister in King Manuel's bed. The story of these two neighbours, swinging through the centuries between enmity and alliance, would become still further entangled. No princess of Spain was to enjoy the luxury of personal happiness, as history would relate.

Larger responsibilities in the mean time found employment enough for Maximilian, King of the Romans and prepared at any moment to succeed a father now reduced to introspective inertia in his transition from senility to death. During 1492 rebellious knights and others in the Low Countries still disputed the Habsburg succession to the Burgundian inheritance and kept open communion with France. Though Maximilian had redeemed Austria from foreign control, and constantly returned to his beloved Innsbruck attired like one of his own peasants, for hunting and mountaineering, he never rested. The Turks, baring their teeth again, now brought him back to that fundamental commitment of his office, the defence of Christendom.

Sultan Bayezid, we recall, had hesitated from daring a full-scale assault upon Europe while his brother Jem, held by the Vatican at an annual fee of 40,000 ducats, still lived. But he now exploited Hungarian disarray for just such a purpose. Hungary had long borne the brunt of Ottoman pressure. It could do so no longer. Jem still lolled his days away in Rome as Bayezid swept into Hungary, Croatia and the Austrian provinces of Styria, Carniola and Carinthia. It was the usual visitation in quest of slaves and plunder, and Bayezid just failed to take Belgrade. Only Maximilian had the will for an encounter. The Turk brought his army to within 100 miles of Venice, but neither the Venetians nor any other power came to their Christian brother's aid. Wasn't resistance to the infidel the sacred task of whichever believer inherited the crown of the

Holy Roman Empire? So they all contended, while offering other justifications in abundance for their passivity. Maximilian would never forgive Venice.

He met the enemy at Villach, at the foot of the Austrian Alps. This time the Fuggers sprang into action in their historic role as money-lenders to the empire. They had a strong personal interest—anxiety to see a well-equipped Christian force protecting their precious silver and copper deposits buried in the local soil. Both sides suffered huge losses. Bayezid then thought the better of it and withdrew. Not long into 1493 and the warriors of Islam would return.

Of course, Charles VIII of France had allowed himself to hope that Maximilian would dig his own grave at Villach. Instead, it had been a small victory, though at heavy cost. Charles, intent upon his foray into Italy, hoped to vanquish the Ottoman Empire with an extravagant scheme that could only find its birth in the mind of a foolhardy ruler with the brain of a child. He would drive a wedge through Italy, conquer Naples and Sicily, then cross the Mediterranean. Like his father Louis XI before him, he had dearly wished to be elected Holy Roman Emperor, but despite the abundant resources of France at his disposal he could not prevent the elevation of the penurious Maximilian. However, wasn't there another historic Christian empire, that of Byzantium, due for liberation from the infidel? He visualized himself capturing the Holy Land from the sea, recovering Jerusalem for the Cross and then swooping on Constantinople in a spectacular rearguard action.

That would indeed bring glory to the Valois monarchy. Italy, so hopelessly divided, appeared easy prey. Charles awaited an appropriate moment to strike across the Alps and enter Milan. It was a great exercise in self-deception. Italy would not offer itself as a trophy; it revealed its true nature as a trap.

And there would be complications with Rome. One week after Columbus took leave of his royal sponsors and departed for destinations unknown, the cardinals (one of them ninety-six years of age) met in conclave. The Pope had died. After the customary horse-trading and intrigue, during which some bishops were bought for cash and others received promises of rich benefices, a successor was chosen. He was the 'Spanish Bull', Rodrigo Borgia, native of Jativa. '*Papam habemus!*' the Roman populace, ever ready for a jamboree, cried. But treachery pervaded the air. Now who dared speak of Italy except with foreboding, and which true Christian would think of the Church without an aching heart?

Chapter Five

MEDICI, BORGIA AND THE ITALIAN PARADOX

In 1489 Pope Innocent VIII created a boy aged thirteen as one of his cardinals. The lad so honoured was Giovanni de' Medici, the clever second son of Lorenzo the Magnificent. This arrangement followed another, also somewhat grotesque, and indeed was coupled with it: the betrothal of Lorenzo's daughter Maddalena (named in memory of a slave girl, parentage unknown, whom Lorenzo's grandfather Cosimo had taken in his bed) to Franceschetto Cibo, son of the Pope. As dowry the groom received substantial estates, including the Pazzi Palace in Florence and a Pazzi country villa, besides 4,000 ducats in gold. The properties had gone forfeit to Lorenzo on the crushing of the conspiracy, already described (see p. 13), that cost the Pazzis their ancestral dignities, their material possessions and, in some cases, their lives. The bride was sixteen, her husband, an insignificant ne'er-do-well, almost forty. Once again, a Supreme Pontiff had grossly abused his spiritual prerogatives in pursuit of earthly favours.

The temptation exists to define the condition of fifteenth-century Italy by the particulars of this transaction. Here lay bared the decadence pervading the Vatican and an example of its exploitation by powerful dynasties, explanation and justification enough for the nemesis in store, both for the country and for the Church Universal. Italy's national ordeal by conquest would come first. The reckoning for Catholicism would await the accession of that juvenile cardinal himself to the throne of St Peter as Pope Leo X, for destiny was saving for him the rebellion to be initiated by Martin Luther against cankerous Rome. Then there would be no halting the persecutions and the wars.

Thankfully, the spectacle of Innocent VIII sinking as low as any Pontiff as he greedily engaged in feathering the domestic nest, enlisting a calculating accessary, illuminates only one aspect of that eventful Italian era. Giambattista Cibo was the first pope publicly to acknowledge his children—he fathered two, begotten before his entry into the religious life. Generally, papal offspring were designated nephews and nieces, as if this excused the regular looting of the Vatican treasury on their behalf. Innocent's successor, Rodrigo Borgia, with a large brood born in the course of his career from cardinal to pope, flagrantly abandoned the camouflage. Innocent somehow lacked the quality of outrageous splendour characteristic of the Borgias. In partnership with his son Franceschetto he dealt in indulgences at street-hawker level. They sold pardons like a potter's wares, granting absolution against a suitable fee for any immorality, including murder.

But the papacy was the product of European, not specifically Italian, degeneration. The Renaissance, on the other hand, was born and germinated specifically here, in this peninsula. It percolated for a century or more through the veins of Italy's anatomy of hopeful, hopeless statelets, where poets and painters were honoured while castle dungeons smothered the cries of a supposed witch, and rivers washed up unwanted infants drowned as casually as sickly cats. Art and letters flourished along with freedom of enquiry, so that it fell to Italy to redeem Christian civilization; though we grieve for its proclivities to evil while celebrating its capacity for good.

The secrets of the Vatican were better known to the Medici of Florence than to any other Italian potentates. They had been its bankers since the chaotic days of the Great Schism earlier in the century, when Florence sheltered successive papal pretenders in search of a throne. The relationship had survived periods of the utmost tension, for the many branches of the Medici bank operated as an unofficial intelligence service, of greater value to the popes than their own legates, who could waver in their loyalties if the price was right. The death in 1484 of Innocent's predecessor, Sixtus IV, a Pazzi partisan smeared by involvement in the assassination at Mass of Lorenzo's younger brother, had closed a difficult chapter. Pope Innocent won the Holy See by the usual shabby means: in his case the purchase of two hesitant cardinals, one the son of the King of Naples, the other a brother of the dictator of Milan. Lorenzo, fearing a renewed anti-Medici trend in Vatican politics, adroitly courted the new Pope, virtually rendering Innocent his captive.

Still, the Pope understood the limits beyond which public displeasure could not be defied. Appoint young Giovanni de' Medici a cardinal? By all means, if Lorenzo desired it. But he would not allow the boy to enter the Sacred College awhile, nor would he hasten to announce the elevation. Giovanni was already a canon of every cathedral in Tuscany. He held the abbacy of Monte Casino and a cassockful of other benefices in France as well as Italy. Surely he could wait, there was no danger of his ever dying of starvation! Innocent ordered the boy away, to study canon law at Pisa. Lorenzo bristled at the delay, fearing the old Pope's demise before the formal induction of his son. Another Pope could well annul the cardinalate. At length, after three years, his protestations succeeded. He was just in time. Giovanni donned the red hat and the sapphire ring in February 1492. Not many months would elapse before Lorenzo and the Pope were both dead.

Michelangelo, himself still under seventeen years of age, was then lodging in the Medici Palace in Florence, there making the acquaintance of Giovanni's old tutor, the humanist poet Angelo Poliziano, as well as the leader of Lorenzo's neo-Platonist discussion circle, Marsilio Ficino. With their encouragement he had already carved his first relief, 'The Madonna of the Stairs', soon followed by 'The Battle of the Centaurs'. By their contrast of subject and style the two works, to this day on display in Florence, might be said to epitomize the Medicean era's metaphysical range: beauty as a spiritual endowment of man, strength as an inheritance of pagan virtues. Lorenzo had discovered the boy artist in apprenticeship at the Ghirlandaio workshop, brought him home and given him a salary, said to be five ducats a month.

Perhaps Lorenzo, tired and prematurely aged, sought in this second son Giovanni and in his protégé Michelangelo vindication of all his exertions as a prince and a scholar. He was neither in title, he was both in aspiration. And doubtless Michelangelo, together with Poliziano and Ficino, kept his true thoughts private to himself as he made his way to Fiesole to witness the service of consecration and blessing of the youngest cardinal in the Benedictine abbey there. The abbey, so near to the garden where Boccaccio set the background for his *Decameron*, had been rebuilt as a present to Tuscany by Giovanni's great-grandfather Cosimo. Another priest, Savonarola, Prior of San Marco monastery in Florence, received the news of Giovanni's elevation with unconcealed revulsion, for it was another sign to him that Satan guided Lorenzo the Magnificent's domination of Florence.

Florence thought of itself as a republic, governed by a Signoria of twelve elected though frequently changing notables whose leader was nominally the sovereignty's first citizen. It had expanded over the previous two centuries and pre-empted the Duchy of Milan from devouring a succession of still tinier autonomous cities, among them Pistoia, Prato and Arezzo, by performing that operation itself. Medici funds helped Florence to acquire more, either by conquest or purchase. Thus did Pisa and Leghorn succumb, and the island of Elba, so that in the fifteenth century Florentine commerce enjoyed shipping facilities untrammelled by the maritime giants, Genoa and Venice. The Medici were not always represented on the Signoria, which had once expressed its displeasure at the family's egotism by locking Cosimo in the bell-tower of the Palazzo Vecchio, where members resided during their term of office. Nevertheless Cosimo ultimately emerged the victor. An important guild of artisans, the Ciompi (meaning they wore clogs), supported Medici politics since the days of an old revolt, when the family championed its cause. Thenceforward Florence fell under near-autocratic Medici rule, with Cosimo recognized as 'Pater Patriae'.

Of Cosimo de' Medici another Florentine, Machiavelli, wrote: 'He not only surpassed all his contemporaries in wealth and authority but also in generosity and prudence . . . Although his homes, like all his other works and actions, were quite of a regal character, and he alone was prince in Florence, still everything was so tempered with his prudence that he never transgressed the decent moderation of civil life. In his conversation, his servants, his travelling, his mode of living and the relationships he formed, the modest demeanour of the citizen was always evident.' True, but it was partly a ploy. The Medici chose to hide behind a humble exterior whenever summoned to perform acts of which they disapproved.

To be sure, there existed a Florentine arrogance rooted in its consciousness of a chosen role as keeper of the Italian eternity. The state's location alone impeded the rivalries of its northern neighbours and hindered the spread of papal territory. Its soil had nurtured the founders of Italian letters and the forerunners of Renaissance art. Florence had bequeathed to Europe a universally accepted coin, the florin, so named because of the city's red lily emblem. Its language became the Italian language. Its cathedral inaugurated a new era in architecture. The city-state confidently preserved its own calendar, New Year's Day being the Feast of the Annunciation, 25 March.

If Cosimo de' Medici wished more from Florence than his city could bestow, this was less out of political ambition than a desire to restore to the Italian peninsula its role, long defunct, as the primal force of Christendom. Throughout the Middle Ages, and while France held cultural and religious sway over Europe, Florence constituted a reminder that

Italy was really one country. How eagerly Cosimo seized the opportunity in 1439 for his city to act as host to the gathering which brought both the western Pontiff and the eastern Byzantine Emperor together on the banks of the Arno! The meeting augured the hope of union between East and West in the face of the Turkish menace to Constantinople; and of a new, triumphant crusade, reconciliation of the Latin Church with the Greek, harmony among all true believers at last. Proudly, Cosimo used the occasion to invite pilgrims of all nations to come and worship in the cathedral, just then crowned by Brunelleschi's mighty cupola with its giant multicoloured marble slabs tapering to its summit. All the experts had scoffed at Brunelleschi's plan. It was impossible of execution, they said. Yet here it stood, soaring heavenwards beside Giotto's campanile and Ghiberti's as yet unfinished bronze Baptistry doors, which would have Michelangelo rhapsodizing about the gates of Paradise.

The historic conclave of reconciliation between the two branches of Christianity had opened at Ferrara, much to Cosimo's chagrin. John Palaeologus, emperor of little more than a single city, offered the East's submission to the primacy of Rome in return for troops and funds in the defence of Constantinople. But doctrinal differences and hurt sensitivities brought an impasse. Then an ill omen: the visitation of plague in Ferrara. So, at Cosimo's urgent behest, the conclave had moved to Florence. Pope Eugenius IV proceeded to Mass in the cathedral together with Palaeologus and the Patriarch of Constantinople, the three of them linked in brotherhood under Christ, the grandeur of the ceremonial charged with deepest pathos. For the Byzantines, with all their tradition, their learning, their outward pomp, came as stricken supplicants.

Plenary meetings took place in the spacious Franciscan Church of the Holy Cross, its chapels decorated with Giotto's frescoes and Donatello's dramatic crucifix set in glory over the north transept. There also their eyes could feast on that gentle sculptor's Annunciation, surely one of the subtlest images of the Virgin in all Renaissance art. It was as if a curtain separating two cultures fell away. The Patriarch and his large retinue of scholars fluently quoted from Greek masters known to the West only as legends. Seminars clarified obscurities of text and ambiguities of dogma that had divided Christians for centuries. Ideas crossed and trans-fertilized, libraries were compared, Greek manuscripts were at last accurately copied. And ever in attendance, an enthralled Cosimo de' Medici. He died in 1464, just before Italy produced its first printed book.

Thus it had by no means proved fruitless, this 1439 Council of Florence, though it terminated with the visitors unable to accept the Pope's conditions for union and returning to Constantinople to defy Islam empty-handed, abandoned except for a small body of Italian volunteers. As we know, within fifteen years Constantinople ceased to exist as a Christian metropolis. Florence alone gained in renown. Cosimo had persuaded some eastern scholars to remain. He offered them lucrative benefices within his gift and employment as scribes and translators in his library. Other patrons followed the Florentine example. When Constantinople reached its desperate end in 1453 Europe felt impoverished, though all Italy was the richer.

Modern Italian children rarely leave school without committing to memory Lorenzo the Magnificent's poem (he wrote many fine ones) with its suggestive opening, '*Quant'è bella giovenezza, che si fugge tuttavia! Chi vuol esser lieto, sia. Di doman non c'è certezza.*' 'How beautiful is youth, and so swiftly gone! Give joyousness its rein, for there is no telling about the morrow.'

Lorenzo was a living demonstration of the sentiment. He reached maturity in the company of artists and scholars who in this period made the name of Florence almost synonymous with the Renaissance. As it spread, throughout Italy and across the Alps into Germany, more hesitantly to England, France and Spain, the Renaissance permeated the halls of the Vatican Palace, the popes themselves ingesting a humanism which presumed to rank secular ideas with the philosophy of ecclesiastics. As we have noted, popes too gave little heed to the morrow, openly enjoying their pleasures as they indulged their Pharaonic dreams.

But where might this end? Patronage of art, literature and architecture could not atone for that other Italy, whose rulers and their acolytes engaged in a *danse macabre*. From his pulpit in Florence, Girolamo Savonarola foretold the retribution on its way. They were trifling with God, he cried, condemning Pope Innocent, Lorenzo de' Medici and all other potentates of the peninsula in the same malediction. Savonarola was not short of material to feed his passionate eloquence. Franceschetto Cibo, son of the Holy Father, son-in-law of Lorenzo, strikingly advertised the disease. Not long married, this dissolute man repaired to the Vatican in quest of portable booty. He believed the Pope had died. On being disabused of this good news Franceschetto sought to abduct Jem the royal hostage, to use him in high-class trade, no doubt, or to pocket the bounty accompanying guardianship of the Ottoman prisoner.

Back in the mists of time a tradition arose that the Emperor Constantine had in the fourth century 'donated' Italy to the Pontificate as a temporal dominion. Scholars had long ago exploded the tradition as a hoax. History however could not be undone, and now the extensive 'Papal States' spanned this country's middle from coast to coast. Here lay the root of the peninsula's regular torments as the prey of acquisitive foreign monarchs, and its painful fragmentation. North of the Papal States Italy developed as European. South of them the winds blowing out of the Sahara and the Orient rendered it specifically Mediterranean, with the result that Sicily and its adjacent mainland, conquered and reconquered by outsiders, preserved an Arab flavour not dissimilar from much of Spain.

It thus transpired that during its exile in Avignon (1309–77) the papacy was compelled to delegate administration of its secular possessions, if administration it might be termed, to nominees, or 'vicars', usually military governors transformed into all manner of baronial despots. Mostly, they concerned themselves with retention of their power. Founding dynasties, they accumulated great wealth while hiring themselves out with their legions to fight anybody's battles, and wide areas fell into desolation and banditry. The popes, on their return to Italy, failed to implant Rome's rule except by reconquest and feverish diplomacy. Even then they could not properly complete the process. Thereby hangs the sorry tale of Italy's restlessness, servility and betrayal.

It was all in the nature of the Italian paradox that the most ruthless of the war-lords—*condottieri*—progressed from lowly origin to the nobility imbued with the Renaissance spirit. The Sforza family comes to mind as the most adept at scrambling its way upward to become one of the great Italian clans, a machinating finger in every political pie. It helped, no doubt, that Jacopo Sforza had twenty siblings to spread round the country in key appointments and fruitful marriages. Jacopo warned his dashing bastard son Francesco never to ride a hard-mouthed horse or interfere with other men's wives. The advice won for Francesco a Visconti bride, of the French blood royal, from the Duchy of Milan; and *his* son Ludovico married into the Este family, immovable from Ferrara since the twelfth century though nominally its temporary keepers on behalf of the Pope. With the fifteen-year-old Beatrice d'Este at his side Ludovico (called *il Moro*, 'the Moor', because of his complexion and Lombardy's mulberry marked on his standard), saw himself in the Medici mould. Firmly established in Milan, he developed the tastes of a Renaissance prince along with his appetite for glory. Ludovico brought Leonardo da Vinci and Bramante, later architectural genius of the new St Peter's, to increase the splendours of a realm where the construction of that marble wonder, the cathedral of Milan, was already a hundred years in the building.

Frustration dogged the papal path at every turn as successive Pontiffs endeavoured, in this cruel arena made into a barnyard of no consistent pecking order, to bring their 'vicars' to heel. The Bentivoglio family would only surrender Bologna, with Europe's oldest university, after an extended struggle against Rome that endured until 1516. Likewise Rimini, whose Malateste rulers are recalled in history for the infamous Sigismondo, known as the 'bold pagan monster'. He abandoned one wife, murdered two others and 'canonized' a mistress. Excommunicated by Pope Pius II (though who more tolerant?), he was then burnt in effigy. Yet this Malateste surrounded himself with poets and scholars. Indeed, the blind Piero della Francesca, on his death-bed in 1492, might well thank Providence for a tyrant, by then long gone, whose patronage had enabled him to produce works of religious radiance that amplified the perspectives of art.

Siena, an independent republic described by the French scholar-diplomat (and Medici spy) Commynes as the worst governed city in Italy, had long resisted annexation by Florence. Its inhabitants had detested their northern neighbour since medieval times, when Florentine troops started a plague by volleying dead animals and excrement over its walls. How in contrast can one adequately explain why the regime of the frightening House of Este, whose scions regularly assassinated each other's heirs, should prove so acceptable to the citizenry of Ferrara? Perhaps a clue may be sought in the clear separation of domestic rivalries from the administration of the little state, which was a model of authoritarian efficiency.

Duke Ercole of Ferrara's two emancipated daughters, Beatrice and Isabella d'Este, excelled as true Renaissance figures in the world of art and learning. Ariosto, the first name in Renaissance poetry and permanently in residence at the court, found all his material, the love, the drama and the satire, by observing the contorted relationships of his patrons. Ferrara fell between the rival appetites of the popes and the Venetians. The result was intrigue of the murkiest. Playing a characteristically dangerous hand, Duke Ercole would one day collude with Milan and Florence to bribe the Turks in the hope of advancing the Serene Republic's destruction. And did Ercole poison his own wife, sister of King Ferrante of Naples? The evidence is ambiguous.

Against the gloom, beacons shone. Rulers there were within the Papal States whose allegiance to the popes never weakened throughout the Avignon period. Without the customary arrogance of *condottieri*, nor their insecurity, the Montefeltro dukes of ever-tranquil Urbino were a model for those times, adored by their subjects. Duke Federigo da Montefeltro is known from the description in Castiglione's prose dialogue *The Courtier*, and by that striking profile, broken nose protruding, blind eye concealed (duelling damage), painted by Piero della Francesca in 1466. As to his library, Federigo procured catalogues from the greatest collections to prove that his was more comprehensive even than those housed in the Vatican, or in Florence or at the university of Oxford. He spent 30,000 ducats over fourteen years to gather copies of every known manuscript. His librarian wrote: 'He made a rule that every book be bound in crimson and ornamented in silver, from the Bible down to the modern authors.' They had to be transcribed on vellum, and each a complete copy without imperfections. Little wonder that Federigo, in presenting his library to the Pope, spoke of the invention of printing with scorn.

Nevertheless successive fifteenth-century Pontiffs, some so reviled as to be threatened with deposition, commonly placed their trust in none except their own kinsfolk. They invested their best energies in family advancement. Making cardinals out of the most worthy (and sometimes the least worthy!), prowling the Christian world for likely marriage connections to royalty, the Vicars of Christ courted a scheme to turn the papacy into a hereditary monarchy all-powerful in Italy. That the Vatican precinct warranted much of its calumny for being an Augean stable they fully realized, though its cleansing invariably languished at the bottom of their priorities.

The city of Rome itself had been brought to order by Sixtus IV, Innocent's VIII's predecessor, but its approaches were still staked out under the domination of rivalling clans, of which the Orsini and the Colonna emerged as the strongest. As with others in Italy, these two families maintained control by virtue of their private armies, today hired out to serve the Pope, tomorrow to war against him. Revenue intended for the papal purse dropped into their own pockets or was side-tracked to cardinals owing them first allegiance. Lorenzo de' Medici married Clarisse Orsini, a Roman lady woefully unequal to the sophistication of Florentine society but a useful conduit of information on the happenings, nefarious and otherwise, back home. Their nuptials in 1469 required five gargantuan banquets at the Medici Palace and three days of festivities, tournaments and theatricals in the Piazza Santa Croce to impress the populace.

Sixtus IV, the Pope who appealed to Ferdinand of Aragon for assistance in dislodging the Turks from Otranto in 1480, had purchased the office of Supreme Pontiff in 1471 and then packed the College of Cardinals with six of his own flesh and blood. His pacification of Rome had been achieved by striking at the House of Colonna, which controlled the city's criminal population as one of its perquisites. Though perennially short of money, Sixtus felt deeply the need to transform the Eternal City into a capital worthy of the Church. The intention was estimable, given the abject conditions of the place, but its implementation earned for Sixtus a reputation for simony that ranked him among the most venal rulers of the time. He charged his nephew Cardinal Piero Riario, Archbishop of Florence, with the task of begging money and troops from the Visconti Duke of Milan, who in return was promised recognition, never fulfilled, as King of Lombardy. Another nephew, the layman Girolamo Riario, was assigned to evict the Medici from Florence and install the Pazzi as first family in the state.

This was not the only time that Florence and the Vatican came close to war. The Medici retained their traditional banking arrangement, efforts to dislodge them notwithstanding, but they lost a lucrative contract for exploitation of the alum deposits at Tolfa near Civitavecchia. Profits were ostensibly earmarked for a forthcoming crusade. In 1476 Sixtus transferred the contract to Genoese fellow-countrymen, beginning a slide in Medici fortunes not immediately apparent to Lorenzo, whose Maecenean patronage of the arts continued as always. He realized only too well, however, that he must repair relations with Rome if the profound Medici influence on Italian affairs was to survive; hopeless even to attempt the task while Sixtus reigned, but fortunately popes did not live forever.

Unregenerate though Sixtus was as a man, and constantly on the search for schemes to turn his holy office to an easy penny, he nevertheless took passionately to the rebuilding and embellishment of Rome. Eyes everywhere focused on the grandeur of Florence, the fame of its Tuscan artists and builders, the status enjoyed by the Medici as its munificent benefactors. Could Rome remain unaffected?

The popes habitually gave thought to a memorial of their Pontificate. For Sixtus it was to be a magnificent chapel to serve the cardinals in conclave. Part of the crumbling Vatican Palace was demolished, and in its place there arose in 1480 the Sistine Chapel, whose decoration would reach the summit in Renaissance art. Parenthetically, it was in this period that Christopher Columbus received inspiration out of Florence for his own project, through correspondence with Paolo Toscanelli, the physician renowned for his world chart indicating a route westward to the

Indies (see p. 47). Work on the Sistine Chapel concentrated in one location the Florentine genius of Botticelli, Domenico Ghirlandaio, Rosselli, Perugino and, awaiting Pope Julius II—another nephew of Sixtus—the culminating masterpiece of Michelangelo's Ceiling. The latter's 'Last Judgment', painted on the Altar Wall, completed the whole glorious enterprise thirty years later.

None of the miseries yet in store for Italy in its tragic progress to nationhood could now halt the transformation of the Eternal City. It would preoccupy the popes for another hundred years: the Raphael Rooms in the Vatican blending inspired representations of secular and spiritual history; the erection of a new cathedral to house the shrine of St Peter's martyrdom and realized according to the awesome concept of Bramante's classical scheme, if not precisely to his intentions; the renovation of Castel Sant' Angelo as a secure papal fortress-home and refuge during times of turbulence; new roads and squares, devotional sculpture by masters of marble, palaces threaded with intricate tracery for bloated cardinals.

The Renaissance, flowing from Florence its mother city and bearing humanism in its voluminous tide, spread, as already stated, to all western Europe. Medieval resistance melted beneath the barrage: Thomas More's *Utopia*; John Colet's iconoclastic lectures on St Paul at Oxford; Albrecht Dürer's emotional realism in art; Johann Reuchlin's dissection of its Hebrew sources in the Bible; the flailing of the Church by Erasmus for its abuses; Jacques Lefèvre of Etaples and his new theology. All these came under the influence of Lorenzo's neo-Platonic school, in some cases by direct personal association.

Shrewd politician he might well have been, but Lorenzo's statesmanship is not what he is most remembered by. However, it reached a peak in the year 1479, when he sailed from Pisa on an extended peace mission to King Ferrante of Naples. The latter, mothered by a half-caste Moor, rose from illegitimacy in the House of Aragon to reign over a kingdom that had been denied to Ferdinand's father (Naples accepted a bastard son, Palermo not, hence the split in the 'Kingdom of the Two Sicilies'). Ferrante's Regno, nominally in vassalage to the Supreme Pontiff, could be invoked to assist Rome with troops if required. Sixtus's determination to remove the Medici was just such an occasion. Ferrante responded. Naturally, the annexation of Tuscany rose instinctively to the front of his calculating mind. He sent his army north, demanding the surrender of Florence. The classic division of north and south in Italy seemed about to erupt in the greatest of the peninsula's civil wars, with complications through external intervention to be dreaded. Siena and Lucca joined the Pope's cause, Federigo of Urbino commanded his army. Milan stayed neutral, and thus Florence found itself isolated. Here was an opportunity the still-living Louis XI of France could not think to lose. Naples had once belonged to his Anjou forebears, so why not come to Lorenzo's aid, crush Ferrante and incidentally place his clawed fist round the foot of Italy?

Louis proffered his velvet glove to Lorenzo: he would defend Florence. Lorenzo's reply was characteristic of the man. 'I cannot set my own advantage above the safety of all Italy,' he replied. 'Would to God it never come into the mind of the French kings to try their strength in this country! Should they ever do so, Italy is lost.'

Lorenzo chose instead to make his personal appeal to Ferrante, risking his life thereby. Ferrante faced him sullenly, but the Neapolitans were entranced by Il Magnifico, so different from their own tyrannical king. Lorenzo spread largesse among them, ransoming a hundred galley slaves with 60,000 florins, handing out dowries to girls of poor families, arguing all the time for the welfare of Italy. A pose, no doubt in part, but it wore Ferrante down. Florence was saved at the price of an indemnity for Ferrante's military expenses and amnesty for those members of the Pazzi family not yet executed. The Turks' sudden perch upon Otranto, sending tremors throughout Italy, aided Lorenzo's mission of reconciliation. Both sides had won, and he returned home a national hero. Botticelli needed no second bidding when his Medici patron requested a commemoration from his brush. It was the 'Minerva and the Centaur', depicting Strife led in submission by Wisdom, Botticelli's finest evocation of pagan allegory. The picture now hangs in the Uffizi Gallery. And as Botticelli gave the work its finishing touches, Lorenzo was sending Leonardo da Vinci off to Milan with his blessing and a gift for its regent Ludovico Sforza, husband of Beatrice d'Este. Ludovico was shortly to acquire the Duchy of Milan for himself through the convenient death of his Visconti nephew, conceivably by poison.

Leonardo was then thirty years of age. The natural son of a proud father bedazzled early on by the colossus within the boy's mind, he had been given a place in Lorenzo's 'Academy' under the pupillage of Verrocchio, whom he rapidly outshone in the artist's trade. Truthfully, Leonardo proved the most brilliant jack of all trades. His achievements combined art with science, relieving God of responsibility for every detailed aspect of matter and man. He painstakingly explored the mysteries of procreation from the foetus in the womb to the decrepitude of old age; then the universe beyond—cloud movement, optics, ballistics, the animal world. The painter was, like Michelangelo, equally sculptor and architect, but additionally an engineer and philosopher. He invented pastel drawing and developed artillery. Leonardo possessed immense physical strength, he could play the lyre, and the gift he brought to Ludovico of Milan from Lorenzo was a lyre made by himself of silver to his patron's order and in the shape of a horse's head. Leonardo's fascination with geometry and mechanics led him to problems of flood control and city sanitation. Despite his deep interest in instruments of warfare he was of the gentlest character, railing against human cruelty to animals and birds, condemning their use as pets. Did Leonardo dissipate his genius in too many avenues of endeavour? Many have said so. But he would not have been Leonardo otherwise.

At the Sforza court presided over by Beatrice d'Este (her secretary noted her death there at the age of twenty-one as 'changing Paradise into Inferno') Leonardo remained, with brief absences, for seventeen years. What survives of his immense output was mainly achieved there, including designs for the flying machine produced in 1492. Ludovico would surely have observed him at work on his 'Last Supper', commissioned by the duke for the Church of Santa Maria della Grazie, though never completed. The painting, being in oil and not fresco, quickly deteriorated. Its composition and spatial effort took art into the High Renaissance. As for the 'Mona Lisa'—'looking closely at her throat you might imagine the beating of the pulse', declared Leonardo's near-contemporary Giorgio Vasari—Ludovico would never know of it. From 1500 he was a captive in the hands of the French, confined for ten years and then to die in a dungeon beside the Loire, his penalty for resisting the invasion of Louis XII after his best generals had deserted to the enemy.

Early in 1492 Lorenzo de' Medici lay sick in his villa at Careggi unable to move without assistance. Italy was sinking once more into its traditional discord. As the storm clouds gathered Florence sustained its independence only with the greatest difficulty, the Medici bank no longer the power it had been, the Medici dynasty fading into decline. Over all vultures hovered, France and Spain. Though just forty-three years of age, Lorenzo was losing his battle against gout, which had racked him for some twenty years, complicated by other physical disorders that no amount of privilege could avert and sometimes encouraged. He insisted still on the companionship of his band of intellectual brothers: the writer Pico della Mirandola, Marsilio Ficino the philosopher, and his closest friend within that circle, the poet Poliziano. He continued to give at-

tention to the Medici library, ordering the purchase of important manuscripts as their existence became known, and also keeping under review
his unique collection of medallions and ancient artefacts. He required
to be informed daily of the business transacted by the Signoria, where
old animosities reawakened with the lightening of the Medici hand over
affairs of state. Crisis was sending its premonitions with every messenger
out of Florence.

Did Lorenzo specifically request absolution from the Prior of San
Marco, or had Savonarola presented himself to administer the last rites
uninvited? We do not know for certain, though the preacher, never one
to be constrained, had by this time magnetized Florence, élite and common folk alike, winning many influential adherents. While persuaded
by the intensity of his piety, they feared of making him an enemy, for
they recognized that in his virtues there simmered a menacing passion.
Savonarola's frenzied denunciation of corruption in public life, not restricted to Florence, gave credence to reports of a curse rather than a
blessing laid by Savonarola upon the soul within the expiring body of Il
Magnifico.

The prior had arrived in Florence from his native Ferrara, scorning
the career offered by his father the court physician, as early as 1481.
Attired in his mendicant's cloak, ascetic and glinty-eyed—see Fra Bartolommeo's portrait still hanging in the convent of San Marco—he
brought stark prophecies of the terrible retribution awaiting Italy for its
extravagances and sinful licence. And since his return to Florence in
1490 after years as an itinerant Dominican friar, the penumbra cast by
that personality had thinned the hedonistic atmosphere of Renaissance
society, bringing a restitution of the severest religious orthodoxy. Car-
nivals, harlotry, painting the human form, studying Greek philosophers,
jewellery, were alike condemned as manifestations of the Italian Sodom
and Gomorrah. Savonarola captivated Botticelli, hitherto a jovial fellow,
by his spell, to the degree of rendering his last pictures an agonizing
spiritual experience for the painter, so that he must abandon art and
voluntarily espouse penury. Pico della Mirandola, a man of outstanding
independent intellect, also fell victim to his oratory, and of course Fra
Bartolommeo embraced the friar's faith and practice in their totality.
Many clerics claimed attainment to a state of godliness higher than
ordinary mortals, though none was believed as Savonarola was believed.
He could have been a cardinal, but Rome disgusted him. In a vision he
saw a huge black cross, signifying God's fury, casting its shadow over the
Eternal City.

During the first days of April 1492, ominous happenings sowed dread among the Florentines: lightning flashing through the cathedral, a fight to the death between lions in their cage, spectres walking over the Arno, witches screaming of Satanic rites at Mass. These were all duly reported to Lorenzo and he sensed the end. Magicians replaced his doctors, but he sank nevertheless. On 8 April he ceased to breathe.

That day terminated the Florentine epic. Piero, Lorenzo's eldest son, just twenty years of age, succeeded as head of the illustrious family. But he was another Ichabod, for the glory had departed and the ark of the Renaissance taken to different air. The Medici bank mouldered from its trunk to its many branches, the name lost its resonance while the city-state came under a new rule, the religious authoritarianism of Savonarola. Piero invited Michelangelo to remain in the Medici Palace as before, with nothing altered. The artist, having experienced the prophet's raging sermons, thought otherwise. He above all had revived the nude as the ideal central to art as during Graeco-Roman times, and Florence was no place to express either the tenderness or the power. Michelangelo allowed himself two years to continue on his immense 'Hercules' in marble (since lost) before he fled the hostile pressures to go in search of other patrons. At length Piero de' Medici was himself compelled to escape, not so much because of Savonarola's whiplash, but to save himself from the French.

In time, events would turn full circle and the two would return, Leonardo da Vinci too. Following its period of travail Florence would greet a restored Medici regime. Soon the august family would be enthroned, dukes at home, popes in Rome, though not specially noteworthy otherwise except on the distaff side: two Medici daughters would leave their imprint on history as regents of storm-tossed France. As we glance over the fate of Italy subsequent to Lorenzo's death in 1492 and deep into the sixteenth century, we shall observe the country's gradual decline, political and economic, into a lifeless entity still at the mercy of other nations' struggles.

The year marking the Medici eclipse allowed another dynasty, the Borgias, to rise and occupy the centre of this unhappy stage. Medici and Borgia may well be viewed as the two sides of the same European coin, the one reflecting the continent's promise, the other its shame. To be sure, not all the good lay on the Medici side, nor all the evil on the Borgias'. Still, the gathering of Catholic eminence into the soiled hands of Rodrigo Borgia just as Christendom's cultural springs were deprived of Lorenzo de' Medici added a particular poignancy to the year 1492. That this should occur precisely when Christopher Columbus sailed from

Palos in Spain to take the continent to a virgin frontier suddenly made Europe appear simultaneously in a condition of decay yet renewal. And between Medici and Borgia, Savonarola constituted a link binding the extremes.

His flaming eloquence consumed all opposition, even in politics. Savonarola chastised the Signoria of Florence for protecting the interests of the privileged, and forced it to introduce election by popular vote. A new Grand Council was inaugurated, open to all. He frightened it, then controlled it. The punishment of the Lord, he prophesied, would take the form of spoliation of Italy by the French. It occurred. He cursed Milan for allowing Charles VIII through the Alpine passes, then himself welcomed that king, notionally on a holy crusade, into Florence. Charles rode in triumph through Rome and proceeded south to overrun the entire peninsula. It would happen in 1494, the French soldiers gazing in wonderment at this inexhaustible national treasure house while regarding its inhabitants with contempt. The invaders talked of liberation, but this was conquest. Would the French leave Italy and sail east to capture Jerusalem, as Charles had contended? No, they tarried, unsure themselves how to proceed, attracting the most unforgiving of hatreds. In the mean time Savonarola, having reduced Florence to numbed obedience to the dictates of his rigid orthodoxy, was turning his wrath upon the recently elected Pope, Rodrigo Borgia, Alexander VI.

This cleric's scandalous Pontificate began with his election. It was August 1492, and few Italians relished the prospect of another Spaniard as Pope: Calixtus III, Borgia's uncle, had done his utmost to render the Vatican a virtual fief of Aragon. Now a strong Genoese candidate, Giuliano della Rovere, nephew of Sixtus IV, waited impatiently in the wings. Rovere enjoyed the preference of the French and the financial support of King Ferrante of Naples, as well as two cardinals from his own highly placed family. Other Italians were in the lists, every one a puppet of influential secular interests. However, as in the case of cardinals bearing the name of Orsini or Colonna, they mainly neutralized each other.

The only way Cardinal Borgia could win, and having attained the office of Vice-Chancellor of the Church at an early age he had long planned for the moment, was to outbid his rivals in acquisition of any votes for sale. Not only was he an outsider surrounded by servile Catalan clerics, his record as a capable administrator could not erase his reputation as a man of irrepressible worldly passions. He had once participated in a celebration at Siena reported to have degenerated into an orgy, and he took no pains to conceal his association with other men's wives. The cardinal's own elder offspring brazenly paraded in Roman society while the younger ones danced lovingly around him throughout the day.

During four long sessions of deliberation in conclave without any cardinal receiving the required two-thirds majority, all contestants fell away except Giuliano della Rovere and, sheltering beneath the substantial coat-tails of his warrior brother Ludovico, Ascanio Sforza. It was thus a case of Genoa versus Milan. Della Rovere, scrupulously keeping to the rules, would not stoop to horse-trading, but bribes and promises distributed among Sforza's supporters held the outcome in balance. Suddenly the latter and his following changed their votes. Four mules loaded with silver had the previous night appeared at the gate of that cardinal's palace, a placebo from Rodrigo Borgia accompanied by an undertaking to confer the Vice-Chancellorship on Sforza. At the next counting all was over, and Borgia, now sixty-one years of age, ascended St Peter's throne as Alexander VI. 'Flee, we are in the clutches of a wolf,' the young Medici cardinal Giovanni was heard to remark. He had chosen the wrong animal for comparison.

With good reason Pope Alexander was known as the Spanish Bull. His palace, built in Rome some thirty years earlier and considered the most luxurious residence in the city—it is now absorbed in the Palazzo Sforza-Cesarini—was compared by a previous pope to Nero's. The bull figured on a gold field on the family standard, for the Borgias, though pretending to ancient royal lineage, were of the minor nobility. In fact, the sobriquet grew from another connotation: his sexual prowess. While a young cardinal Rodrigo had fathered children by various anonymous mistresses. Later he formed a steady attachment with a lady of property in Rome, Vanozza dei Catanei, a name indicative of noble rank. She bore him four of his nine identifiable sons and daughters, among them Cesare and Lucrezia. The eventful lives of those two in the service of their devoted father added much colour if little propriety to the Renaissance scene. We have the Florentine historian Guiccardini's record as the only evidence of another son, Giovanni, being the product of the Pope's incestuous relationship with his own daughter Lucrezia. Renaissance historians, be it said (Machiavelli included), notoriously lent themselves to polemical propaganda on behalf of their patrons, and any tale blackening Alexander became grist to his enemies. The allegation of incest was never satisfactorily substantiated. Certainly in the evening of his life (Alexander died in 1503) he fathered two sons of Giulia Farnese, a beautiful young Orsini wife whose marriage in 1489 the Pope had, as cardinal, presided over with great pomp in the Borgia residence. Guiccardini also charged him with taking young boys into his bed.

If the artist Pinturicchio, in depicting a pious Alexander in profile worshipping the Risen Christ to decorate the Borgia Apartments of the Vatican (future popes refrained from occupying them for hundreds of years), gives little indication of his character, we have another of the frescoes offering the sacred Egyptian bull Apis as fanciful ancestor of his strength. He was undoubtedly of robust health and dignified in deportment, quick-witted, and regarded by those of his cardinals not absolutely detesting him as a wise statesman. There never was a pope with his stamina for a long day of work and a longer night of relaxation. He became enslaved, however, by one obsession that could only be pursued through descent into a morality ranging from deceit and simony to complicity in murder: the advancement of his numerous family to the peaks, not excluding the hope of a secular crown. Alexander spoke Spanish, or rather Catalan, in public as well as privately; so did his son Cesare, whose personal authority increased with every day of Alexander's papacy. By his early twenties Cesare ranked among the most powerful men in all Italy. Among those made to bow before his ambition and dangerous whims was his own father.

Remove, if we can, considerations of moral turpitude to which the Pope was prone, and there remained a diplomatist and administrator of no mean accomplishment. Later, as we shall see, he invoked qualities of mediation never before required of any pope to satisfy the competing interests of Spain and Portugal in world-wide exploration. Earlier, as Cardinal Archbishop of Valencia in the service of Sixtus IV, he journeyed to Spain and, playing the wise statesman, hastened the termination of the civil war caused by the Catalan insurrection against King John of Aragon, Ferdinand's father. He acted out of the particular concern to strengthen Spanish support for the Vatican against the hostility of France. How better to do this than to bring the blessing of his master the Pope on the contemplated marriage of Ferdinand to Isabella of Castile? He therefore produced an authentic instrument of papal dispensation allowing the union between cousins to replace the original forgery (see p. 45). He then worked effectively against Castilian opposition to the match.

Sixtus had by no means been an easy superior to serve, yet his Vice-Chancellor succeeded also in detaching himself from the anti-Medicean policy of the Pontiff during the Pazzi conspiracy in Florence, and simultaneously maintained good relations with Ferrante of Naples. This facilitated Lorenzo's peace-seeking mission to Ferrante, so it counted as something of a coup for Borgia. On his election as Alexander VI he might have concentrated on purging the Curia of the corruption paralysing the ecclesiastical apparatus. Such was his stated intention, but he neglected it. Instead he proceeded with the inherited struggle to reimpose Pontifical control throughout the entire territory of the Papal States. Each Italian sovereignty—Venice, Florence, Naples particularly— looked for pickings there, and every internal vassal princeling ploughed a private furrow. Needless to say, Alexander became embedded in intrigue and led himself into a morass. Withal, he dared not ignore the enmity of his defeated competitor for the papacy, Giuliano della Rovere. No man would confidently choose such an opponent. Incorruptible, able and aggressive, this cardinal dedicated himself to undermining the Pope and usurping his tiara. Playing an old Italian game, della Rovere worked upon a foreign monarch to assist him, no matter the cost, in performing the operation. In this case it was Charles VIII, light-headed son of the French king whom Lorenzo de' Medici had once rebuffed, Louis XI.

It thus transpired that in the year 1492 a long period of relative peace in the peninsula, forty years, terminated with the passing of Lorenzo de' Medici and the arrival of Rodrigo Borgia. Now came the settling of accounts. A hardened cynic could justifiably view the only truly permanent Italian characteristic in the succeeding half century to be the country's instability. Alliances rapidly dissolved and reformed. Wars, not inordinately costly in lives due to the employment of halfhearted mercenaries, punctuated the decades. In the process Savonarola would defy the Pope, suffer excommunication and make a pyre of easy-living Florence with his 'bonfire of the vanities'. Nude statuary, books of secular learning, the *Decameron*, ornate costumes, playing-cards, mirrors, 'sinful' pictures readily contributed by their artists Botticelli and Fra Bartolommeo, were all cast into a tremendous heap and burnt in front of the Signoria Palace. Then the extraordinary preacher himself, repudiated and tortured, would in 1498 be roped to a scaffold and put to the torch. Martin Luther was to divide the Church, a later French king would be taken prisoner by the Holy Roman Emperor at Pavia, while in 1527 Rome would undergo sacking by German troops. Ultimately, Italy's greatest pride, its culture, languished with little sign of revival.

Pope Alexander, while still cardinal, had pestered Ferdinand of Aragon to reward him for services rendered to Spain. Ferdinand reluctantly elevated Borgia's eldest son Pedro Luis (mother unknown) to the dukedom of Gandia. The Spanish title passed to a son by Vanozza dei Catanei with that duke's premature death. On his Pontificate, the father swiftly organized for Cesare 'purification' from his illegitimacy so as to crown the wild youth's career in the Church as Archbishop of Valencia, his own former See. This did not concede dispensation for a cardinalate but the omission was soon repaired, and Cesare, along with a cousin, received the red hat in the earliest nominations to the Sacred College. Neither were Alexander's other children neglected. Lucrezia had been betrothed successively to two Spanish noblemen before turning thirteen, eventually marrying Giovanni Sforza, who ruled Pesaro ostensibly on behalf of the Pope his liege but in reality for his cousin Ludovico of Milan. Two more marriages for Lucrezia would progressively enhance her status, after deep implication in the scandals of the Borgia clan, till she came to rest as Duchess of Ferrara and died aged thirty-nine.

Her precocious womanhood worked in the papal interest, as Lucrezia well understood. Her first marriage to a Sforza obtained for Pope Alexander a pathway into the friendship of the Milanese court. The intention, to cause anxiety to King Ferrante of Naples, succeeded. The latter, who was known to have wept at the Borgia promotion to St Peter's, grew alarmed, for the Milan alliance brought a powerful enemy close to Rome, one who could neutralize his own substantial influence on Vatican policy. Hastily, Ferrante offered a selection of Neapolitan princesses as brides to whichever Borgia sons remained available. The choice alighted on Jofrè, still in his teens and preparing for the priestly life. This was soon rectified. Jofrè found himself joined to a Ferrante granddaughter as Prince of Squillace in Calabria—hardly a significant price for the King of Naples to pay for security on his long frontier with the Papal States. Doubtless Machiavelli was impressed. Only this was poor guarantee of any security.

France always intended to make quick work of conquering Naples, regarded as French property by that old Angevin connection. Thus we return to Charles VIII's endeavour. As recounted in the previous chapter, he had extricated himself from Flanders, collected Brittany, paid off England and conceded unimportant borderlands to Ferdinand of Aragon as well as to Emperor-to-be Maximilian, so as to clear his way of outside opposition. By the end of 1492 Charles felt all but ready for this, his great enterprise. Possessing a virtually open invitation from Milan to march through Lombardy, he now desired the Pope's blessing. Alexander had just made his peace with Ferrante, and therefore played for time— rather, he was playing with fire, for Charles had on his side the Pope's bitter personal foes: Cardinal della Rovere and, still at that time, Savonarola. Their attitude placed Genoa and Florence in the French king's pocket. More, della Rovere counted on the support of all those cardinals unable to abide the Spanish Bull either for his nationality or his excesses. Yet again, coaxed by a petticoat, Alexander had appointed as another puppet cardinal Alessandro Farnese, brother of his youngest mistress. 'The man knew neither shame nor sincerity, neither faith nor religion,' wrote Guiccardini. By the way Pope Alexander handled the French would depend his survival or his deposition. Another complication: he could not look for succour from Maximilian. The King of the Romans, as he was still designated, hoped for French help to punish Venice for encroaching upon his Austrian domain.

Who was left to encourage the Pope's resistance? All the calculations pointed Alexander towards the country of his birth, Spain, where he and the monarchy instinctively washed each other's hands. True, Charles had bribed Ferdinand with restitution of two Pyrenean regions contested between their respective fathers. However, the Pope was soon to deal a stronger card. He would be able to do Spain its greatest service, with his benediction forming a Catholic arch over the new doctrine of imperialism.

On Rodrigo Borgia's election as Pope Alexander VI we had left Columbus and his little flotilla sailing down the Rio Tinto from Palos. How had he fared?

Chapter Six

THE VOYAGE

I have decided, Sovereign Princes, to make a daily record of this journey, carefully setting down all that I may do and see and experience. In addition to noting each night what had occurred during the day, and each day how I sailed in the night, I intend to draw a chart of all the seas and lands of the Ocean, in their true places and according to their bearings. Also, to compose a book and illustrate everything in a true picture, by latitude from the equinoctial line and by longitude from the West. Above all I must forget my sleep and give the greatest attention to my navigation, which is essential. This will be a great task.

he original of the journal is lost, though it was incorporated, in part or whole, in various records made shortly after Columbus's four voyages to the Indies and it may well have suffered from editorial licence in the process. The most notable sources include the *Life* of his father produced by his younger son Ferdinand, and the detailed account of the explorations given in the *Historia de las Indias*, the work of Bishop Bartholomew de Las Casas. The bishop knew Columbus personally and defended him in the controversies that grew around the Discoverer's exploits. He had settled in the New World himself to become one of the earliest champions of native rights. Las Casas also wrote a description of the man: 'More than average height, long face, an air of authority, aquiline nose; blue eyes, light complexion. His beard and hair were red in his younger days, but soon turned grey from his labours. He was affable and cheerful in speaking, eloquent and boastful in negotiation but of a modest gravity and discreet in conversation. He was sober and moderate in eating, drinking, dress . . . a Catholic of great devotion.'

Of his limitations as a leader, we shall learn. Columbus's journal is meagre in acknowledging the contribution made by others to the success of the voyage. Disagreements evidently occurred from time to time with his captains, Martin Alonso Pinzón of *Pinta* and his brother Vicente Yañez Pinzón of *Niña*. This would have been inevitable. The captain-general, as he termed himself, was not of Spanish blood and suspected the others' ways. The two slender caravels made better time than the labouring *Santa Maria* and tended to drive too far onward against his command that the three ships sail abreast, keeping each other in sight during the day and by the light of charcoal-burning braziers at night. Columbus feared their stealing the least fraction of his credit should one or the other reach the Indies first. Steering problems encountered by *Pinta* shortly after departure on 3 August 1492 gave rise to suggestions of sabotage.

They sailed a steady course south-west, aided by the north-eastern trades, always within sight of the African coast. Familiar as he was with the North Atlantic, Columbus distrusted its fierce headwinds. In any case he proposed making for the Canaries as a first, easy stage. The islands fell on a latitude of 28 degrees, which by his calculation placed them exactly east of Cipangu, Marco Polo's Japan. Between the Canaries and Japan he anticipated early landfall at Antilia, the island of seven Christian cities, rich in precious stones, whose church steeples reached high in the sky. It was believed, in Toscanelli's graphic account, to have been settled long ago as a refuge from the Moors. Of course, no such island existed, but its name survives in the Antilles.

Seven days of uneventful navigation brought the Canaries in sight. Columbus steered by the North Star, the sun's position and his own dead reckoning. Compass, astrolabe, simple quadrant and half-hour glass measured with tolerable accuracy direction, speed and time. As it happened, he overestimated their speed by some 9 per cent, so that all distances calculated were too short, while direction barely erred. But the vessels averaged just over 8 knots, which meant they covered a respectable distance, some 142 nautical miles, almost every 24 hours. Becalmed for two days outside the Canaries, *Santa Maria* was then able to enter Gomera by oar while *Pinta* put in at Las Palmas for repairs—her rudder had broken. In the mean time the flagship and *Niña* restocked with victuals of bread, cheese, dried fish and pickled beef, as well as casks of fresh water and wine. Collective prayers and hymn-singing marked morning and dusk, and always a recital of the Creed. These were solemn moments for the mariners. They knew that despite the skill of their leader, his conviction and their fortitude, the fate of the expedition rested in the keep of an unseen pilot, the Blessed Virgin.

On 2 September all three ships stood anchored off Gomera, on the western extremity of the little Canaries archipelago. A young widow, Doña Beatriz de Bobadilla, commanded the tiny island as hereditary governor in the name of Queen Isabelia. The appointment apparently descended first upon her late husband in order to distance the wife from the attentions of King Ferdinand. The little expedition seemed to tarry there rather longer than necessary, and reports tell of another love affair, perhaps exaggerated in the recounting, between this attractive noble-woman and the captain-general. Four days later his flotilla weighed an-chor and by daybreak they discerned as their last vision of land in Christian ownership, though still inhabited only by Guanche natives, the volcanic peak of Tenerife.

The next ten days gave plain sailing due west. Now the crews grew restless the more water they covered without sight of shore. Troubled by doubts regarding the wisdom of the enterprise and their own rash participation in it, many sailors surrendered to a spirit of pessimism. Shouldn't they retrace their way home while still able, confess to failure but safe in body and soul? They had in fact travelled further, according to Columbus's true reckoning, than they were actually told, since he was bent on reassuring his crews as to the distance separating them from Europe. He kept two logs. Ironically, because of his miscalculation of speed, the false reckoning proved more accurate than the secret one.

Imagination fed their hopes and anxieties as they intently scanned the horizon. Wasn't that a tropical bird passing across their bows, and didn't this signify they could be no more than 25 leagues from land? On the night of Saturday, 15 September, a tired look-out observed a gleam, like a flame, fall into the sea—surely a bad omen! Then frequent floatings of a yellow seaweed convinced some that they were about to crash against rocks. Columbus knew better. Land still lay a long way off. Yet he himself was half persuaded two days later, when a seaman brought him a live crab picked off the seaweed. It suggested to the leader that they were approaching water of less salinity, a sure sign of land, perhaps Antilia. Disappointment again, and continued monotony.

Whenever the wind dropped a fear arose of their entering a watery vacuum, dooming them to a ghostly end. Slightly changing course, they caught a head wind, the sails clapped and, wrote Columbus, 'it was as with the children of Israel led out of bondage, when they murmured against Moses.' For they rode upon the waves again, and the spirit of the seamen recovered, for one more day.

Columbus picked his favourites on *Santa Maria* to spy among a group of trouble-makers. On 24 September they reported talk of mutiny. He and his officers slept below in their private quarters, while the others bedded down wherever they found shelter. The grumblers were discussing a plan to throw the captain-general overboard. Couldn't he have fallen on taking bearings from the stars? It would justify their turning about. According to Las Casas, Columbus refused to heed the whisperings. But he yearned for good news. Periodically he would communicate with Martin Alonso Pinzón, eldest of the three brothers with the expedition, by attaching a message to a line thrown over to *Pinta*, sometimes a chart fixing position. Martin Alonso insisted on 25 September that, according to his calculation, they were approaching some islands, 25 leagues (about 80 miles) away. Columbus agreed, and altered direction south-west. That evening Martin Alonso bellowed success from *Pinta's* poop. He had descried land, and without ado claimed the reward promised to the first one sighting it. Hurrahs echoed across the ships, while Columbus himself rendered gratitude to the Lord. It proved on closer inspection to be nothing but a heavy storm cloud, and in deep gloom they re-sumed their course due west. By Monday, 1 October, they had sailed almost 2,000 nautical miles from the last point of the Canaries, yet except for the occasional dolphin below and stray gannets above, they could see only the limitless ocean. Drenching rain fell. Quarrels increased.

On 4 October a happier day at last: birds in great number springing out of the skies to settle on the ships, petrels mainly, but also a single gull. Their island nestings most surely be near. Martin Alonso affirmed it must be Cipangu, as marked on their chart, therefore they should steer southwards. However, the captain-general now refused to divert from his fixed course. Only on 8 October, a Monday, would he consent to navigate west-south-west, lest the Indies elude them. Clearly they were sailing in the neighbourhood of land now, for the bird-life appeared frequently, and in many varieties. Soft warm breezes stroked their weath-ered faces, speed was good, and he ordered the other two vessels closer, undoubtedly so that his own look-out, from the highest mast, would make the first sighting of the Indies. He warned them all against false claims.

They had been at sea for thirty-two days. The vessels' creaking grated even more strongly on their nerves. Where might Columbus be leading them? The Pinzón brothers themselves, by one account, wished to turn back now. Their crews were openly rebellious. Columbus begged their patience for three more days. If nothing then appeared on the horizon he would give the order to reverse direction. But the reports conflict: another historian, not Las Casas, insists that Martin Alonso encouraged Columbus to proceed when the captain-general was in his turn on the point of weakening. Since several days he could not trust his compass; it became subject to magnetic variation, the needle wavering in a fashion unfamiliar to voyagers in this alien hemisphere. Instinct took over, and they followed the flight of birds. Tension reduced them all to silence. Floating branches with green leaves and the rare strip of plain, rotting wood persuaded Columbus of the nearness of land, to a degree that on 11 October he thought he saw a distant light, 'as though from a wax candle'—his mind playing tricks. But *Pinta*, against orders, kept forging ahead.

And at 2 a.m. on Friday, 12 October, the caravel's look-out, Rodrigo de Triano, observed a gleam of white reflected in the moonlight. Land! '*Tierra! Tierra!*' he cried. Martin Alonso ordered a gun fired, their agreed signal, for this was no mirage. They were approaching a low cliff face. Now the crews of the three craft hugged each other in release and, once again, sang their evening hymn, '*Salve Regina*'. They shortened sail, almost drifting towards a coral reef. On first light trees, their foliage a welcoming living colour, met their eyes. It was time to hoist all their flags, and to hang shields over the deck sides. Would they face an enemy? Perhaps monsters. Diego de Harana, the trusted armourer, prepared pikes and battleaxes, while the officers kept hands to their swords. But all fear vanished as they observed a group of naked men splashing towards them, curious for a clearer sight of the strangers and those sea-borne things with great white wings out of which they emerged.

Christopher Columbus, bearing the royal standard and attired in the uniform he chose to wear in recognition of his prospective title as Admiral and Viceroy, was rowed to shore, bearing gifts. Soon, with his two Pinzón captains as witness, and in the legal presence of Rodrigo Sanchez representing their Catholic Majesties, he solemnly claimed this place in the name of Queen Isabella of Castile, so bringing America into Christian history. Doubt never entered his mind. They had attained the fringe of Asia, the Indies, and these natives were therefore Indians.

The sunny isle upon whose western coast he set thankful foot belonged to what would later be known as the Bahamas. He named it for the

Saviour, San Salvador. The people to whom he attached the description Indians were in fact Tainos of the Arawak language group. They called this Atlantic home of theirs Guanahani. They had no words in their vocabulary either for the strangers or for their vessels, which seemed capable of yielding a limitless array of wondrous things as they observed them being carried to their land. One more small matter not immediately realized by the tan-skinned, youthful-looking men with painted faces and short, stiff hair 'almost like the hair of a horse's tail': they had bartered their island for a few coloured woollen caps, tiny hawks' bells that rang amusingly in their ears, and handfuls of glass beads.

Controversies, with which we need not trouble ourselves, later arose over a claim by Grand Turk Island in the Turks and Caicos, the self-governing group still today of the British West Indies, that it was really the one originally described as San Salvador (Watlings Island to the British). This is located some 200 miles south-east of Watlings. Other islands in the vicinity make a like claim to the glory of being the first European step upon America. We may never know the exact truth, though the general truth of the discovery of the Caribbean Archipelago on 12 October 1492 is of course beyond dispute.

But the treasure Columbus and his men had come for, where was that? According to Marco Polo gold and jewels beyond Europe's computation abounded for the picking here, yet little of this was evident except for the thin golden circlets some of the natives suspended from their noses. From the gestures they made, and they appeared as generous with their information as with their presents of food and parrots and clay instruments, gold would be found in the north of Guanahani and in neighbouring islands. Columbus therefore wasted no time. He circumnavigated the coastline, sending his men to reconnoitre by boat, and himself investigated the structure of the terrain. The natives made a bread from the cassava plant, they cultivated corn and yams, and showed how they easily reached other islands by paddling the hollowed-out tree trunks serving them as 'canoes'—their word. Some sailors dallied inland. They exhibited excessive interest in the naked women, but this was hardly the time.

So, repaying the Tainos' hospitality by taking six of them back to the flagship and holding them, much against their will, to serve as guides, the leader ordered anchors weighed after two days. They must hasten to Cipangu and Cathay proper, great lands promising great rewards. Within some hours' easy sailing they arrived in the shelter of what he named as Santa Maria de la Concepción—today's Rum Cay. Thence to a chain of further islands, all of which Columbus appropriately christened to signify God's blessing and Spanish ownership—names they retained until the British, their earliest foreign settlers, took formal possession long afterwards on behalf of King George III. The admiral found sweet fresh water and encountered plenty of goodwill. But no gold.

Two weeks had by this time elapsed since their arrival at San Salvador. They were island-hopping on a zigzag course throughout, but nowhere found indication of a continental shore. His guides explained in their way to Columbus of their closeness to Colba, a very great country indeed. Rich in gold? Of course, and much else! Columbus reckoned he must now be in latitude 42 degrees north, and the place referred to could only be Cipangu, with its khans, magnificent temples and great civilization. In truth, he was at latitude 21 degrees, and they were navigating through the shallows into Cuba. They entered a harbour on 28 October which the admiral was to describe as the most beautiful he had ever seen, its coast lined with an exuberance of blossoming flora.

At every staging the explorer, hand to breast, distributed tokens of goodwill, then enacted his little ceremony of peaceful annexation on behalf of his sovereign. Martin Alonso Pinzón of *Pinta* was however growing impatient with the routine. They were rounding the north-east of Cuba point by point, always meeting the same bland curiosity of the natives, whose gesticulations Luis de Torres the interpreter, master of Hebrew and Arabic, could only translate by guesswork. But they were shown nothing of real value to impress a European fortune-hunter. Columbus, mindful of future colonization and to prove the success of his expedition, gathered samples of vegetation and creature life to take back home. He made copious notes regarding the natives' docility, their lack of religion and the prospects (excellent!) of their conversion to Christianity.

Such conduct of the endeavour did not satisfy Martin Alonso, particularly as he could divine Columbus's own sense of disappointment. Against the express order of the captain-general *Pinta's* commander took off to find his own gold. In the mean time Torres was despatched inland at the head of a party to verify the existence of a great city, perhaps the capital of a kingdom. Torres carried the usual store of worthless objects as goodwill tokens should he encounter a monarch. And as he waited, Columbus sensed the ebbing deference his men accorded his person. On first making landfall they almost fell over themselves in worship of his achievement. Now they were questioning his judgment, which promised riches tomorrow, or the day after at the latest. Why did he not face the

unpalatable truth? This was no Cathay, no Cipangu, nor indeed anywhere of like importance. Idling was not good for sailors. Columbus put
them to work caulking the keels of *Niña* and *Santa Maria*. The time
dragged. He vowed to punish Martin Alonso of *Pinta* for his desertion.

At length, on 5 November, Torres returned from the Cuban interior.
He reported merely that they had been hospitably received by a native
chief—the '*cacique*'—living in a primitive village together with his people. On receipt of this intelligence a general mood of hopelessness swept
over the enterprise. Torres told of shrubland and abundant fresh-water
fish, but little to justify their further delay in Cuba. Oh, he informed
Columbus, one strange practice: the group had rested among Indians
sucking leaves held in their mouths, and applying a flame. Smoke emitted
from their nostrils as if their heads were on fire. The native term for
those leaves? *Tobacos*.

The expedition had to proceed in search of objectives granting higher
compensation. Less the two vessels could not do, since the captain-
general refused to entertain defeat, despite the general feeling of anticlimax. Columbus had already seen enough of the fir trees proliferating
on Cuba to assure him that ocean-going vessels could be built on this
spot. His thoughts began visualizing future *hidalgos* in this place, mar-
shalling battalions of natives in organized servility for the enrichment of
Spain. He understood his Indians better now, enough to remain sceptical
of their insistence of gold and pearls (he showed them samples) in plentiful supply just waiting to be gathered on yet another island landscape
not too far away.

Perhaps the innocents in those parts were overanxious to please their
new friends, who were so generous with their hawks' bells and, for all
the natives knew, might have dropped from the sky. The island of which
they now spoke lay beyond the eastern edge of Cuba, a day's distance
by oar. Convincing as they might appear on the gold available there—
though they failed to comprehend the strangers' obsessive search for the
yellow metal—they warned Columbus against the country. Its inhabitants lived ferociously. They would venture forth to seize prisoners from
more peaceful places and then eat them. The word 'cannibal' had not
yet reached European speech, for it was born in this region. Columbus
was not too disturbed. He had weapons enough to match their bare
hands. He determined to investigate.

The short voyage proved unusually stormy for *Santa Maria* (they were
in fact battling the narrows of Windward Passage). It required all the
arts of seamanship, but they anchored on 6 December to have their lust

for treasure rewarded at last. Triumphantly, the hunters detected a message escaping from the rocksides—gleams of brilliant yellow, and specks of washed gold in the river shallows. Furthermore, the aspect of the place made it a joy to behold. The admiral felt redeemed in all senses. They had reached a heavily populated island for the first time, with innumerable inlets facilitating easy harbourage. The natives displayed grains of gold beaten into flat shapes to adorn their bodies. Revealing not the slightest sign of hostility, they proffered the aliens dustings of the precious metal and pointed inland to indicate their source of supply. Enchanted, Columbus emphatically declared this to be the gateway to Cathay, naming it La Isla Española (Hispaniola, the Spanish Isle).

They had of course arrived in the country later to be divided between Haiti and the Dominican Republic, a land inhabited by Caribs, who appeared a degree closer to sophistication than the simple Tainos, from whom they most probably stole it. A European could achieve his heart's desire here, for the seamen noted the readiness of the women to please. Natives led a party to their *cacique*, whose name they took to be Guacanagari. He proved to be a dignified young man bearing himself as a chieftain, the party reported. As appreciation of its paltry gifts he sent back a girdle with a large gold buckle for their leader.

In its recovered enthusiasm the expedition set about exploring with a will along the coastline of Hispaniola and offshore into Tortuga, always handsomely entertained and never failing to collect fragments of gold in their forays to the interior. Christmas was nigh, and it promised a bounty. So far their harvest could not be reckoned as likely to impress any ruler back home. Once divided up there was hardly enough to guarantee comfortable retirement for one old *marinero*, let alone two crews of them. But hopes ran high, and the ships attracted admiring sightseers by the hundred.

The Caribs obliged their guests with women and feasted them to exhaustion while *Santa Maria* and *Niña* lay at anchor close by the reefs east of present-day Cap Haitien. Wine by the barrel came out of store in exchange for their delicious pineapple fruit and other unfamiliar delicacies. The men on watch, regularly changed, tended to relax, at least on *Santa Maria*, so that a fatal lapse of command ensued. During the night of Monday, 24 December, while her tiller was entrusted to a young apprentice, she ran on a reef. Soon the flagship was shipping water badly. Every effort to refloat her, in which the crew enlisted willing hands despatched by *cacique* Guacanagari (who thereby achieved a place in the history books) proved of no avail. Thankfully, *Niña* was safe.

Columbus's own account of this disastrous, humiliating affair, as related in his son Ferdinand's biography, blamed the ship's master—her legal owner, Juan de la Cosa—for neglecting the watch and disobeying an order never to leave the tiller in the hands of a boy. Ferdinand quoted Columbus further: 'The tide was on the ebb and the ship was in danger. I had the mast cut away to lighten her so that we could get her off the reef. But the water became ever shallower. The ship would not move and began to list.' A vessel which had sturdily braved thousands of miles of uncharted ocean lay a pitiful wreck in a few feet of low tide.

Ever alert for heavenly omens, the admiral now rose to the situation. He decided he was appointed by Providence to create a permanent Christian settlement here and mark it as the birth of Spanish colonization. Logic lent reason to the divine command, for the only use to which he could now turn the hopelessly battered hulk of his flagship was to salvage its timbers and construct a fort. Of course! This was the birthday of the Lord Jesus, and this place must therefore be Navidad. The task was completed in all haste, by thirty-six volunteers electing to stay under governance of the man closest to the leader, Diego de Harana. At home these seamen were nonentities; here they would be rich, and the masters. The remaining stores not transferred to Niña, calculated to last a year, were ferried on to dry land. Not for a single moment did the pioneers doubt their capacity to survive, and rule all they surveyed, and build their individual hoards of gold while awaiting the stream of fellow-countrymen who would surely follow. They rescued Santa Maria's guns, and emplaced them at key points on the stockade.

Columbus interpreted the settlers' role somewhat differently. He nominated two officers, Pedro Gutiérrez and Rodrigo de Escobedo, both from the royal inspectorate, to reside with them so as to ensure proper accountancy of treasure discovered or won in the course of trade. The two would protect Queen Isabella's interests. Lest this appear too modest a base from which to initiate the conquest of an unexplored realm, the admiral ordered Niña to fire a volley into what still remained of the wreck, thus registering Christian supremacy over the barbarians.

Christopher Columbus had declared victory. He had reached the outposts of Asia where China and Japan broke into a thousand islands, each and every one claimed for Castile. Wondering if he would ever meet Pinta again, he prepared Niña for the return crossing. Styling himself according to his royal contract as Viceroy of the Islands of the Indies and Admiral of the Ocean Sea, he departed on 4 January 1493. He was bringing his six captive Indians back, together with specimens of animal and vegetable life as well as gold. Then, hugging the shoreline in search of *Pinta*, he began composing his report of the expedition, in the form of a letter addressed to Luis de Santangel, whose intercession with the queen had launched his fleet on its historic voyage to the other side of the world.

To his immense relief, *Pinta* came in view off the headland newly baptized as the Monte Christi peninsula. It would be unwise at this stage to start recriminations. Therefore Martin Alonso Pinzón was forgiven his desertion, except where it could wound him most, by receiving little credit for his contribution to the success of the enterprise in the official record. He now reported faithfully on his own harvest of gold, more significant by far than the quantity stored in the admiral's treasure-chest. It came from the interior of Hispaniola, called the Cibao. Columbus had feared *Pinta* would forestall his triumph by an earlier arrival home. Not only was that anxiety allayed, but with *Santa Maria* down, the two caravels, each skippered by a Pinzón, would now offer security to each other on the return across the ocean.

Only one more brief halt now, before they sailed away. This may have been where *Pinta* was instructed by the admiral to put in for the purpose of releasing her own captives, two of them women. If so, the moment held more significance than they knew, for the landing-party was received by hostile men adorned with feathers, evidently a sign of violent intentions. They brandished bows and arrows. The first resistance! Needless to relate, the Indians could not match the others' steel, which drew blood from some slight contact with an unwary native's skin, and away they all scattered. It was a sobering experience nevertheless, and the location is recalled to this day as Golfo de las Flechas (Arrow Gulf).

Gentle breezes carried *Pinta* and *Niña* northward, where they could benefit from the friendly currents of the Sargasso Sea. The two caravels had had the best of it on the voyage westward to the Indies, more comfortable than the cumbersome *Santa Maria*. But homebound, they fixed a passage higher in the Atlantic and its heavy breakers gave them a succession of unexpected shocks. The hulls of both vessels, which had been inadequately scraped and caulked when opportunity allowed, began to feel their age, taking copious quantities of ocean water. *Pinta* had neglected to repair a broken mast and *Niña's* troubles began from insufficient ballast; she tossed violently upon the swell. Also, their outward voyage had been a summer cruise, now they laboured against angry winter squalls that drove them off course. Two weeks of this, and Columbus calculated to his bitter regret that the first land to be sighted due east would not be the Canaries but the Azores—not Spanish territory but Portuguese. Even then, he sensed the possibility of losing the struggle against the elements.

On 13 February, after twenty-six days of arduous navigation with deceptive instruments, and much of it fraught in dread of evil spirits menacing with siren calls from the deep, the ships became separated and lost each other. Once again Columbus suspected Pinzón of treachery: Martin Alonso was a skilled and daring captain, could he not be planning to speed ahead with the intention of arriving first with the good news, to rob the glory and perhaps the rewards? We know the depth of Columbus's resentment. His log (the edited versions that exist) tells how he now wrote a summary of his discoveries on parchment, which he wrapped in waxed binding, sealed in a cask and dropped overboard. Should *Niña* go down and he not survive, perhaps this testament would be found, so that he would be remembered as the first who dreamed of a western passage to the Indies, and, against every discouragement, reached that distant shore. His two sons would succeed to the dignities and wealth of which he was cheated by death. For all we know, that parchment still lies in its watery grave.

The seas lashing into *Niña* refused to subside. The admiral summoned the entire crew to join him in a special appeal to the Holy Virgin. They must vow that whoever came through his ordeal would, on reaching land, make a penitential pilgrimage to the nearest shrine of the Mother of God and offer thanks for his deliverance. The following morning, 15 February, they sighted the island of Santa Maria in the Azores.

Trembling with the joyful anticipation of appearing in his new guise as civilization's greatest mariner, Columbus prepared himself for a ceremonial reception: what a dramatic story he ached to tell the Portuguese here! No European had seen what these men of the *Niña* had seen, no ship had sailed where she had sailed. But no man could be more mortified than when he tried to give some indication of their adventure. Instead of a welcome, the island's governor made preparations to take them all in custody, in the name of his King John. These weathered Spaniards had surely been on some pirate voyage, probably to West Africa, which the world knew was a Portuguese preserve. The governor dismissed protestations of a Castilian expedition to the Indies; he had heard nothing of such a mad affair. As for the landing-party sent ahead by Columbus, it was already locked in the island's jail, and the so-called Admiral of the Ocean Sea had better come quietly.

In the ensuing angry exchange with the governor Columbus made threats of his own, to use *Niña*'s guns against the place. More persuasive, however, was his passing to the other of his royal warrant, unmistakably engraved with the sovereign seal. Mollified, the Portuguese commander made honourable amends with an offer of hospitality and fresh provisions for the ship. Then they all landed and, stripped to their bare waists as true penitents, proceeded to their promised devotions in the nearest chapel.

The spirits of the deep continued to trouble *Niña* on the final stage of the voyage. She still had to negotiate 800 miles of buffeting gales, which grew more fierce the nearer they approached continental Europe. Columbus intended to sail round Cape St Vincent, steering clear of Portugal altogether and making direct for Palos, womb of the great enterprise. It was not to be. The overworked vessel could do no more than limp into the Lisbon roadsteads and, to the profound relief of all, drop anchor off Belém. To those who sailed in her, *Niña* was by now almost a breathing creature. For over thirty weeks she had kept them, miraculously, safe in mind and body. As for their forty-one-year-old leader, he drew himself up at the dockside like an impatient conqueror awaiting obeisance.

No sign here of *Pinta*, and Columbus hastened in despatching a courier overland with his official report to Isabella and Ferdinand, then in residence at Barcelona. When the Spanish text was first printed, in April 1493, it was styled *Columbus's Letter to Santangel* and addressed to 'The Keeper of the Privy Purse'. To it was appended a postscript relating to his enforced delay here at Lisbon. The only extant copy of this edition is to be found in the New York Public Library. Various Latin versions, each text slightly altered, perhaps deliberately, quickly followed.

Columbus wrote with unconcealed pride of his 'great victory'. He described the voyage, his discoveries, the character and physical aspect of the natives, and of the terrain. He had not, he said, encountered any wild creatures nor people of extraordinary physique (i.e., headless, or three-legged, etc., as the fables told) but he had been advised of man-eating savages who preyed upon the rest, of an island (probably Martinique) said to be inhabited exclusively by women, and of another whose inhabitants grew tails. A miscomprehension for monkeys?

He had been well received everywhere, Columbus continued, and in return made it his practice to treat the natives, a simple, timid folk but by no means unintelligent, with generosity and courtesy. As he had observed it, private property did not exist. Women, however, were seen to work more than men. They had no religion but gave every prospect

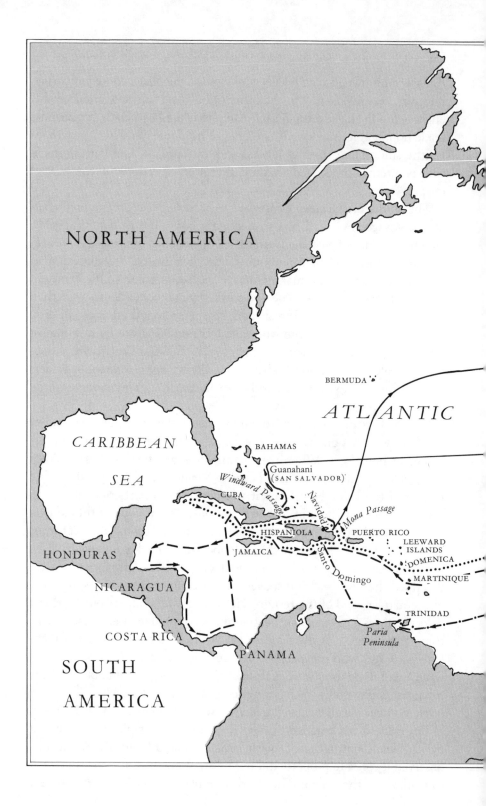

NORTH AMERICA

BERMUDA

ATLANTIC

CARIBBEAN

SEA

BAHAMAS

Guanahani
(SAN SALVADOR)

Windward Passage

CUBA

Navidad

Mona Passage

HISPANIOLA

PUERTO RICO

LEEWARD
ISLANDS

JAMAICA

Santo Domingo

DOMENICA

HONDURAS

MARTINIQUE

NICARAGUA

TRINIDAD

COSTA RICA

Paria
Peninsula

PANAMA

SOUTH

AMERICA

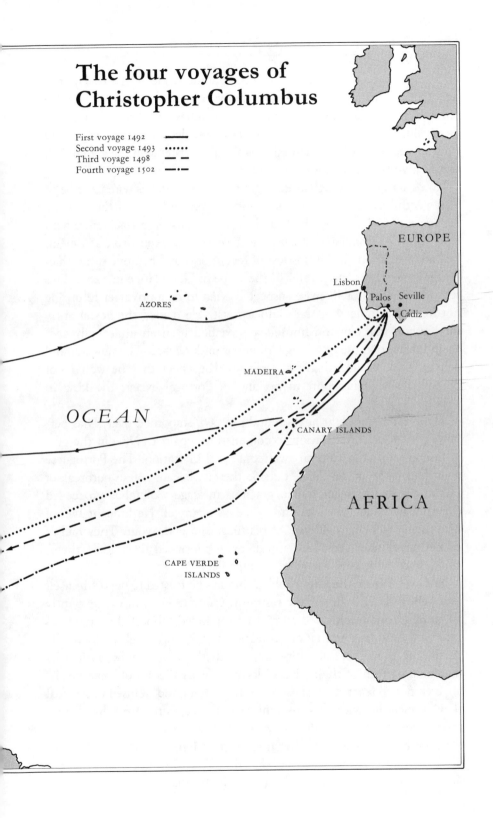

The four voyages of
Christopher Columbus

First voyage 1492
Second voyage 1493
Third voyage 1498
Fourth voyage 1502

EUROPE

Lisbon

AZORES

Palos   Seville
Cádiz

MADEIRA

OCEAN

CANARY ISLANDS

AFRICA

CAPE VERDE
ISLANDS

of conversion to the faith of our Lord. Should it please their Majesties he would return and carry forward the work he had begun at Navidad of establishing the Castilian nation in the Indies, and bring back abundant gold, 'as much as they should want', besides slaves to any number from among those who remained pagan. All Christendom, he concluded, should give thanks to the Holy Trinity.

Now that he had touched Portugal proper, Columbus dared not be so disrespectful as to ignore protocol and sail onward without first paying his respects to its monarch. Dared not? He relished an audience with King John, so dismissive of his project years ago. Even here, at Belém, he had been afforded the frostiest of receptions, and by none other than Bartholomew Dias, discoverer of the Cape of Good Hope in 1487. This renowned navigator likewise suspected Niña to be a privateer returning not from the Indies but the Guinea coast. He denied the vessel entry into Lisbon harbour and himself approached it in an armed pinnace, again for the purpose of taking Columbus under guard. The new admiral delivered a cool and dignified reply, to the effect that he would not be trifled with but report to no one in Portugal except the king in person.

The business of identification and protocol smoothed over, Dias permitted Vicente Yañez Pinzón to commission repairs to Niña in the port of Lisbon while the admiral awaited a royal invitation. The Portuguese court had taken up residence outside the city because of an outbreak of plague there. On receipt of a gracious message Columbus proceeded overland by mule, 30 miles and two days of travel. He brought two of his Indians as living evidence of his successful endeavour. They had of course never seen such beasts and, once persuaded to straddle them, could do so with only the greatest difficulty.

Not even before the king could Columbus be trusted to deport himself as it behoved, with diplomatic restraint. Quite the contrary. Arrogantly adopting a tone of elevated reproof he reminded John of their previous interview, and its termination in rebuff. The king, though undoubtedly nettled by the other's intelligence, which the two natives verified by making a pattern of their islands' location with the aid of some beads, affected not to react. His advisers, on the other hand, refused to conceal their displeasure with this insolent Genoese captain. What had all he related to do with Castile, they asked? Ownership of islands in the Atlantic had been settled, after long negotiation. Surely Columbus was aware of the treaty of Alcaçovas, signed by Portugal and Castile in 1479, and the edict of Pope Sixtus IV (his bull Aeterna regis, 1481) whereby any such islands south of the Canaries and west of Portugal belonged to this country? Columbus professed ignorance of such a bull. His expedition had been blessed and financed by the Queen of Castile, in whose name he proclaimed their ownership. The territory might well have gone to Portugal once. Now no longer.

Infuriated, the courtiers conferred privately with their king during a recess in the audience. Portuguese records tell of their plan to rectify the historic mistake. Why not silence Columbus by having him killed? Spain would not then know of his return from the Indies. Fortunately, John, balanced and capable statesman that he was, scotched the foolish idea. In fact he sanctioned a visit by the explorer to his own Queen Leonor, then in retreat at a nearby convent, because she had requested a first-hand account of the great adventure. The episode nevertheless opened Portugal's eyes to a changed world. Oceans successfully navigated meant oceans controlled. Who would ultimately own them?

Could there be any mistaking the answer when Columbus, officially promoted and ennobled, received a message from Ferdinand and Isabella addressed to 'Don Cristóbal Colón, their Admiral of the Ocean Sea, Viceroy and Governor of the Islands he has discovered in the Indies'? Collecting his two sons (Diego thirteen, Ferdinand five), he was splendidly welcomed at court. Honours and wealth were now his, and for his descendants in perpetuity. The queen invited him to sit beside her at her right. His Indians were scrutinized and interrogated. Whether or not they understood the questions, which concerned Jesus, they nevertheless knew the Castilian for 'yes' and used it frequently. Then they were made to kneel before their Majesties and were received, with the royal couple and their Infante Don Juan as godparents, in baptism.

In a tone of redoubled fervour Columbus declared the two Indians to be the first of many, many others awaiting the blessing of Christ. For he would return to Navidad in Hispaniola with all despatch, at the head of a large fleet bringing colonists and priests. Another Spain was due to arise among the barbarians—a great Christian civilization in fact, out of which the good word would spread through Asia even unto the terrified ears of the infidel conqueror of Jerusalem. Spain, he intimated, could assert itself anew: the world's greatest, richest power—metamorphosis indeed for a fragmented nation under alien rule until, as it were, the day before yesterday!

What had begun at Palos must end at Palos. Before repairing to Barcelona Columbus returned to *Niña*'s home port, where he arrived on 15 March 1493. Amazingly, that very same day Martin Alonso Pinzón

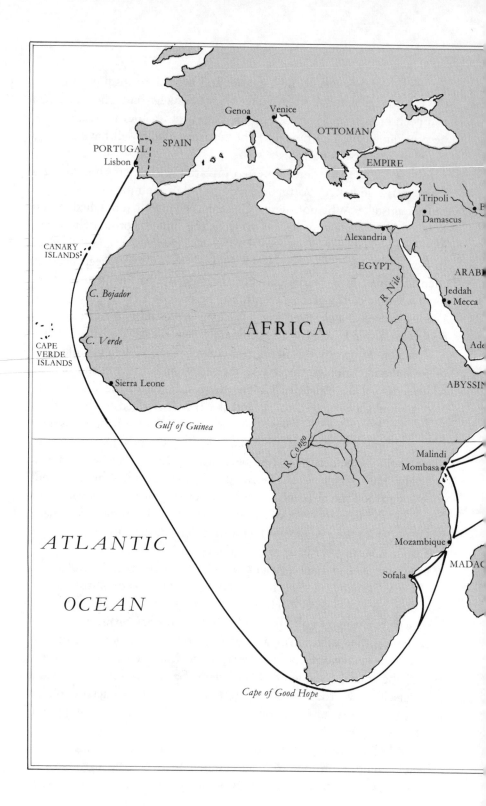

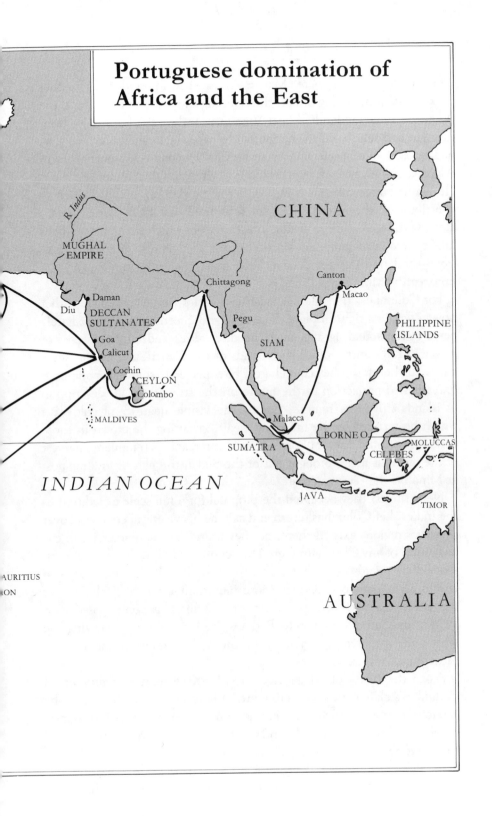

Portuguese domination of Africa and the East

brought *Pinta* to rest there. Martin Alonso had forestalled his brother back to Spain by sailing direct, thus eluding the fierce storms around the Azores and making landfall near Vigo just north of the Portuguese frontier. He had sent word to the monarchs begging an audience. But they had refused him, preferring to await the Discoverer's report. Martin Alonso, now a very sick man, could not withstand the painful rejection. He too had undertaken a voyage of heroic proportions and had much to contribute to the record. It is also recounted that *Pinta* carried home, along with its treasure, a deadly infection from which the native Indians might have been immune. Martin Alonso died shortly afterwards, possibly—and nothing could have been more tragically ironic—the first European victim of syphilis.

For Columbus, the role he had invented for himself a decade earlier now entered its rightful place. The king and queen did not immediately perceive the actual significance of his discoveries. Indeed, they were not as yet in full control of all the islands of the Canaries, Castilian since 1481. Furthermore, they could hardly be expected to share their admiral's unrestrained projection of the future on the strength of his description of islands still more remote, nor by the visible quantity of gold with which he testified to the untapped wealth awaiting the crown in those parts. In contrast, John of Portugal had been reaping an immense harvest of the precious metal brought out of the Sudan through his trading post at Mina on the Guinea coast.

Nevertheless they accepted the proposal for a full-scale expedition to the Indies. Let Columbus return and assume his viceregal command over whatever regions existed there, be they islands or mainland, not in the possession of any Christian ruler. They consented to settlement by thousands of Spaniards—yes, but Castilians only, Isabella insisted—so as to ensure permanent occupation. More important than this, salvation of the natives must proceed apace. It was a solemn obligation imposed upon every truly Catholic monarch. Perhaps the hypocrisy interweaving the sentiment appeared less blatant in those days than in the empire-gathering of subsequent eras.

As to the treaty of Alcaçovas, cited by King John in refutation of Columbus's claims, this had terminated a Portuguese-Castilian war. The two royal houses now worked at harmonious relations—indeed, the eldest daughter of Isabella and Ferdinand was the widow of John's son. It would be folly to reopen an unhappy chapter now for the sake of faraway places that might well hold less promise than Columbus, in his optimism, supposed. Isabella might believe that an injunction to carry the gospel to pagan races would explain the innocence of Castile's endeavour, but Ferdinand realized how the very word Indies roused the strongest proprietorial instincts of the Portuguese mind.

Decidedly so. Not only had their explorers, since the time of Henry the Navigator, been engrossed in discovering a seaward passage there, but plans were in hand at that moment for an expedition to consummate the heroic voyage of Bartholomew Dias and chart the ocean he had discovered round Africa so as to reach the Indies across those eastern waters. Portuguese travellers had ventured overland across Africa further than any other Europeans in search of the realm of the priest king Prester John. Moreover, had not King John of Portugal been advised by the Italian cartographer Toscanelli long before Columbus sailed, and had he not appointed the Salamanca astronomer Zacuto, immediately following the expulsion of Jews from Spain, his own Astronomer-Royal? All this activity proceeded in the spirit of the bull *Aeterna regis* of Pope Sixtus. Surely the authority of His Holiness was binding on Castile?

True, but Rome had a new pope, elected as Columbus sailed out of Palos the year before—Alexander VI, Ferdinand of Aragon's Borgia ally, protégé and compatriot. And never was a lord spiritual more in need of a powerful lord temporal than now. As we have seen, Alexander lived in fear of deposition. His unrelenting enemy Giuliano della Rovere, with the connivance of others of the College of Cardinals, was in conspiratorial association with the French king, Charles VIII. They intended to make the projected French invasion of Italy the occasion to destroy that unworthy Pope. Alexander therefore needed Ferdinand as much as Ferdinand needed him.

The Pope's hand slipped as if by nature ordained into the one extended by Ferdinand. A conflict between Spain and Portugal over places distant from Europe? Hadn't it all been settled by one of his holy predecessors years before? No, these were other islands, newly discovered by an Italian under commission of Castile. The Pope must arbitrate over their ownership, remembering also that further lands could be involved, the Indian mainland in fact. And he should not overlook the particular interest of his native soil, and of his most dutiful servant Ferdinand.

Now the carrot. As King of Aragon Ferdinand had made Alexander's eldest son Pedro Luis Borgia Duke of Gandia, succeeded since his death in 1488 by another son, Juan. Ferdinand was now prepared to fulfil a promise to give this young duke his own cousin Maria Enriquez as bride. As we know, Alexander schemed tirelessly to lift his beloved progeny on to the brotherhood of royalty.

Thus was the bargain struck. In the sententious vocabulary of these things, the bull *Inter cetera*, issued on 3 May 1493, spoke in part of:

our dear son in Christ, Ferdinand, king, and our very dear daughter in Christ, Isabella, queen, of Castile, León, Aragon, Sicily and Granada, whose devotion to the Catholic faith has recovered the kingdom of Granada from the Saracens, having chosen our beloved son Christopher Columbus, a man assuredly worthy of the highest recommendations and fitted for so great an undertaking . . . to make diligent quest for these remote and unknown mainlands and islands through the sea where hitherto no one had sailed . . . We, of our own accord, by the authority of Almighty God conferred upon us in blessed Peter and of the vicarship of Jesus Christ . . . give, grant and assign all islands and mainlands, whether in the direction of India or towards any other quarter, found one hundred leagues west and south of the Azores and Cape Verde, to the kings of Castile and León . . . with the proviso that none of the islands and mainlands found and to be found, discovered and to be discovered, be not in the actual possession of any Christian king or prince up to the birthday of our Lord Jesus Christ just passed, from which the present year one thousand four hundred and ninety-three begins . . .'

It was Alexander's third or fourth attempt (backdated) at drafting a bull satisfactory to Ferdinand. He had cut the world in two like an orange, half the continents beyond Europe to Spain, half by implication to Portugal. It was as if no other power, Christian or otherwise, could contemplate building a ship that might sail an ocean. King John accepted the exalted ruling, but only after his geographers nudged him into persuading the Spanish, in the treaty of Tordesillas, June 1494, to move the demarcation line 270 leagues further west of the Azores. John evidently knew something of which Ferdinand, even Columbus, was ignorant. For by doing so Brazil was shifted east of the line and therefore allocated to Portugal, together with the true route round Africa to the true Indies.

Chapter Seven

DREAMS AND REALITIES
OF EMPIRE

ach of Columbus's subsequent three voyages left him progressively more disillusioned with his royal masters and their advisers. He suspected misunderstandings and treachery at every turn, and was destined to die in 1506 a profoundly disappointed man.

The conviction that he had brought Asia within reach of Europe from the west never deserted him, though really his mistake was only slight, purely an error of designation. He had discovered a new continent, yet he continued to insist that it was the eastern extremity of an old one. Columbus was not alone. The first map of the world based upon his explorations, made in 1500 by the cartographer of his second voyage Juan de la Cosa (not the master of *Santa Maria*), still showed a landmass extending uninterrupted westward round the globe. No mariner sailed into the Pacific until 1513, when Vasco Nunez de Balboa, the first great *conquistador*, crossed the Isthmus of Panama to sight this other ocean, so close to the point where Columbus turned away during his fourth voyage ten years earlier. A further seven years would elapse before Ferdinand Magellan negotiated that immense waterway and gauged the distance separating America's western seaboard from Asia, though without himself surviving to tell the triumphant tale.

Magellan, undoubtedly the greatest seaman in all exploration, nevertheless did not achieve what Columbus achieved: point history in a new direction. All who followed after his planting of the Castilian standard upon Navidad in Hispaniola were spurred by that act rather than any other feat of navigation. The performance verged on the superhuman. Columbus defied tradition, theory, religious limitations and the entire store of known experience, not to mention the blockade of discouragement. Subsequent exploration of the world's surface derived from his original inspiration, and immediately. Most significantly, it was Christian exploration, bringing supremacy to the Christian monarchs it served. As a consequence, Islam, Christendom's collective enemy, became contained within the Old World. It could advance deeper into Europe and fringe all of Asia besides a large portion of Africa. Yet its bounds were locked. The year 1492 decided that Islam, be it ever so successful, would be fated in the end to halt its conquests, retreat and decline.

For the Turks would require the subjugation of Europe before they could move into the Atlantic, as was assuredly their intention. A final reckoning of forces still belonged to the future, since the struggle between the rival civilizations would not conclusively be resolved for another two centuries. And by then the world beyond was already appropriated as the vassal of western Europe. Here, within its own paradox, lay the secret of Europe's accomplishment. The Christian nations were divided and bent upon each other's humiliation, even destruction, whereas Islam militant embraced a monolith ruled by a despot from its summit at Constantinople. Soon the Turkish ruler would pronounce himself not only Sultan but Caliph, thereby personifying an authority denied in Christendom to any Supreme Pontiff and Holy Roman Emperor combined.

By contrast, mutual distrust drove the western European powers to continuous, costly conflict. Yet it also rendered them an inner dynamism. They improved their ships, armies and techniques not so much to triumph over the infidel Turk as rather to frustrate their Christian neighbours. Spain's incentive to conquer an empire sprang from its fear of Portugal's appetite, and vice versa, though both would be supplanted by other European nations in due course. The Turks however suffered no considerable competition within Islam, rivalries notwithstanding. Thus qualities that hitherto gave them strength turned to complacency and weakness while that chronic malady of Christian Europe, discord, provided the traction force necessary for innovation and strength.

Call America Las Indias, or indeed by any other name, its discovery was the starting signal that sent Spain and Portugal on a race against each other and conveyed the coming century to them. To be sure, they exhausted themselves in the process and so forfeited their global role to France, England and the Dutch, who similarly strove, each of them, to spread their national wings before their neighbours might forestall them. These nations likewise possessed the supreme advantage of a window on the west. Turkish fleets roamed the Mediterranean but expansion could only be via the Atlantic Ocean.

There intervened also that blind element so frequently overlooked as a factor in history: accident. All except tiny Portugal conceived their struggles as lying within Europe, where every acre of contested land was deemed to be worth a battle. Yet continents could be secured by the daring of a single intrepid individual. A dozen explorers won the world for rulers who themselves perspired over trivial sovereignties within this imperilled Christian promontory hanging over the ledge of Asia. Little wonder the Turks stormed forth whenever Europe left its rear unguarded.

Although Ferdinand went along, albeit halfheartedly, with the resolve of Columbus to establish Spanish rule in the Indies, he did so less in the expectation of creating a Greater Castile there than in the hope of gaining the riches to pursue his specific Aragonese ambitions. He and Isabella now enjoyed a title, 'Los Reyes Católicos' ('The Catholic Kings'), bestowed by their friend in Rome, Pope Alexander. True, Ferdinand's plans were so devious as to cloud the logic of his actions to the observer, though clearly he wished to increase his possessions in Italy, at the expense of the minor princelings governing their separate portions of it. Columbus sailed—this time from Cadiz—in September 1493 with no fewer than seventeen ships carrying 1,200 soldiers, craftsmen, settlers and *hidalgo* adventurers. Christ was represented by half a dozen priests. The admiral astonished Europe with the courage of the endeavour, its magnitude, the effrontery of it. No such armada destined for deep water had ever left a European port before. One month earlier, that late survival of medievalism Frederick III of the Holy Roman Empire had died after a reign enduring fifty-three frustrating and inglorious years. The two events stood oddly in juxtaposition. Spain was now an empire despite itself while the other, proclaimed as such, barely existed outside its collective memory, serving purely as a term of convenience.

The German people, so long disguised as a nation by this grandiose Holy Roman camouflage, looked to Frederick's successor, his thirty-four-year-old son Maximilian, for signs of a revival of their golden age. If any ruler could bring them some unity of purpose, Maximilian was that man. Undoubtedly he could be the victim of his astonishing naïvety and, as Machiavelli wrote, anyone could cheat him without his knowing it. But he had recovered Austrian territories from the Hungarians and kept the French out of the Netherlands and western Germany. It irked Maximilian that the German people occupied so insignificant a place in Europe when, because of their talents and prosperity, they merited its leadership. All they possessed—mountainsides rich in ores of silver, copper and tin (Martin Luther's father worked as a miner-, industrious artisans, inventors, scholars and bankers, a location covering the heartland of the continent—could not atone for their single lack, the formula for national identity: in a word, statehood.

Maximilian proposed to give it to them, by strong leadership, a national army, efficient taxation and a Church solidly behind the temporal power as was now the case with France, Spain and England. Italy might be fragmented but Germany lay divided into a thousand particles and, Maximilian warned, if it failed to rehabilitate itself it would be sucked dry by the French and then swallowed by the Turks. Such talk fell as music on his subjects' ears, but the new emperor had no significant income and was beset at the periphery of his realm by restive peoples in linguistic blocs with separating instincts of nationality. He could hardly protect his own duchy. Venice had acquired a large slice of territory on the Italian mainland by denuding Austria of it.

In the Imperial Diet, the Reichstag, representatives of the many principalities led by Bavaria, Württemburg, Brandenburg and Hesse rubbed shoulders with much smaller fry sent by the imperial cities to shout the others down. A goodly portion of Germany, perhaps one third, belonged to the Church and was ruled by archbishops, bishops and abbots who generally enjoyed protection through family connections with the huge nobility. Some members of the Reichstag never turned up at all, among them the late Emperor Frederick himself, who did not once meet the Diet during the last thirty years of his reign. The Holy Roman Empire spread itself over Europe, a somnolent behemoth stricken with seemingly incurable organic diseases. Nevertheless its crowned head inherited rights and dignities envied by every other monarch as the highest in Christendom.

Could this confederation recapture a sense of cohesion? The new emperor would do his utmost, and end his days without recognizing his failure. Or perhaps it was not failure at all, for the seed of change had already been planted, the seed of Maximilian in the womb of his beloved wife Mary of Burgundy, dead since 1482. Their son, Duke Philip of Burgundy, was fifteen years old in 1493. Adorned with his feudal title, this Flanders-raised adolescent displayed pronounced independent views. So the epic story of the Holy Roman Empire by no means belonged to the past. Young Philip carried the strain of a Frenchman, Charles the Bold, whom we remember as hoping in vain to acquire the resplendent crown for himself. What that grandfather of Philip could not achieve, a grandson of Maximilian would fulfill, and the power of the House of

Habsburg, blended with Burgundy, would multiply a thousandfold. Charles V, son of Philip, was destined to reign over the greatest of all realms. But we anticipate . . .

Despite the ovations he received as a national symbol on his appearance in Germany, Maximilian began displeasing the Reichstag from the outset of his reign. It refused to vote him money for an imperial army because, it contended, he conducted himself like an emperor while blundering like a Habsburg. His ambitious ideas for an army included substantial expenditure on artillery, in which he made himself an expert. But according to the princes expected to pay for it, Germany had no need of such weaponry. Their defence problems had shrunk in purpose, limited to protecting a river frontier here and a forest there, or to suppressing internal unrest. Put bluntly, Maximilian was preoccupying himself with problems particular to his own dynasty. He fretted over Turkish depredations in his Habsburg territories and yearned to expel the Venetians from his traditional Italian possessions, thus restoring his personal inheritance after the ravages it suffered under his father Frederick. Such objectives would involve full-scale war, so let Maximilian underwrite the cost himself or concentrate his thoughts on the administrative reform of the Reich. It cried for centralized government. It offered him the loyalty of a prosperous confederation with himself responding to advice from experienced councillors. Foreign wars were to be avoided, and certainly he must not indulge in military adventures for family advantage that had no relevance to the nation as a whole. It desired no repetition of that folly of 1488, when Maximilian had to be rescued by an imperial army from a Bruges prison, the ignominious consequence of a Flemish quarrel with France.

So that was it. He intended to reign as the divinely chosen emperor in the fullest sense (Dürer painted him anointed by the Virgin) while the Reichstag saw him as a parliamentary servant. Allowing the discussion, a bleak pedantic debate in his estimation, and purely an occupation for the lawyers, to take its languid course, Maximilian went his own way. Now that the French ceased to menace the Netherlands his first move was to transfer his authority as regent there to his son Philip. He could therefore assure Charles VIII of France that he would not oppose a march through Italy and his installation in the kingdom of Naples, which incorporated the southern half of the peninsula excluding Sicily. Charles considered he had legal right to its crown descending from his Angevin forbears. In return, Maximilian expected French passivity in a campaign of his own against Venice. As for money, he found a solution to that problem too. A bride was available with a dowry appropriate to an emperor's hand.

Bianca Maria Sforza was married in Milan to Maximilian in a proxy ceremony for which Leonardo da Vinci designed suitable wall draperies and arranged a splendid décor. It was another of those Italian parodies of holy matrimony. Nothing could assuage the feeling of offence the marriage caused among Europe's tightly defined caste of interconnected royal families: first at the cynicism of it and then at the spectacle of the emperor's union with a woman tarred as a commoner. Bianca was the niece of Ludovico il Moro, regent of Milan, but what were the Sforza clan if not parvenu mercenary captains risen from humble stock? This troubled Maximilian not at all. Ludovico, the rich ally of Charles VIII, would prove equally helpful to Maximilian's Venetian plans. Historically, Milan lay within the empire, and Maximilian lightly exercised his prerogative as suzerain to invest Ludovico with the formal dukedom. The 'Moor' had long pursued the ancient throne (Charlemagne wore the Iron Crown of Lombardy) by a complicated route that included the mysterious death of his Visconti nephew. In 1494 Bianca Maria presented herself at the nuptial bedchamber in Innsbruck with treasure and possessions valued at 440,000 ducats, the inventory recording a chamber-pot in solid silver and knitting needles of gold.

Maximilian was not yet ready to take on Venice. However, in September 1494 the French king had Ludovico open the Alpine passes through Lombardy and allow him to lead a large invading force virtually uncontested down the Italian peninsula. Charles's cousin Louis of Orleans brought a fleet into Genoa that had virtually been purchased from that same city. Twenty-two years of age, an ungainly, loping man with a stutter, and afflicted by smallpox, Charles VIII too had extracted money from Ludovico, though he treated the newly crowned duke with all the contempt an Italian might expect from a Frenchman. Piero de'Medici, son of Lorenzo, threw up his hands and, as we know, escaped just before the king, attired in gilded armour and wearing his crown, rode into Florence. It had suited Fra Savonarola perfectly, for he could now presume to greet the most unpleasant-looking invader as God's own messenger despatched for a predestined Italian Judgment Day.

Charles's preparations seemed well made. As he advanced through the country both Ferdinand of Spain, who also ruled Sicily, and Maximilian, ostensibly the Habsburg defender of the empire, honoured their undertakings by averting their eyes. It was more a victory parade than a war.

On the appearance of Charles's formidable gunnery, drawn by 12,000 horses and followed by Swiss mercenaries, the cities in their path lost no time in opening their gates. The king anticipated an enthusiastic welcome on his arrival in Naples, for he counted on strong support from its barons, some of them of French origin and all aggrieved by the tyrannous work King Ferrante had made of Neapolitan rule. Venice, true to its tradition, remained neutral. Pisa, Leghorn and Bologna capitulated while the Colonna and Orsini families, whose troops supposedly maintained the security of the papal realm, went over to the enemy and cleared his road to Rome. Cardinal della Rovere was at Charles's elbow, intent on manipulating French power into declaring Pope Alexander's election void and instituting the much needed cleansing of the Church.

What was Alexander to do? He was pledged to assist Naples, over whose king the occupant of St Peter's held suzerainty, but so far Neapolitan resistance had proved derisory. Its navy had engaged the French fleet outside Genoa with such disastrous consequences as to impel the king's abdication. (This was no longer Ferrante, who had died, but his son Alfonso, who now passed the crown to *his* heir Ferrantino; theirs was a cadet branch of the House of Aragon.)

Given the classic Italian syndrome, wherein internal rivalries and grievances defined relations with a foreign predator—'Never mind Italy, is he useful to me?'—Alexander found himself in the toils of a dilemma. His duty, both as Pope and as a temporal monarch ruling a great slice of Italy at its middle, demanded a stand against the enemy, with excommunication of Charles the least of its punishments. His reputation as a corrupt pope deep in simony and womanizing scandalized Europe, and this warned Alexander of the consequences should Charles prove victorious: deposition from his sacred office and relegation no doubt to some obscure bishopric like the anti-popes of old, with Cardinal della Rovere reigning in his stead. What this could entail also for the various Borgia appointments he had made, and the Borgia children he had fathered—banishment and possibly even death—gave him pause. A French detachment had already found the Pope's young companion Giulia Farnese on the road to Viterbo and taken her prisoner together with his favourite cousin Adriana de Milo.

Alexander, moreover, hugged a guilty conscience. He had stooped so low as to intrigue with the infidel who threatened all Christendom. The Pope had advised Sultan Bayezid of Charles's contemplated crusade, utilizing the occasion to venture a hint of blackmail—the Jem factor. What if Charles embarked upon his crusade with the sultan's brother, freed from papal custody, at his side? In fact, introducing a potential usurper to bear on the Turkish situation. Alexander would therefore guarantee to hold Jem secure and not surrender him to Charles, on certain conditions: more Muslim money for the Pope—not merely the regular retainer as hitherto—and Bayezid to press Venice to launch an attack on the French from the rear. Such was the ambivalence with which Christian rulers regarded their supreme enemy. However, Alexander's letter bearing this nefarious proposal was intercepted by French agents. Charles was informed. Alexander's fears redoubled.

On the other hand Charles might be seduced, for Alexander was no mean charmer. The Frenchman would need the Pope to legalize his investiture as King of Naples, and might well refrain from endangering his claim to Naples by substituting a della Rovere for a Borgia in St Peter's. Choosing the better part of valour, Alexander consequently played a diplomatic hand. He ordered Ferrantino of Naples to clear his troops out of Rome and gave instructions to the cardinals to surrender the Eternal City to Charles (they would have done so anyway!) while he betook himself to his fortress beside the Vatican, Castel Sant'Angelo, as Charles assumed possession of the Palazzo Venezia. Polite messages passed to and fro.

Alexander gambled on the deference due to his Holiness. Affecting to bless Charles's contemplated crusade to redeem Constantinople and Jerusalem, he decided to speed the other on his way by surrendering his Turkish prisoner Jem. The Pope's son Cesare Borgia, nineteen years of age though already Cardinal Archbishop of Valencia, brought the Muslim prince to French headquarters. Cesare was deputed to remain as papal legate to the king, in the realization that he would be retained in any event, as guarantor of his parent's goodwill. This done, Alexander rode out of Castel Sant'Angelo in all his dignity to meet Charles in the Vatican.

He enacted a gesture of friendly condescension by withholding his hand or foot so as to spare Charles the necessity for either a kiss of allegiance or an act of conquering insolence. The king registered his Christian piety by undertaking to erect a splendid new house of God surmounting the Pincio hill. Approached by a monumental stairway, the Spanish Steps, it rose to dominate the heights as the Trinità dei Monti.

More encounters followed, Alexander resorting to all the contrived ploys of which he was capable to avoid serious business. Reform of the Church never entered their discussions, which terminated without a papal statement on Charles's right to the Neapolitan crown or otherwise.

French troops, packing the city, occupied themselves in frolic among the women and inspection of the artistic treasures of the place. Then, amid general relief, they moved out along the Appian Way to Naples unobstructed except by the dust of their horses' hooves. Ferrantino now beat a hasty retreat to Ischia while Cesare Borgia, cardinal, emissary and hostage, made good a well-timed escape. Alexander, as ever true to himself, paid a ransom of 3,000 ducats to receive back his two ladies. They seemed none too distraught after their enforced sojourn with a French regiment in Viterbo. Alas for poor Jem! Pending his further utilization in a crusade, he had been despatched to captivity in France, only to die a sudden death in a matter of weeks. The Pope's enemies insisted that he had been served a fatal potion secretly delivered from Rome. Doubtless Alexander wasted no pity on the fate of Naples, whose king had regularly insulted him by paying no papal tribute additional to the annual presentation of a white palfrey (see p. 15).

Clutching his Anjou pedigree like a passport divinely issued, Charles marked the capture of Naples by stealing the great bronze door at the entrance of its castle. Soon his courtiers were usurping splendid palaces throughout Campania. They had left a trail of dislocation all along their route from Milan, reducing the Florentine Republic to a rump—important cities, Pisa among them, having availed themselves of the opportunity to snatch their independence—and adding disgust to the local population's hatred. There was no denying brutal Swiss mercenaries the fruits of a swift and relatively bloodless victory. To Italy's shame, Charles had demonstrated how its hedonism and disunity invited conquest by any aggressor so determined. In this regard two lines of thought brought Ferdinand of Spain to urgent action.

He was himself an Italian ruler, Sicily being a jewel in the Aragon crown. Only a narrow strip of water separated this island from Calabria in the kingdom of Naples, and Charles's appetite, if unrestrained, would surely look upon it as a tempting morsel. Moreover, what that brainless French king could do, so could he. His house too had once owned Naples (who hadn't!). Why not again? Half of Italy would thus fall to Ferdinand, whatever befell the rest. First of all Charles must be evicted and Ferdinand's own kinsman Ferrantino provisionally restored. The consummation of his scheme could safely await another day. In the mean time Ferdinand deposited a formidable army in Sicily under his general Gonsalvo de Córdoba, conqueror of Granada in 1492.

Charles had entered Naples on 22 February 1495, but he was already feeling insecure. In their wide estates the local barons, even those of

French descent, were voicing bitter discontent at the arrogance of the occupying power. They plotted with Ferrantino hiding away in the Bay of Naples. Similar waves of resentment stirred in Lombardy, rousing Ludovico of Milan to contrition for his intrigues with the French. Venice too was shaken by the speed of conquest and revealed another attitude. It was all grist to Pope Alexander's mill. He assisted Ferdinand in organizing an alliance. Now Emperor Maximilian joined them, and the League of Venice took shape 'for the peace and tranquillity of Italy, the welfare of all Christendom, the defence of the honour and authority of the Holy See and the rights of the Holy Roman Empire'. Proud words, but Florence, most firmly under French control, stayed apart.

Only Ferdinand could spin such a web, though it required a humiliation on the scale administered by Charles VIII to start the first thread. Here was Milan actually aligning itself with Venice, and the Venetians motivated by a conscience for Italy as a whole. Their *rapprochement* owed not a little to the skill of Ludovico's brilliant consort Beatrice d'Este, who the previous year had led an embassy to Venice and argued eloquently for an end to the rivalry between the two northern city-states. Most significant for the destiny of Europe, the League of Venice brought the House of Aragon into its blood compact with the House of Habsburg. Ferdinand bargained for a multitudinous force under the Holy Roman Empire to wreak destruction upon the enemy common to them both. He put everything he cherished into the offer of a dynastic union with the Habsburg, a double marriage: his own heir Juan betrothed to Maximilian's daughter Margaret, given as a child to Charles of France but then cast out; and for Maximilian's heir Philip of Burgundy he had a daughter on his side available, the Princess Joanna. The arrangement would close the ring around France, for Ferdinand had already promised his fourth daughter, Catherine, as consort for the heir of Henry VII of England. Wasn't such achievement worth a hundred empires in the Indies?

Maximilian consented with alacrity to the brilliant double match. Like Charles of France, he too awaited his coronation by the Pontiff, as Holy Roman Emperor. With Rome's participation in the League of Venice, surely that gesture, to which Maximilian had set his heart, could not be long delayed, whereupon he and Ferdinand would command Italy between them. The emperor considered that he, not a French king, was the true champion of Christendom who by right must lead all Europe in a crusade against the Turk. He dreamed lavishly, seeing himself as head of a universal monarchy. We know, from a letter he later wrote to his more level-headed daughter Margaret, that this did not exclude Maximilian from ultimate election to the Papacy itself. He told her that Ferdinand favoured the proposition. Some naïvety there!

In Naples, Charles naturally became aware of the formation of the League of Venice. He was caught uncomfortably far from home at the foot of Italy and without an ally—a devastating turn of events. Ludovico of Milan had betrayed him; Maximilian, to whose son he had restored territory in Flanders, likewise. Finally there was Ferdinand—whose claim to contested provinces in the Pyrenees he had graciously accepted—organizing the entire conspiracy. Charles wisely concluded that he should make good his extrication while he could, delaying in Rome only long enough for the Pope to anoint him king of this Neapolitan fief and returning another day to deliver a proper lesson to Italy. The putative crusader began his retreat as an army of the league assembled in the north to confront him. Meanwhile Gonsalvo de Córdoba made swift work of cleansing Naples of the enemy and leading Ferrantino back to his throne. Perhaps the Turk alone could see the joke.

What of the Pope? Alexander would not this time expose himself as an instrument of Charles's plans, despite an offer of 150,000 ducats in return for legitimizing the latter's annexation of Naples. But he lacked sufficient troops to defend Rome, since the Colonna and Orsini families, its traditional guardians, still adhered to the French king. In the event, a farcical game of hide and seek transpired. As Charles entered Rome to a cold welcome Alexander took off to Orvieto, traditionally a papal stronghold. Orvieto lay on the French line of retreat and Charles hastened to catch the Pope there. Before he arrived Alexander was away again, this time to Perugia, still in the Papal States. The city was beyond French reach, though no safe harbour for Alexander, not with the Baglioni family in tyrannical control—they hated him. By now Charles feared to waste further time. A punishing forced march along the Apennines faced his troops.

They had gathered so much booty in the shape of artistic treasures and other plunder as to require a baggage train of mules a mile in length. At Fornovo, half-way between Bologna and Milan, the major Italian battalions mustered in readiness for the French. They were commanded by Francesco Gonzaga, Duke of Mantua and husband of that other redoubtable Este sister Isabella. The French army, its pride gone, its Swiss and other hirelings homesick and deserting, should have proved an easy opponent. Gonzaga, however, held his fire pending the arrival of Maximilian with his Germans, and thus permitted the enemy time to rest and regroup. But Maximilian never arrived, so on 6 July 1495 Gonzaga engaged battle alone. The action proved indecisive, with heavy casualties on both sides. Most of the French scurried home in disorder via Piacenza and over the Alps, to leave their store of plunder behind and turn the entire campaign into a fiasco.

Maximilian had intended to lead as the supreme army commander, only to find himself detained at Worms where the Reichstag, typically, consumed weeks in debating whether or not to vote him the funds to raise a force: once again, no laurels for the head of the Holy Roman Empire. Nevertheless Italy gained the realization that the French, despite their superiority in arms and their long military tradition, were not invincible. On their side no Italian had had cause to put a fully equipped army in the field for the previous forty years. Nothing except the false Turkish alarm at Otranto in 1460 had disturbed their private rivalries during that period. Sadly, the peninsula would now be as Savonarola had foretold, and suffer the crush of foreign domination for centuries to come. The French returned within the decade.

Still, political domination could not impair Italy's own cultural as-cendancy over Europe. The French, the Germans, the Spanish, all fell captive to Italy's creed of humanist, artistic freedom. The true victor of the wars of aggression beginning with Charles VIII was the Renaissance.

Ferdinand could in 1495 afford the greatest satisfaction. He had not so much pushed Spain into first place in the question of Italy, as raised the stature of his own Aragonese kingdom to the position to which it always aspired: a Mediterranean power poised to overtake Venice and lead the challenge against the Turks where they felt all-powerful, on water. His father, who could barely hold Aragon itself except by com-promise with its constantly disaffecting provinces, would have revelled in the achievement. It is impossible to escape the conclusion that so far as Ferdinand saw the disposition of strength it lay here, in this inland sea, and not in that western ocean which obsessed the Portuguese and involved Castile in costly maritime adventures that seemed only to end in a question mark. The League of Venice had yielded immediate tangible results by humiliating France. Ferdinand already knew that dividends from the Indies, if any, would not flow for years, perhaps decades.

The ink was hardly dry on the Venice pact when an event occurred on faraway Hispaniola to open a new era in the affairs of humankind—the first organized resistance of the aborigines against the white man's penetration of their soil. Some natives had deduced that these visitors who materalized in giant winged canoes from nowhere, demanding gold, bellowing thunder from their machines and ordering them to serve, were an evil power. An important *cacique* was challenging their right of entry. The mood had changed drastically since the Discoverer made his first landfall that October day in 1492 on the tiny island of San Salvador to a friendly reception from its surprised, timid inhabitants. It was now the end of March 1495. Since leaving Europe on his second voyage eighteen months earlier Columbus for his part had become a man much chastened by experience.

He was disappointed in not having the support of his brother Bartholomew on this voyage; only the much younger Diego was with him. Bartholomew, it will be recalled, had been deputed to secure the patronage of King Charles of France or Henry VII of England during the long interval before Ferdinand and Isabella gave their consent. Not having met with success, Bartholomew was instead retained as cartographer by Anne of Beaujeu at Fontainebleau. He had not yet returned to Spain. Christopher consequently left a letter for Bartholomew at Seville, with the request that he join the expedition at Hispaniola. Full navigational instructions were included.

Considering the magnitude of the undertaking, the most meticulous preparations had been required. The expedition was intended to be self-supporting for six months and the monarchs placed the task of fitting it out in the charge of Juan Rodriguez de Fonseca, Archdeacon of Seville. This man was beginning a long career of involvement with the Indies as personal counsellor to their Majesties, and whatever Fonseca might lack in expertise he made up in absolute devotion to the letter of his assignment, regularly referring difficulties with Columbus for royal arbitration. As a consequence the Discoverer, still the august admiral, champed at every delay. He regarded Fonseca as an enemy of the enterprise. In his mind the priest was deliberately frustrating progress, easily said when Columbus himself was absent from Cadiz for a large part of the time. Some of the vessels, regular Noah's arks, took on horses and farm animals, savage dogs to terrify obstreperous natives, cats and chickens. They shipped salted meats, flour to make biscuit, charcoal, seed and roots for planting, crossbows, muskets and small field guns, together with two years' supply of wine. Stories now being retailed of the easy pickings to be had in the Indies were such that far more volunteers sought enlistment than could be accommodated. Columbus convinced himself also that dishonest trade was transacted at Cadiz. He later complained of the inferior breed of horses (mounts for a detachment of lancers) and leaking barrels. The wine turned sour during the voyage.

The fulsome reception everywhere accorded him while he travelled about Spain had certainly turned the mariner's head. He had regularly attended court to advise the sovereigns on their negotiations with the Pope for a bull favouring Spain over Portugal. Ever the devout Catholic, he made a pilgrimage to Guadaloupe, sacred for the appearance of the Virgin to a cowherd and associated with a victory over the Moors. The two sons of Columbus were now enrolled in royal service as pages to the Infante Juan while he himself affected the comportment of a nobleman, with a coat of arms and a mysterious signature written in the form of a pyramid. He wove an aureole round his name, which could translate as 'bearer of Christ', St Christopher being the patron saint of travellers. Great ceremony, including an escort of Venetian galleys, accompanied the fleet's auspicious departure from Cadiz when it sailed in September 1493.

Sadly, among the casualties of this catastrophic second expedition we must count the leader's own log. Its non-survival, not even in the form known to us in the case of the earlier voyage, impairs the fullest assessment of the results. Eye-witness reports are not however lacking, for a detailed record was made by Michele de Cuneo, a childhood intimate from Genoa, who sailed purely for the experience without signing as a member of the company. His constituted a vivid, personal narrative undistorted by special interest, essential for checking against the accounts given by the surgeon, Diego Chanca, and others. Columbus's flagship, registered as another Santa Maria though generally called the Mariaga-lante, was captained by Antonio de Torres, the man assumed to be second-in-command. Torres governed Las Palmas in Grand Canary for Queen Isabella when Columbus briefly rested there at the outset of his first voyage. Mariagalante carried the heaviest cargo. Another craft bobbing in the waves was none other than faithful little Niña, battle-scarred from the previous venture, albeit without a Pinzón. That family was not represented this time.

Though much maligned, Fonseca had no cause for self-reproach in spending five months to organize those seventeen ships for the voyage. It was a feat. Each vessel carried sealed instructions should it lose the convoy. Strikingly, the admiral kept them all together without mishap. As before, first port of call was Gomera in the Canaries, colourfully decked out in the admiral's honour by its governor, the widow who, according to Cuneo, had been Columbus's inamorata.

His primary destination would of course be Navidad in Hispaniola, to

Ferdinand and Isabella of Spain adoring the Virgin with their eldest children Prince Juan and Princess Isabella, both of whom predeceased them.
Representation also of Saints Thomas Aquinas and Dominic

Alfonso of Portugal kneels in veneration of St. Vincent. His heir Prince John behind him with Prince Henry the Navigator

Christopher Columbus. Posthumous portrait attributed to Sebastiano del Piombo

Pope Alexander VI. Detail from Pinturicchio's Resurrection fresco in the Vatican

Columbus taking leave of Ferdinand and Isabella at Palos in 1492. Idealized in an engraving of 1594. The monarchs were not present

ALEXANDER EPISCOPUS

SERVUS SERUORUM DEI

Cariſſimo in Chriſto filio Ferdinando Regi:
& Cariſſimæ in Chriſto filiæ Eliſabeth
Reginæ Caſtellæ , Legionis , Ara-
gonum , Siciliæ , & Granatæ,
illuſtribus , Salutem , &
Apoſtolicam bene-
dictionem .

INter cetera divinę Majeſtati benepla-
cita opera , & cordis noſtri deſiderabi-
lia , illud profecto potiſſimum extitit , ut
fides Catholica, Chriſtiana religio , noſtris
præſertim temporibus exaltetur , ac ubili-
bet amplietur , & dilatetur , animarumq.
ſalus procuretur , ac barbaricę nationes
deprimantur , & ad fidem ipſam reducan-
tur . Unde cum ad hanc ſacram Petri Se-
dem Divina favente clementia (meritis
licet imparibus) evecti fuerimus , cogno-
ſcentes vos tamquam veros Catholicos
Reges , & Principes , quales ſemper fuiſſe
novimus , & a vobis pręclare geſta toti
pene jam Orbi notiſſima demonſtrant , ne-
dum id exoptare, ſed omni conatu , ſtudio,
& diligentia , nullis laboribus , nullis im-
penſis, nulliſque parcendo periculis, etiam
proprium ſanguinem effundendo efficere ,
ac omnem animum veſtrum , omneſquᴇ

Beginning of an early printed version of the historic
bull of Alexander, *Inter cetera*, 1493, whereby all
undiscovered pagan lands were divided between Spain
and Portugal. The Treaty of Tordesillas, 1494, revised
the demarcation line westward, thus allocating Brazil
to Portugal

Dürer's portrait of Maximilian I, Holy
Roman Emperor, at the age of sixty, just
before his death. The pomegranate
symbolizes hope of eternal life. The
imperial arms bear the Order of the
Golden Fleece, inherited from Charles the
Bold, Duke of Burgundy

Detail from Michelangelo's David

Lorenzo de' Medici, the Magnificent. *Left*, polychromed stucco by Verrocchio's studio; *right*, by an unknown artist

A 1577 woodcut of Cesare Borgia

Portrait medallion of Lucrezia Borgia, aged 24, after her marriage to Alfonso d'Este. Reverse depicts a blindfold, bound Cupid

Execution on the pyre of Savonarola in the Piazza della Signoria, Florence, 1498. Unknown artist. The Duomo at left

Suppression of the Aztecs of Mexico by Cortés : burning of prisoners

Charles V, Holy Roman Emperor, attired
for battle. Titian's portrait

The young Cardinal della Rovere,
later Julius II, at audience with his
uncle, Pope Sixtus IV. Vatican
librarian Platina kneels. By Melozzo
da Forli, Vatican

relieve its little garrison under Diego de Harana and initiate the era of colonization. But not directly, for he now knew that the shortest distance across the Atlantic led to the Leeward Islands of the Lesser Antilles (as they were subsequently described), south-east of Hispaniola and in Columbus's optimism richly endowed with gold. Twenty-two days out of Gomera and the fleet arrived. This being a Sunday, Columbus named the first island they touched Dominica. Then his procedure of taking everything within reach into the formal ownership of the Castilian crown resumed.

Roughly six weeks passed in cruising through the chain of islands, all quickly prospected, blessed in the name of the Holy Mother and mapped on a chart as possessions of the Spanish Indies: Guadaloupe (redeeming a pledge given at the shrine), Montserrat, Antigua, Redonda, San Martin, San Jorge (St Kitts), Santa Anastasia, Santa Cruz (St Croix), the Virgin Islands group, so named in commemoration of St Ursula and the legendary 11,000 maidens massacred by the Huns.

Not surprisingly, the admiral's authority was tested to the full by his motley contingent of explorers. Soldiers ventured against orders far afield in quest of easy sex and booty, necessitating rescue by search parties. The *hidalgos* would not stoop to physical labour—they received no pay— and these were islands of the man-eating Caribs. Human bones were in gruesome evidence everywhere. Stray women, young girls mainly, some thickened in pregnancy or with babes in arms, indicated that they were of the Taino tribes escaping from Carib enslavement. Their babes would be eaten if caught. Older boys showed the marks of castration. Sinister as the scene appeared, eerie the silence (large dogs, strangely mute, roamed), what mainly perturbed the seamen was the absence of any sign that these were gold-bearing islands. Carib women, domiciled in their villages, were taken on board, ravished and discarded. But where were the Carib men? Gestures by the women explained their absence: out in their canoes hunting Tainos to bring home for dinner. Fishing was unknown.

It all argued for the greatest wariness. The Europeans hardly intended to make this hazardous voyage across the Atlantic to end up in a stew pot. Indeed, while at anchor at Santa Cruz the flagship was pelted by a shower of arrows, one of which mortally wounded a seaman. The volley came from a canoe containing several men and women with two slave boys so recently castrated their wounds were as yet unhealed. Cuneo described the incident:

We pursued the canoe in our boat. Fortunately we all had our shields, though an arrow pierced one of our crew who in three days was dead. We captured the Caribs, intending to bring them back to Europe. One of them, wounded by a spear, appeared as though he had died. We threw him back into the water but in fact he began swimming away frantically, so we caught him with a grappling iron and axed off his head.

Cuneo further relates how the admiral gave him 'a very beautiful Carib woman, naked as they all are', whom he took to his cabin for his pleasure. She resisted fiercely at first then cooperated 'with all the experience of a qualified whore'. How frequently such couplings took place we can but surmise. Certainly the first recorded epidemic of syphilis in Europe (the probable cause of Martin Alonso Pinzón's death) is dated from the return of this second expedition. The disease manifested itself among King Ferdinand's soldiers, veterans of the Indies, commanded by Gonsalvo de Córdoba in Sicily. Cuneo alone wrote frankly of sexual encounters during those early days in the Indies.

On 19 November 1493, when the fleet drew into Puerto Rico, called in the Arawak language Boriquen and by Columbus St John the Baptist, the admiral knew he must be just east of Hispaniola. They rested for two days, fished, took on fresh water and sailed onward again through the gale-swept straits to reach an unfamiliar stretch of its coast. Navidad would surely have grown into a solidly established township, contentedly awaiting his arrival, anticipating the stores he had brought, truly an outpost of Christian civilization. Columbus could barely suppress his impatience. He would replace and reward its faithful keepers and with others continue exploration of the Asian mainland starting from Cuba, which he considered too large to be an island and therefore an extremity of Cathay or Cipangu. There could well be a meeting with the Great Khan. Poor Columbus already lagged behind the times. Few European scholars still entertained the idea that China and Japan lay in these regions. Indeed, the expression 'New World' was already current. It appeared this same November written by Pietro Martire d'Anghiera, the Italian humanist employed at the Spanish court, in a letter to Ascanio Sforza, the cardinal bribed for his vote by Alexander VI but already the Pope's enemy.

The imagination of Columbus leapt ahead to a joyful reunion with Diego de Harana and to the accounting the royal representatives on Navidad, Gutiérrez and Escobado, would render of the gold and spices accumulated in the interval. The reality proved otherwise. As the fleet closed in on Navidad they beheld a ghost town: no trace of people, Indian or European, and only the charred remains of the fort erected out of the wrecked *Santa Maria* as evidence of a previous existence. Columbus sent a detachment forward to reconnoitre. It came upon a macabre sight—four decomposed bodies, two of them showing beards. These could only belong to Europeans; the natives did not grow beards.

But there was life. Some Caribs drew their canoe alongside the flagship and demanded to speak with the admiral, who was known to them. The two races could communicate better now. A Taino brought to Europe on the previous voyage and baptized was returning home to serve as a tolerable interpreter. When satisfied as to Columbus's identity the Indians told their sorry tale. He remembered their *cacique* Guacanagari? He is my friend, replied Columbus. Apparently Guacanagari had led his people into battle against a rival, a savage *cacique* named Caonobo, to defend the European beachhead but had been defeated. Caonobo thereupon destroyed Navidad together with its inhabitants. Guacanagari had escaped. All this was related as occurring because of strife within the European camp. Gutierrez had deserted the post to head a band of Spaniards in a foray for this yellow metal seemingly so important to them, and of course to seize women. Yes, they too were slaughtered. No Europeans remained alive. So the Caribs, who previously had shown their amenable side, could indeed be as fierce as Columbus had been warned.

A pall descended upon the enterprise, followed by fierce recrimination. The leader's assurances of friendly inhabitants, divine protection, good living, were revealed as a fraud. The grandees, vociferously supported by the priests, were particularly incensed. They wished to track Guacanagari down, execute him for treachery and take every Carib they found into slavery. Columbus would not have it. They must proceed as originally directed, settle down, plant their crops, convert the heathen and teach him the virtues of honest toil. Theirs must be a peaceful occupation. Only those Indians refusing to work diligently, or scorning baptism, should be enslaved. That was the civilized Christian way.

Against further protests he declared his determination never to desert Hispaniola. Somewhere in the interior, which he knew as Cibao, enough gold existed to assuage discontent and provide handsome revenue for their sovereigns. He, Christopher Columbus, was their appointed viceroy and he intended to rule justly, as commanded. Brave words, but they disguised a profoundly discomfited leader uncertain of loyalty in the angry ranks.

Guacanagari, it transpired, was in hiding. Columbus ordered a party, including Chanca the surgeon, to take a native who would guide them to the *cacique's* settlement. They found the chief lying on a bed of reeds slung between two posts—these were the people who taught the seaman's world the virtues of the hammock. Ostensibly incapacitated by a wound in his leg, which was bandaged, Guacanagari delivered himself of a somewhat confused account of the happenings, and how they terminated in a massacre. Chanca examined the wound, reluctantly uncovered, and it proved to be trivial, almost nonexistent. Still Columbus would not have the man executed. Instead he despatched an invitation to Guacanagari to visit him, which the other accepted, though the sight of the horses hardly reassured him. He decided they fed on human flesh. On another occasion, when Columbus sent the *cacique* a message, his village was found to be abandoned.

Navidad, he now concluded, could never have survived as a suitable colony for Europeans anyway, it was too exposed to the elements. He sailed eastward in search of a bay offering good shelter and fresh water. The location chosen was given the name Isabella, in honour of the queen. Trees were felled, and the carpenters hammered rudimentary housing together in the plan of a square, for greater protection. Columbus took a larger structure for his own use as viceroy's residence, and in the centre they built a chapel. A few of the *hidalgos* reluctantly put their hands to building and planting, much to the disgust of other grandees. This was January 1494. One day, Columbus vowed, this encampment would grow into a second Cadiz.

More immediately, Isabella would prove a graveyard. The stock of provisions in no way equalled the requirement. Chanca's medicines ran dangerously low. Cattle and horses died, native workers ran away at the first opportunity, morale sank. With disillusionment sapping the endeavour, Columbus counted the mouths he had to feed and realized the expedition had been launched on too ambitious a scale. Until the crops ripened they would suffer hunger. Some of his men had already fallen ill through eating poisonous fruit and suspect fish. It would all come right in the end, of that he was convinced, although nothing would help more than an early discovery of abundant gold. Cibao beckoned.

A detachment was organized for the trek inland to find the deposits of which the Indians, who were to do the actual mining, spoke. The group scrambled its way across the rivers and over hazardous rock slopes, through dense rain forests and into marsh, dragging their horses and encouraging the natives along with beatings and, in one case, cutting off a man's ears. Here at last they struck gold. Nuggets of it the size of beans gleamed out of the heavy soil. The guides and labourers toiled away for four weeks, panning and dredging to bring out a considerable hoard—at any rate enough to raise everyone's expectations for the future. Columbus now decided the time was propitious for Antonio de Torres to set sail for Spain, in command of twelve of their vessels. He must bring the booty to the notice of the monarchs, inform them of the magnificent progress achieved, and implore the shipment of more supplies without delay. Carrying a letter from the viceroy detailing all particulars, Torres also transported human booty restrained in manacles—slaves, if the truth be told, though Columbus maintained they were intended to learn Castilian and return as interpreters.

Thus in one important respect at least the entire enterprise had lost its original exalted purpose. Columbus had proclaimed the endeavour at its outset to include the noble mission of spreading Christianity over the Indies and taking pagan Asia within the orbit of civilization, culminating in a crossing of the continent on a victorious crusade for the liberation of Jerusalem. It was the usual pretext to sanctify many a mean intention in those days. He had seen himself as the instrument joining the Catholic Monarchs in brotherhood with the mighty rulers believed to exist in palaces set in magnificent cities. The possibility was by no means rejected even now. But he had also promised the king and queen concrete rewards for their patronage, and his thoughts settled ever more purposefully on those two baser elements of civilized desire—treasure and slaves. In earlier times Columbus had voyaged to the Guinea coast of Africa and observed the profits of Portuguese exploration. Portugal disregarded actual colonization. It established fortified trading posts specifically for the bartering of European merchandise for gold, slaves and spices. Lisbon flourished as no other city as a consequence. The memory came to affect the Discoverer's judgment, rendering him more calculating, less scrupulous, and erratic.

A wiser leader would have hesitated before sending gold of such paucity. Assayed at Cadiz to the value of 30,000 ducats, this was hardly a harvest to excite a king. As for the natives, of whom only twenty-six survived the voyage, had they been baptized? (They had not.) If yes, this was not Christian treatment. If no, Columbus had ignored the queen's request for kindness to the heathen, for these people were now her subjects. In delivering the list of necessities Torres had been instructed to remain silent on Navidad's fate but to stress that everything despatched from Spain to strengthen the enterprise would be handsomely repaid in gold and a continuous supply of Carib slaves. The latter detail was not in the least welcome to Isabella's ears.

Yet Columbus judged the situation so improved he could safely move on to Cuba with three of the remaining five caravels. He therefore allocated 500 of the strongest men to continue exploration in the hills of Hispaniola while he delegated his brother Diego to command the rest, assisted by Friar Buil, a Benedictine monk so far unemployed as a baptizer. Why Diego? Surely he was too mild for such a responsibility. According to Cuneo, his ambitions lay elsewhere than as a leader, since he expressed a desire for the priesthood. Perhaps Diego alone merited the viceroy's absolute trust: four Spanish desperadoes were already clamped in irons and confined to the flagship, which was now anchored in Isabella Bay to serve as a prison.

During the Discoverer's five-month absence from his base at Isabella the situation there gradually slid towards anarchy. Illness and deprivation extracted their price in a mutiny. Those working the deposits in Cibao were led by Alonso de Hojeda, a strong personality (he later commanded a separate expedition which reached Venezuela), and were equally affected by the severe conditions. Hojeda's Indian labourers, already enfeebled, died at an appalling rate. They starved, or contracted typhus, smallpox and other infections that had been imported by the Europeans as a kind of grim exchange for the syphilis they were destined to take away. In the event Hojeda, himself sick, brought his men back to base virtually empty-handed. The sorry-looking prospectors clamoured for home.

Luckily Columbus knew little of this. Selecting some veterans of his first voyage, with Juan de la Cosa to map the coastline and his sardonic friend Cuneo for Italian companionship, he set sail for Cuba aboard little Niña. He was once again the intrepid explorer, again high in optimism and grandiose plans. Columbus never completed the circumnavigation of the island and so could not be disabused of his contention that Cuba broadened into continental Asia, probably southern China. Constantly seeking clues from holy writ, he defeated his own navigational instincts, which could be superb, by identifying Old Testament scenes wherever he journeyed. Thus Cibao in Hispaniola might well be the Ophir associated with the super-abundance of gold rendered to King Solomon of Ancient Israel. And the beauties of Cuba, its stately palms and aromatic plants, its many varieties of edible fruits, and the glory of flamingos in flight, all told him that the Garden of Eden could be located somewhere in these parts (and confirmed absolutely on his third voyage!). Indeed, he nominated a group of tiny islands, today a mangrove swamp, the Queen's Garden. They sailed along the southern shore of Cuba without mishap, all the natives encountered returning goodwill with goodwill. They gratefully accepted the usual gifts proffered by the white man—hawks' bells, woollen caps, coloured glass. These were Taino Indians of a sturdy stock, meat-eaters who slaughtered the docile non-barking dogs for food. They demonstrated how they caught turtles. Tame sucking fish held by a long leash fastened themselves on to the turtles and in they came. Food was shared with the seamen, though when questioned about gold the natives shook their heads with incomprehension. Vaguely pointing southward across the sea they spoke of a rich island. Off the treasure-seekers went again, in rough water and against fierce trade winds, to discover Jamaica.

It was not a happy experience. The Jamaican Arawaks resisted entry into what is now St Ann's Bay, threatening an ugly situation. They could only be dispersed with the aid of cross-bows assisted by the explorers' own savage dogs. And of gold, not a trace. Three months had now gone by on this wild-goose chase, sometimes with insufficient water to ration the crews even to a cupful a day. Yet they resolutely sailed back to Cuba and continued ever westward, endlessly, endlessly reconnoitring the land in desperate search for the whereabouts of China. Occasionally a sailor would hallucinate, professing to see fully-clothed men in white, and the tracks of large animals such as could only exist in the wildest imagination.

Time seemed to be standing still for Columbus, the world revolving around him. Guided by hasty calculations of his longitude, totally inaccurate as it happened, he reckoned they had sailed half-way round the globe since leaving the Canaries, and as Cuba was too extensive to form an island they must indeed be coasting along the immense shore-line of China. His men refused to believe it, but they were exhausted by their privations and lack of sleep, and so humoured him. This was China, they accepted, and on his insistence each man took an oath on it. Only then would he give the order to turn about and begin the task of coaxing the three little ships into the more familiar waters circling Hispaniola.

August was already upon them when the admiral himself began to develop strange symptoms. He had long battled against chronic arthritis, but these signs were mental, and accompanied by a high fever. He could not properly concentrate or recall conversations just a few minutes old. During one spasm he fell into a coma, in others he complained of being unable to see. No doubt about it, Columbus was breaking under the strain of stretched nerves. Such was his malady as described in his son Ferdinand's biography, which states how others took command as the caravels, all in urgent need of overhaul, finally hove to in Isabella Bay on 29 September 1494.

Good news now: Bartholomew, not seen by his brother Christopher for six years, was there to welcome them and help restore the admiral's health. The king and queen had sent Bartholomew off with their blessing and plentiful supplies in five caravels for the garrison. It was the best medicine for the sick leader. This brother was businesslike, and absolutely dependable. He listened to no tales and told none. The bad news, however, was the chaos reigning in the pathetic little version of a transatlantic Cadiz. Friar Buil, supposedly Diego's deputy, had conspired with a substantial disaffected group to desert and, commandeering three of the new seaworthy vessels brought by Bartholomew, they were embarked for home.

Incapable of firmness, Diego was left powerless while skirmishes broke out between Spaniards and Indians. Caonobó, the warrior *cacique*, had combined with others to place the life of every European in peril, armed though he might be. In fact, Caonobó had achieved the inconceivable: he had mobilized a force united in their hatred of the conqueror. The 250,000 mainly Caribs believed to inhabit Hispaniola at that time were generally at each other's throats. Even now many of them eluded Caonobó and dutifully performed for the Europeans without protest. Still, Diego faced a coordinated threat to wipe the Spaniards off the landscape.

The challenge acted upon Columbus to contribute to his cure. Together with Bartholomew and Hojeda he led 200 men into the interior. They had their hounds and plenty of fire power in the shape of arquebuses. Lancers mounted on their fresh horses preceded the attack. Caonobó was captured and his army routed. This was the battle fought just as the League of Venice had formed to defeat the French. Historians may well continue to debate which would go down as the more significant victory. The pacification of Hispaniola henceforth proceeded apace, by a strategy of terror—the sight of a horse was alone enough to reduce some natives to suicide.

Antonio de Torres had by this time recrossed the Atlantic with more supplies and, in concession to humanity's other requirement for permanent, stable residence, the first European women. Masculine demand for sexual partners had finally been accorded its right. Torres also brought instructions for the admiral. He was to return home and advise on future plans in the light of Portuguese claims written into the treaty of Tordesillas. Did a line 270 leagues further than the original 100 leagues to the west of the Azores cut into the Indies? However, Columbus decided his presence was essential for creating more strong-points and thoroughly prospecting Cibao, so he sent home a deputy in his stead. A year passed in imposing total dominion over Hispaniola and in accumulating a very considerable quantity of gold.

Yet Columbus erred in not returning home when requested. Friar Buil and the other malcontents had wasted no time in reporting the admiral's shortcomings as viceroy, his arrogance, and the abysmal condition of the colony. It was in fact no secret in Spain that all was not as it should be, but quite the reverse. To Columbus's dismay, a royal inspector arrived, with powers to investigate the situation on behalf of the sovereigns. He gave the impression of being superior to Columbus, and the latter responded badly, diagnosing intrigue reaching to the highest circles of the court.

The inspector could not have chosen a more inauspicious time to appear, for the endeavour had lately suffered a further disaster, contributed as it happened by the forces of nature. In June a fearful gale suddenly blew in from the Atlantic and tore a devastating path through the island, uprooting trees, washing away structures and flooding the land as rain lashed down in torrents. '*Huracán!*' cried the natives, speeding off in search of shelter. The swollen tide sent three ships keeling over in the harbour, with all hands lost. We are now familiar with the impact of these visitations, which regularly forge destruction upon the eastern seaboard of the Americas. But for this expedition of Columbus the cyclone was a frightening phenomenon. Could it be divine retribution for the genocidal treatment meted out to the simple barbarians?

In the course of that first year of Hispaniola's total subjugation every Indian over the age of fourteen was 'taxed' four hawks' bells of gold dust, with the *caciques* delivering an additional collective quantity. Those deserting were hunted down and killed. Las Casas wrote of the torture and executions: 'When each day they saw how their people perished from the inhuman cruelty of the Spaniards, how they were ridden down by horses, torn asunder and eaten by dogs . . . the Indians resigned themselves to their fate and gave themselves over to their enemies without a struggle.' Little wonder that in the four years since this place first came into the possession of the Spanish crown almost half of them had died; in another four years, although the treatment improved, and the yields demanded were reduced under pressure from home, the Indian population again dropped by half. A small reservation in the Dominican Republic now confines their few descendants. Chief Caonobó died in fetters on a caravel transporting him to Spain.

Nowhere, in any statement attributed to him, did Columbus express compassion for these people, for in his culture their enslavement was a Christian right. In resisting the power vested in him by his royal masters they spurned the grace of God. Christendom still dictated such rules, as did Islam. Something must have told him, however, as he departed Hispaniola in March 1496, aboard *Niña*, and sailing in tandem with one other vessel, that his days as a national hero were over, lost in a whirlpool of hardships, conflicts, false dawns and greed. Few good words were being uttered of his discoveries at the court of Ferdinand and Isabella, of that he was convinced. And he feared the cancellation of the entire endeavour as a lost cause. Nevertheless he refused to admit defeat.

One admission: his excess of pride. We do not know enough about the state of his mind, though indication is provided by his adoption of an attire quite other than that proclaiming his status as Viceroy and Admiral of the Ocean Sea. Henceforth, whenever he appeared in public the Discoverer chose to dress in the sombre brown habit of a Franciscan friar. February 1495 saw the first auction of Indian slaves on the Lisbon market.

Chapter Eight

LEADERS IN THE HANDS OF FATE

hile Christopher Columbus floundered, in October 1495, beneath the weight of his responsibilities for imposing the Catholic Monarchs' peace upon Hispaniola as the starting point of colonization in the Indies, King John II of Portugal lay in his last agonies at Alvor in the Algarve. When death finally took him it was after a sea bath, the physicians' prescription for his dropsy. This sagacious ruler was known to his people as the 'perfect prince'. John had tolerated no nonsense from his arrogant nobility and refrained from interfering in the affairs of Castile, a practice ending disastrously for his predecessor on the Portuguese throne. He sought to avoid colonial rivalry with the neighbouring kingdom, though the determination with which Queen Isabella affected to assume her newly found authority in the Indies disturbed him. Ambiguities remained as to the exact identification of the lands across the Atlantic.

However, John considered the treaty of Tordesillas a satisfactory solution in the matter of exploration and ceased to concern Portugal directly with the western approaches. What had he to fear when Africa's entire oceanic coastline came within his sphere? The Portuguese would continue unimpeded round the Cape of Good Hope, seeking a route offering connection with the Indies where they were proven to exist, in the east. Spain respected Portugal's trading monopoly in Africa and all that stemmed therefrom. Conversely, Aragonese ships cruised possessively along the Mediterranean littoral of the Dark Continent, and if they could elude the Barbary pirates, thought John, good luck to them.

Tragedy had cheated John of a son and heir when the Portuguese Crown Prince Alfonso had died after a fall from his horse in 1491. This had occurred shortly after Alfonso's marriage to the Infanta Isabella, eldest daughter of the Spanish rulers. God granted near-divine privileges to royal families, but then punished their children with brief life-probability, through deliberate violence, unlucky accident or congenital disease—all suffered fatalistically as the price of kingship. A similar accident had struck down Maximilian's young wife Mary of Burgundy outside Bruges in 1481. King John's other son, his favourite, was illegitimate and barred from succession to the throne. He had therefore visualized Alfonso as progenitor of a union between the Iberian powers, with Portugal as the senior partner. Harmonious relations with Castile were its essential prerequisite. Some Castilian advisers of Queen Isabella on their side had strongly favoured such a combination even before Ferdinand contributed Aragon to the joint realm. They disliked their queen's consort then and whispered against him still.

Spain was seeking treasure, hitherto with no significant success, in the West Indies while Portugal's bounty from the yield of Sudanese gold pouring into Lisbon via the Guinea trading stations expanded from year to year. One fifth of it flowed directly into the royal coffers. Since the rounding of the Cape by Bartholomew Dias in 1488 John knew that territorial conquest in the Orient lay within Portugal's grasp, and would not transgress any treaty arrangements with Spain. His death in 1495 spared him knowledge of a challenge arising from other quarters.

It therefore fell to the new King of Portugal, John's brother-in-law Manuel, to license the voyage that revealed what the maps obscured and Venice dreaded—the sea route to India. Vasco da Gama sailed out of Lisbon on 8 July 1497 in command of four tiny ships. A tough warrior who since 1492 had preyed upon French merchantmen straying into Portuguese waters, and enriching himself thereby, Gama took fourteen weeks to reach the Cape. Once in the Indian Ocean he found he was not alone. Muslim seafarers ranged as far south as Mozambique. Indian craft lurked in that ocean too. Both were suspicious of his intentions, shots were exchanged and the hostile incident scattered the Arab dhows at Mombasa. Elsewhere on his landings, however, Gama lulled opposition away by offering the African primitives a looking-glass. They loved that article of another civilization's vanity; observing their reflection in the mirror they enjoyed the joke.

Little in motivation had altered since the mariners of Henry the Navigator first ventured forth sixty years before: cold acquisitiveness shrouded in a Christian pretext. The spoils known to be available in the Orient, an alliance with a fabled Christian king, conversion of the pagan, the reconquest of Jerusalem—all these combined to spur Vasco da Gama on his way. Already in King John's time individual Portuguese explorers had crossed the African jungle in search of Prester John. One of them, Pero da Covilham, penetrated as far as Ethiopia. He was said later to have touched the coast of India in an Arab vessel. Gama may have known of the feat, though Covilham himself never returned to Europe and the evidence is unclear. The immediate purpose of this latest expedition, however, was to capture spices at their source. Until now Arab ships carried the valuable produce to Egypt for trading with Venetian merchants and distribution at a huge premium throughout Europe, thus consolidating the economic power of the 'Most Serene Republic'. But what if Columbus, over there in Hispaniola, had really hopped the islands fringing the Asian mainland? What if his claim to have found Cathay were verified? Given the geographical incertitude inherent in the papal bulls (where did the West begin and the East end on a globe?), the discoveries of the Genoese explorer could well argue Spanish ownership of the Indies. Whatever the true situation, prudence urged the Portuguese craft on.

Gama dared lose no time in staking the claim. He stood his flotilla, its sails limp, off a river-mouth at Malindi, unsure where Providence might set his eastward course. The prospect looked awesome, for these deep waters evoked dread. His crews, ridden with scurvy, had grown mutinous. Fortunately, a Muslim scholar-navigator, Ahmad ibn-Majid, offered himself as pilot. Delaying no longer, Gama ploughed the dark, buffeting waves for twenty-three days. On 20 May 1498, breathing with relief, the survivors (a third of his 150 men died on the voyage) sailed into Calicut on the Malibar coast. Whatever Spain may have gathered to itself across the Atlantic, this was no *terra incognita* barren of civilization but India proper.

Calicut, ruled by a Hindu *zamorin*, revealed itself to Vasco da Gama as a hive of mercantile activity dominated by Muslims. Centuries of development beyond Christendom's reach, besides successive conquests, migrations and linguistic cross-fertilization, had crystallized into an Indian civilization as advanced in every respect as the explorer's own, and in some ways, of which he was woefully ignorant, superior. In fact, on being welcomed ashore by a great beating of drums, he prayed in a Hindu temple believing it to be a church. Islam had not yet spread its influence to the far south of the Indian sub-continent.

Without a notion of this land's history beyond the imaginative tales of Marco Polo, Gama knelt before the *zamorin* at some disadvantage. The gifts he brought as tokens of friendship from his European king could hardly impress such a chieftain. They were the usual shabby truck intended to propitiate a barbarian, but this man, bedecked in pearls and rubies, residing in a richly ornamented palace, would not be fooled by cheap tricks with a mirror. The Hindus understood trade, and the benefits and complications arising from it. Little wonder the local merchants notified the Portuguese that he had no business in these parts. They warned him off. Sensibly, he took the hint, departing after a stay of some weeks in the realization that force would be necessary to plant King Manuel's standard in India.

Nevertheless the latter felt by no means discouraged when Gama returned home at last in July 1499, having put in at the Azores for medicines in a vain attempt to save a dying shipmate specially dear to him—his brother. And despite the inauspicious nature of Gama's report, Manuel lost no time in proclaiming himself 'Lord of the Conquest, Navigation and Commerce of Ethiopia, Arabia, Persia and India'. Far from being an empty boast, to a large extent this was shortly to become a reality.

Already, too many summers had passed for Spain and Portugal to harvest the whole wide world beyond Europe as their private cornucopia. England and France did not inhabit another planet, nor had they been asleep. Brooding much of his time away in monastic retreat at Seville, Christopher Columbus meticulously compiled a report meanwhile on the results of his second voyage, emphasizing its achievements and the promising vista he could discern for large-scale settlement in the Indies with the consequent enrichment of his royal patrons. He guarded his trophies—articles of gold, exotic birds, a converted native decked out in coloured feathers and a crown to signify his high Carib rank—in readiness for a summons to court and the order to fit out a third expedition. It seemed long in coming.

During the interim argosies returning from regular visits to Hispaniola released hundreds of disappointed voyagers to haunt Seville and other harbours, scotching the Discoverer's assertions of gold-rich soil across the sea and substituting a version that lacked nothing in the meanness of its telling. They spoke as virtuous men injured by disease and mosquitoes and lazy savages reluctant to serve. Yet small quantities of gold were indeed being delivered to Seville, as well as Indian slaves for auction on the Lisbon market. Among those witnessing the scenes, French and English merchants as familiar with Seville and Lisbon as with their own home towns, and of course Italian mariners waiting to sign with a ship of any nationality, the inevitable questions arose. What had the Spanish

Pope actually divided between the Iberian kingdoms? Water? Sky? Weren't the elements God-given for all mankind? Simultaneously, other explorers, potential and actual, began looking to the possibilities. One of these, a Genoese of Venetian citizenship, claimed he had once visited Asia trading for spices, and was certain he could reach that continent again by sailing westward. The credentials of John Cabot may have been spurious, but they nevertheless persuaded Henry VII of England to license him to cross the Atlantic under the English flag.

Cabot set sail from Bristol in 1497 some weeks before Vasco da Gama departed from Lisbon. In a month he had made landfall on the North American coast, somewhere between Labrador and Maine, possibly Nova Scotia. Wherever, he called the place Asia. King Henry, not a markedly generous man, had financed only one vessel, the *Mayhew*, barely large enough to crew two dozen hands, among whom Cabot's more famous son Sebastian subsequently recorded himself as a member. They encountered not a single human being, nor could they exactly establish their location, but John Cabot nevertheless took possession in the name of his sponsor.

Such a claim for the voyage, more a boast than a conviction, failed to disturb the Hispanic monopoly as expressed at Tordesillas. And as a gesture placing England among the Atlantic powers it held little more significance in history than the appearance of the Norsemen along these coasts 500 years earlier. Cabot sailed again the following year with five ships, all of which encountered a fate remaining a mystery to this day, for none returned. However, Henry VII had signalled an alert: greed knew no frontiers. The secrets of transatlantic navigation ceased to belong to Spain alone. Isabella the Catholic could not prevent those waters from becoming a vast international hunting ground. Soon, Europeans would not encounter as fierce an opposition from the indigenous populations as they would from other Europeans.

To be sure, these matters had their connection with developments in the old continent, arising from the ill-disguised preoccupation of the Atlantic states with their ambitions nearer home. In brief, while Portugal, vaunting its prosperity, sought that bonding alliance with its Iberian neighbour, the Aragonese half of Spain indulged its traditional adventurism in Italy. Ferdinand could not keep his fingers out of the country. Besides, he was pledged to frustrate every threatening move the French made in that direction. Henry VII, though still not absolutely secure as King of England, courted respectability for his parvenu dynasty by endeavouring to join the quarrelling club. Old misunderstandings with France had not completely evaporated in England—would they ever?—and Henry played his hand as junior partner to Ferdinand. On their side the French, allied with Scotland, backed Perkin Warbeck, pretender to the Tudor throne.

With important issues of war and peace fixing Ferdinand's attentions upon Europe, his neglect of the Viceroy and Admiral of the Ocean Sea languishing at Seville was understandable. Columbus recognized perfectly how his endeavours commended themselves more fervently to the queen than to her consort, evidenced in the reports he sent back while abroad. These never failed to include the participation of God in the capacity of co-pilot, as it were, protecting his expeditions from disaster at sea and against the ubiquitous perils he confronted on land, or in guiding his judgment when a mere mortal would, unaided, falter. Ferdinand may well have suspected a touch of religious mania in the despatches. Not so Isabella. She understood. To her, life being a permanent crusade, everything undertaken on her behalf must reflect the Christian imperative.

Columbus worried deeply lest the king and queen forget him. His brother Bartholomew, able though he might be, could not be left indefinitely in command of Hispaniola as if it were some tranquil, blossoming island in the Mediterranean. His tenancy of the governor's residence was purely a provisional arrangement, and the rough men braving the wilds there were unlikely to endure it with any tolerance. Bartholomew's warrant as the viceroy's deputy still awaited an official imprimatur. More, the tales circulated by Columbus's enemies regarding the quality of his own administration of the Indies had manifestly succeeded in undermining the confidence of the court. A royal caprice could lose him everything, the material fruits of his endeavours no less than his august appointment.

Thus had winter 1496 dragged over to spring 1497, yet still without decision on a third voyage. Would he ever sail again, he fretted? Indeed he would, for in the summer of 1497 Vasco da Gama departed Lisbon, his intended destination still a well-guarded secret. Anxiety thereupon jolted the advisers of Isabella and Ferdinand. Perhaps the Portuguese explorer was embarked upon a voyage encroaching upon their preserve. Prevarication therefore ceased. Columbus received his authorization at last.

We return to the situation on Hispaniola. Conditions there had gone from bad to worse. Bartholomew, as deputy governor in his brother's absence, found the maintenance of control beyond his powers when the man appointed chief magistrate by Christopher, Francisco Roldán, led a rebellion against 'Genoese' rule. Betaking himself with seventy disenchanted settlers to a stretch of territory in Hispaniola's south-west, and as it were declaring independence, Roldán offered its native inhabitants release from forced labour provided they acknowledged his rule. Of course, they would gladly agree to anything removing the whiplash from their backs. At this time Diego, youngest Columbus brother, had resumed charge at Hispaniola, for Bartholomew was engaged, on Christopher's order, in establishing another beachhead—it would be the third—at a place in the south more adequately sheltered from the Atlantic storms. This location, well chosen, detained Bartholomew for months in its reinforcement for permanent occupation. Named Santo Domingo, the settlement took sturdy root. In fact it remained the base of Spanish-American colonization for the next sixty years, and flourishes still as capital city of the present-day Republic of Dominica. Bartholomew's absence there allowed Roldán the opportunity for his revolt. By way of justification, he had received intimation from the royal inspector lately in Hispaniola falsely alleging that the era of the Columbus family was ended. The man declared that Christopher no longer enjoyed the sovereigns' favour.

His grievances assuaged by confirmation from those sovereigns of his rights and offices, Columbus was at length enabled to sail again on 30 May 1498. Two years had passed since he had returned from his second voyage. He commanded six caravels, their crews falling somewhat from the standard expected by a man perceiving himself as a messenger from Christ. There were some who had emerged from the jails with a free pardon as reward for enlistment. Others looked forward to a life's ease among delectable women in a moral borderland. A time-keeper endowed with supernatural powers would have noted the date as ten days after Gama's arrival at Calicut in India.

For Columbus, everything he cherished depended upon this third expedition: his reputation as an explorer, his family fortunes, his ranking in the hierarchy of royal favourites. A different route across the Atlantic tempted him this time. According to Aristotle, the world's subterranean riches lay most plentifully close to the Equator, a truth demonstrated surely in the treasure won by the Portuguese trading as far south as the Gulf of Guinea. Once clear of the Madeiras and Canaries, and having loaded stores, Columbus therefore divided his fleet, despatching a squadron of three ships direct to Hispaniola while he steered the rest down towards the Cape Verde Islands before squaring west. Seeking loyalty as much as seamanship in his choice of captains, he had placed Alonso de Carvajal in command of the advance squadron. Carvajal, an old friend, had sailed with Columbus on the second voyage and had laboured at Seville to speed up preparations for this one. The other two ships under Carvajal were entrusted to Giannetto Columbus, the admiral's cousin, and to a brother of his mistress Beatriz de Harana, whose own cousin Diego lay buried at Navidad.

As to himself, Columbus had studied Marco Polo's account of a strait dividing Asia into two great regions; it was the southern half that now attracted him. Four weeks out and his look-out sighted three hills in the distance—material evidence of the protection of the Holy Trinity. They approached an island and, confused once again in his longitudes, Columbus thankfully baptized the place Trinidad. So close, almost bumping the shoulder of the immense sub-continent of South America, yet the Discoverer failed to realize what lay within his grasp!

It was only the first miscalculation of this unhappy voyage. Carvajal, who seems to have been burdened with the worst of the coerced jailbirds, covered the ocean uneventfully enough but failed to locate Santo Domingo, their agreed destination. Embarrassment turned to horror when he discovered he had made landfall in Roldán's territory. Perceiving the danger, he made about and embarked on a frenzied exploration of Hispaniola's shoreline, though not before half his men, preferring to take terra firma where they found it, deserted Carvajal for the comforts proffered by Roldán.

The north-western corner of Trinidad faced a narrow strip of land just 7 miles away, a tongue of the country shortly to be designated Venezuela. It formed a gulf with the wide delta of the plenteous Orinoco. Columbus actually dropped anchor there and thus set foot in fact upon the continental mainland. Here, native women, all wearing necklaces of pearls, flocked around the ships. Those pearls were enough to convince Columbus and his seamen that they ploughed the waters of the Far East. Had they lingered, they might have gathered great quantities of the jewel, as valuable as gold in European hands; but the admiral, in the belief that he was navigating yet another island, refused to tarry. So they sailed along the jagged peninsula (to be called Paria), and then put back into the open sea. It was now time to make speed for Santo Domingo. Suddenly a single caravel hove in view. To the immense joy of Columbus it carried his brother Bartholomew. The deputy-governor of Hispaniola was in search of Carvajal's flotilla, sighted out at sea but moving in the wrong direction.

Now Columbus learned at first hand of the troubled history of Hispaniola since his departure in March 1496. Santo Domingo itself looked a creditable specimen of what he was straining to achieve in the Indies: an air of peaceful confidence, accommodation firmly built and well sheltered, docile Indians tending newly planted clearings under the direction of their Spanish masters. But the Roldán factor overhung the scene. Bartholomew informed his brother that the rebellious magistrate, too strong to dislodge, still defied the law and threatened the deposition of the Columbus family. Christopher decided to treat with him. It was a blunder, emphasizing the viceroy's limitations as an administrator.

Throughout the next year he offered terms, until Roldán extracted an undertaking from Columbus restoring his official position as law officer. He would also be permitted to retain possession of the area under his control complete with its native inhabitants. They could cultivate the land and extract its gold in serfdom—almost, though not quite, slavery. So it transpired that by this agreement, negotiated with a traitor, Columbus was no longer plenipotentiary in a region where he had demanded, and been awarded, exclusive rights. The 'treaty of peace' nullified the royal charter under which Columbus had begun his great enterprise in 1492.

Once this intelligence travelled back to the ears of the king and queen, their viceroy inevitably forfeited their trust, almost completely. Yet what could they do, given the harassment of affairs closer home, than order another enquiry? The man they chose for the task, the crown official Francisco de Bobadilla, was given the widest powers over the Indies. Only in August 1500 could he reach Santo Domingo, at the head of a fleet of six well-armed ships. A man of integrity, though haughty to an extreme, Bobadilla would not live to see Spain again.

In Spain the detractors of Columbus now outnumbered his supporters, to the degree that he was derided as 'lord of the Mosquitoes' even by men whose admiration he had formerly earned for his courage and spectacular seamanship. Having solved the Atlantic conundrum and opened up the territory for Castilian aggrandisement, the Discoveror seemed to belong to the past. Rival explorers, likewise bent upon wealth and glory, entered the scene and rendered whatever decisions Bobadilla might reach irrelevant.

They could not indulge in free-lance exploration without government sanction, but they nevertheless enjoyed the support of Juan de Fonseca ('the enemy' according to Christopher and his filial biographer Ferdinand Columbus). Fonseca had incurred the explorer's ire while provisioning the ships of his second voyage—that ambitious expedition which sailed from Cadiz in a blaze of confidence in September 1493. Now a bishop, and the sovereigns' personal representative on the councils dealing with all aspects of Las Indias, still so-called, Fonseca received for preservation the reports and charts regularly despatched by Columbus. He evinced little deference for the latter's prerogatives, never having tried to understand his complex character. Without hesitation he passed these confidential documents to Alonso de Hojeda, Columbus's old lieutenant in the crushing of the *caciques*' rebellion. Thus fortified, Hojeda was enabled to fit out an expedition and set a course directed principally to the pearl fisheries in the little Gulf of Paria. Shrewdly, he recruited Juan de la Cosa, cartographer of the transatlantic islands, to accompany him. The Indies, far from their original concept of a Columbus monopoly, were now spreading like a public feast before the eyes of any ambitious adventurer entrusted with the handling of a ship: Amerigo Vespucci, for another example.

Florentine by birth, Vespucci was the most enterprising member of Hojeda's expedition, perhaps also the most literate. An employee of the Medici bank for many years, latterly in Seville, he was long acquainted with Columbus, from whom he gained valuable nautical intelligence— mounting an expedition, how to elude becalming in the doldrums, and what might be expected on approaching the other side. Vespucci shipped with Hojeda from Cadiz in May 1494. Then, the crossing achieved, he detached his vessel from the convoy so as to explore on his own account. While Hojeda, benefiting from Columbus's experience, prospected along the land-mass adjacent to Trinidad, naming it Venezuela ('Little Venice', apparently because of the native dwellings erected on stilts), Vespucci probed its southerly shallows, claiming to have explored beyond the Amazon. He produced an account of his experience that adjusted his voyage retroactively as of 1497. Based on this fallacious datum, subsequent retailing of those same exploits gave him credit for discovering the mainland before Columbus. Furthermore, Vespucci featured in a 1504 publication as the star explorer of the New World as a whole. It was an early example of the unfamiliar and deceptive power of print. The work went into a score of swift editions, multiplying his fame accordingly. Columbus paled before Vespucci's reputation: identification of the entire continent soon attached to the latter's forename Amerigo. Vespucci at least buried finally the illusion that Las Indias bore some geographical relation to Cathay or Cipangu.

Hot in the wake of Hojeda and Vespucci, Vicente Yanez Pinzón, captain of *Niña* on her first voyage under Columbus and returning to Palos with the admiral, arrived in the Gulf of Paria. A question remains as to whether he made landfall on the Brazilian shore before any Portuguese mariner. Certainly he sailed up the Amazon to sample its fresh water nearly 100 miles inland. Before making for home Pinzon retraced his course to Hispaniola and other islands discovered during those heroic days with Columbus, to receive a kinder place in the history of oceanic exploration than his elder brother Martin Alonso.

One may be tempted to conclude that the Catholic Monarchs were allowing development in the Indies to slip out of their control. This was never the case with Queen Isabella, in whom conversion of the heathen ever occupied a foremost place in her heart. Moreover, by proclaiming an empire, she determined to preserve Castilian supremacy in the Iberian constellation of nations. On the other hand Ferdinand continued his more passive role in the progress of the oceanic endeavour. From the moment of the integration of Provence within the kingdom of France, Ferdinand's ears sharpened particularly when Aragon's traditional adversary threatened to usurp his country's strategic inheritance as a Mediterranean power. As already noted, nothing troubled Ferdinand so much as French designs on Italy. Hence his intimacy with the Spanish Pope, his sedulous wooing of Maximilian the Holy Roman Emperor, and the desirability of keeping alive England's hoary disputes with its cross-channel neighbour. Each of these would be of the greatest assistance in preventing France from taking Italy within its grasp. Surprisingly, France would not cease from driving a claim up that Sisyphean hill, despite repeatedly coming to grief in the process.

Suffering from a similar disease, Ferdinand could not be reconciled to the permanent abandonment of any region that had once been in the possession of his house. Naples particularly goaded his instinct for dressing rapacity as self-justification. It irked him that Naples, a kingdom comprising almost half the Italian peninsula and formerly joined with his own island kingdom of Sicily, existed as a separate state by virtue of illegitimacy within his family. The misdeed made Naples the property of Aragonese cousins whom Ferdinand despised. Nevertheless he could be a patient man, and happily his chase after a greater Aragon interlocked comfortably with Castilian interests. The French had come to the reluctant realization that Aragonese participation in the joint Spanish throne inevitably neutralized their own influence upon the affairs of Castile. Naples boasted some of the richest cornfields in Europe, whereas Spain hungered through dearth of cereals.

In drawing the strands together Ferdinand engaged the fate of all his four daughters. Their mother Queen Isabella impressed upon them the significance of their respective roles, to which they dutifully acquiesced. A husband for a princess of an important power must first be selected in the interests of the state. Whatever conjugal happiness issued from the match could only be incidental, a fortuitous luxury. While she still possessed them Isabella held her daughters close. The country had no fixed capital as yet, so the court was perpetually on the move. The girls were present at Granada for the ceremonial entrance of their parents in 1492. They travelled together as a family to Valladolid, where they spent much time, and to Barcelona, chief city of Aragon, and to Toledo. The long, arduous journey across the dusty, mountainous terrain for that memorable mission of piety to the shrine of Compostela kept them on the road for months. The sisters received an education that paid service to the humanist age—Pietro Martire, the Italian Renaissance scholar, tutored them—but the atmosphere they breathed was politics.

The youngest, Catherine, named after Isabella's English grandmother Catherine of Lancaster, celebrated her sixth birthday in the newly captured Alhambra at Granada. A shadow hung over the festivities and marred the day. Catherine's eldest sister, another Isabella, had recently returned to the household heavily veiled, a widow of twenty. It had been a brief marriage indeed, Isabella's to the Infante Alfonso, heir to King John of Portugal. The sudden bereavement inaugurated a pitiable succession of swift tragedies that would cross this family throughout the parents' lives. So much had depended upon the match, more than could be gained by a victorious army in the field, and no one knew this better than Ferdinand and his wife, except surely John of Portugal himself. A dark episode of regal history had haunted that monarch's reign since 1485. To render his crown secure John had forced himself to kill with his own hand his queen's elder brother. By so doing he staved off a powerful conspiracy of Portuguese nobles, but on his son Alfonso's accidental death the succession fell nonetheless to the queen's younger brother Manuel. This one would in due course claim his nephew Alfonso's Castilian widow Isabella for himself.

The healing process between Spain and Portugal had to be sustained, despite the conflicts already germinating in their scramble for overseas possessions. But the bereaved Isabella took a long period to acclimatize herself to the idea of sharing another Portuguese bed. She had given up hope of any existence for herself except one of pious contemplation in a convent of the Poor Clares.

Since the age of three little Catherine had been bespoken, and it amused her that her sisters already teased her by her future title, Princess of Wales. As long as she could remember, Catherine was destined for a life in England as consort to Henry VII's heir Prince Arthur. She understood enough now to realize she too must function as a pawn in the family power game against France, and as the youngest she must go to Spain's least significant ally, that cold northern island where the Tudor, whom some contended was not absolutely of the blood royal, had recently fought his way to the throne. She saw no reason to question the story given to her that this Prince Arthur's pedigree reached back to the gallant Arthur of the Round Table, for weren't all kings descended from such ancient heroes?

Henry VII would be the last to scorn a Spanish bride for his son, since he ached for respectability within royalty's magic circle. There lay something of a thieves' compact behind this betrothal of two innocent children. Arthur was not yet two. It sealed a treaty negotiated in 1489 whereby Henry and Ferdinand each agreed to guarantee the other's territorial aims in France. The English, having solemnly surrendered their right to the French throne, found it difficult to discard their practice of fishing in troubled Gallic waters, particularly when the French were dipping in their own.

For peace of mind regarding the future of their own house in Spain, the hopes of Ferdinand and Isabella reposed in their son Juan. As he grew to manhood the succession seemed assured. Juan's marriage at Burgos in 1497 to Margaret, Ghent-born daughter of Maximilian, cemented the alliance with the emperor forged by the League of Venice. In fact, Ferdinand made extra sure of it by pairing his second daughter Joanna with Maximilian's heir Philip of Burgundy, now ruling in the Netherlands. And this being a double marriage, tedious negotiations over suitable dowries were conveniently obviated. As for Margaret, she had little cause for complaint. Hadn't she endured a virtual kidnapping when the French took her away from Ghent for house-training as future queen to their Charles VIII, only to be rudely discarded as surplus to requirement (see p. 75) in favour of Anne of Brittany? Juan and Margaret made a handsome couple, auspicious for Spain, in their official residence at Salamanca, where the two sons of Christopher Columbus, Diego and Ferdinand, served as pages. And that left Maria, the fourth daughter of Ferdinand and Isabella, still unaccounted for. Four years senior to her sister Catherine, Maria awaited her turn, in reserve as it were, for some future combination to take the Hispanic destiny to another corner of

Europe. Alternatively, a mishap in the dynastic scheme could necessitate Maria's substitution for one of her sisters.

Were he to recover Naples, Ferdinand of Aragon's kingdom would scotch French competition and thrive almost unchallenged in the Mediterranean, dwarfing Genoa and outstripping Venice. He would stand as Christendom's true champion against Islam. Difficult though it might be to penetrate the maze of his devious thinking, we can comprehend why Ferdinand perused the reports emanating from the Indies somewhat cursorily. Those distant lands promised much but rendered little. Yet the intensity with which Ferdinand envisioned himself as master of Europe's inland sea can be gauged by his manipulation of his Borgia friend the Pope to grant to Catalonia (hence, Aragon) exclusive rights to establish trading posts along the Islamic North African littoral. This occurred in 1494, compensation after a fashion for Aragon to balance his wife's arrogation to Castile of all rights in the Indies. North Africa thus became a sub-section in the division of the entire globe among the three Iberian powers. East of Fez as far as Ferdinand would dare was appropriated as an Aragonese interest matching Portugal's exclusivity from Fez all the way down the African coast as far as Portugal could reach. Not long into the next century and Ferdinand converted his trading posts into actual conquests. The creeping annexation of the Maghreb shore was in train. Where might it terminate except in Egypt, still unconquered by the Turks and assuredly awaiting a 'protector'. Could there be a better jumping-off ground to snatch the Holy Land from the infidel? The world was heavily populated in those days with potential crusaders. If only noise could capture Jerusalem, as with Jericho of old, David's city would be Christian many times over.

However, tragedy would strike once again to interrupt Ferdinand's grandiose dream The Infanta Isabella, dissuaded by her mother from making her vows to the Poor Clares, finally agreed to marriage with Manuel, King John's successor in Portugal; though not before her God had put into the princess's head a demand that Manuel purge his country of the impurity from which her own had latterly cleansed itself, in 1492. He must expel the Jews. To this he consented, though with extreme reluctance. Manuel had inherited trusted Jewish counsellors from his predecessor, including the royal astronomer Abraham Zacuto, formerly Spanish, whose knowledge Columbus had turned to benefit for his transatlantic exploration. The Jewish question did not evoke so much Catholic passion in this country, and the Portuguese state council warned against the measure. Jews expelled from Spain in 1492 had been eagerly received in Islamic lands, especially Turkey. They were teaching the Muslims secrets that aided the enemies of Christendom. Their influence in Antwerp made their goodwill vital to Lisbon's further commercial expansion. Having itself granted refuge to large numbers of exiles driven from Spain, how could Portugal now follow that ferocious example? It could and it did.

The younger Isabella was duly delivered to her new husband in 1497 while the decree of expulsion from Portugal was being implemented. Professing Jews would be allowed until October of that year to depart, and any Christian discovered concealing one of them after that month would forfeit his property. The Jews themselves could take theirs away with them, but the full implementation of the decree carried zeal to an inhuman extreme: their children between the ages of four and twenty would be retained for compulsory baptism. Seizure of this entire younger generation began on the first day of Passover, March 1497, amid the protests of several bishops, and indeed of many other citizens. Ordinary people now defied the law, incurring severe punishment for hiding children and so enabling them to accompany their parents into exile. Such acts reversed Manuel's intention. He was using the children as bait to compel their parents' conversion. Many did so, though Bishop Fernando Coutinho, most vociferous of the protesters, wrote of scenes he personally witnessed of parents and children choosing martyrdom and dying together with a Hebrew prayer on their lips.

Further horrors: shipping ordered by King Manuel as transportation for the exiles was delayed so that finally some 20,000 Jews stood on Lisbon harbour, stranded without a passage. These were taken into custody and offered the alternatives: conversion at this twelfth hour or slavery as the king's property. Thousands chose servitude. But among those able to depart were two illustrious brothers of the Caro family, one of whom, Joseph, settled in Palestine where he produced the authoritative code of rabbinic law still in regular use. Another *émigré* was Zacuto himself. Many settled in Amsterdam, which thereby assumed a bustling 'Portuguese' atmosphere. Intervention by Pope Alexander, an act of true Christian compassion that has earned the Borgia redemption in the Jewish martyrology, gave those forcibly converted a further breathing space. Alexander brought them under papal protection, much to the indignation of the Dominicans. The friars inspired new persecutions, resulting in an unknown number of Jews killed before Manuel terminated the slaughter and punished the guilty.

A period of calm followed, until 1531, when the Medici Pope Clement

VII authorized the Inquisition in Portugal. The hunt for secret Jews (Marranos) was then resumed, and Portugal at last satisfied Spain as its equal in Christian diligence. Contemporaneously the Moors left in Spain, both the converted ones (Moriscos) and those openly Muslim, were being driven from this homeland through repression, forced conversion and social ostracism. So much for the Catholic Monarchs' promise of religious tolerance given on the surrender of Granada. Formal expulsion was yet to come.

On that day in 1497 when the Spanish rulers gave their widowed daughter Isabella in marriage to Manuel, they received news of the illness of the Crown Prince Juan in his residence at Salamanca. Together with his adoring wife Margaret Juan had maintained a truly Renaissance establishment there, close to a university renowned for its poets and scholarship and deeply influenced by the humanism emanating from Italy. Ferdinand and Isabella hastened directly from their daughter's nuptials to Salamanca. Too late. Their only son was dead. Thus did fate play its tricks upon princes. They had allowed their hopes to build a great kingdom around Juan: from his mother, Castile and an Atlantic empire; from his father, Aragon and a grand Mediterranean design. Now a shroud sufficed.

But Margaret was with child. Perhaps Juan's son . . . ? They dared not utter the thought, for Margaret also was in a state of shock. And when her babe was born, prematurely, it too was lifeless. Juan's seed died with him. This gave the Spanish succession to Manuel's Queen Isabella, their eldest daughter, with everything ultimately falling into the lap of Manuel to bequeath to his Portugese descendants. If this was God's inscrutable will, so be it. But what of Margaret, waylaid by that same divine purpose on her journey to the throne of France, then to the throne of Spain? This highly intelligent and independent woman would survive to assume a role of no small significance as regent of the Netherlands. It was her native land. It formed part of her father's Holy Roman Empire. She would serve it well.

Worse could befall the mourning Ferdinand and Isabella than for a Portuguese grandchild to enter their line of succession. And much worse transpired, for they were not to be spared. Bereavements followed each other in relentless succession. Their daughter and heir Isabella duly conceived but in 1498 she succumbed in the delivery of a son. Two years later this child, Miguel, followed his mother to the grave. Who had laid this terrible curse upon the family! In synagogues throughout Europe, in Turkey and the Maghreb, and in the mosques likewise, Jews and Muslims were convinced of the answer. Sadly also, Maria, the daughter of the monarchs not yet bespoken, knew that her destiny was now written. Little Catherine, mentally Princess of Wales already, saw the look in her sister's eyes. Maria must one day allow herself to follow the dead Isabella and be enclosed in the empty arms of King Manuel of Portugal.

In 1498, a busy year for the Reaper, it was also the turn for Charles VIII of France to die, thus releasing his people after a fifteen-year reign from any further consequences of his ineptitude and extravagant posturings. He had not yet attained his twenty-ninth year. Nature had never been kind to this king, in whose body all the congenital ills of the Valois dynasty seemed to find a home. Actively disliked by his father Louis XI, Charles had married Anne of Brittany on the order of his dominating sibling Anne of Beaujeu, without the union providing his country with an heir. An accidental knock on Charles's head as he stumbled against a wall proved mortal and gave the crown to his cousin, the Duke of Orleans. He would be Louis XII. One feature the new king of France shared in common with Ferdinand of Aragon. Both could summarize their foreign policy in a single word—Italy. Ferdinand could therefore afford little time in mourning for his son and his daughter, nor for the affairs of Columbus, who had sailed away on his third voyage in May of that year.

Louis XII (his father the humanist poet Charles of Orleans spent twenty-five years in an English prison as penalty for his capture at Agincourt) had performed service for his predecessor during the disastrous Italian campaign. No love was lost between King Charles and Louis. As Duke of Orleans the latter had, like his father before him but for a purely domestic reason (a slight case of treason), been incarcerated, a prisoner of his own king and cousin. Charles's good fortune in his marriage to the attractive and seemingly demure Anne of Brittany contrasted with Louis's sense of injustice in having Charles's second sister, Jeanne de France, a virtuous woman but dreadfully deformed, foisted upon him. Were it only possible, Louis would expunge the last twenty years from French history. But he could rectify what could not be avenged. Two matters demanded urgent action: a divorce to free himself of Jeanne so as to substitute the widowed Anne as his wife and queen; and a victorious campaign in Italy to wipe out the disgrace of the French débâcle there.

Already thirty-five years of age on his coronation, Louis had outgrown a somewhat turbulent youth. He now gave the impression of a monarch prepared to forget inherited Orleanist grievances, and he spoke like a statesman. The French appreciated his regal composure. Unhappily, little marked ability lay behind that dignified facade. Louis's intelligence re-sided in the cool head of the ambitious Archbishop of Rouen, Georges d'Amboise. The prelate had St Peter's in his sights. What Amboise wanted for France became the king's policy. Louis coveted Milan (a Visconti grandmother gave him successor's right to the duchy over the Sforza, who issued from a bastard princess), as well as Naples because of its Angevin past. Bring him those, thought Amboise, and take the Holy See for himself, then all Italy would fall to France and its manifest destiny as maker of a new Europe would be assured.

One small matter, the reorganization of traditional alliances, stood in the way. However, in concerns relating to Italy and the papacy old wounds could be made to heal rapidly. The preparations began. Ludovico Sforza could not swallow the indignity of bowing once again to the French. He determined this time to renovate his reputation and give fight. An incidental sacrifice: Sforza ordered Leonardo da Vinci to sur-render the immense quantity of bronze reserved for a contemplated eques-trian monument of the 'Moor's' father Francesco. It would now go to the foundry for conversion into cannon. But nothing helped. Milan was overrun.

Would King Louis succeed in overturning at a stroke everything achieved by King Ferdinand in creating his League of Venice in 1495? Despatch of Charles VIII had largely been the Spaniard's work, and he intended to follow that success with his own seizure of Naples. In planning a strategy he yielded to none in his capacity for a role reversal. The germ of an idea blossomed into a scheme: supper with the devil. Ferdinand decided that he and Louis could divide the spoils by a joint campaign. Others, in whose calculation the welfare of Italy played as little part, would hasten to their side: Venice, ever suspicious of Sforza arrogance in Milan and tempted with a bribe of more space on the mainland, suffered no pangs of conscience in supporting the invasion. As for Pope Alexander, he was ready to sell whatever soul he possessed to embroil France in an operation to consolidate his rule in the disaffected Papal States that would simultaneously foster the interests of his family.

We spare a thought for the dilemma in which the Holy Roman Emperor now found himself. Maximilian's duty lay with his wife Bianca's uncle Ludovico Sforza in defending the integrity of Milan against Venice and the invader. But his son Philip, reigning in the Netherlands as Duke of Burgundy, studiously nurtured good relations with France. Furthermore, Maximilian did not relish a war against Louis to protect Italy. Not only would it displease the Netherlands, it would offend his Imperial Diet. Surprises were in store for one and all, as we shall shortly discover. Ferdinand and Louis signed a treaty at Granada in November 1500. The French were already in Milan. One way or another, the independent kingdom of Naples was doomed.

In the mean time, Vasco da Gama returned in triumph from India, while Ferdinand, with Queen Isabella tugging at his elbow, was begging their emissary Francisco de Bobadilla to hasten his departure for the Indies, *their* Indies, and install order out of chaos. Gama's report suggested great opportunities for Portugal in the true, rich India once the insolent natives came round to respect Christian strength and accepted the evidence of Christian civilization's superiority. What a contrast with the reports brought back from Hispaniola, since 1492 a drain on Castile's exchequer! The queen was moreover incensed by the practice of returned seamen, in defiance of her wishes, bringing their human booty for sale to the Lisbon slave market. Not until August 1500 could Bobadilla, empowered if necessary to depose Christopher Columbus, disembark at Santo Domingo.

The immediate spectacle that confronted Bobadilla on landing was an array of seven bodies—Spanish, not Indian—strung up on the gallows. Diego, the youngest and least competent of the Columbus brothers, sheepishly explained. These men had been sentenced to death by the viceroy for treason. Indeed, both Christopher and Bartholomew, Diego informed Bobadilla, were at that very moment in different parts of the island at the head of armed detachments hunting other mutineers. Five miscreants were under guard awaiting execution, said Diego, inviting the newcomer to a personal inspection.

Bobadilla intended no such waste of time. He instructed Diego to release the prisoners, without so much as a cursory investigation of the crimes alleged against them. Diego refused, pending authorization by his brother. Whereupon he was seized and placed under arrest while Bobadilla took possession of the viceroy's house, impounding Columbus's effects and all documents found there. He then had Christopher brought back to base under duress, when he slapped the Discoverer in irons. Bobadilla gave no explanation. The disgrace was complete.

Bartholomew's turn was yet to come. According to the account published by Christopher's son Ferdinand, Bartholomew's first instinct, when apprised of the situation, was to resist. He had men of his own, and spirit enough. But Christopher absolutely forbade defiance of the monarch's emissary. So Bartholomew too was placed in irons and the three Columbus brothers, thus restrained, were sent home to await a royal decision on whether they should stand trial.

For what crime? Certainly he had pressed his luck too far. Columbus had delegated authority to his brothers over more experienced men, and he should have anticipated how this would alienate even the most loyal among them. The brothers were Genoese, but Hispaniola belonged to Castile. On the other hand, an official edict had appointed him governor and viceroy for life, the dignity descending in perpetuity to his heirs. Both Christopher's brothers had been ennobled by the Catholic Monarchs. True he was a man of poor judgment in administration, wavering in his decisions, as in the sparing of Roldán, when firmness was required. Nevertheless his situation was unique, in territory hitherto unknown, and remote from the centre of government. Authority over such men as he commanded, all of them difficult to control, some of them desperadoes, others *hidalgo* gentry unaccustomed to discipline or even hard work, every one a fortune-hunter, could only be tenuous at best.

For all that, these same men were shocked by his treatment at the hands of Bobadilla. Both Christopher and Bartholomew were sent home on the caravel *La Gordas* whose captain was apparently eager at least to spare their dignity and release them from their fetters. Columbus would not allow it. He wished all Spain to observe his humiliation, the king and queen too, so that the full measure of ingratitude could be known to posterity. He had brought a new world into the patrimony of Castile, yet, as he later wrote to a friend, 'if I had stolen the Indies and given them to the Moors I could not have encountered more enmity in Spain'. Bitterly, he observed to his son Ferdinand that those manacles would be interred with his bones.

Chapter Nine

DISHONOUR ABOUNDING

exual licence and Christian religiosity lived in easy association in Renaissance times; not more so than during the Middle Ages but certainly to greater public indifference. Keeping a mistress and raising illegitimate children in a high-born family evoked few affectations of horror, except when issues crucial to the interests of others were at stake.

Bastardy itself carried no stigma, though it raised profound legal difficulties in questions of inheritance and the granting of honours. Royal husbands were of course especially privileged in this regard, due to the mystical essence of kingship. Retiring for the night with a concubine being a recognized practice, complications occurred only if the woman interpreted her unofficial place in the bedchamber in a political sense, as sometimes occurred. Wars, great and small, erupted through the claim to a throne by a natural son (or daughter) against a relative born in wedlock. Powerful dynasties came into existence through illegitimacy and suffered extinction thereby. Few more labyrinthine exercises confront the historian than to determine the family connections of the regional despots, significant and otherwise, who proliferated in a fragmented Italy at the mercy of foreign predators.

And as the Renaissance loosened the disciplines of chastity many women of rank likewise asserted the right to take lovers beyond the sacrament of the marriage vow. To be sure, tolerance imposed its limits. Royal wives could not be expected to defy instinct and view with generous indulgence a husband's infatuation with a second mate outside the matrimonial home. Queen Isabella worried over her consort Ferdinand's frailties; indeed, she took steps to separate from their court any woman upon whom the king's roving eye might linger. John II of Portugal, as already narrated, loved a natural son above one born of his queen, thus causing an estrangement without repair until their reconciliation at John's death-bed.

The Church could always be relied upon to stretch the rules when influential men desired the appointment of a bastard son to the priesthood. Papal dispensation was regularly granted. In one respect, however, the law demanded more rigorous application: a man born out of wedlock could not achieve elevation to the College of Cardinals. But as we know full well, many a bastard wore the red hat, either through the falsification of records, or nepotism at its most blatant, or consequent upon a pope's pursuit of political favours. Such a one, Cesare Borgia, joined the College in 1493 at the age of eighteen.

He was the ablest of Pope Alexander VI's numerous progeny—the ablest, the most calculating and the most ruthless. Cesare received church appointments from his eighth year, before he could properly write his name and without first entering holy orders. He was nominated a canon of Valencia Cathedral, an archdeacon, a rector, all salaried benefices in Spain, a country he had not as yet even visited. While pursuing his university courses at Perugia and Pisa—by all accounts a brilliant student—Cesare was made Bishop of Pamplona and awarded an estate with a lay title in Italy. At Pisa a fellow student of the same age and close acquaintance, Lorenzo de' Medici's son Giovanni, would one day, in his Holiness as Pope Leo X, serve excommunication upon Martin Luther.

Cesare's father, while Cardinal Archbishop of Valencia and Vice-Chancellor of the Church, had secured from Pope Sixtus IV dispensation to have this son purified for the priesthood. The cardinalate was another matter entirely. This Alexander could only organize himself, against the scruples of the entire College led by his relentless enemy Giuliano della Rovere. The Pope blandly issued a bull stating that Vanozza dei Catanei, Alexander's long-time mistress, was a married woman at the time of Cesare's birth. Indeed she was—her priestly lover found her three husbands in turn. But none of these had fathered Cesare, nor Juan, the Duke of Gandia married to a cousin of Ferdinand of Aragon, nor Lucrezia, matched at twelve with a Sforza to foster one political purpose of the Pope, nor Jofrè, joined for another political purpose to an illegitimate granddaughter of the King of Naples. Documents already existed testifying to their true parentage. Vanozza remained a faithful and loving mother to her children by the Spanish Bull, unprotesting while the needs of his clamorous flesh took him to younger women.

As Supreme Pontiff, an ordinary human being would surely consider himself to have achieved the summit of ambition. Not so Alexander, who was a man cast in a most particular mould. He owed his ecclesiastical ascent to his uncle, Calixtus III, and in his son Cesare he nurtured a still greater design, to render the Pontificate an office hereditary within the Borgia dynasty: Vicars of Christ in St Peter's and lords absolute of the Papal States bestriding the waist of Italy from coast to coast. His further offspring could reinforce the structure, through their strategic coupling, already in swift progression, with other ruling houses. Supremacy in the spiritual world linked with the political mastery of Italy would wedge the Borgias into a situation of boundless power. Was this madness? Hindsight provides the answer. Alexander's papacy made a cataclysm inevitable: the Reformation.

However, Cesare Borgia himself was to shatter the dream, though not the symptoms which gave it birth. The relationship between caring parent and dutiful son exploded in conflicting aspirations when a moment arrived that Cesare, from being an extension of the Pope's will, turned into the partnership's dominant force. He did not wish for St Peter's throne. He had no desire to remain a cardinal. The Church bored him. He craved the earthly glories of a temporal prince, for he had to be the leader nonpareil in every venture, even in the *Palio* at Siena. When his rider's victory in that horse race was disputed, he took it as a personal affront.

Cesare observed with envy how the Pope's favourite son Juan, second Duke of Gandia (he had inherited the title together with a duchess from his half-brother Pedro Luis, prematurely dead), assumed a place in the firmament of the august. The Pope had summoned the arrogant, shallow duke back to Rome in 1496 and, despite his deficiency in every masculine quality except sexual hubris, appointed him, at the age of twenty, Captain General of the Church. Gandia took the papal forces into the field against the rebellious Orsini clan, which had deserted with its army to Charles VIII of France on the latter's invasion. An encounter had terminated without clear victory for either side, though Gandia was slightly wounded. Now Alexander rewarded this son with two Orsini cities as hereditary fiefs. Every cardinal saw the gift in the context of the Pontiff's corrupt scheme for family aggrandizement. Still, few openly protested. Some had themselves purchased the red hat with half their fortunes, while others lived in fear of the notorious Borgia poison, a white arsenic compound expertly delivered when required to silence a dissident voice.

A bright June night in 1497 removed the Duke of Gandia from Cesare's path to greatness. The brothers, accompanied by another cardinal, their cousin, had dined with Vanozza in her villa on the outskirts of Rome. They were riding back to the Vatican when suddenly Gandia excused himself and rode off with his two attendant servants. The obvious reason was to visit a courtesan, and so it was reported. But two days later the duke was discovered dead in the Tiber. Nine stab wounds punctured the body of the Pope's most loved son.

Although assassination at the behest of a Borgia was no rarity, sus-picion did not immediately fall upon Cesare, who was among the last to see Gandia alive. In common with the rest of the family, the young duke had accumulated many enemies, both personal for his philandering way of life as well as political in the papal service. And the Orsini, having forfeited estates to the Holy Father's favourite son, were top of the list. As regards Cesare, was it conceivable that he would raise a murderous hand against a brother? Yet strangely, the grief-stricken Pope called off the search for the killer after just a few days, while Cesare's subsequent record of extreme violence on a caprice brought his unexplained role on that particular evening into eternal debate. He was never fully exonerated of complicity, even though the general circumstances more surely con-victed a hired Orsini assassin of unknown identity.

Unconsolable Alexander remained, to the degree of detecting a warn-ing from Providence against the stench generated by his papacy. Con-trition demanded action. He thereupon established a commission of cardinals to formulate a radical reform of the Church, beginning with the Curia: a regimen of austerity in all practices, the elimination of corruption in appointments, a stronger spiritual bulwark against the in-trigue that swamped God's work in the bishoprics. Alexander addressed the commission thus: 'We would give seven tiaras to recall the Duke of Gandia to life. God has given us this punishment for our sins . . . We will begin the reform with ourselves and so proceed through all levels of the Church till the whole work is accomplished.'

Pressed with greater determination, such a cleansing might well have halted the Reformation, perhaps forever. But Alexander's zeal, inspired by fear for the Borgia destiny, foundered on the perilous rocks of that same Borgia selfish interest. Nothing of significance changed. The welfare of the Church ranked low beside his family's well-being. Louis XII's succession to the throne of France in 1498, and the decision of Cesare Borgia to renounce holy orders, fostered the kind of hopes and fears that kept the papacy cavorting like an insatiable monster in one of Dante's circles of degradation. Alexander and Louis XII needed each other, while Cesare needed them both. Having already sent tremors through all Italy by staking his claim to Milan and Naples, Louis XII sought papal dispensation to annul his marriage to Jeanne, his unloved childless queen, so that he might replace her with Anne of Brittany, widow of Charles VIII. The opportunity thus arose for Alexander to balance Cesare's renunciation of the Church (he might have made the third Borgia Pontiff) with a place close to the centre of temporal affairs.

At a stroke, the Pope could put Louis in his debt and set Cesare on the road to power. He dealt out his soiled cards accordingly. The son was hastily unfrocked and despatched on a mission to Chinon in France, the necessary dispensation for the king's divorce and a red hat for Archbishop Georges d'Amboise in his baggage. The one would not be appeased without the other. Anne of Brittany duly returned to her former throne while Jeanne de France, doubtless with considerable relief, founded a religious order and buried her past beneath a new name, Sister Gabriella Marie. Cesare was himself furnished with a grand title as Duke of Romagna in the Papal States, not to mention a ceremonial sword in preparation for his coming appointment as the next Captain-General of the Church. The sword was inscribed with the motto *Aut Caesar aut Nihil*—either Caesar or nothing.

He arrived at Chinon in a velvet cloak of embroidered splendour, escorted by a detachment of cavalry with armour bearers and flanked by his personal entourage (mostly Catalan). Cesare's posture could well have qualified for a meeting of emperors, though the French, who ordered these things much better when required, found the spectacle somewhat ridiculous. However, more hung on the mission for Cesare. He was additionally on the errand of claiming a royal bride. The woman in question was Carlotta, the daughter of King Federigo of Naples. The latter had succeeded his nephew Ferrantino in a welter of rapid changes that gave Naples five kings in three years. Carlotta resided at the French court.

In no circumstances would she accept the Borgia upstart so recently released from a life of supposed celibacy. Her father, already ensnared in the Pope's family schemes—his niece Sancia being married to young Jofrè Borgia—encouraged her refusal. Carlotta, in love with a Breton nobleman, had fled from Chinon and was now beyond recall in Brittany. As for Cesare, he had no intention of returning to Rome without the prize of a royal bride. Long negotiations proceeded and finally he was given, on Louis' orders, Charlotte d'Albret, sister of the King of Navarre. A French title now seemed appropriate, and the erstwhile Archbishop of Valencia became transmogrified into the Duke of Valentinois: as the wags had it, a Valentino to the last. Navarre, that buffer Pyrenean region perpetually contested between France and Aragon, was then a French protectorate. Ferdinand the Catholic had it in his sights and would indeed possess it before he died.

If all this hinted at parody it nevertheless covered an underlying compact of grim intent. Cesare Borgia had won the valuable trust of Louis; for repayment he agreed to participate in the campaign to dislodge Ludovico Sforza from Milan. His papal force, comprising in the main mercenaries hired at Vatican expense, would be sprinkled with French troops, while in turn he could count on French assistance to sweep the Romagna clean of the cluster of princelings defying papal authority in a region which, historically, lay within the ultimate jurisdiction of Rome.

Neither Ludovico of Milan nor Federigo of Naples, enthroned in rich but rickety statehood, prime targets of the second French visitation within a few years, could immediately assess what business was keeping the Pope's headstrong son at Louis' court. Neither could Ferdinand over in Spain. Alexander assured them all of the innocence of the mission and cited ecclesiastical arguments to justify Louis' unseemly divorce. Far from supporting a French conquest of Italy he wished merely to reimpose the Holy See's control over papal territory. During Charles VIII's violent incursion too many of its vassals betrayed their suzerain and fell over themselves to grant the invader passage. Meanwhile, Ferdinand's own treacherous scheme (doubly treacherous in fact) was ripening independently. Once Milan fell, he and Louis would partition the large Neapolitan kingdom between them. Still, it would be foolish to alienate the Pope, whose blessing was necessary to legitimize Ferdinand's intended final stroke—uncontested sovereignty over undivided Naples.

For the moment the scramble for an initial foothold in Italy sufficed to preoccupy the wolves. Virtually a *condottiere* in the French service, Cesare Borgia crossed into Lombardy in July 1499. If he was to satisfy his hunger for a crown he would need to hurry, for the parent he used as a doormat to the portals of fame and fortune was approaching his seventieth birthday in a state of crippling obesity that indicated he would not be long for this world. Venice seized the opportunity to share in the feast and with Louis' consent took a bite out of eastern Lombardy. By the century's expiry all was over for Ludovico il Moro, archetypal Renaissance prince. He fled from Milan with his gold, then returned to the battlefield leading 10,000 hired men after encouragement from Maximilian, Holy Roman Emperor, only to be defeated, captured and condemned to the French dungeon from which he never emerged.

What of his nephew Giovanni, lord of Pesaro and the husband of Lucrezia Borgia? He had long been discarded as superfluous to the Borgia interest. Their divorce provided the gossips with the kind of joke that never failed to make a Roman holiday. To arrange this particular annulment the Holy Father decided the grounds: non-consummation due to Giovanni's impotence. Lucrezia, it was solemnly sworn, remained a virgin. Giovanni had hotly protested to his uncle as head of the Sforza confraternity. Ludovico, more urgently engaged at the time, drily observed that the slander, if such it was, could be refuted by a public exhibition. The truth lay in another direction. Giovanni had been cuckolded in favour of a Vatican chamberlain, Pedro Calderon. As it happened Lucrezia had borne a child, probably by that unfortunate Spaniard, who was shortly to end his days, like Gandia, prematurely in the Tiber. The paternity of Lucrezia's child might of course have belonged to another of her lovers. (Whispers ascribed it to Cesare, or the Pope himself.) At all events, Lucrezia was soon to marry the Neapolitan Duke of Bisceglie, whose sister Sancia had already joined the infamous family as Jofrè Borgia's wife. Bisceglie was not to be her last husband. When it suited the Borgia dynastic strategy Cesare, already a tyrant in his own right, had him strangled in the Vatican.

Military appetite feeds upon victories, and Cesare grew intoxicated by his meteoric rise to generalship. Following the Lombard triumph, which was hardly his alone, he instinctively looked greedily towards Tuscany. Nothing barred his way into Florence—except the French. They guaranteed the old Medici preserve its security, with Piero, son of the Magnificent, soldiering in King Louis' grand army. So wiser counsel prevailed. Having discharged his obligation to Louis, at least in part, Cesare focused his martial endeavours upon his own duchy, Romagna. Distribute the ironies: here was Louis in Milan marvelling at the genius of Leonardo da Vinci as revealed in his Last Supper, painted on the order of the artist's sponsor Ludovico, while there was the artist himself obligingly entering the employ of Cesare Borgia in the capacity of engineer and artillery expert. Italian patriotism, such as it was, would sleep for 300 more years before it emerged even in a regional form. Think of Machiavelli, himself a Florentine observer at Cesare's camp, writing glowingly of the Pope's son as the Italian soldier-statesman *par excellence*.

The powers ravished the country and art held itself aloof. Thus war proceeded while Michelangelo tussled in Rome with the problem of his Pietà, one day to be the glory of a newly built St Peter's: how to sculpt

the Virgin bearing the Saviour as a fully grown man in her arms? Cesare
Borgia had purchased Michelangelo's recumbent Cupid from a dealer
who passed the figure off, engrained with clay, as an original salvaged
from the ruins of ancient Rome. One day Cesare would present the
sculpture to Isabella d'Este. It has vanished long since.

Ludovico's realm had crumbled not through any special prowess on
the part of his enemies. He naturally anticipated help from Maximilian,
husband of his niece, but as on other occasions, the emperor failed to
arrive. Worse, the Swiss mercenaries, on discovering they had been
leased by both contending sides, refused to fight each other. Those
employed by Ludovio drifted home.

Cesare Borgia pressed forward, not a professional soldier in the French
service now but truly Captain-General of the Church. He sowed terror
wherever his troops encountered opposition in the Romagna, that wedge
of the fertile Italian landscape stretching northward from the Adriatic
coast to beyond Bologna. Eventually the entire region, pockmarked with
its petty vassals turned independent, dropped into papal submission—
all except Bologna itself. There the Bentivoglio family gained a respite
by conceding one of its strongholds and consenting to fight alongside
the 'Valentino' in suppressing baronial resistance against their suzerain.
At Pesaro, seat of his ex-brother-in-law Giovanni Sforza, Cesare slept
in the palace briefly occupied by Lucrezia. Faenza, before succumbing,
held out against a long winter siege during which the Borgia's Italian
and Spanish mercenaries, goaded by mutual detestation, almost fought
a battle against each other while his French allies surveyed the scene in
disbelief. Rimini fell like an over-ripe apple and deservedly so, brutalized
as it had been for a century by the blood-stained Malatesta dynasts.

On the other hand Forli and Imola, both ruled by the tigress Caterina
Sforza as a consequence of her marriage to a nephew (murdered) of Pope
Sixtus IV, proved a more strenuous proposition. Even after Imola finally
surrendered Caterina, who had once captured Castel Sant'Angelo in
Rome, betook herself to Forli, refusing to submit. Cesare personally
approached the walls of her citadel and threatened to kill all her children—six at that time—unless she ceased resistance. The story goes that
Caterina appeared on the battlements, raised her garments to reveal her
nakedness and cried: 'Look, this body is young enough to produce still
more.' Three weeks into the siege of Forli yet the Italian Boadicea continued to hold out. She tried, unsuccessfully, to set herself on fire with
gunpowder. Her eventual surrender to the Captain-General produced
the usual crop of anecdotes: 'Cesare raped her! No, the virago seduced

him!' Caterina might well have perished in her prison cell beneath Castel Sant'Angelo had not the French demanded her release, with a guarantee extracted from her captor of chivalrous treatment. She survived to bear three more children in marriage to a Medici.

The best part of three years was devoted to pacification of the Romagna and the other insubordinate provinces forgetting their allegiance to Rome. Cesare's troops required constant reinforcement, draining the papal treasury. But he proceeded deaf to Alexander's calls for the campaign's termination. Machiavelli wrote of him: 'In the pursuit of lands and glory he never rests, recognizing neither fatigue nor danger.' Surely he had no justifiable cause to advance upon Urbino and evict the reigning Montefeltro duke, whose father, the celebrated Federigo, had been honoured by England as a Knight of the Garter and was called 'the light of Italy'! This Federigo had given successive popes unswerving loyalty as a faithful warrior in their service. Cesare established himself nevertheless in the gracious Montefeltro palace, a masterpiece in combined Gothic and Renaissance style, while Federigo's son Guidobaldi—no soldier he— took off to the shelter of Mantua in fear of his life. Cesare actually used the title Duke of Urbino himself. Nothing confirmed Cardinal della Rovere in his hostility to the Borgias so much as this arrogance, since a Rovere nephew was in line for that particular title. From a safe distance Guidobaldi Montefeltro loudly demanded the return from the Vatican of the priceless manuscript library presented by his father. Rightly so, exclaimed Isabella d'Este, who presided over the Mantuan court of her Gonzaga husband. Despatching an indignant reproof to Cesare Borgia she castigated the conqueror as a thief as well as a murderer. It was by way of assuagement that he made Isabella the gift of Michelangelo's Cupid (which, incidentally, he no longer owned). During this period Isabella would need to stomach the contortions of the Borgias at their zenith by witnessing the marriage between her brother Alfonso d'Este, heir to Ferrara, and Cesare's sister Lucrezia.

As Italy echoed to the noise of gunfire and Cesare Borgia's ruthlessly acquired renown, King Federigo of Naples awoke to the plot germinating between his cousin Ferdinand of Aragon and Louis of France. He found himself utterly friendless. He no longer dared to trust the Borgias, under whose aegis the Vatican combined the operation of an irregular family business with the horrors of a charnel house. Venice? Paid off by Louis to stay away. Florence? A broken reed. Federigo's only ally, Ludovico of Milan, was heavily engaged in his vain attempt to safeguard his own throne. Federigo's mind now worked as others before and after him did in similar resentments. Deprived of Christian friends, you resorted to an infidel—the sultan of course. A naval onslaught by that monarch upon Venice might save his kingdom. Federigo notified Constantinople, where the very name of Venice raised a furious wind, that should a Turkish fleet choose this moment to sail up the Adriatic and besiege the Most Serene Republic it could do so unmolested by any vessel flying the Neapolitan standard.

Death had removed Sultan Bayezid's brother Jem as a threat to the throne of the Sublime Porte. Although keeping up the pressure on Hungary, Bayezid had steered clear of Italy since 1482. But this was an opportunity not to be missed. It thus transpired that in 1499 a full-scale naval war ensued, during which the Venetians suffered a resounding defeat in the Ionian Sea. The republic lost important coastal outposts for ever in that stretch of the Mediterranean. Soon the Turkish galleys, accompanied by corsairs hunting easy booty, swarmed into the Adriatic; and from bases on its eastern shore delivered stiff punishment upon the Venetian hinterland. The white of their sails sufficed for the panic evacuation of villages to safety deep inshore. French help was invoked, as well as a Spanish flotilla under Gonsalvo de Córdoba. Then the customary Turkish caution came to the rescue of Venice. Complications developed for the sultan at home and he reluctantly withdrew.

Bayezid achieved more than he knew. The costly naval encounter heralded the impending twilight of Venice. Its Oriental commerce already imperilled in consequence of Portugal's discovery of the Cape route to India, the republic now surrendered preeminence in its own traditional waters. Of course it was defiant enough to fight again and retrieve its place, for a while at least, though in the oceanic epoch just dawning it would struggle merely to survive, let alone challenge the world. On his part Federigo of Naples, as we shall see, failed with his gamble to save his kingdom. But he suffered an infinitely lighter fate than the one in store for his nephew the Duke of Bisceglie, whose murder in 1500 rendered Lucrezia Borgia available to marry Alfonso d'Este. On his downfall Federigo departed to an honourable exile.

The huge expense notwithstanding, Cesare's achievement in subduing the Romagna earned him the Pope's deepest gratitude and made him the toast of the fickle Roman populace. Alexander's heart melted whenever his son returned to the city, as periodically he did in high ceremonial state. The Captain-General of the Church, robed as Duke of Romagna, would kneel to his Holiness and report his latest victories, testified by the important prisoners languishing in the Castel Sant'Angelo awaiting ransom or death. Would not Alexander's Pontificate enter history as one of the greatest, for restoring long-lost territories to the Holy See?

Appropriately, the jubilee year of 1500 brought hundreds of thousands of pilgrims, many of them from foreign lands, to the Eternal City, all in a euphoria of piety and eagerly purchasing indulgences for themselves, their children and their dead forebears. Replenishing the coffers of the Church assured them all perpetual bliss in heaven. Further, the pilgrims contributed munificently to the crusading tax, ostensibly to be used one blessed day for the reclamation of Jerusalem. Money poured into the papal exchequer in such a flood of benevolence no one could calculate what percentage leaked into the cavernous pockets of the army of Borgia favourites haunting the Vatican, though a small papal flotilla did in fact join the Venetian fleet in the Ionian Sea.

Alexander loved festivities, circuses, bull fights, but he remained very much the Pope none the less with a finger on the pulse of the Catholic world. He never tired either of discussing with his cardinals, especially those newly appointed in honour of the jubilee, the dream of building a new cathedral church, the most splendid of all edifices, to enshrine the earthly remains of his earliest forerunner St Peter. Alexander knew he would not live to see it rise except from his own eternal resting-place. But already the young Florentine Michelangelo had carved his noble Pietà out of a huge slab of Carrara marble. It was destined for the new cathedral, so one might say the work was begun, praise the Lord.

Simultaneously, reports of the Borgia scandals spread far and wide to rock the Vatican: courtesans disporting themselves in the palace, assassinations perpetrated and gross trafficking in the distribution of papal offices. Cesare's princess, Charlotte d'Albret, remained a faithful wife, albeit from a distance as she never joined her husband in Italy. He was to be seen everywhere with his mistress, the rich courtesan Fiametta de' Michelis. For the most spectacular orgy of the time, recorded in the careful diary of a man incapable of exaggeration, the Curia's master of papal ceremonies Johannes Burchard, we repair to Cesare's own apartments. It was All Saints' Eve in 1501, and Burchard recorded:

A supper was held at which 50 honest prostitutes, those termed courtesans, were present. After supper they danced with the servants and others, first clothed then naked. Later the candlesticks were placed on the floor and chestnuts were scattered among the prostitutes. They had to pick up the chestnuts by crawling around the lighted candles. The Pope, the duke and his sister Lucrezia were among those observing the scene. Then prizes—boots, caps, silken cloaks and other articles—were awarded to the men who made love to the prostitutes the most number of times.

Such spectacles may not have been extraordinary on the seamier side of Renaissance society when the Italian nobility made merry. However, another account tells of this event's macabre epilogue. Alexander and his daughter watched at a Vatican window while Cesare had a band of unarmed criminals turned loose in the courtyard and then proceeded to shoot them down one by one.

King Louis remained in Milan while his army trampled across the Papal States to take up the conquest of Naples. His arrangement with Ferdinand of Aragon for division of the spoils involved his possession of the city itself together with the northern portion of the Regno, the Catholic Monarch receiving the rest. Except that Ferdinand had other plans than those engrossed in the treaty signed with France at Granada. Gonsalvo de Córdoba commanded a formidable force in another part of the kingdom, waiting to pounce.

The French army, which included a small Romagnol detachment under Cesare Borgia, encountered no opposition until it reached Capua. There, the local militia, bravely led by *condottieri* of the Colonna family, made a determined stand. That ancient town, hitherto recalled in history for its association with Hannibal, now assumed a more gruesome fame, in the mournful remembrance of which the cathedral bell still tolls an annual knell. Some 5,000 inhabitants were slaughtered in the sack of Capua and though the French fastened guilt for the massacre on Cesare's troops, they themselves could not have been completely blameless. Resistance ceased throughout the entire state after this holocaust. On his part Federigo of Naples, sickened by the deceit perpetrated on him by his cousin Ferdinand, surrendered the kingdom entire to the French and departed to exile. Gallantly, Louis awarded him the Duchy of Anjou in compensation. As to the guilty partners, they soon fell out and resorted to battle. Gonsalvo then showed his hand.

Once again France paid for its violation of fractured, impotent Italy by bringing disaster upon itself. Gonsalvo confronted his monarch's so-called ally on the banks of the Garigliano river late in 1503, when the days were short and the winter particularly severe. It rained incessantly. Displaying brilliant generalship, Gonsalvo trapped the army of Louis in the swell of the flooding river. Men, horses and cannon were washed away in the torrent or sank in the swamplands of the plain. Among the perished lay Piero de' Medici, elder son of Lorenzo the Magnificent, serving with the French host in the hope of regaining Florence thereby. The survivors, many of them completely naked, stumbled along the roads north, hungry, frozen and demoralized, their bodies stinging as though afflicted by the plagues sent to chastise Pharaoh's uncomprehending Egyptians. No Italian would give succour to a French soldier begging for water or a crust. To escape the intense cold they would bury themselves up to their necks in the dunghills. In this fashion did the straggling remnant of Louis' proud force drag its weary feet into Rome.

Ferdinand had at last regained for Aragon and Spain a province 'stolen' from his father forty-five years before. Triumphantly, he joined Naples to the kingdom he shared with Isabella of Castile, the kingdom that was to hold the key to Europe and dominate the century just begun. Already, events showed every indication that Ferdinand's dream as a young prince on marrying Isabella in 1469, to make his dynasty the greatest in Christendom, was approaching realization. However, in rounding out the achievement of denying Naples to the French this account has run ahead of itself. Turning the clock back three years to October 1501, we observe Catherine, the youngest daughter of the Catholic Monarchs, arriving at Plymouth Hoe to commence her new life with the heir of England.

It had been a long and arduous journey for the princess of fifteen years, over the hard and dusty roads of the arid Spanish interior, then across the hazardous Bay of Biscay only to reach the English Channel in one of its angry moods. Certainly the match with Prince Arthur of Wales, settled some twelve years earlier, counted as one of Ferdinand's most astute diplomatic strokes. France being the principal obstacle to Spanish expansion, and enduringly suspicious, what could be more convenient than to entice England to his side, for was not the northern kingdom ready at all times to trespass upon France when beckoned, practically at the crook of a finger? Catherine of Aragon on the English throne, and London no further distant than Naples! Ferdinand could not wish for a better ambassador. She was escorted to the Tudor court by a large and imposing retinue that included two archbishops to stand proxy for her parents. Arrangements for the transmission of Catherine's dowry, and the method of payment (200,000 crowns in two installments and partly taking the form of the bride's jewellery and household effects) continued in laborious negotiation with the penny-pinching Welshman then reigning in England. Doubtless that would straighten out in time.

Ferdinand had taken tidy care of his own interests in yielding up the girl. On the other hand she herself was more naturally concerned with the human aspects of her destiny. He was rather small, this Arthur, and of a delicate pallor, particularly when standing beside his puffing younger brother, ten-year-old Henry, Duke of York, at the marriage ceremony in St Paul's Cathedral. And there is little more to relate at this juncture, except that misfortune struck at poor Catherine within a lapse of months. In April 1502 her husband contracted the sweating sickness and died. The younger brother, succeeding Arthur as Prince of Wales, was immediately and bluntly notified, to his profound disgust, that duty would require him to marry this somewhat precise and over-dignified Spanish princess six years his senior.

In the years until he eventually consented to do so, shortly after his coronation in 1509 as Henry VIII, Catherine grew into a woman much weathered by her isolation in a country that forgot the courtesies due to her royal state. She sorrowed in lonely exile when her mother Isabella died in 1504. Her father rarely wrote. Then, as Queen of England, the anguish of her child-bearing: six times, and Henry clamouring for an heir. Yet only one survived, the girl Mary. What years these were for Catherine, with banishment to the damp East Anglian fens still to come! The king cut the Roman knot in 1533 in order to divorce her, by which time most of those featured in this narrative would be in the grave, save a nephew who refused to abandon her: Charles, son of Catherine's sister Joanna (called La Loca, for she lost her wits). Charles would prove a champion not easily dismissed. Having inherited his Austrian grandfather's title as Holy Roman Emperor, and his mother's realms in Europe and America as King of Spain, he obstructed papal dispensation for the divorce during four difficult years. But what could Charles ultimately do to lighten his aunt's miserable situation? Catherine died in 1536 with no memories to sweeten her last thoughts except in the recollection of her distant Spanish childhood.

She was as yet an unmarried princess justifiably contemplating a happy prospect when, in October 1500, Christopher Columbus found himself at Cadiz manacled like a common criminal. He had fallen from the summit to the nadir of any man's fortunes. The Discoverer, remote from those alarums which kept Europe astir with fluctuating alliances and constant war, lost no time however in requesting an audience with Ferdinand and Isabella. They delayed their consent. Their preoccupation with the Italian venture, the secret negotiations with France, their grief at the succession of family tragedies still unrelieved, gave them little inclination to concern themselves with the discontents of an incompetent Viceroy of the Indies.

However, the honour incumbent upon their aureole of majesty had to be preserved. This never allowed a subject of theirs, no matter his insignificance, to feel slighted on their account. It could not permit the sovereigns to sanction the continued humiliation of Columbus now that he had arrived on their side of the Atlantic. They ordered his immediate release. Whatever the intention to the contrary of their emissary Bobadilla in Hispaniola, Columbus was not to forfeit his entitlements earned for bringing the Indies into the possession of Spain. After all, the contract making him Admiral of the Ocean Sea, with a perpetual stake in the treasure and trade of those parts, carried the royal seal. Let others disparage Columbus's achievements, but not they. Truthfully, Ferdinand and Isabella felt no desire ever to meet him again, yet a formal audience as demanded by protocol would not be denied. He would not be returning to the Indies, of that they were sure.

Columbus was aged but by no means old in 1500—just forty-nine, like the queen herself. No less than his body, his mind had lost its agility in those years as a leader alone, ever wrestling with the elements, chancing life and limb against hitherto unknown hazards. The old arthritic pains still troubled his body balance. More recent illnesses, all exacerbated by deprivation, lack of sleep and chronic anxiety, had made of him a man in the grip of a complexity of obsessions drenched with self-pity. Like so many other leaders fixated on the memory of their early success he had outlived his usefulness yet refused to face the unpalatable truth. How could he pass on the mantle with so much more still to accomplish for Christ in that pagan world, so much more to bring to Spain!

The sovereigns, having signed the cynical treaty with France in Granada for the dismemberment of Naples, proposed to spend their Christmas in the Moorish city. Just before the festival they steeled themselves for a meeting with their importunate admiral. He arrived with his two brothers, and a pathetic spectacle he made, so obviously unwell yet pleading to be granted another expedition to the Indies. He begged for the retention of his title and privileges, to the degree that both brothers Bartholomew and Diego found the scene unbearable. They decided then and there to finish with all exploration. Christopher's sons too were compelled to stand by as uncomfortable witnesses. The elder, Diego, an experienced twenty-year-old courtier by this time, knew the sovereigns' intentions. Ferdinand and Isabella planned that Columbus should be paid off and retired with a suitable estate in Spain. Further decisions regarding Hispaniola would exclude him.

To their credit, the king and queen heard the explorer out. In reply, they reiterated their assurance of his rights to a share in the wealth of the Indies and displayed sympathetic understanding for Columbus's complaints against Bobadilla, who in any case was to be replaced. He had sequestered a chestful of money belonging to Columbus in Hispaniola? They would ensure its restoration. However, on the subject of another voyage they kept their silence.

The man eventually appointed to replace Francisco de Bobadilla in the Indies was a soldier long in royal service. Nicolás de Ovando would depart with a clear brief: to crush rebellion in Hispaniola, hold the natives to forced labour in exchange for conversion and protection, and apply himself to the better exploitation of the island's riches. Only when Columbus discovered the details of the appointment, whereby Ovando bore the insignia of Governor of the Islands and Mainland of the Indies, did he realize that his own title was now a facade, empty of all significance.

Nevertheless, in one most important respect, after his long bombardment of the monarchs with letters and depositions, copies of which went to his son Diego at court and the San Giorgio bank in Genoa—for they included a meticulous accounting of what was financially due to him—Columbus had his way. They granted him permission to sail once more, though under specific conditions. In no circumstances was he to interfere with Ovando's operations at Santo Domingo. More, he was not to disembark there except with the governor's permission. Two officers of the realm, the brothers Porras, were to sail with him. Who? They were unknown to the Discoverer. Diego and Francisco Porras boasted a sister influential at court, the mistress of the Royal Treasurer no less, so she practically held the purse strings. One of the brothers was to captain a caravel, the other would represent the crown as the expedition's comptroller. So it was agreed. Ovando departed in February 1502, three months before Columbus was ready, commanding a fleet of thirty vessels. In contrast four small caravels were allowed the redundant viceroy.

It had been conceded as a sop. Bartholomew understood this better than his elder brother, and would only sail when implored to do so by Christopher. The latter laid great store on vindicating himself as the one true navigator of the oceans notwithstanding. He portentously designated this his 'High Voyage', by which he would chart the exact course leading from the waters lapping China to the heart of Asia and there on. It was not unlikely he would encounter Vasco da Gama, who had lately set sail from Lisbon on a second expedition eastbound for India. A rendezvous would signify the joint mastery of the two Iberian powers, allied by the marriage bond, over the seaways of the globe. Would not this be an historic meeting, satisfying the skeptics beyond doubt in his claim to having opened the western route to the Indies?

Perhaps Ferdinand and Isabella were impressed (more likely Isabella alone), for they furnished Columbus with a letter of credentials addressed to Gama, should they meet. It ran:

> This is to inform you, Captain under our Son the Most Serene King of Portugal, that We are sending Admiral Don Cristóbal Colón, the bearer of this letter, with certain ships on their customary course, sailing to the West. And since We have learned that our Son, the King of Portugal, is sending you with certain ships to the East, and since by good fortune you may meet at sea, We have instructed the said Admiral Don Cristóbal Colón that you are to regard one another as friends and as the captains and subjects of Kings who are bound together by so much kinship, love and affection. Wherefore we beseech you to do likewise on your part.

Manuel of Portugal had taken the Catholic Monarchs' last available daughter Maria in marriage in 1500, consequent upon the chain of bereavements afflicting their two houses as previously described.

Despite the contrast with Ovando's magnificent fleet, with its holds plentifully stocked to supply every foreseeable need, a complement of veteran soldiers aboard, and under the navigational command of Columbus's hardy old shipmate from his second voyage Antonio Torres, the little squadron made a brave picture. Columbus was undertaking the crossing for the fourth time in ten years. He brought along his thirteen-year-old younger son Ferdinand for the experience. One of his caravels, *La Gallega*, was piloted by Pedro de Terreros, who had trusted Columbus for a safe landfall on that pioneering voyage of 1492 and signed with every one since. Bartholomew Columbus was on board the *Santiago de Palos*, nicknamed the *Bermuda*, together with the Porras brothers, though without any function specified. He was not listed on the treasurer's payroll. The name of the leader's vessel remains unknown to this day, except as the 'flagship'. Smallest of the four, displacement 50 tons, was the *Vizcaina* ('Biscayan'), entrusted to the command of Bartholomew Fieschi. A Genoese, Fieschi enjoyed friendship with Columbus dating from their youth in Italy. The Bible packed with the admiral's personal belongings bore an inscription for which he was profoundly grateful. It had been sent to him by Pope Alexander. No interpreter accompanied the expedition, though the Church was represented by one lowly friar.

Thus began the High Voyage. And it was just as well for Columbus that he could share the hazards with a few staunch allies besides his young son, who took to the seas like an old tar, and of course his brother Bartholomew. Christopher fell ill a day or two after setting sail, while the Porras pair gave trouble from the start. Nevertheless, after three uneventful weeks afloat the four ships made landfall at Martinique, which the Tainos called Matinino. Three days later, guided as much by instinct as deliberate intention, the little convoy hauled in off Santo Domingo, careful to remain outside the bar. And there a chain of catastrophes began, with the cruel sea choosing Ovando's expedition as its first victim.

Columbus would not be welcomed by Ovando, this he well knew. In any event he did not propose to tarry, but to exchange *Bermuda* for a craft better adapted to the high winds he anticipated. Also he desired Ovando's authorization to send letters back with the fleet of twenty-five ships which, having unloaded at Santo Domingo, were now due to return to Spain. Then again, Columbus recognized signs of an approaching hurricane. Having already experienced their ferocity in these parts he wanted the precaution of temporary shelter. Terreros rowed to shore with these requests, at the same time advising Ovando of the oncoming danger. Prudence, according to Columbus, demanded postponement of the big fleet's departure.

Dismissing the warning as if it came from a dreamy old mariner feigning superior seamanship but speaking through his second childhood, Ovando ordered his fleet away—eastward out of the harbour, through the Mona Passage and into the open sea. It proved a miscalculation of the most tragic proportions. As if commanded by the devil, the weather suddenly changed from relative calm to the epicentre of a pitiless storm. Twenty ships went to the bottom that day, taking 500 men with them. Francisco de Bobadilla, returning from his royal assignment, was drowned together with the rebel Roldán. Ovando's captain-in-chief Torres went down, and some native Indians, including a *cacique*, on transportation for some criminality. Survivors numbered a handful. Treasure lost comprised a substantial amount of gold. An irony: the only ship to ride out the elements and enter tranquil waters back to Spain was the tiny *Aguja*, which fortuitously carried Columbus's personal property restored.

As to the four little craft under his command, they were soon able to make their departure against the storm, still driving hard. Kinder weather allowed them the shelter denied them by Ovando close by the coast of Jamaica. Columbus then led them across the Caribbean Sea for a distance of 360 miles, until they came upon the Bay Islands cresting the mainland of Honduras, where the ships anchored. It was now 27 July 1502, and the crews were nearing exhaustion. This was *terra nova*, a puzzle to be resolved only by a sixth sense. It told Columbus that the skein of land just visible to his look-out aloft must indicate the strait leading to an unbroken expanse of the great continent of Asia. It would mark the discovery he had long striven for. Unhappily, his sixth sense erred. In reality they had arrived in the territory of the Guaymi tribes. From an encounter with a long, well-constructed canoe the explorers received evidence of a native civilization that knew how to weave cloth and smelt metals.

Were he in search of trade, this would doubtless have proved a profitable halting place. But the punishing last few days had so taxed Columbus's strength, and undermined the seamen's morale in general, that he felt it unwise to delay. Instead, he seized the canoe's leader and ordered him to pilot them to the mainland. This done, the Indian was released. Studying the stars, consulting his charts and dipping into his Bible, the admiral calculated their location as the vicinity of the Malay Peninsula. Therefore the much-desired channel could not be far away. In describing the voyage many years later, Ferdinand Columbus spoke of his father's conviction that this would be the Malacca Straits.

It tells of the stubbornness of the man no less than his fortitude that Columbus continued as navigator while developing a fever so intense as to prevent his leaving his bunk for days on end. They were plying an eastward course. 'For an entire month,' he wrote, 'we struggled against a never-ending storm—rain, thunder and lightning. Sails tore to shreds, anchors, rigging, cables, boats and stores were lost. Many old hands whom we regarded as brave men lost their courage. What I felt most was the suffering of Ferdinand, my young son.'

The worst of their problems was the dreaded woodworm. It rotted the hulls. But the men were surely superb mariners, for their ships continued to perform as directed. After six weeks they managed to round the cape called by the leader Gracias á Dios, and to turn south to present-day Nicaragua. Negotiating a river mouth cost two lives, the first casualties. They arrived at Costa Rica, at that time the territory of friendly Talamanca Indians. These people appeared so anxious to engage in trade they sent young girls up to the great canoes in a gesture of goodwill and peace. Columbus, more concerned to reach his strait, ordered the girls to be covered and put back on shore. The distraction of women hampered marine discipline.

However, of this they could be certain: they had discovered gold-bearing terrain. The Indians briskly exchanged their personal adornments, which transpired to be forged in an alloy of gold and copper, for whatever the visitors had to offer. Imperiously, the admiral cut the trading short. 'The channel, where is the channel?' he queried, in no language or gesture the others could comprehend. He made diagrams, repeating the words 'Indian Ocean' like an incantation capable of inducing a spell, always without success. So they sailed on, ever along the coast and oblivious of the one geographical feature that would solve the mystery. They were fringing an isthmus, perhaps the wettest region of the world. Barely 40 miles over the nearby cordillera lay not the Indian Ocean but the Pacific—only 12 miles once they ventured into the widest bay. Columbus would never know of it, for Nuñez de Balboa sighted the glistening deep only after the Discoverer's death.

Of course he wished to bring back gold, but given his state of mind Columbus thought first of proving his Asian thesis, and that meant pursuing his quest for a corridor. Besides, the shorelands being permanently inundated by the rainfall, they could not make fast landing long enough to search for treasure. Even the natives seemed powerless against the force of water; one careless step could drown a man. Sadly, the High Voyage was turning into a floating purgatory. Food ran short, and as Christmas came and went the only available fresh nourishment, against which there was fierce prejudice, had to be cut from a beached shark.

When finally Columbus yielded and considered establishing a trading station, in the district of Veragua (Mosquito Gulf), opposition arose from hundreds of well-led Indians. Willingly would they trade with the strangers, but at the sight of their soil being prepared for a settlement they turned violent. Thus it happened that Diego Tristán, accompanied by ten men and a wolfhound, was ambushed while venturing upstream by boat to collect fresh water. The entire party was killed. The loss was all the greater for Columbus as Tristán, a comrade from his second voyage, captained the flagship. In another hostile incident Bartholomew Columbus and a landing party found themselves marooned. Luckily they were able to improvise a raft, which delivered them across the shallows to the ships beyond. Courage was not lacking during these tormenting days, and was frequently opposed by courage on the Indian side. On the other hand those official representatives, the two Porras brothers, could take no more of it. They demanded to return home.

Misfortunes piled upon adversity. First one ship, *Gallega*, sprang too many leaks and had to be abandoned, then *Vizcaina*. They were now reduced to 116 seamen, mostly sick in body and sullen in spirit, all crowded on the two remaining weather-beaten caravels. Yet Columbus still refused to admit defeat, even though the situation called for a change of plan. He decided that willy-nilly they must make for Santo Domingo, refit and head for home to obtain reinforcements. Thus resuscitated, the High Voyage would continue where it left off. He would achieve his purpose in every particular: suppress pagan opposition, unearth the precious minerals their reconnaisance had revealed, explore the Asian hemisphere and crown the endeavour by returning to Spain via the Indian Ocean. Grand the vision!

The most their vessels could be persuaded to do took them limping to Jamaica, as far as St Ann's Bay. Columbus had discovered the inlet previously and had baptized it Santa Gloria to mark its Spanish possession. Realizing now that the two craft were on the point of giving up the ghost, he ran them aground and fixed them so as to perform the functions of a fort. It was summer-time once again, 1503. He must face the inevitable and somehow get word to Governor Ovando at Santo Domingo and beseech a rescue operation.

In the event, the party would be doomed to languish in Jamaica for another year. No longer were these men of the calibre from which colonies sprang. Throughout that period they neither fished nor planted, relying on native goodwill for provender—cassava bread, rodents, sea food—purchased with their own famous treasures, coloured beads and hawks' bells. Improvisation was the seaman's trademark, but these failed even to hollow out some tree trunks for canoes, acquiring them instead from the Indians. However, they retained their weapons, and a cageful of dogs, in the event of contingencies.

Three experienced sailors assisted Columbus in holding the castaway band together: his brother Bartholomew, his friend Fieschi and a gallant *hidalgo* adventurer, Diego Méndez. Without them all force would ebb from the leader's command. Santo Domingo in Hispaniola lay across 108 miles of water, not an impossible trip for a seaworthy canoe, but a strong man needed to take charge of it, one loyal to Columbus and able to cope with any hostile encounter. The possibility of losing direction and succumbing to hunger and thirst could not be excluded. He had to be chosen therefore from among the three.

Méndez volunteered, bearing a message for the Catholic Monarchs in which Columbus craved permission, should he reach Europe alive, to proceed on a pilgrimage to Rome. Méndez took a small crew to guard the Indians press-ganged into paddling the boat. At first an unfriendly native demonstration foiled his attempt. The second time Fieschi, better armed, accompanied Méndez in another canoe with an additional crew while Bartholomew in a third escorted them out to open sea. Bartholomew realized his presence was required at Jamaica should a threatening situation arise which Columbus was in no condition to handle on his own. When several weeks had elapsed without word from Méndez or Fieschi, and it seemed the rescue operation had foundered, serious trouble began.

Diego and Francisco Porras declared rebellion against the admiral. Collecting half the complement, forty-eight men, they announced their determination to proceed on their own to Santo Domingo in several canoes they had somehow acquired, together with Indian prisoners to work the paddles. They would throw themselves on Ovando's mercy and implore transportation to Spain. True enough they departed, only to be caught after a couple of days by a heavy thunderstorm which drove them back to shore. These were men made desperate indeed. Losing all their provisions in the process, they had thrown their Indians overboard lest hunger and thirst made the natives mad and likely to slaughter the Spaniards. Now the mutineers defiantly pitched their camp away from the main beachhead and ravaged the countryside for food and water.

Month succeeded month in agonized waiting, and still no word. The island's soil contained no gold; that was common knowledge among explorers, since Columbus had reported as much after his previous investigation of Jamaica. Consequently no ship was likely to happen by. Winter returned, and the natives grew restive. Would these strangers, unwelcome in the first place, stay among them forever, demanding food, capturing prisoners, stealing their women? Why not starve them out?

One day they refused to 'sell' any more food to Columbus—an unmistakable hint of a war of attrition. It could result in the early death of the vastly outnumbered Spaniards, or their enslavement at the very least. Sick man though he might be, escaping from such an eventuality was not beyond Columbus's competence. He resorted to a brilliant subterfuge, praying all the while that God watched over his destiny. Astronomical tables which he customarily consulted came to his aid, for he was able to calculate that the next day, 29 February 1504, should see a total lunar eclipse. He therefore summoned the tribal chief and made him understand that the Christian deity would steal 'his' moon, and that very night, if the food supply ceased. Thankfully, the eclipse occurred. The moon changed colour before disappearing entirely in the firmament, terrifying the natives. Columbus had no trouble from them thereafter.

But a small war remained to be fought against the Porras faction. Eight months into the year of the enforced sojourn on Jamaica a caravel appeared in St Ann's Bay. Its purpose was not rescue but reconnaissance. The captain told Columbus of Ovando's strict injunction to take no one on board. He had arrived purely to bring a letter from Diego Méndez together with a deceptive sweetener from Ovando for the admiral: a gift of wine and bacon. Undoubtedly, the mission's true purpose was to ascertain only whether the sick Columbus was alive or dead. The governor certainly wished the latter. He feared lest the survival of the explorer would ultimately endanger his own position at Santo Domingo, possibly bringing his replacement and the restitution of the man who had initiated the colonization of Hispaniola. By this time the colony had taken root as a reasonably thriving accessory to the Spanish kingdom.

One can well imagine the reaction of the castaways to their desertion when the only sail besides their own that they had seen during two hard years disappeared over the horizon. Their despair would indeed have been complete, were it not for the Méndez letter. It remarked on the infamous attitude of Ovando, but brought consolation nevertheless. Méndez was in the process of chartering a rescue vessel from an independent trader in Hispaniola on the strength of a document of authorization he possessed from Columbus. All was not lost.

What of the mutineers? Bartholomew, with an armed guard, was despatched to their camp to demand their surrender against an offer of pardon. They would all leave together as free men on the day of salvation. Foolishly, Francisco Porras imposed his own conditions: a separate ship for the rebels if two arrived, or absolute division of space, stores and command if there was only one. He therefore left no alternative but to fight it out, with spears mostly because little ammunition now remained for the arquebuses. Such a spectacle it made for the onlooking Indians, the god-men in hand-to-hand combat setting about each other's destruction! Bartholomew led the loyalists. A few men on either side died, including Pedro de Terreros, captain of the ill-fated *Gallega* and Columbus's comrade in every season, kind and cruel, since 1492. All was over by sunset, the rebels suppressed and forgiven—though not Francisco Porras, who was put in irons.

The day of relief dawned in June, when an ancient caravel hove in view. Its decrepit timbers would never have survived an Atlantic crossing, but who cared? Laboriously the ship carried them to Santo Domingo, a return to civilization of sorts, on 13 August 1504. An icy encounter between Ovando and Columbus ensued, the one in full possession of his dignity, the other a relic of the man whose instinct and courage twelve years earlier had inaugurated a new epoch in history.

Ferdinand Columbus described the scene: 'The Governor received the Admiral quite hospitably, accommodating him in the official residence. However, it was like the kiss of a scorpion, for he also released Francisco Porras, ringleader of the mutineers, and declared his intention of punishing those responsible for his imprisonment.' It was one more wound for the battered spirit of the Admiral of the Ocean Sea.

Another chartered ship carried him home, along with his brother, his son and just twenty-two of the complement with which he had confidently embarked on this fourth voyage. The rest, like the lotus-eaters of mythology, elected to abide awhile—happily so for them, as the return proved a 16-day misery punctuated by fearful tempests and heart-stopping mishaps. The caravel made tiny Sanlucar de Barrameda near Cadiz on 7 November. Two weeks later Queen Isabella died. This event, as much as any other, signalled the end of the mariner's epic career.

She had succeeded to the throne in 1474 as ruler of the minor kingdom of Castile. She left it much enhanced, the dominant power bordering the Mediterranean. In its united state the realm, crossing the line from medievalism to modernity, assumed an exalted rank in Europe by virtue of the energy and skill with which the monarchs thrust themselves into the business of government. They also evinced a capacity for cruelty, as in their treatment of Muslims and Jews, and Isabella had finally agreed, in 1503, the enslavement of Indians due to their widespread cannibalism. They were therefore beyond Christian redemption. But this would bring upon the monarchs posterity's condemnation. It was not the verdict of contemporary society, which shared Spanish attitudes of intolerance without the same opportunities for their practice. Ferdinand had generally served his queen well.

Yet in a totally unexpected turn of events, revealing more about their marital state than ever could be discerned during her lifetime, Isabella bequeathed her crown not to her co-ruler and consort, but to their daughter Joanna, wife of the Archduke Philip of Burgundy in alien Ghent. It was all the more inexplicable since this daughter's mind was totally unhinged. She brooded in silence for days on end, opening her mouth only to speak in fantasies. When her thoughts settled on her husband's inconstancy, her violence required curbing by armed guards. Truly, Joanna did not realize what she had inherited. Not so her husband. He intended to hold firm to the fabulous endowment that came with her person. It brought Castile into union with the Netherlands.

Naturally, Ferdinand remained the crowned head of Aragon. But then, Joanna was his daughter and lawful heir too, therefore his kingdom must eventually go the way of Castile, to a foreign prince. Not only was Ferdinand wounded personally by the terms of his wife's testament, the broader implications wrought devastation upon his plans, so carefully laid, for Aragon to assume the leadership of Christendom. Now his kingdom could well be reduced to a mere province ruled from a distant capital. Had he dreamed and schemed over the years in order for all his achievements to fall into the hands of this son-in-law, a Habsburg! Was this a trick God played against him when taking his own dear son? He had nurtured the opposite purpose in engineering the dual marriage of his children with those of the Holy Roman Emperor. Dare he remain impassive while the son of Maximilian clambered over the incapacity of Ferdinand's sick daughter to occupy this august throne, of which he was the principal architect?

There could only be one answer: Ferdinand must begin his calculations afresh. If no longer King of Castile he was nevertheless its designated regent, acting in the absence of Joanna and her husband Philip, who were still detained in the Netherlands. This could buy him time enough to take a second wife for himself and produce another, more appropriate heir—specifically, a son.

The thought allowed him little inclination to bandy arguments with Christopher Columbus, an admiral irremediably embittered now, and unemployed except for the agitation he sedulously pursued for recognition of his dignities to the full and to extract the maximum income due from the empire materializing from his endeavours. The last two years of his life would pass in inglorious controversy over his gold. Columbus held Ferdinand to the letter of his 1492 contract, asserting that Bobadilla first had cheated him, then Ovando. Moreover, he stood loyally by his companions of that fourth voyage. The seamen had accumulated considerable back pay in credit from that arduous expedition, yet every base device was being introduced to deny it to them.

His strength receding, Columbus followed the regency in residence from Segovia to Medina del Campo and thence to Salamanca until, worn out, he retired to Seville. Ferdinand, observing during an audience reluctantly granted that the man was nearing his end, sanctioned a more than adequate settlement of all claims. It made the house of Columbus among the wealthiest in Spain.

Prayer brought the Discoverer solace as religion increasingly dominated his personality. Thus he set funds aside for a crusade, for charity and other sacred causes. His gold endowed a chapel in Hispaniola. Offices were to be recited in perpetuity there for his soul. Columbus died in

Valladolid on 20 May 1506, aged fifty-six, never conceding that his 'Indies' lay in a part of the world remote from Asia. His funeral took place without the presence of a bishop and lacked the ceremony commensurate with the farewell to a great man.

Three years later the lustre of the name revived, for his son Diego succeeded to all his dignities with appointment as Governor of Hispaniola and the Islands. The family additionally received Veragua as hereditary duchy, so gaining title to that Panamanian region where the last expedition had drawn breath before grinding to extinction on the island of Jamaica.

Christopher's ashes probably rest in the cathedral of Santo Domingo, though Spaniards debate the issue to this day. On the order of his descendants the casket certainly crossed the Atlantic, but the records are obscure as to whether Hispaniola was his ultimate burial place. Many believe the casket now lies within his elaborate nineteenth-century monument in Seville Cathedral. It is as though the spirit of the Discoverer continues to wander between the Old World and the New.

Chapter Ten

TWILIGHT
OF THE LESSER GODS

he spark ignited by Columbus in 1492 fired Spain and Portugal to build colonial empires unimpeded for a century before any rival could seriously enter the field. And having fastened a Hispanic girdle round the world the Iberian powers captured the global mercantile destiny for Europe. The first to navigate the oceans, they could lay claim to the remote territories still beyond others' reach. It was *their* ships that criss-crossed the tradeways, *their* gunpowder that coerced native peoples into service, *their* monopolies that funnelled back the riches.

Little did Spain and Portugal realize how the power so swiftly attained could just as easily fade. They had bitten off more than they could digest. But they demonstrated a truism which, strangely, had lain unperceived since the Norsemen's epoch: communities washed by the wildest seas could build vessels stout enough to ride the storms and reach horizons hitherto uncharted except in legend.

Therefore, when the time arrived for Spain and Portugal to surrender their supremacy, this had to descend to their only significant opponents, likewise Christian and equally positioned close to the Atlantic. Inevitably, capitalism followed in their tracks. Monarchs proposed, bankers disposed. Capitalism operated in an arena of intricate arithmetic, with trust transcending national boundaries. The requirement of long-term credit obeyed arcane laws of profit and loss. The Europeans who possessed those secrets were rarely from the same expansionist countries. In any event, here was a combination that made the smallest of the planet's continents the greatest.

That other spark, the Renaissance, ignited by Florence and brought to its flaming Italian splendour by the time of Lorenzo the Magnificent's death, also in 1492, ensured that Europeans similarly dominated the world intellectually, by virtue of their cultural and technological achievements. Italy as a spiritual force, like Spain and Portugal in physical strength, would fail to maintain its leadership. It too passed the torch on. Nevertheless all else flowed between these two powerful engines of change. Henceforward whatever progress occurred in distant parts, whatever the languages of enlightenment and commerce, the administrations created, the tyrannies imposed, would grow out of Europe. So it remained until the twentieth century, when the struggle for global domination reached its climax and neutered the contestants, thereby availing the countless millions of Europe's subject peoples across the world the opportunities to discover their own identities and choose their separate destinies.

We have already observed the European paradox that in retrospect appears as an irony of cosmic proportions. In 1492 this continent, despite its plenitude of innovation and energy, was not yet strong enough, nor did it possess the collective will, to protect its own eastern borderlands. Europe was not divided from Asia by any broad stretch of water in the way that the Mediterranean blocked off Africa. What Iberia achieved for itself by courtesy of the ocean, Europe could not do where its soil mingled with the soil of a contiguous civilization. As water granted Christendom the physical advantage at its western extremity, so land bestowed this upon Islam in the East. Bottled up in the Mediterranean as a result of the Spanish recovery of Granada, Islamic power was thus deprived of expansion into the western hemisphere. In the East its religious spread gathered many different races under its spell, but this did not equate with political domination. Not that the Muslims had by any means abandoned Europe. On the contrary, the white continent in 1492 still represented an attainable prey to an ever-aggressive creed that thought of itself rather than Christianity to be elected by God as supreme over the earth.

As previously noted, Venice was no longer capable, by 1492, of holding the Turks at bay in the Mediterranean. Once the guardian of the continent's vulnerable underbelly, the maritime republic had now to preserve its strength for its own survival, letting the sleeping dogs of war lie. Only most reluctantly would it challenge the movement of Ottoman fleets. A new Christian champion, Ivan the Great, had successfully contained the Muslim drift across the steppes, though a mass of unfinished argument with Poland and Lithuania (a composite kingdom) lay ahead before the Duchy of Moscow could be synonymous with Russia. Ivan might well proclaim himself the heir to Byzantium and Rome, but he commanded a population woefully behind the times in the European sense. Thus beneath the flow of Christian verbiage promising resumption of war against the Saracens and its intended culmination in the reconquest of the Holy Land, excuses multiplied. Spain, having expelled Islam from Andalusia, the place in which that civilization had turned passive, and despite pretensions to the contrary, had thereby completed its anti-Muslim mission except where Moorish North Africa beckoned. So had France, whose European consciousness did not match its other immense accomplishments. England was as yet unready for a substantial military role.

As much by default as desire, responsibility for the expulsion of the Ottomans from Europe descended upon whoever wore the regalia of Holy Roman Emperor. In 1492 the thirty-three-year-old Maximilian, King of the Romans, already felt the weight of this charge. His liveliest interest and deepest loyalty centred on his native Austria. Much of that inheritance his father, the Emperor Frederick III, had lost to the Hungarians during one of those somnolent interludes of his long reign. Maximilian, we recall, had recaptured the territory, except for the portion swallowed by Venice. However, the Turks lay in waiting nearby. One long jump and they could repeat the Hungarian feat of seizing Vienna. Another and they could plunge the Muslim dagger into western Europe's heartland while doubtless its numerous monarchs would still be debating the allocation of blame.

Happily for the fate of Europe, Sultan Bayezid became immersed, after his 1503 truce with Venice, in a civil war in Anatolia. That ferocious Sunni-Shia struggle, compounded with a holding operation in western Persia, was destined to occupy Bayezid virtually until his death in 1512. Still, who could be sure? An atmosphere of agonizing uncertainty in Poland, Hungary and the Empire hung over the respite, for the Ottoman mission demanded continuous *jihad* against the Christian infidel. Bayezid's successor, Selim I, made preparations for an assault. He exercised his kingly prerogative of putting his brothers and nephews to death—manifestly protecting his rear. Fortuitously, a more pressing objective then consumed his energies: conquest of Syria and Egypt. Selim (the 'Grim Sultan') never ventured beyond the fortresses guarding his dominion over south-eastern Europe. The Emperor Maximilian would therefore end his reign without being tested in this greatest of labours. His military exploits, involving the usual recurring cast of characters, were restricted to a lesser theatre, Christian against Christian.

His frustrations as head of an amorphous empire lacking all united purpose explain a good deal of Maximilian's well-meaning though erratic behaviour. His son Philip ceased to recognize his father as regent of the Netherlands (the Burgundian inheritance) by the age of sixteen—Philip's coming of age in 1494. Philip was not the son to Maximilian that the latter had been to Emperor Frederick, and he widened the chasm separating himself as a western European sovereign from his parent as head of a central European confederation. Philip's disposition led him naturally to friendship with France. In one of his several capacities, Count of Flanders and Artois, he owed allegiance to Louis XII, not his father. Furthermore, Philip was smoothing the path and clarifying his obligations for his eventual possession of Castile, and then Aragon, through his mentally sick consort Joanna.

Louis reciprocated the warmth Philip evinced towards him because the Netherlands, once freed of Maximilian's influence, ceased to constitute an avenue for the possible invasion of France. The situation was quite otherwise in regard to Philip's relations with Ferdinand the Catholic. As we know, the latter clung to the hope of depriving his Habsburg son-in-law of the Spanish patrimony. He saw the younger man as devoid of character, yet arrogant. Ferdinand had bested worthier rivals. How infuriating that the Castilian grandees adopted a kinder attitude to this foreigner than to himself, architect of the country's greatness! Given the everchanging pattern of alliances blighting European harmony, we need to register that such was the position in the year of Isabella's death, 1504, when Philip also took pains to strengthen relations with England. Flourishing commerce between the island kingdom and the Netherlands determined it; diplomatic support for Philip's accession to Spain demanded it.

Philip contrasted with his father Maximilian in his desire to avoid war at all costs. He endeavoured, fruitlessly, to mediate between Ferdinand and Louis in their opposing claims to Naples. As though Ferdinand would permit his Flemish son-in-law to nullify his intentions there! Again, it troubled Philip not in the slightest that Louis remained ensconced in Milan, an imperial fief, after his expulsion from Naples, although this pained Maximilian as much as the Venetian hold on his Austrian inheritances located in northern Italy. So, inevitably, we are drawn back to that complex country. Much had changed in that cockpit, principally arising from the death of Pope Alexander in 1503 and the consequent collapse of Cesare Borgia's influence as the shadow behind the Holy See.

If his many enemies were to be believed, Alexander's departure from this life was no ordinary human occurrence. One diarist wrote of his demise as being signalled by the devil, in the shape of an ape, stealing through a window of the Pope's bedchamber. The sultry summer of 1503 brought an epidemic of plague to Rome. Death permeated the Vatican no less than the squalid dwellings of the poorest neighbourhood. Both the Pope and his son fell violently ill and this, noted the sensation-mongers haunting the great palace, could hardly make for coincidence. Had they inadvertently served each other with a lethal potion intended for some Borgia victim? However, Cesare recovered while, on 18 August, Alexander perished. According to that meticulous supervisor of pontifical protocol, Johannes Burchard, the Pope suffered prolonged agonies un-attended, since no one would willingly approach his bed. Cesare marked verification of his father's death by directing his servants to ransack Alexander's apartments, removing everything of value, including a great quantity of personal treasure. The action was reminiscent of the at-tempted plunder by Franceschetto Cibo when he calculated, mistakenly it transpired, that his father Pope Innocent VIII had just died.

Another gruesome picture: Alexander's body. It lay in the bare dark chamber overnight without caring watch, swelling to distortion, the face grotesque and turned a deep purple. The flesh required mutilation to squeeze it into its casket. Further details were related by a gloating Francesco Gonzaga of Mantua in a letter to his duchess Isabella d'Este:

> He was carried to the grave with little honour, his body dragged from the bed to the sepulchre by a porter who fastened a cord to his feet, as no one would touch him. His funeral was so miserable, the wife of the lame dwarf at Mantua received a more honourable burial. Scandalous inscrip-tions are written over his grave every day.

The indignity of it all corresponded with the moral depths to which the papacy had sunk during the reign. Alexander's better traits soon went beyond recollection while the tales of infamy entered history. Cesare retained his Captain-General's place as master of Rome for two months more, thanks to the fidelity, worthy of a better cause, of a clique of influential cardinals.

Georges d'Amboise, the cardinal whose hand guided every movement of Louis of France, reasonably anticipated he would be the next to wear the tiara. His credentials included a substantial detachment of French troops stationed in Rome. And surely Cesare would now repay his many debts to Louis by intimidating the conclave. Unluckily for Amboise, an equally formidable candidate was making his presence felt in the Eternal

City—Alexander's old rival Giuliano della Rovere. He claimed the hour belonged to none but him. Another foreign pope? They dared not elect the Frenchman, he argued, for the sake of the holy Church, and Italy's pride. Evidently della Rovere hoped his own previous investment in French patronage was forgotten, or forgiven. Deadlock resulted amid the usual unseemly scramble for favours, and the impasse eventually terminated with the election of an aged compromise candidate, Francesco Piccolomini, as Pius III. This Sienese nephew of the versatile humanist scholar (and sometime author of love stories) Pius II tottered to the throne, only to survive for three brief weeks.

Promptly returning to the fray, della Rovere abandoned those scruples impelling him to chastise Alexander all the twelve years of the latter's reign. Some cardinals he bribed, others he threatened. Cesare Borgia received conciliatory overtures, encouraging the Duke of Romagna to deceive himself into believing his rank and person were safe. Della Rovere thereby won the unanimous vote of the conclave, and as Julius II celebrated his first Mass in the Lateran at last on 1 November 1503. Immensely energetic and confident, a secular statesman as well as a prelate, this Pope wore armour as comfortably as a surplice. In fact he revelled in warfare and was castigated accordingly by Erasmus, who flailed the Church for its unchristian practices in the bitter satire *In Praise of Folly*. Machiavelli, by contrast, admired Julius unreservedly.

The Church now found itself with a leader indeed. Julius began by cleansing the Vatican of many malpractices. He plunged into the recovery of the remaining portions of the Papal States—Bologna from the Bentivoglio, Perugia from the Baglioni—as well as other cities whose rulers had retained a vestige of independence by toadying to Venice. Rome underwent a dramatic change. Cesare was left friendless in the capital and deprived of an army of his own. Loyalists of the Orsini and Colonna families returned in strength, with the two clans, overbearing as ever, restored as traditional guardians of the city and thirsting for revenge against the Borgia. Cesare escaped to Ostia in the hope of negotiating some favours from the Pope. But Julius stripped him of his papal titles and sent men to take him under arrest, though prudence told Julius to keep the general, once so renowned, among the living.

Painful times ensued for Cesare Borgia. He was allowed a small measure of freedom, which he employed in storing his prodigious wealth in the Genoese banks and in seeking the protection of Gonsalvo de Córdoba, Ferdinand's viceroy in Naples. If he expected a friendly reception from that quarter he was disappointed. The Borgia family were finished as a power and Ferdinand the Catholic was now paying court to Julius, historically his suzerain in respect of the regained kingdom of Naples. Why alienate the new Pope for the sake of a fallen idol? Even Louis discarded Cesare.

On Ferdinand's instructions Gonsalvo made Cesare captive and transported him to Spain, a prison in Valencia—the diocese which its quondam archbishop had never previously entered. This was not quite the end. As ever a fighter, Cesare attempted to escape, only to be caught while trying to kill a warder. He was then transferred to a fortress in Medina del Campo, from which he succeeded in liberating himself. Reaching Navarre, whose king was Cesare's brother-in-law, he enrolled in the royal service, finally meeting his death during a local civil war in 1507.

For an epitaph, we recall the marriage of Cesare to Charlotte d'Albret, mother of his child, Louise. The widow never saw her husband again after their first few months together. Nevertheless she now mourned him deeply. The term is to be read literally, for Charlotte attired herself in black, covered the walls of her chateau in black, and even her bed linen. Every article of daily use was somehow fringed with the colour of grief. Louise, rescued from the sombre abode by the death of her mother in 1514, married Louis de la Tremouille, a French soldier of eminence.

Thenceforward the House of Borgia wove into the fabric of the era's multitudinous nobility, part Italian, part Spanish, part French. As Duchess of Ferrara Lucrezia achieved a second personality without radically altering her conduct. Always admired for her beauty, she gained the respect of the Ferrarese by her charitable works. There were various related bastard children to care for while she tended her Renaissance garden. But Lucrezia could not tolerate boredom and during her husband's frequent absences found diversion in a succession of love affairs, one of which, with Francesco Gonzaga, brought the wrath of her sister-in-law Isabella d'Este on her head.

A grandson of Juan, Duke of Gandia, retreated from baser tumults to enroll in the Society of Jesus, serving with such pious dedication as to be appointed General of the Jesuit Order. He ultimately achieved canonization. Another dimly connected descendant further brightened the family escutcheon on his election in the next century as Pope Innocent X. The civil war in Navarre that claimed Cesare's life had arisen because mutually hostile branches of the same French dynasty disputed the state's possession while being universally abominated by the true, Basque originating, Navarrese. Straddling the Pyrenees, desperately poor, the little kingdom packed a long and violent history within its narrow geographical confines. For some three centuries it had been dominated and protected on both sides of the mountains by the French, the terrain producing an isolated pastoral society riddled with superstition and devil worship. (One future day it would offer much employment to the Inquisition.) Rising steeply on the French side, the range was difficult to traverse and thus formed an ideal natural barrier to the advantage of Spain, though the opposite was the case from the south. Here it gave more gradually on to the Ebro plain, inviting easy invasion of France—one of the reasons why Ferdinand ardently desired Navarre for himself.

Ferdinand's father, John of Aragon, had previously ruled there as consort to its Queen Blanche, his first wife (not Ferdinand's mother). We need not pursue the complicated interrelationships concerned with Navarre: the Albrets, their kinsfolk the Foix and the French royal house (an Albret yet unborn would ascend the throne of France as Henry IV and marry Marie de' Medici) though naturally Ferdinand observed their situation with the sly interest of a participant. Was he not a virile widower with a crown of his own to bestow? With just a little stirring of the dynastic mixture he might well turn the succession to Navarre back to the House of Aragon. He thought of marriage again, and of another son perhaps, born of this second wife. In the happy prospect lay also the possibility of preventing Philip, Duke of Burgundy, from reaping the monumental bonus of Castile, and ultimately of Aragon too, by virtue of Philip's union with the inadequate Joanna, Ferdinand's daughter.

A twenty-three-year-old beauty, Germaine de Foix, appeared in his sights. She was a niece of Louis XII and Ferdinand's own remote kin. Germaine accepted his proffered hand. If this involved a complete volte-face in regard to France the old chess-master was more than ready. Discarding friends and burying troublesome hatchets came as second nature to Ferdinand. He and Louis signed a treaty of alliance in October 1505. In so doing, Louis' special relationship with Philip changed to hostility.

Ferdinand married Germaine six months later, when he was fifty-four. Now for a son, to be legitimate heir to Aragon, Naples, the Balearics and Sardinia and, with God's blessing, Castile too. The dynasty would thus survive through the male line, to take within its compass the numerous crowns Ferdinand had accrued, whether as inheritance, by wedlock, in battle and through cunning, or anticipated as a consequence of Columbus's discoveries—all, in fact, that now seemed on the point of slipping through his fingers. What he had to do was skip a generation.

Jeanne D'Albret, daughter of Marguerite d'Angoulême, (sister of Francis I) was mother of Henry IV

Fearful of the sudden change of wind blowing through his intentions, Philip sailed with Joanna for Spain from the Netherlands with a considerable fleet for the purpose of declaring formal possession. He had earlier crossed to Spain overland through France, a route now ruled out of the question because of Louis' new attitude towards him. It was January 1506, and the Channel was so tempestuous that the Flemish ships were driven on to the English coast near Weymouth. But this was an experience Philip welcomed, for the shelter granted the opportunity for a meeting at Windsor with Henry VII.

To record that the two sovereigns collapsed into each other's arms would exaggerate. Nevertheless they had long sought a meeting to bind even closer the commercial ties between England and the Netherlands. Henry played the benevolent veteran statesman. He outwitted Philip— not a difficult manoeuvre—and won more than he gave, promising English naval support in the event of an armed struggle against Ferdinand over Castile. Two unhappy sisters were occasioned a brief reunion: Catherine, the homesick young widow marooned without an English friend and not yet accepted by the younger Henry; Joanna, the wife already made haggard by her mental condition and the cruel neglect she suffered from an uncaring husband.

Eventually Ferdinand and Philip met face to face in a village near Valladolid, the older man warmly embracing his daughter and displaying polite deference towards the Habsburg. Joanna, if nothing else a fruitful wife, had already given birth to her Habsburg heir in the Prinsenhof at Ghent. The boy Charles was under the care of Philip's sibling, now known as Margaret of Austria. That much-bespoken lady had returned to the homeland of her youth childless, following the death of her second husband the Duke of Savoy.

In choosing his young French bride Germaine de Foix Ferdinand had overlooked the Castilian reflex. As we know, he had never been popular with important sections of the ruling caste there and now he lost still more in public esteem. Germaine in no sense satisfied the grandees as a worthy successor to their Queen Isabella, whose memory and pious image the Castilians had come to revere. A psychological factor entered the equation, for Ferdinand appeared to have shrunk back in their eyes to his Aragonese origins, with the old animosities rising to the surface. The qualities that made him an ideal consort and a premier statesman of Europe now gave way in Castile to that other impression, disreputable wiliness. Contrariwise, in his own kingdom anti-Castilian sentiment gained strength. He was their man. The loyal Cortes of Barcelona had long written into its statutes that a legitimate male heir of Ferdinand, no matter the mother, would automatically succeed to the kingdom of Aragon.

Ferdinand almost achieved an arrangement with Philip. They would rule Castile jointly, he proposed, and should Joanna recover her mental balance, as a triad. It would form a close family compact. On reflection, however, Philip reacted stiffly. The Castilian mood was thoroughly opposed to the old fox and Philip needed to carry his new subjects wholly with him. The answer was No. It was the last the two men saw of each other. Angrily, Ferdinand withdrew to Aragon and avenged himself by purging that kingdom of its Castilian officials. Shortly afterwards he took his pregnant wife to reside in Naples, where one of his earliest measures was to expel its Castilian viceroy, *el Gran Capitan* Gonsalvo de Córdoba.

As so often elsewhere in this narrative, the fates intervened to reduce the scheming of their playthings to naught. In September 1506, Philip of Burgundy, ruler of the Netherlands, died at Burgos. The young man of twenty- eight had barely savoured one Spanish summer. Such a bizarre relationship, his marriage with Joanna! One of her peculiarities was never to allow him out of her sight, for a single moment. She had trailed his movements continuously, even to the beds of other partners more to his preference. Nonetheless that unfortunate woman, unable to distinguish the world she inhabited from the world of her wild imagination, bore Philip six robust children, two of them sons. Charles, domiciled in Brussels, had not as yet seen his younger brother Ferdinand, born in 1502 during Joanna's earlier visit to her family in Spain. This boy, remaining in the charge of Spanish guardians, spoke their language while Charles was nurtured in French.

All of Joanna's offspring would in time wear royal crowns. Sacrificed to reasons of state and shifted around half the thrones of Europe like pedigree cattle at an auction, the princesses resided in palaces without number, none of which warranted the description of a home. And all the while their mad mother occupied only one, more a prison than a palace, at Tordesillas. Was it a mercy that she herself would be spared for a further half-century? During the first fourteen years, locked in the obsession that the day was about to dawn when Philip would quicken into life, she refused to surrender his embalmed body for burial. Meanwhile the young consort of King Ferdinand performed as behoved a royal bride and duly gave birth to a son. Sadly, he survived just a few hours. And so the cards needed to be shuffled afresh, since Joanna was now, during Charles's minority, the sole legitimate monarch of Castile.

In the circumstances, the vacuum of authority there demanded a strong administrator of the highest prestige. As it transpired, one such was available. Power in the land rested in the capable hands of the Archbishop of Toledo, Jiménez de Cisneros, later to be elevated to the cardinalate. We have already encountered the prelate. During the entire history of the long Muslim presence in Spain few Christian names are recalled by that abused people with greater revulsion, because of the zeal with which he persecuted the Moors left in Granada subsequent to the elimination of their independent kingdom (see p. 60). Cisneros now occupied the office of Inquisitor General, an appointment he owed to the religious and political influence he had exerted over Queen Isabella. Her dying wish, to carry the Christian banner against the Moors into Africa, led Cisneros to organize the siege and capture first of Mers el-Kebir and later Oran on the Barbary Coast. While still engaged on this ostensibly holy war he grew anxious for the future of Spain itself should the country be inundated by Netherlander officials once Charles came of age. As a fanatic for the purity of Hispanic blood he dreaded the importation of Flemings, Walloons and Jews from those hybrid Burgundian lands.

Cisneros implored Ferdinand's return from Naples, overriding Castilian objections on the grounds that Isabella's testament specified such an arrangement in the contingency of Joanna's affliction proving permanent. He regarded Ferdinand as the least of all evils. Constitutionally, the erstwhile King of Castile assumed the office of the country's regent. Now he could resume an active Spanish foreign policy, attending more closely than previously to problems in the Indies, controlling the campaigns in North Africa and keeping steady watch over the confused situation in Navarre.

Most immediately, Ferdinand's thoughts returned to Italy, a country perennially caught in the toils of unfinished military business. To be sure, one of the city-states preferred it that way—Venice. It had always profited through the rivalries engendered by the peninsula's helplessness. But the Most Serene Republic thereby alienated almost all other rulers with a stake in Italy. Ferdinand, Louis of France and the Emperor Maximilian had as much cause to join forces as they had grounds to clash with every change in the Italian political climate. Pope Julius was not averse to using them, together or severally, to pull chestnuts out of the fire on his account; such was the papal privilege, hallowed by tradition if not by God. Julius determined to activate their identity of interest again. He was in the process of recovering for the Papal States those towns remaining within Venetian shelter as a consequence of Cesare Borgia's fall. Thus once more the pendulum swung.

Louis XII cherished Milan for its artistic heritage, a legacy of the Sforzas, no less than for its solid commercial eminence. He was grateful to Leonardo da Vinci for overlooking the alien occupation of Lombardy and remaining in Milan to accept commissions as official artist and engineer. In the conviction that the duchy would stay French for ever Louis was keenly seeking an occasion to relieve Venice of the various chippings of Lombard soil it had progressively appropriated. Ferdinand experienced a like resentment because Venice, during the descent of Charles VIII upon Naples years before, had insolently occupied Brindisi and other Neapolitan ports on the Adriatic coast. As for Maximilian, his quarrel with Venice was longstanding, and related specifically to stolen Austrian inheritances on the Italian side of the Alps. Early in 1508, and ill-prepared as he never failed to be, Maximilian brushed his infantry against the Venetians, intending repossession. The outcome was a débâcle, for he lost still more in the process, including Trieste and Fiume (Rijeka), Austria's only outlets on the Adriatic. Maximilian was now licking his wounds.

That Louis and the emperor could indeed suppress their instincts of mutual hostility and converge in purpose was mainly due to the negotiating skill of Maximilian's daughter Margaret. She was appointed regent of the Netherlands on the death of her brother Philip pending the coming-of-age of his heir, Charles of Ghent. Always a steadying influence on her father, Margaret worked for peace between Habsburg and Valois, signing an agreement at Cambrai that same year of 1508 with Cardinal d'Amboise. Ferdinand lost no time in joining. The combination would drive Venice off the Italian mainland to where it truly belonged, within its own lagoon. Each partner secretly hoped for something more out of the pact, for these were indeed fair-weather friends and all three aspired to supremacy in Europe. Maximilian had not yet been crowned by the Pope as Holy Roman Emperor. He chafed at the delay and believed he could now speed matters up.

To expect such an alliance to sustain itself was of course beyond credence. Few battles were fought and fewer alliances survived. Maximilian met with a blunt rebuff from the Reichstag when requesting money for his share of the campaign, the Germans being disinclined as ever to empty their pockets in an Austrian cause. What he borrowed from the Fugger bank enabled Maximilian to win back Trieste before his withdrawal beneath a mountain of unpaid bills. Further, he never succeeded in being crowned, remaining 'Emperor-Elect' to the end of his days. Ferdinand gathered up the Brindisi littoral and that sufficed for him.

Campaigning alone, the French pursued the struggle against Venice with such effect that Louis emerged as the strong man of Italy. His aspirations extended far beyond the object envisioned at Cambrai, and a troubled Maximilian feared he could lose to France whatever Austrian lands were still due from Venice. Pope Julius too recognized in Louis the immemorial scourge of his fragmented country. Two years after the signing of that agreement, now looking so bleakly transparent, he took the initiative in turning the tables.

A more serious order of battle came into operation: Venice and Rome in a so-called Holy League isolating France and supported by Ferdinand. Maximilian opened the Brenner Pass to enable the Swiss, who had been losing important trading interests to the French, to sweep into Lombardy. Coming up from the rear, young Henry VIII of England, newly enthroned and itching to make some impact on the European scene for purposes of his own, attached himself to the re-formed alliance. Louis, recognizing here the desperation that comes with envy, despised them all and brought up an army led by his superb cavalry of 3,000 horses.

Determined to illustrate the perils of treating too lightly the ancient French claim to Milan, Louis made of his isolation a challenge to the spiritual supremacy of the pugnacious Pope. He summoned his French cardinals, besides other bishops harbouring a grievance against Julius, to Pisa, there to constitute a general council of the Church with the object of unseating the Holy Father. Here was war in earnest, Louis remarking that they were making a Moor out of him. Julius was equal to the situation: he could take an army into battle, he could administer the papal dominion as no one before him in a hundred years, and whatsoever his past record he lamented the indignities thrust upon Italy. He called a council of his own (the Fifth Lateran Council, 1512) where he made a grand showing of all the authority implicit in his office against the French king. He even mooted the idea, fortunately not proceeded with, of pronouncing the throne of France vacant and replacing Louis with Henry VIII. Julius was hardly the man to tolerate the insubordination which had created schism in the Church and the proliferation of 'anti-popes' in times past.

The rival armies clashed at Ravenna on 11 April 1512. The French, ably led by a heroic young general, the prince of the blood Gaston de Foix, managed in a bitterly fought engagement to defeat a strong force of Spanish and papal troops. All France grieved when it learned of

Gaston's death in action, but not France alone. Germaine, his enemy Ferdinand's queen, mourned the most. Gaston de Foix was her brother. Louis' army then turned back to face the Swiss, but failed to hold Milan. So once again the French withdrew from Italy, badly mauled after Ravenna by the wounds dealt them by this most iron-willed infantry of all, not mercenaries for once but rather operating in their own interest. A puppet Sforza returned to assume nominal rule over the duchy as a client of the cantons. A Medici was restored to Florence. However, this by no means completed the circle. Another generation would inherit the conflict.

Ferdinand the Catholic, fitful ally but unforgiving foe, sprang to the occasion in Navarre on the news that Gaston de Foix had perished. Did this not render Germaine first in line to the throne of the little kingdom? On the pretext of his wife's right he invaded, hence recovering the last of the lands constituting his agenda for the House of Aragon. In this regard he employed a characteristic stratagem, utilizing the goodwill stored in the marriage, performed at last, of his youngest daughter Catherine to Henry VIII. Ferdinand invited this English son-in-law (who did not require much persuasion) to mount an assault on Guyenne, that south-west corner of France once belonging to the Plantagenets, while his own troops entered Navarre. The harebrained Tudor expedition, equal in pointlessness to the attack Henry's father made upon Brittany in 1492, ended in disease and ignominy for a pathetically ill-equipped body of Englishmen under the Marquis of Dorset. All it achieved was to hold a French army immobile, guarding the Atlantic coast, as the deed of swallowing Navarre was done. 'Basse Navarre' over the Pyrenes subsequently returned to the Albrets, within the terms of a later agreement concluded with France.

Immortality not being among the supernal qualities inherent in sovereignty, all the leading participants in the ongoing international pageant of ambition and deception, dreams fulfilled and expectations dashed, were shortly due to change. Louis, but recently married to his third wife, Henry VIII's sister Mary, died in 1515, Ferdinand one year later. Pope Julius, whose mind adapted eminently to campaign strategy even as he worked at transforming Rome into the greatest Renaissance city, preceded them both, in 1513. He had initiated the construction of the new St Peter's and, at the price of 10,000 ducats, commissioned his own tomb from Michelangelo to rest in it. Julius intended his sepulchre to rise as a colossal sculpture embracing forty biblical figures, though when ultimately executed the work would dwindle in magnitude, if not in power, as the noble 'Moses', and be housed in the lesser basilica of San Pietro in Vincoli. The fee also shrank in the process, the Pope's heirs paying only 4,800 ducats for the marble masterpiece. Julius survived long enough to watch over the completion of Michelangelo's Sistine Ceiling and observe Raphael begin his decoration of the Vatican apartments.

Maximilian, Archduke and Emperor, was not quite for the grave. He would live to see his Flemish grandson Charles enter his maturity in the Netherlands and take upon his shoulders the many realms of his other grandfather Ferdinand, with still more to follow. On Ferdinand's death Cardinal Cisneros returned to the regency of Spain, reluctantly as it happened, pending Charles's coronation. The stern cleric had spent his freedom from affairs of state, as well as his personal fortune, in supervising the redaction at Alcala of his Polyglot Bible—the Testaments in their most authoritative Hebrew-Aramaic, Greek and Latin texts. This achievement of scholarship set a standard in linguistic studies that would in time penetrate through the clamour of the kings who swore by the Bible but failed to live by it.

Chapter Eleven

HABSBURG OVER EUROPE

espite Maximilian's failure to reconcile his sacred pledge as Holy Roman Emperor with his efforts to foster his own Archduchy of Austria as a European power comparable with France and Spain, he never lost his personal popularity as leader nonpareil in the eyes of Germany as a whole. He was the figurehead of noble mien and strong racial motivation. They loved Maximilian precisely for those characteristics that hampered him as an autocrat: accessibility, lightness of touch, a man of the people simultaneously radiating extraordinary qualities of personal grace. And so striking a contrast to his wholly unendowed father Frederick III! This conglomerate of a nation, the most numerous population in Europe, approved of the direction in which he wished to take them—towards unity of purpose—but not to the point of surrendering the rights and privileges they had dragged over from the feudal system.

The various princes, knights and free cities, altogether comprising some 360 individual units, acknowledged no horizon beyond themselves. Secluded within the continent and blinkered against change, they conceded the necessity for security, but the conflicts between the powers over possession of this or that peripheral territory left them cold. German princes other than Maximilian felt little concern, and no sense of obligation, towards the satellite countries recognizing him as their titular suzerain. The Empire was an elective monarchy and the long occupation of the throne by the Habsburgs notwithstanding, its crown was not bestowed through automatic succession. In theory any Christian king could ascend to it. Indeed, some still tried.

In his capacity as sovereign duke over Austria, Maximilian folded his responsibility there, with its Italian and Slav extensions, into the larger

imperial scheme. To defend the one, he maintained, necessitated defence
of the other. Moreover, given a large and publicly financed German
army, the Empire could resume its implied role of yore, near to the
concept of a universal Christian monarchy. That's where the Reichstag
balked, rendering the twenty-six years of Maximilian's reign a succession
of failed enterprises and humiliating demonstrations of impotence. It had
long been thus. The Habsburgs would acquire rich territories through
marriage but little by military conquest. Maximilian could cite the Ottoman menace as demanding a united effort of resistance and, before his
death in 1519, raise to the Reichstag the danger of expanding Muscovite
power. It was to little avail. Russia appeared too far away, and calls for
a crusade hardly activated the German Church, thoroughly unimpressed
as it was by Rome. The army he finally organized, the Landsknechte
modelled on the Swiss pattern, fought well when it chose but, like the
Swiss, responded unpredictably to orders, often chasing after booty rather
than an enemy.

Confronting a France restive with designs upon the Low Countries
and Franche-Comté, both formerly Burgundian, and Venetian penetration of Italy, and the vulnerability of Austria itself as feeble Hungary's
neighbour, Maximilian distributed his energies in a multiplicity of Habsburg causes. Hungary shared a crown in common with Bohemia-Moravia,
a Slav constituent of the Empire. On their side the Magyar population
of Hungary regarded the Habsburgs and the Turks with almost equal
repugnance. Concurrently, the emperor's difficulties inside Germany
largely stemmed from the fear of his brother princes there that Austria,
an empire within the Empire, limited their own independence as members of a free confederation.

Not so many years were past since 1491, when he had recaptured
Vienna and the Lower Austrian provinces from Hungary for Frederick
III while the Magyars stood in daily fear of Ottoman invasion. The sultan
already possessed Serbia. The son had won his father's lands back, it will
be recalled (p. 74), from a Magyar kingdom suddenly destabilized by the
death of its warrior ruler, Matthias Corvinus. Maximilian could have
marched into Hungary then and there against little opposition, except
that his unpaid German mercenaries refused to go on. In any case the
conquest was not absolutely vital, since Hungary was already mortgaged
to the Austrian future. As early as 1463 Frederick had arrived at an
arrangement with Matthias, subsequently reaffirmed, that failing male
succession Hungary would accept the Habsburgs. Old Frederick had in

fact legally adopted Matthias Corvinus as his son, thereby regularizing possible annexation in the guise of family right.

Still, the existing line had held, through the Jagiello dynasty ruling Bohemia, Poland and Lithuania in parallel, and this provisionally saved the situation so far as the Magyar nobles were concerned. They were adamant in refusing the succession to a Habsburg. Maximilian, equally intent upon securing the kingdom, negotiated the obstacle in a pact ludicrous and cynical to our eyes but in those days regarded as a practical act of state. Before an unborn Jagiello child was due, sex unknown, he undertook to give an available granddaughter Mary, fifth offspring of Joanna and Philip, as its consort. The Jagiello babe, born prematurely in the death of its mother, mercifully proved to be a boy. To keep the infant warm and breathing he was enclosed in the bodies of freshly killed animals. Thus a Habsburg queen for a future King of Hungary and Bohemia was assured. He would become Louis II in 1516, at the age of ten.

The reigning Hungarian monarch already had a young daughter, Anne, and to make doubly certain of the succession Maximilian pledged one or other of his grandsons, Charles or Ferdinand (it was 1506, the year their father Philip of Burgundy died; Charles was six, his brother three) as her husband. These were heady days for marriage brokerage. The emperor, now a widower for the second time following the death of Bianca Sforza, agreed to take Anne for himself should neither of his grandsons claim her. Cautiously, he later enacted a ceremony of betrothal with the girl (twelve years old) in St Stephen's Cathedral at Vienna. Simultaneously, Louis of Hungary betrothed Mary, in whose veins flowed the blood of two dynasties, Spanish and Austrian. However, a grotesque union between Maximilian and the child Anne of Hungary was rendered unnecessary, for she went to the ever-agreeable Ferdinand.

Achieving these ends needed resources well beyond Maximilian's own capacity. True, Bianca had brought him wealth, but it was long gone, due both to his extravagance and to hers. The sovereign with the most august title in Europe was also among the poorest. Riches in plenty existed beneath the ground of Bohemia and Hungary, more even than in the Austrian Tyrol. These minerals had gradually come under the control of the Augsburg bankers, especially the establishments of Fugger and Hochstetter. German miners had laboured consistently for centuries in these parts. They formed the core of the East European industrial force, just as German merchants constituted its economic elite. Additionally, the age had seen the ubiquitous spread of the German clergy, into whose possession, much to the dismay of the Hungarian baronial class, had fallen extensive church lands. Tolerance of other races had always distinguished Jagiello rule, with the result that their respective kingdoms not only provided a good livelihood for Germans *en masse*, but contained the densest ghettos of European Jews since the early Middle Ages.

Inevitably, then, Hungary and Bohemia were destined one day to fall into Habsburg possession, thus terminating the long connection with Poland and Lithuania. Bohemia in particular contained rich seams of coal, tin, copper, iron and even gold. Little wonder the Fuggers hastened to the aid of the Habsburg whenever beckoned. Their interests were mutual. Habsburg rule might have been specifically designed to protect Fugger preserves, even though the bankers' investment appeared, on occasion, perilously long-term. For the rest of Maxmilian's reign Hungary was not to be a Habsburg province, the Magyars continuing to harbour strong objections to so absolute a German takeover. It would require a punishing exhibition of Ottoman strength, with Hungary broken in spirit and territorially in smithereens, before these objections could be overcome.

He aged rapidly, this Austrian hero who promised more than his subjects desired. Short of breath, the strong Habsburg jaw of Dürer's famous portrait now given to a tremble, Maximilian dared not rest as those two disruptive elements, Martin Luther of Wittenberg and Francis I of France, emerged to disturb the small residue of life left in him. Luther, the Augustinian friar with the vitriolic turn of phrase, hurled a bombshell against the all-embracing canopy of Christendom, which the emperor above any man had sworn to defend. Luther was said to have nailed his ninety-five theses to the door of the Castle Church at Wittenberg. More probably he brandished the document before the throng in the town square. The effect nonetheless was the same, a challenge to the doctrinal absolutism of the Pope with a manifesto against Catholic ritual that was to carry Europe into the blood-soaked era of religious wars. The ferment overlapped trouble in Italy yet again.

For the third time in twenty years a French king led his army across the Alps in a bid to bring Lombardy to heel and snatch Genoa in the process. Francis I succeeded his uncle Louis XII in 1515. He patched a truce with Henry VIII of England (already in the wind as evidenced in Louis' marriage in late life to Henry's sister Mary), signed an alliance with Venice and obtained the blessing of the new Pope, Lorenzo the

Magnificent's son Leo X, for his right to the Duchy of Milan. Francis made an easy bargain with Leo: he would protect the Medici, who had recently passed through the revolving doors of the Signoria in Florence for another period at the helm.

Achieving all this at a stroke, the French king incidentally demolished a hope cherished by the Swiss of rendering Lombardy a creature of their own. By destroying a powerful Swiss force in a day and a half of continuous slaughter south-east of Milan at Marignano, Francis put an end to any future pretension of the cantons to play an independent role in Europe. They lost heart for participation in its struggles other than as disinterested mercenaries. And never again would a Sforza rise in the old military tradition of the family to place his mark upon the history of Italy. The peninsula continued to produce outstanding generals, and soldiers prepared to serve with valour; but the country as a whole was incapable of raising an army in the defence of a principle so nebulous as a national cause.

With Ferdinand the Catholic dead, no substantial opponent immediately existed to contest the new young Valois king, though reputedly he inherited more of the weaknesses of Charles VIII than the strengths of Louis XII. His profound Gallic sentiment desired glory for France, so naturally crusader's rhetoric dropped frequently from his lips. The Pope originally thought to rally the Holy League of his predecessor Julius against him, but then the old strain of Medici subservience to France came through, and Leo signed a Concordat with the king that reinstated the French bishops, so recently rebellious, to favour in Rome. In return Francis (he bore the title 'Most Christian King') recognized Leo's authority, limited withal, in various matters relating to the Church in his own realm.

Of course, Maximilian could not suffer a revived French Duchy of Milan. With whatever troops he was able to muster against the inertia of the Reichstag, he forced his way into the ever-prospering city and actually held it for a day. His grandson Charles, who formally succeeded to the throne of Spain on Ferdinand's death in 1516, was not yet ready for an overseas expedition, due in part to some domestic opposition to his accession. In fact he reached an agreement with Francis to which an exhausted Maximilian was compelled to adhere, and as a consequence the emperor abandoned further military adventures, in Italy or elsewhere. Not that this signified Habsburg acquiescence to the sight of the Valois indefinitely trampling over the Italian peninsula at will. Charles would shortly take up the challenge, and bring a reckoning that Francis would find more devastating than anything either of his predecessors had experienced.

Maximilian's life terminated with every major problem of his *imperium* still unsolved. Primarily, he had not secured a firm undertaking from the Electors to recognize his grandson as King of the Romans and hence the acknowledged heir to the Empire. Already, the minds of a motley of rulers, never seriously contemplated as emperor by the German princes, buzzed with the possibility of succeeding him—among them Henry VIII, whose Lord Chancellor Cardinal Wolsey nurtured a dream of the papacy. Francis, however, was not of that ilk. The Most Christian King was a powerful candidate. He could afford the luxury, and so expended a large fortune in bribes to win the crown. Some Electors, their palms well-greased, reminded Maximilian that he himself had not as yet been ceremonially anointed by the Pope, so in any case it was surely premature to predetermine the succession for Charles.

Ever brave in the midst of a storm, optimistic to the last, pursued as always by his creditors, Maximilian departed from a meeting of the Reichstag at Augsburg to make his way back to Vienna. He must prepare for his official coronation and proceed to the fulfilment of Christendom's greatest responsibility and his dearest wish: a crusade to expel the Turk from the Balkans, then from Constantinople and at last—Jerusalem! He rested at Wels, 100 miles still to go. But his journey was over. He asked that his heart be taken to Bruges and placed in the tomb of Mary his first wife, the consort of the emperor's blushing youth and the daughter of the last medieval Duke of Burgundy. He left little to posterity, except a legend.

Without any intention of rocking the papacy, Martin Luther continued his lecturing at the University of Wittenberg, a true Catholic by his lights and by no means a rarity in the Germany of humanist thought. All he wished was to reassert the sacred message of St Paul. But the noisome seeds planted beneath the Vatican by the Borgia Pope were sprouting weeds, and Leo X was hardly the Pontiff to uproot them. That frugal man Pope Julius had saved and scraped to ensure that his successor inherited a full exchequer. In addition, taxation flowed copiously to Rome from the cities now recovered for the Papal States. It was nothing like enough for debt-ridden Leo X. Pleasure-loving, cynical and a recklessly extravagant prelate requiring 700 employees for his personal court and many thousands of ducats to spend each month on entertainment, he needed money on a scale hitherto unknown during the most profligate of Vatican regimes. He therefore turned the sale of indulgences into a highly organized commerce. In Germany this was conducted by a Dominican friar and administered, on commission, by Fugger agents. Leo's personal expenditure was not of course the only budgetary liability. Wealth was being poured into the construction of the new St Peter's as into a bottomless pit.

A generous payment for an indulgence could spare the penitent 100,000 years in the limbo of purgatory—surely a dispensation devoutly to be wished. But Luther pondered how such traffic reconciled with the Gospel. It was as though God's forgiveness (i.e. 'justification') did not require absolute faith, for the gates of heaven would open to any sinner in return for monies donated ostensibly for good works, or as a sign of repentance—all by courtesy of a churchman acting indirectly in the name of the Holy Father. Leo had conveyed the archdiocese of Mainz to a priestly nobleman for 24,000 gold crowns, not inordinately expensive considering that the appointment granted the new archbishop status as Primate of Germany and a vote in the Imperial Electoral College. Such a vote merited an immense bribe in the auction pending for Maximilian's successor. In Mainz particularly the sale of indulgences reached proportions disgusting Luther to the point of composing his ninety-five theses and launching his bitter protest.

He soon went further, publishing a document describing the Roman Church as 'the most licentious den of thieves, the most shameless of brothels, the kingdom of sin, death and hell'. The fire-breathing Wittenberg professor was enunciating a verdict on the papacy which, if not on many German clerics' lips since the accession of the Borgia Pope in 1492, came frequently to their thoughts. In this regard northern Europe strongly contrasted with the Mediterranean south, producing an underlying strain of mysticism in Christianity at once more analytical and less paganized than in sunnier climes.

The inspiration Italy gave to Germany as the model for literature and art, blossoming as the northern Renaissance, was balanced by the revulsion experienced there for the pomp and self-glorification associated with the Vicar of Christ in Rome, whom theology accepted as intermediary between God and man. Germany probably enjoyed a higher literacy rate than any other nation. It printed more books, studied the sacred texts more devotedly and generated more resentment on the part of the common people against the aristocracy than anywhere else. Germany was also a country plagued by murderous bands of robber knights. One sensed the wrath of God in the atmosphere. Ploughing a fertile furrow, Martin Luther attracted a large following. His seditious pamphlets threatened by their fevered prose to split the country, always a political hotchpotch, into two rival religious camps.

Six months after Maximilian's death in 1519, the nineteen-year-old Charles, King of Spain, prevailed against Francis I among the Electors and won the nomination as King of the Romans and consequently Emperor-Elect. Naturally, the news was greeted throughout Europe with as much displeasure as approval. If the Reich hardly knew how it could possibly refuse him, a man who shared their racial ancestry and whose territories dwarfed every other ruler's, the Pope feared the implications both for his spiritual office and for his temporal power. The French king in his turn saw his country diminished and circumscribed by a monarchy extending beyond all previous geographical perspectives. As for Spain, it was to a degree thwarted because instead of the locally bred Ferdinand, whose second grandfather and namesake had groomed him for the Iberian throne, the people found themselves shackled to a ruler of many irreconcilable loyalties and into the bargain unable to speak their language.

Charles V could justifiably proclaim, in a description much later appropriated by the British Empire, that the sun never set on his domain. His titles: King of the Romans, Semper Augustus, King of Spain, Sicily, Sardinia, Jerusalem, the Balearic Islands, the Indies and the Mainland on the far side of the Atlantic; Archduke of Austria, Duke of Brabant, Styria, Carinthia, Carniola, Luxembourg, Limburg, Athens and Patras; Count of Habsburg, Flanders and Tyrol, Count Palatine of Burgundy, Hainault, Pfirt, Roussillon; Landgrave of Alsace, Count of Swabia, Lord of Asia and Africa.

Little remained over which Charles, or his blood, might not extend their sway, for his brother had married the heiress to Hungary (their sister Mary already its queen), and their aunt Catherine was Queen of England. Two more aunts, then a sister followed each other in turn as consort to King Manuel of Portugal, leaving a third sister available for the latter's heir and a fourth for the King of Denmark, Norway and (briefly) Sweden. In the course of the many (and so confusing!) dynastic couplings of Spain and Portugal Charles himself married Manuel's daughter Isabella. He could therefore visualize the inevitable consummation of every monarch's apocalyptic dream: a universal Christian monarchy, and a Habsburg paramount at its helm. Some irritating problems still remained unresolved, but God's world would be restored to the unity, piety and plenty of the Garden of Eden. As regards the spiritual side, Charles anticipated no obstacles. He had already chosen the successor to Leo X. The next Pope would be Adrian of Utrecht, his old Dutch tutor.

Uppermost in Charles's mind, therefore, was the integrality of the Church. Defending it was implicit in his office. Yet over in Wittenberg a Saxon priest was giving public utterance to heresies that impressed a growing number of Germans, prominent among them an Imperial Elector, the Archduke Frederick of Saxony. Criticism of Rome could be tolerated in this humanist age, as most notably demonstrated by the scholar and satirist Erasmus and his English friend Sir Thomas More. But none took Luther's overtly mutinous path. He went so far as to invite the German princes in a body to cease their contributions to the papal treasury and inaugurate the reform of all Catholic practices. Even the uneducated peasantry adopted Luther, much to his ire incidentally, as their champion against the cupidity of those Imperial Knights who wished to expropriate the land of the peasant classes and reduce them to serfdom. Luther was no social revolutionary; quite the reverse.

Late in 1620 Leo took this monster in monk's clothing by the horns and published a bull of excommunication against Luther. The latter was burning the works of canon law on a bonfire at Wittenberg and, to the applause of the student body, he dramatically added the bull to the flames. Emperor Charles dared no longer ignore the situation. When the Pope demanded the heretic's execution as an outlaw he summoned Luther to appear before the Imperial Diet, then in session at Worms. It was a mistake of grievous proportions. Charles hoped to achieve a reconciliation, bringing Luther's recantation and the Pope's forgiveness. In the event the 'wild boar', as Leo described him, utilized the occasion for an historic challenge to the existing religious order. He apologized for the intemperate language of his writings but refused to retract his views. More important to him than the pleading of an emperor was the call of his conscience.

It should have meant Savonarola's fate, death on the pyre for Luther. But the law had to be content only with his effigy, for he escaped, under the protection of the Elector of Saxony, to the shelter of Wartburg Castle. He continued to write compulsively, subverting the sacraments, condemning the peasants for their rebellion against their predestined place, reviling the Jews for spurning Christ, cursing the Fuggers as usurers. Luther married a former nun and made his beautiful German translation of the Bible. Politics and religion were feeding upon each other, soon to grow indistinguishable in war.

Charles, ensnared as he was by conflicts both inherited and new, quickly realized they were beyond the wit of any one person to solve. He enlisted his family to share the responsibilities of the realm. Thus he transferred the Archduchy of Austria to his brother (so also keeping Ferdinand distant from supporters in Spain) and retained his former guardian Aunt Margaret as governor of the Netherlands. When Margaret died, in 1530, his equally sagacious sister Mary, Dowager Queen of Hungary, became available for the office through her widowhood. Even Germaine de Foix received the emperor's trust in an executive appointment: she was made viceroy of Valencia. Still, Charles was nevertheless destined to spend his life in the saddle and eternally on the move, as judge, military commander and diplomatic fire-extinguisher.

The struggle between the two great dynasties of Habsburg and Valois, prolonged deep into the sixteenth century with consequences for all Europe, might have been terminated by the mutual exhaustion of France and Spain were it not for the constant intervention of the religious element and the self-flagellation of Germany. A Lutheran league of German princes enveloped ancillary quarrels in its train.

Worse, Islam recovered its earlier momentum under a dynamic new Turkish leader, Suleiman, called the Magnificent, who succeeded to the sultanate in 1520, the year of Charles's coronation as King of the Romans and the beginning of the Reformation. The peasants' revolt in Germany ('murderous, thieving hordes,' wrote Luther), crushed in 1525 with the utmost savagery, started a social process whereby the common people would first find their voice, then their strength. How characteristic of the time that in their national wars monarchs treated their royal foes with chivalric deference, though when it was a case of civil war waged against their own, mercy vanished!

So it transpired, also in 1525, as an imperial army met Francis I of France in battle at Pavia and proved the overwhelming advantage of artillery against cavalry. The French suffered a shattering defeat, largely because of the defection of their leading soldier, the Duke de Bourbon, to Charles. Among the French dead lay General Louis de la Tremouille, husband of Cesare Borgia's daughter Louise, and Richard de la Pole, last of the Yorkist pretenders to the English throne. Milan was retrieved for the Empire. Or so it was said, though its citizens, ruefully observing the looting German conquerors, might have described the situation otherwise.

Francis was himself taken prisoner and brought to Madrid. However, Charles forbade any public rejoicing of the victory since it involved the capture of a Christian king. Instead, he expressed thanks to the Lord by expelling the Jewish inhabitants from Naples. The kingdom had never been contaminated by the Inquisition. As for the Duke de Bourbon, Constable of France, whose defection brought the victory, Charles refused to give him his favourite sister Eleanor, widow of the King of Portugal, in marriage. Hadn't the Bourbon shamed his royal blood in betraying his liege monarch? Yet one day Charles's enemy Francis would have her.

There was no halting Francis, even after Pavia. No sooner had the French king ransomed himself by conceding, in a treaty with his conqueror, all past and current acquisitions, Burgundian and imperial, gained by France from the Habsburgs, than the tables briefly turned again. Leaving his two sons in Spain as hostage, Francis renounced the agreement and then wooed the mercurial Henry VIII back to his side of the dispute. He also enlisted the support of the Pope—another Medici, Clement III, the Dutchman Adrian having died after only two years in the Vatican. Francis moreover enjoyed the ephemeral loyalty of Italy's renowned admiral Andrea Doria, who put the Genoese fleets to valuable French service. Doria blocked the movement of Spanish ships in the Mediterranean while Francis went for Naples. Venice, detecting a new Spanish menace (shades of Ferdinand the Catholic!) in Charles's victory at Pavia, joined the invader.

Like a siren charming the unwary into a whirlpool, Italy foiled the designs of France for a fourth time. At a critical moment Andrea Doria switched from Valois to Habsburg, so leaving a French army in distress and reestablishing Charles as master of the volatile peninsula. The emperor's triumph was soured, however, by the conduct of his troops, mainly German Landsknechte. In 1527 they fell upon Rome, and with a savagery reminiscent of the Vandals during the last agonies of the old Roman Empire, sacked the Eternal City. It was a repeat of their cruel behaviour in capturing Milan, only more so. Constable de Bourbon, the French traitor, marched his soldiery to the walls and himself led them in the first assault. He perished from a cannonball fired, the story went, by Benvenuto Cellini, the Florentine goldsmith, sculptor and incomparable memoirist. The pillaged city, deserted by the Pope and his courtiers, by most of its poets and painters too, seemed as though struck by an earthquake. In all probability, the Bourbon general deliberately embraced his death there. Since his humiliation at the hands of Charles he no longer desired a command, least of all an ill-disciplined German horde.

The emperor would not live the atrocity down. Nor would Francis for a personal act deemed just as heinous: a betrayal of the faith. He colluded with Suleiman, stamped by Christendom to be the instrument of Satan.

As negotiated by a petty princeling in quest of some minor advantage, such a deed was not unknown; but this ruler bore the papal title 'Most Christian King'. Francis was obsessed with avenging Pavia and crippling the Empire. How better than to encourage the Sublime Porte to synchronize with the French in a lunge from the Balkans, bringing destruction upon the Habsborgs' eastern marches while he himself usurped Italy.

Suleiman had not idled his time as though awaiting a fiat from Francis. A close student of European politics, he was the only sixteenth-century potentate with a stature equal to Charles V, twenty-five years old on his succession and already engrossed in a strategy for the defeat of the West. This could only be achieved by the swiftest action, for an army of the sultan dared not tarry on any one front, their own Muslim periphery being prone to sudden eruption. Suleiman led a heavily armoured force out of Serbia in 1521, liquidating Hungary's southern positions and capturing Sabacz and Belgrade. The latter city had stood firm against the Ottomans since 1456, but would not now recover its freedom for another three and a half centuries. Then he landed on Rhodes, an island base from which the Knights Hospitallers had long harried Muslim traffic and robbed the Mecca pilgrims. They resisted stubbornly for 145 days, those pirate Hospitallers, and won generous surrender terms (i.e., they were allowed to live), departing for Malta. Now, spurred by French encouragement, Suleiman would have little difficulty in bringing Hungary to submission. The kingdom was still ruled by Louis, kin to the Habsburgs Charles and Ferdinand through marriage to their sister Mary. At the crucial moment no outside military assistance was available to Louis, either from Bohemia, Hungary's sister kingdom, or from the emperor, despite their close family connection. Louis faced the Turk with his insignificant army standing alone. Hungary's doom inevitably struck at Mohacs in 1526, not so much a defeat as a massacre. The twenty-two-year-old Louis himself lay among the fallen.

Suleiman's victory placed all central and eastern Hungary into Muslim hands. Buda the capital fell without a struggle, while a puppet Magyar was allowed to reign in the east (Transylvania) in return for vassalage and military service against the Habsburgs. Venice had also not intervened, on account of its humiliating accord of neutrality signed earlier with the Porte that included an annual tribute to Constantinople of 10,000 ducats. Poland wished to help, but was locked in a survival struggle of its own.

Three centuries earlier the Magyars had laboured to rebuild their national existence after being crushed by the Mongols. Now came the

Turks, to reduce their state to a rump of land fast by Austria. Still not spent, the advance of the infidel overran their southern plains and was approaching the walls of Vienna. No other choice was left to the Magyars than to face the unthinkable and accept the Habsburg Ferdinand as their king. By courtesy of his brother the emperor he was already Archduke of Austria. Ferdinand's election to the kingdom of Hungary (whatever was left of it) of course gave him Bohemia too. Nominally at least he now possessed a Habsburg Empire of his own; nor would it collapse until the conclusion of the Great War of 1914-18. But even its capital was as yet far from secure. The Viennese could smell the smoke of Ottoman camp fires across the forest.

Suleiman had demonstrated his powers as a fighting ruler, but he was also a statesman. To its credit Islam did not sanction enforced conversion and captive peoples were largely left to their own devices provided they dutifully buckled under the authority of their masters. Suleiman saw the wisdom of preserving his conquests by indirect control rather than physical occupation, and by the regular payment of tribute. For the moment, he decided he had gained as much as he could digest, especially as the campaign in Hungary had inflicted severe punishment upon his troops. This was less on account of the military opposition than because of the terrain, where heavy flooding trapped the janissaries, immobilized his horsemen and played havoc with his baggage trains.

Vienna, rendered almost impregnable, could withstand a siege of virtually indefinite duration. The sultan refused to gamble with time. He therefore signed a truce with the archduke, scorning Ferdinand's offer of a subvention for the release of all Hungary. Instead, Suleiman judiciously permitted his Magyar pawn, anti-Habsburg to the last, the privilege of locating his court at Buda and keeping up the pressure on his conqueror's behalf. As a caution, the Turkish navy swept the Emperor Charles's Neapolitan fleet out of the eastern Mediterranean which, due also to the stifling of Venice as a maritime power, thereupon became an exclusive Muslim sea. If the protector of the Holy Roman Empire believed himself divinely selected not merely to defend Christendom but to wield authority over the entire world, the claim must have sounded risible in Suleiman's ears. When he wrote to his ally the King of France, he described himself as 'Shadow of God on earth, distributor of crowns to the monarchs of the surface of the globe'.

Charles V nevertheless soared above his Christian peers not only for the breadth of his responsibilities but also for his sagacity and nobility of intention. Truth to tell, he never vaunted his own array of titles, bearing them as it were with the stoicism of a courageous man born with a limp. If he left Europe no better a place than when he inherited his role, and in some respects worse—acrimonious and quarrelsome still, blinkered and violent to the end, deeply in danger—it was because he was at odds with his time. The Empire lacked the first element of cohesion, communality of interest. Medievalism had not completely died while modernism was not yet properly alive. In seeking to effect a reconciliation between Catholic and Protestant this royal admirer of Erasmus was prescribing for Christianity a tolerance not achieved till this day. Discussion and criticism of the rights and wrongs of colonial rule in Spanish America was unrestricted during his reign and freely published.

The Medici popes with whom Charles clashed preferred him as their adversary than as their champion. He exerted himself to protect the Holy See, yet by an irony the army of which he was the ultimate if absent commander subjected Rome to shocking ravishment. Besides the seismic fissure in the Church, granting the continent new pretexts for persecution and paralysing Germany as a political force, Charles began his imperial reign in 1520 with an uprising in Castile, a revolutionary situation in Valencia and this resurgent aggression of Islam. A recalcitrant rebel in the Low Countries preoccupied him with the internal problems of their seventeen individual provinces for years—all this, and the collision with France, whose king ignored history's lessons and twice repeated the blunders of his predecessors with calamitous invasion of Italy. The crown Charles wore made him a slave. Struggling to discover the ancestral Castilian streak in his character, he even applied himself to mastery of the language—no mean exercise for a man of poor education.

Still, he never acted but people would suspect his motive. When trouble took him to the Netherlands, Spain complained it was to accord the Low Countries preferential treatment. In calling for a crusade, was Charles speaking less from a desire to liberate Jerusalem than to relieve his western half of the Mediterranean of pressure from the eastern Islamic half? Even so, he imposed his personality upon the epoch.

While the separate portions of his realm rejected his concept of a universal Christian monarchy, knowing it to be a sham, each in its different way took the Flemish ruler to its self-seeking heart. This was no mystery. Within Germany itself he inherited the aura of his grandfather Maximilian. More than this, the Holy Roman Empire generated economic dividends, mostly at the expense of Spain. Spanish wool made the rich Low Countries wealthier still, despite the turbulence created there by one of their princelings, the Protestant Duke of Guelders. The

Low Countries exported their manufactures to Seville in ever-increasing quantity, for onward transmission to that other Spain across the Atlantic. Back to Antwerp flowed the bullion reaped by the *conquistadores* as they sped over Mexico and Peru, so lubricating the money market that dominated the commerce of the world from the Netherlands.

The Spaniards were ill prepared to adapt to the onset of capitalism, and foreign bankers lost no time in occupying the vacuum left by the Jews in 1492. Then how was all that specie, profit of Spanish colonization, put to work? It served to pay the lion's share of Charles's campaigns. Nonetheless, even as his Spanish subjects dolefully observed their doubts confirmed in accepting this Habsburg, they appreciated his devout Catholicism, anticipating he would bring them much of Islamic North Africa, a prize far more valuable than the recovery of Jerusalem could offer. To them he would always be King Charles the First, not Emperor Charles the Fifth. He captured Tunis in their name in 1535 and kept the Barbary corsairs, allied to Suleiman, distant from the Spanish coasts. But an expedition to seize Algiers failed, and the expectation of a Spanish empire in Africa as companion colony to America ultimately proved sterile.

On the other hand Italy, perennial bone of contention, fell almost in its totality to Spain. Though at what cost! The son of Francis, Henry II, endeavoured finally to snatch Milan and Naples, besides much else, for France. More costly, enervating conflict ensued, to the point of breaking the financial backs of both exhausted powers. Neither could repay its accumulated debts. Only then did France accept Spanish domination over the peninsula. The contestants signed the Treaty of Cateau-Cambrésis in 1559, granting Italy a hundred years of respite from the clash of foreign armies on its soil. A clock thereupon stopped—the Italian clock of daring innovation, cultural energy, sublime architecture. Epitomizing the national dullness, Pope Paul IV ordered the covering of nudities displayed in Michelangelo's 'Last Judgment'.

By this time the Emperor Charles V was dead. Worn out like his grandfather before him by his endeavours, and disillusioned into the bargain, he had in 1556 passed on to his brother Ferdinand of Austria his imperial title, and relinquished his Spanish crown in favour of his own son Philip II. The latter had married Queen Mary of England and would at an appropriate moment respond to every Spaniard's atavistic urge and effect the annexation of Portugal. But he was destined to lose his invincible Armada in a vain attempt to wrest the English throne from Mary's half-sister Elizabeth.

Charles had chosen to make his abdication speech to his disparate people in Brussels, where he was Duke of Brabant. In a final disappointment the hitherto deeply devoted Ferdinand shattered the fraternal bond. He divided the Habsburgs by refusing Charles's plea to write a testament bequeathing the Holy Roman Empire, which Ferdinand had inherited, to Philip. It had declined in any event to little more than a bloated title, the Reformation having washed the reality away. Charles was the last emperor to be crowned by the Pope.

Progressively, the sixteenth century anchored the outermost world to Europe but kept the continent itself in the heat of Reformation and Counter-Reformation. Roman Catholicism might be authoritarian in the extreme, but Protestantism developed even deeper intolerances among fanatics of its own. Recurring strife so bled the body politic as ultimately to leave England, though still a minor power and used by others purely as a makeweight for their ends, a formidable competitor in the Indies, East as well as West. France, and a Dutch Republic severed from Spain, were already in the race. This would leave a portion of the Netherlands (approximately today's Belgium) still attached to the Habsburgs, except that Calvinist Amsterdam would usurp Antwerp's pride of place as the financial centre all-powerful in global trade.

European introspection meanwhile permitted the Ottoman Empire to consolidate its conquests and achieve still further expansion. At its zenith, shortly after Suleiman's death in 1566, the Crescent of Muhammad flew in three continents, embracing all of south-east Europe as far as Buda, huge stretches north of the Black Sea, and the broad belt of Islamic territories between Mecca and the western shore of North Africa. Just a small portion of the once large kingdom of Poland kept itself free in exchange for heavy tribute exacted by the Turk. As we have seen, thanks to the extinction of Islam in Andalusia, Muslim power could never break out of the Mediterranean funnel at Gibraltar and compete for the Atlantic. Miraculously, Vienna, awaiting the turn of the Islamic tide, held for the Habsburgs. The moment of decision leads us far into the next century.

In the summer of 1683 a mighty Turkish force mustered noisily in the approaches to the beleaguered city for a final strike, to be followed, the Grand Vizier Kara Mustapha declared, by the conquest of Rome. The reality in Central Europe, depopulated and begrimed by the Thirty Years War, mocked the posture of Christendom. During two months of preparation the Turks, with their complement of Kurds, Tatars, Bosnians and Mamelukes, harnessed their Christian captives to dig emplacements while they plundered the neighbourhood and gathered thousands of women and children for eventual transportation as slaves. And as the Grand Vizier established himself in style with his harem and its guardian eunuchs, Vienna emptied itself of its inhabitants. The defenders of the city numbered some 14,000 under the command of Charles of Lorraine. Win or lose, it would be the Empire's decisive act of justification. The Pope begged the Sun King, Louis XIV of France, for help, in vain. The enemy of his Habsburg enemy could do his worst. However, the princes of Germany sent reinforcements, another 30,000 men.

Suddenly a Polish army, led in person by King John Sobieski, appeared to the rescue. It had crossed the lower slopes of the Tatras in small groups, losing much of its artillery on the way but overcoming its fears of the consequences of defeat. The combined force of Christians routed the enemy. The Ottoman guns were melted down to make the great bell of St Stephen's Cathedral in Vienna, for on that Sunday, 12 September 1683, the white continent was permitted to survive. The long menace of Islam began to recede from Europe as the growing empires of Holland, England and France forced Turkey into a backwater.

Poland, however, was granted but a century of freedom before itself being devoured, this time by her Christian neighbours. One of them happened to be the empire of the Habsburgs that Poland had contributed so much to preserve. *(Austria, Prussia, Russia cut up Poland among themselves)*

Chapter Twelve

THE IBERIAN ZENITH

lready by 1500, the year of Charles V's birth in Ghent and the return of a manacled Christopher Columbus to Spain following his disastrous third voyage, it seemed that the political and economic destiny of Transoceania was settled. And with remarkably little controversy. All had been signed and sealed between Spain and Portugal, Pope Alexander VI acting as 'honest broker'. To Spain, ownership and exploitation of the earth's unplumbed riches in the West; to Portugal, the bounty of Africa and the Orient. Gold, silver, gems, pepper, spices, cotton and silk, with an abundant labour supply shackled into service, would elevate the Iberian Powers to mastery over the globe. God's will should be done. Their mariners were instructed to proceed on further exploration in implementation of the respective claims without stumbling into each other's path. The world was much better understood geographically than just a decade earlier, if by no means as yet reconnoitred.

Despite the union of the Infanta Joanna with the Emperor Maximilian's son Philip, and the birth of their Habsburg heir Charles, the Iberian monarchies dared still to anticipate their fusion one day into a common Hispanic dynasty. We have already recounted King Manuel of Portugal's ventures into matrimony with the daughters of Isabella and Ferdinand, of which his second experience, with Maria, also took place in 1500. The bond was tightening.

Not that rivalry had ceased: separate interests ever needed protection. Vasco da Gama had doubled the Cape of Good Hope to reach India in 1498, but the feat could not dissolve all future argument. Where might the Indies proper be located in relation to the Tordesillas line? Differences would thus intrude, but there seemed little to disturb the Iberian mental picture of the general shape of things to come in remoter regions, however others might dream of redesigning the pattern of Europe itself.

On the evidence, Portugal was favoured with the better bargain. The western lands, only tentatively explored so far on their Atlantic edge, remained terra incognita, largely uncharted except for the discoveries made by Columbus. The navigator Pedro Alvarez Cabral, apparently with no business in the vicinity, verified the existence of Brazil as a landmass jutting into Portuguese space in 1500. And although Cabral sent news of his triumph back to Manuel, his orders had been to set course for the Cape route to India, so ownership of that region rested on a mere assumption.

In contrast, the Orient was a book already more than half-opened by Marco Polo 200 years earlier, with Muslim and Hindu traders subsequently turning further pages. Intrepid European travellers had also glimpsed its treasures in days long gone by, since the times of the old Greek and Roman empires in fact. But they had taken the overland route, now blocked. The Muslim Near East constituted a bridge, culturally besides physically, between Europe and the Orient—a bridge and a barrier. In this regard Vasco da Gama had placed a priceless asset in the hands of Portugal. His voyage round Africa changed the economic power balance, eclipsing Islamic might at its explosive epicentre. We sense Lisbon's dazzling transformation into the world's busiest seaport, and the corresponding decline of Venice, with Manuel momentarily Europe's wealthiest monarch as the old century melted into the new. Exotic new tastes in luxury foods became cheaply available. The vanities displayed by the bejewelled women of the merchant classes gave ubiquitous evidence of the continent's access of prosperity.

The thirty years following Columbus's death in 1506 exceeded everything that transpired both before and since in the realm of exploration. Europe grew tentacles to feel out nature's limitless largesse, hitherto beyond reach. Simultaneously, Europe established its intellectual hegemony over races unfamiliar to the Christian mind. This is not to disparage or condemn. The picture is uneven, for civilizations rise and fall, and brilliant societies existed elsewhere during Europe's extended epochs of darkness.

Spain was to take possession of an America peopled by folk easily subjugated. On the other hand the Orient, with its capable rulers, efficient armies, culture of moral imperatives and continuous tradition of technical innovation, knew how to resist penetration. Spain therefore conquered, absolutely, while Portugal preyed. Neither country contained excess populations bending to the enticements of migration and colonization, Portugal possessing little more than a million souls. To be sure, Spaniards crossed the Atlantic in a flow adequate to give the old-new world they encountered a Latinized complexion through its usurpation by a European caste imposing a slave system. And what sorry specimens of civilization those colonists frequently made! Vagabonds, fugitives from justice, restless veterans of the wars in Granada and Italy, these vastly outnumbered the *hidalgo* soldiers of fortune—not that the latter set standards of honourable conduct in the frontier communities germinating out of the wilds.

The Portuguese constructed an entirely different empire. They excelled in creating a network of fortified cities as impregnable bases along both lengths of Africa and on the Indian Ocean's indented shoreline, all connected to the mother country via aggressively defended shipping lanes.

A story of rapacity entirely unrestrained? Not quite, for one civilizing legacy bequeathed by the Europeans endured. It came from the Church, specifically the mendicant orders dedicated to missionary and educational endeavour. Franciscan and Dominican friars, later followed by the Jesuits, constituted partners in conquest. But they roused the conscience of the colonization process and worked with a desperation to limit the worst cruelties. Yet the friars were powerless, in those early years, against the cataract of evil. The indigenous population of Hispaniola was the first to succumb. Those stultified primitives were virtually exterminated by 1508, victims of inhuman working conditions, stricken by the newly imported smallpox, reduced to starvation, or simply killed off when troublesome. Thereupon the conquerors raided the islands of the Bahamas and imported 40,000 of their Arawaks, leaving deserted villages and collapsed tribal societies in their wake. Before long these too died out, to be replaced by Negro slaves transported from Africa. Priests returning home raised an outcry. They induced Ferdinand, while regent of Castile during his grandson's minority (Aragon, it will be recalled, had no standing in the matter), to jerk the imperial rein with his Christian hand.

The Laws of Burgos, 1512, registered the first attempt to codify the rights of the Indians. The decrees did not in any sense apply to the black African work-force, which merely constituted another form of merchandise acquired from a continent deemed a preserve of Portugal. But Indians, the laws determined, were to be regarded as subjects of the crown and therefore free men and women. Upon the Christians lay an obligation to 'rescue' them for God's ultimate redemption. This was to be achieved by peaceful means, not coercion. Though compelled to pay tribute in the form of labour and the surrender of gold in their possession, Indians were entitled to protection as His children. Only those refusing baptism or defecting from their ordained tasks could be punished by enslavement. The Laws of Burgos might just as well have come down from Sinai for all their effect on the first generation of settlers. Such ordinances had no teeth until Charles himself, exasperated by so much unashamed lawlessness, introduced new, toughened measures in 1542. These finally brought the *conquistadores* to heel, though too late to avoid a genocidal catastrophe.

The settlers, allocated consignments of natives to work the land they occupied by a system known as *encomienda*, howled their complaints against every restriction on their freedom. Was this to be Utopia? Indeed the friars, profoundly influenced by Thomas More's projection of an earthly paradise, which they could read in the original Latin from 1516, hugged such a notion. One man hoped to make it a reality.

Among the earliest champions of the Indian, Bartholomew de Las Casas arrived in the New World with an expedition to subjugate Cuba. The evidence of his eyes so outraged him as to change his attitude to life. In the course of a fierce agitation against the cruelties of his fellow-colonists he resigned his *encomienda* and, in 1512, took the vows of a Dominican. He ended his days as a bishop in Mexico still pleading the natives' cause. Las Casas' famous indictment, a gruesome catalogue of colonial bestiality called *Brief Account of the Destruction of the Indies*, published in 1539, is said to have made so profound an impression on the king-emperor, whose confidence Las Casas enjoyed, as to lead to the legislation described above. Translations were subsequently turned to good effect as anti-Spanish propaganda when France and England duly contested Iberian possession of the American treasure-house.

Las Casas wrote of the methods employed to instil docility and servitude in the Indians: random murder of hostages, frequently by decapitation; throwing humans to hungry dogs for a perverted sport; hanging, burning alive, severance of hands, nose and ears to teach lessons in obedience; snatching of women by the dozen to fill a settler's harem. The practices continued on the Central American mainland and into Mexico and Peru, till an estimated 30 million Indians had expired and every heap of skeletons betokened a recent European presence. Only then were the new laws enacted allowing the survivors to live in theoretical freedom and relative peace. As there would be no forgetting, and despite Las Casas' late awakening to the depravity of Negro slavery, Africans inherited the collective ethnic martyrdom in the centuries ensuing.

In the mean while, exploration pressed ahead. By about the year 1512 all four islands of the Greater Antilles—Hispaniola, Cuba, Jamaica and Puerto Rico—had yielded to Spanish control, more or less completely. In the case of the last-named, inhabited by both Arawaks and the more intractable cannibalist Caribs, pacification required further arduous operations that brought to the fore a Spaniard of hitherto only modest achievement. Juan Ponce de León is believed to have joined Columbus's second expedition, in 1493. He subsequently assumed various appointments in the viceroyalty of Nicolás de Ovando, the Discoverer's old enemy who, unmoved, had left Columbus to rot in Jamaica. Ponce de León became governor of Puerto Rico and was seated contentedly in his residence there in 1511 when he was suddenly deprived of that minor outpost of the empire.

This occurred because Ovando's appointment as Viceroy of the Islands and Mainland had terminated, to be followed by that of Diego Columbus, triumphant at last in an unrelenting campaign to inherit his father's honours and privileges. Thus was it signified in Christopher's contract of service 'to be enjoyed by his heirs in perpetuity'. Diego finally wore King Ferdinand down. He assumed the position (it related however to the islands exclusively, not the mainland) in 1509. Hence Ponce de León's notice to quit.

By the unwritten rules prevailing in those pioneering days, when a personality clash could rapidly turn into a blood feud, aggrieved servants of the crown were often allowed to depart on further exploration. This would usually be in quest of that elusive channel believed to bring the fabled wealth of the other Indies within western range. An assuaged Ponce de León led three vessels on such a mission. He sailed from Puerto Rico plying a north-westerly course in 1513 and, by way of the Bahamas, made landfall on Florida. It was the first point of North America taken into European possession. Believing Florida to be an island, Ponce de León retreated on the first encounter with native resistance without founding a permanent colony. Nevertheless the expedition proved of great significance for another discovery: the Gulf Stream. The warm water current originating in the Gulf of Mexico would provide a far more easily navigable route eastward to northern Europe, an advantage readily seized later by the French and English. On a second venture at a permanent landing on Florida in 1521, Ponce de León received a wound from an Indian arrow that proved fatal. Florida, to be bloodily contested in time by France, Spain and England, would never sell itself cheaply.

But we are still in the era of the *conquistadores*. Spain had required all of seven centuries to clear an invader from its own soil, while here a handful of intrepid men won for their country a huge empire within the space of a generation. Santo Domingo in Hispaniola continued as the base from which toilsome expeditions were launched to Honduras, to Nicaragua and along the Isthmus of Panama, whose perilous swamplands, rich in pearls, Columbus had touched but never crossed. Settlers hungering for treasure willingly became *conquistadores*. They bristled with frustration at the slow rewards to be gained by ranching, their cattle denuding the land of the vegetation that now ceased to grant subsistence to the natives. Rivalries among the colonists stunted the growth of orderly administration of the occupied areas.

Personal ambition stimulated Vasco Nuñez de Balboa, a ruthless adventurer, to fight his way in 1513 across the almost impenetrable isthmus and establish the city of Darien, later abandoned, *en route*. Hitherto the region had proved a jungle cemetery for hundreds of less experienced path-finders. Nuñez executed obstructive Indian chiefs, deprived others of their stores of gold ornaments and then, accompanied only by his dog, climbed the peak that looked upon that other ocean, which he described as 'South Sea'. In all he captained a force of sixty-seven on the expedition, one of his lieutenants being Francisco Pizarro. There was a price on Nuñez' head: he had wrested command of the enterprise from its appointed 'licensee'. Yet he was no mean leader and lost not a man. This explorer's diverse qualities extended to a talent for mollifying the Indians, due to his understanding of their respect for a certain rough justice. And he was skilful also in seducing them from their traditional loyalties.

The sighting of the Pacific revitalized the urge to discover the longed-for western passage to the Orient. Inevitably the frontier society claimed the life of Nuñez; it was given to Pizarro to make the arrest, on the grounds of treason. Nuñez was executed in 1519, the year in which Ferdinand Magellan secured a commission from the young Charles, just elected King of the Romans, to cross the Atlantic in search of the Indies of Marco Polo.

Here was another story beginning with wounded egotism. Magellan, of a Portuguese family in royal service, had already sailed twice to the Orient, where he hardened himself in combat against an Egyptian fleet at Diu on the Indian coast and at Malacca against the local potentate.

The Portuguese, it will be recalled, were deeply preoccupied during the period of the Franco-Spanish tussles over Italy with a drive to conquer Morocco—their own, ultimately fatal, obsession. Magellan, soldiering also in those North African campaigns, foolishly fell into disgrace with King Manuel over some illicit business in cattle trading. As a consequence he was refused sanction to take an expedition to the Moluccas (the Spice Islands) where there already existed a fragile Portuguese presence. Undeterred, he switched loyalties and addressed his suit to Spain.

Spices, because of their compactness as transportable cargo, guaranteed rich dividends. Magellan insisted to Charles that he could reach the Moluccas by the western route, so that the Spanish monarch might fairly claim them as lying within his country's prerogatives according to the Treaty of Tordesillas. To be sure, this was the usual quest for a strait leading into the 'South Sea', still undiscovered by any explorer. Only the argument relating to Tordesillas was different, though it was a mischief. Charles could not resist the attraction.

Thus began the most dramatic voyage of all from the point of view of navigational enterprise and Herculean endurance. A fair wind took 240 volunteers manning five vessels out of Sanlúcar de Barrameda close by Cadiz on 10 September 1519. They touched Brazil and rested unmolested by the Portuguese there (unlike the French privateers already roaming the Main) and began a slow progress southward into a seemingly oceanic infinity. Weeks passed, the crews turned mutinous, and still no sign of a strait. When finally, at the continent's extremity, they reached an aperture in the coastline it met them as a wall of water thundering opposition. Amid general consternation Magellan signalled his fleet forward. They were four ships now, one having been wrecked off Patagonia. A second refused the challenge and turned tail. Magellan piloted the remaining three through the horrors of the strait—thirty-eight days of hourly peril, till the safety of the South Sea, which thankfulness told him to baptize the Pacific.

Their ordeal was only just beginning. Four months more, during which nothing hove in their sights except two uninhabited islands; no fresh water, only rats to eat and slow death from the dreaded scurvy. Then at last landfall on the place we now call Guam in the Marianas where natives stole their possessions. Another ten days and they were in the archipelago of the Philippines, as yet unnamed and termination of Magellan's personal voyage through life. He died during a skirmish with Malay islanders that took also forty of the explorer's diseased and malodorous men. Thus the expedition was now down to 108 survivors, in two vessels of the original five, and commanded by the Basque Juan Sebastian de Elcano. He took them limping into the Moluccas and just succeeded in loading up with spices and provisions before making his return via the Cape of Good Hope. A crew of eighteen, spent in health and morale, clinging to the rails of their only ship still afloat, lived to step upon a Spanish shore. Three years almost to the day had passed since their embarkation. They had completed the circumnavigation of the globe. The disputes among themselves, the plunder of defenseless Malays and seizure of their women, the narrow escapes from Portuguese men-o'-war on the look-out, found their way into a thousand tales. De Elcano's was a brilliant achievement, but the name for ever to be associated with the epic would be Ferdinand Magellan.

He had not disappointed Charles. The Moluccas in the East Indies, with much else besides, must indeed be Spain's. The Habsburg king-emperor declared himself their natural ruler, his prize surely for solving the conundrum of a passage westward to the Orient. Not, however, in the eyes of King Manuel. Charles was trespassing over the acknowledged hunting-ground of merchantmen flying the Portuguese ensign.

Though vexing, the argument hardly justified a war between the two monarchs so kindred close. Charles was deeply enough engaged both by his problems in Europe and, no less, by the arrogance of his *conquistadores* in the New World. Some of the latter seemed to take their concessions of estates to imply hereditary ownership, independent like the feudal barons of divided and impoverished Spain in the era preceding the unification. Charles therefore ceded all rights to the Moluccas to Portugal, receiving 350,000 ducats by way of compensation. Still, an agreed Asian demarcation line 15 degrees east of the Moluccas left his entitlement to the Philippines undisputed.

As it happened, Spain felt no urgency to garrison the Philippines, certainly not while the New World, despite all the costly endeavour, was yielding only meagre returns to the crown. So much more remained to be explored there. Vague rumours of an inland region blessed with limitless treasure, and said to be captive to a mighty mainland empire, continued to tantalize the settlers in America. Argonauts in plenty were ready to take up the search. All they lacked was another Jason.

Close to Cuba, which was now rendered tranquil with Havana a capital in embryo, some flourishing sugar plantations, and even rewards of a sort from gold mining, lay the Mayan lands of Yucatan. Occasionally visited, they were as yet virtually untrodden. The reports that sent covetous thought racing emanated from this peninsula. Yucatan's coastline revealed little evidence of a great civilization ever existing in these parts, though such had once been the case. It lay mostly beneath the dust. The long continuous history of the Maya was recorded in a hieroglyphic system on stelae, with a calendar calculated in arithmetical exactitude so as to mark a date corresponding to 13 August 3114 BC as the beginning of time. What we now know of it is the product of recent excavation and research. But early Spanish mariners (one or two surviving there for years following shipwreck) brought back snatches of the most suggestive intelligence. Undoubtedly, these people of Yucatan had once been a multitudinous nation, formed into a highly organized state and inhabiting large cities built by their slaves. Mayan kings had defeated powerful enemies. Why had it all disappeared?

Mayan Indians could be understood to relate that their nation, with others, had succumbed through some catastrophe centuries before, be it climatic inducing famine or more likely as the result of military defeat and deportation. The same word frequently returned to their trembling lips: Aztec. These were the people who now ruled the earth.

Whatever the truth, Diego Velasquez, governor of Cuba, picked Hernando Cortés in 1518 to reconnoitre Yucatan for a corridor to the Orient (Magellan had not yet sailed) and secure all the adjacent territory. Should it be found to be ruled by a pagan king, convert him to the Gospel; if it contained gold and precious stones, all the better. In any case Cortés was to proclaim the overlordship of their ruler Charles. Though a leading citizen of little Santiago, Cortés was not altogether trusted there. He owned cattle and mined for gold, simultaneously acting as local magistrate.

This most celebrated of all the *conquistadores* was born in 1485 of the lesser Spanish nobility. He had arrived in Santo Domingo at the age of nineteen, a lawyer of sorts but yearning for a more adventurous life. He had therefore joined Velasquez, with whom he periodically quarrelled, in the pacification of Cuba, but settled down there nevertheless. It was in fact to rid himself of a nuisance that Velasquez appointed Cortés for this further expedition, in which he was enjoined to deal justly with the Aztecs and impress upon them the benevolent interest of his master, King Charles of Spain.

Cortés leapt at the opportunity. He slipped away in 1519 before Velasquez, who suddenly changed his mind, could stop him. Cortés commanded an enterprise of some magnitude: eleven ships led by a chief pilot whose experience in the Indies dated from service under Columbus, nearly 700 mariners and soldiers, some guns and sixteen horses. What more? Only his self-confidence, nurtured to abundance.

Cortés failed to discover much to detain him on Yucatan except for a capture above the price of rubies: his devoted mistress, soon given Christian baptism as Doña Marina. Apparently of high rank, she came to him following a brief skirmish with Indians whose defiance turned to obeisance at the sight of mounted horses. Here was a phenomenon to be explained only in terms of the supernatural: humans sealed in a single body with four-legged creatures (centaurs?).

Now the natives willingly delivered their gold to Cortés. They brought him food and their young women. Cortés chose Marina for himself not only because of her comeliness but also on account of her comprehension of two dialects, the Aztec tongue Nahautl as well as Mayan. The explorers had come upon the region of Tabasco, midway between the baselands of the two peoples. Cortés' complement included also a Spaniard acquainted with Mayan. The communication problem was thus solved, allowing the invaders an introduction to the native culture. Apparently they worshipped a king of their ancient past, Quetzalcoatl. According to the Aztec time cycle, this god was due for imminent reappearance. Could the visitors be his messengers? Certainly those sixteen horses added the magic touch to adorn the legend.

From this beginning, Cortés proceeded to elicit the information that made him restless to advance. Somewhere in the interior, he was assured, there stood a royal Aztec capital of unsurpassed splendour. Into it flowed the riches of the earth, delivered as tribute by vassal tribes. The Aztecs engaged in close land cultivation, growing maize and the sweet potato. They built monuments and palaces of stone flagged with stucco. The economy of their empire rested on slavery and flourished by barter, while their religious rites involved human sacrifice of a particular barbarous kind—tearing the heart from a living body. Little wonder the Aztecs instilled terror in the peoples spread over the vast area they controlled. Cortés learned which of these subject tribes would resist his trespass over their land, which he could suborn, which were the ablest warriors. It was as though he was being transported back in time to the civilization of the Pharaohs, miraculously surviving half a world away from the Valley of the Nile.

Then, at a place he named Vera Cruz, Cortés executed his single most spectacular act: the scuttling of his fleet. No, he was not mad, he informed his comrades. It was to demonstrate that, while there might ensue regrets and recriminations, even conspiracies, they were committed to an expedition from which there could be no retreat, not until he had placed every one of his men among the world's richest. Many were outraged and dismayed. How, even if they managed to survive, would they succeed in returning home to enjoy their wealth? Cortés put their anxieties at rest. He had ordered one vessel, laden with treasure, back to Spain, to present its booty entire to the king, deducting nothing for themselves. With this grand gesture would Charles, an emperor on one continent, learn of his empire in another. It implied more. Authority needed to be propitiated. Cortés had gone so far as to create the legal fiction of a municipal council at Vera Cruz, to regularize his position and bypass Velasquez as Charles's pro-consul in these parts. However, contrary to his instructions, the ship anchored briefly at Havana and notified Cuba's governor of the situation across the water. Cortés was promptly sentenced *in absentia* to the direst punishment for criminal behaviour.

A force eventually did arrive at Yucatan, not to rescue the expedition but to take its leader into custody and restore the authority of Velasquez. By this time Cortés had, in a charade of cunning ceremonial, won over the credulous Aztec ruler Montezuma and made a puppet of him. The Spaniards assumed mastery of his capital Tenochtitlán ('cactus land'), a wondrously planned settlement risen apparently out of an inland sea. The Aztecs had set it upon the valley of drained swampland, to be approached via causeways. Tenochtitlán, divided at its centre by a wide cemented avenue, with splendid stone residences on either side and humbler dwellings of adobe on the perimeter, the whole intersected by canals, served as much as a shrine as a city. It contained their sacred pyramids whose peaks lifted into the clouds, doubtless to mark their dedication to the sun and moon. Cortés left control to others while he hastened with a detachment back to Vera Cruz, there to subdue the force intent upon his arrest and, genius that he was, make an ally out of the Spanish enemy.

The enterprise and the costly price it exacted—slaughter of native armies as they defended their terrain; death of many, many more through starvation and the poisonous legacy of European disease; the brief recapture of Tenochtitlán and the Aztec execution of Montezuma for his betrayal; how the *conquistadores* destroyed the capital path by path and brick by brick—all these events have been described in many vivid versions, never more stirringly than by William Hickling Prescott in his *Conquest of Mexico*, first published in 1843.

Prescott was writing at a time when the study of anthropology and archaeology was in its infancy. Still, he drew copiously from contemporary sources, principal among them missionary despatches (the least partisan) and the vivid record made by Bernal Díaz, comrade of Cortés on the long march to Tenochtitlán. Little written since has added greatly to our knowledge of the savagery and glory of the Aztec civilization and its collision with this other society of Christian predators. The Aztecs might have been to the Maya what Rome was to Greece, conquerors and conquered.

They had enjoyed 200 proud years of hegemony before they too succumbed, Cortés having substituted what he termed 'New Spain' in their place. He ransacked habitations for their great quantities of gold, destroyed monuments, took possession of artefacts intricately worked in silver, copper and clay, then speedily rebuilt, herding to the work battalions of labourers forced into misery. Alone among the Spaniards, the friars exposed a humanitarian side to European rule as they erected missions to convert and to educate. They found the Indians receptive to the message that the Christian God desired them to destroy their totems and desist from eating human flesh.

Cortés concerned himself with matters of more immediate import. By exploiting tribal grievances against the Aztec domination he fomented internal conflict and so facilitated his grand strategy of annexation. Convoys of vessels heavy with booty made their way back to Seville—that is, those that weren't first intercepted by the privateers infesting the Caribbean waters. The capital of New Spain, Mexico City, rose where Tenochtitlán lies buried.

Though ultimately forgiven his arrogation of authority and awarded a marquisate, Cortés lived out his life a disappointed, embittered man, so frequently the fate, since Columbus, of Spanish empire builders. His able lieutenant Bernal Díaz died in penury. Not uncommonly the *conquistadores* came to a violent end, victims, as we know, of their own lust, rivalries and debasement. So it transpired with Francisco Pizarro, who subjugated the Inca empire of Peru. There were in all five Pizarro half-brothers engaged in pacifying the warrior peoples of the Andes, but only one of them, Hernando, survived the experience, and he ended his days in prison.

Theirs had been an obscure childhood: they were the offspring of an infantry officer's dalliance with simple peasant women in Spain's stark central plateau near Portugal. Francisco never learned properly to read or write. As a consequence, he left no personal testimony to compare with the celebrated five letters Cortés addressed to their monarch. A shepherd boy, Pizarro dreamed of the glamour of the Indies, which he reached as a crew hand in Ovando's fleet of 1502. Subsequently he joined Alonso de Hojeda, Columbus's old shipmate, in exploring the mainland. What turned Pizarro into a leader was his association with Nuñez de Balboa and that discovery of America's second ocean in 1513. It was as though the Pacific beckoned him to challenge the fates. He therefore settled where land lay in intimate communion with the wash of that mysterious sea, in Panama. Fellow-colonists on the isthmus spoke enviously of the discoveries made by Cortés in the north. They were as nothing, their Indians intimated, compared to the riches of the great kingdom in the south.

Pizarro led three expeditions in quest of this fabulous wealth, in 1524, 1526 and, the triumphant one formally sanctioned from Spain, 1531. Three ships, 150 men and thirty horses besides some cannon comprised its strength. Already on the second attempt, by picking its way over the spurs of the Andes, a small force had ambushed the Inca ruler Atahuallpa (he had usurped the empire from a brother) and received, as a first instalment, a huge quantity of gold, silver and precious stones in ransom for the royal prisoner. Now they knew that Inca rule extended far into the regions we designate as Ecuador, Bolivia and northern Chile. The *conquistadores* named them collectively as New Castile.

Like the Aztecs, the Incas had imposed domination through an elaborately connected system of strong-points. Their cities lay high in the mountains and they trained the llama as a beast of burden. They shared with the northern empire ignorance of the wheel, but with this animal, strange to Spanish eyes, the Incas had the advantage over the Aztecs in dispensing with human labour for the portage of their supplies over long distances. Under their rule a population of 15 millions could cultivate food in the lowlands of a variety that filled their stomachs the season round. The same cannot be said to this day of some parts of the world with a similar climate.

In some respects the Incas were more primitive than the Aztecs. They had no writing or conception of arithmetic and were less skilled in metallurgy. Yet cannibalism and human sacrifice had long since been abandoned. Vassal tribes existed in peaceful association with their masters. Initially receiving the Spaniards as friends, they evinced a capacity for defiance that made Pizarro's campaigns, in the course of which he executed Atahuallpa, infinitely more arduous in operation than those of Cortés, and with even greater slaughter. The commander, on one return to Panama for reinforcements, was compelled to enter into agreements for the sharing of booty and allocation of *encomiendas*. The result was inevitable: Spaniard against Spaniard, the conflicts graduating to a full-scale civil war fought out with the pitiless desperation that only estranged brethren are capable of, allowing no quarter. Their encounters would be observed by astonished Inca tribesmen waiting at a discreet distance to pounce on the blood-soaked bodies strewn over the battlefield and strip them naked. To Indian eyes it seemed as though the minerals so important to the Europeans were making them mad. Peru had silver enough to buy a continent.

Complete subjugation of the dispersed tribes required a further decade of campaigning throughout the length and breadth of the Inca dominion, and the establishment of a new capital at Lima beside the coast. The native capital, Cuzco, was located deep inland. In 1538 Pizarro put to death his close comrade in arms, Diego de Almagro, for turning enemy and raising a rebellion to claim Cuzco as his own. Now the commander himself lived in daily peril of assassination. Outlaws in the pay of Almagro's son (they were known as the 'men of Chile' and he was born of an Indian mother) carried out the sentence in 1541. Spanish women for a long while remained few in Latin America, Peru particularly. Consequently Indian women continued to be taken in marriage or concubinage. They produced a new hybrid race of people distinguishable till the present in the social and economic structures that marked the sub-continent's evolution into a society of individual nations.

What of the Portuguese in the mean time? As a maritime empire in the making they incurred no impediments of frontierland rivalries nor anguish over moralities. Everything hinged upon the logistics and security of communication and supply across vast stretches of water. The Portuguese sucked the riches out of the Orient from strategic harbour stations that terminated the sea lanes from Lisbon to China, at length intruding also upon Japan. A myriad islands bathed in the currents where the Indian and Pacific oceans swirled against each other, testing to the utmost the unique navigational prowess of the epoch's premier sailor race. Exceptionally, the Portuguese were prompted to place early colonists on Brazil. This was intended to discourage the attentions of the French, who cruised along the exposed Brazilian coasts to plunder the forests of their rare, extra-hard timber. Indigenous populations being sparse, and gold at this time hardly to be found, little else attracted foreign poachers to Brazil. Plantations, worked by African slaves, would bring the place a certain life, though not immediately. African women were used, and abused, to multiply the generations.

In 1500, the meticulously planned expedition to India under Pedro Alvarez Cabral (the voyage during which Cabral 'happened' upon Brazil) established Lisbon's pre-eminence as entrepôt for the spice trade. The royal exchequer granted him finance for thirteen caravels, 1,200 men and consolation, if required, in the shape of nine priests. The nine were quickly afforded employment, for six of Cabral's vessels, one of them commanded by Bartholomew Dias revisiting the scene of his historic first venture into the Indian Ocean, went to the bottom with all hands on that expedition.

Cabral's arrival at Calicut served bombastic notice on Muslim traders that their monopoly of commerce in this hemisphere was at an end. Arabs and others of their faith had sought out the markets of India since the early Middle Ages, then promoted themselves into slave raiders and conquerors, all with no small success. By the thirteenth century, they were entrenched in India with a sultanate at Delhi and smaller dynasties throughout the north. Conversion of the Hindu had accompanied further Muslim penetration southwards, leading to an intermingling of population in principalities acknowledging both religions. Hinduism and Islam managed to react upon each other peaceably, and at times actually synthesized after a fashion to create new cults. But despite what appeared as separate development in relative harmony, their conflicts were never far below the surface. And into this fermenting situation, shortly to result in Mughal supremacy over all India, the Portuguese arrived to stir anxieties, resentments and divisions.

Cabral soon realized, like Vasco da Gama two years earlier, that the Portuguese flag was not exactly welcome in these waters. At Calicut, Hindu territory but a Muslim trading base, he therefore resorted to the traditional Portuguese practice of advertising their future intentions by firing a few volleys into the town. A harbour skirmish ensued. Cabral then departed for Cochin and Cannanore, between which Calicut was somewhat uncomfortably sandwiched. Here, with better diplomacy, he won the rulers round to conducting trade. These were first promising steps, facilitated by his success in generating hostility towards the *zamorin* of Calicut. Discreet intrigue evidently carried empire-building Europeans a long way on alien shores, as others would be quick to learn.

Not surprisingly, Cabral on his return to Lisbon found few there besides himself prepared to sing his praises: half his fleet wrecked, and forty-eight men lost at Calicut. King Manuel preferred to accord the honour of leading the next enterprise to Gama, who took the Malabar coast of India wholly into Portuguese 'protection', with Calicut obstinate to the last. As the king now viewed the situation, all Africa and India, with the islands surrounding them and the waters in between, were rightfully Portugal's. Thus was it signalled to whomsoever it might concern in the appointment of a Viceroy of the East, Francisco de Almeida. Manuel, whose standard bore the five wounds of the Stigmata, lost no time in despatching heavily armed fleets to obstruct ingress from any quarter, be it Arab, Turkish or native Indian. As yet no other Christian power equal to the challenge had risen over the horizon.

Henceforth nowhere did the Portuguese secure a foothold but they left storehouses and factories walled into the harbourage, all strongly garrisoned: round Africa's perimeter as far as the mouth of the Red Sea, on the Persian Gulf and down the Indian coast, not forgetting Ceylon and the Maldives, northward again via the Coromandel shoreline to the delta of the Ganges, then across to Burmese Pegu. From Pegu confident pilots took their vessels through the Equatorial passage linking Sumatra with the Malay Peninsula and into thriving Malacca, where pepper and spices from the Moluccas equated with gold. Every caravel could substitute as a man-o'-war, every seaman worked with a musket near to hand. The Portuguese roamed almost at will no matter where, so long as they came upon good shelter and could drive away the opposition. Naval battles were fought, townships burnt. Glorification of the mother country required every other trading people to be the loser—Venice too. The Most Serene Republic financed an Egyptian fleet to set against these domineering fellow-Christians, an act of desperation that served Venice to little avail. Almeida destroyed the Egyptians off the Indian coast in 1509.

And all this within the span of some forty years, with Chinese cession of bases still to come. Justly could the national poet Camoens write in his epic *Lusiads* of the Portuguese achievement: *Speak no more of Greece and Troy, and of their voyages. Speak no more of Alexander and Trajan, for I sing of the Lusitanian, who made Neptune and Mars his slave.* Ah, but for how long? Portugal's Oriental expansion unwillingly enmeshed its administrators in regional power politics and local wars, necessitating punitive expeditions far beyond the kingdom's military or financial capabilities.

Viceroy Almeida, fresh from his victory over the Egyptians, was himself killed during an encounter with Bantu tribesmen at the Cape while on his way home. His successor, Alfonso de Albuquerque, developed Goa into the capital of the entire transoceanic enterprise. A realistic administrator (yet capable of fantasies—he dreamed of conquering Mecca and trading the Muslim shrine for Jerusalem), Albuquerque well understood how victories incorporate future perils whereas defeats send nations into the sleep of history. Those extensive lines of communication, the cost of fortifications and the burdens posed by the constant threat to the Portuguese, both on the high seas and on land, could overwhelm the tiny motherland. He therefore encouraged actual Portuguese settlement, as had already begun in Brazil, in India first and then in Africa, with Catholic marriage to local women. This would strengthen the individual personal stake in the empire. Commerce was ostensibly a government monopoly—a fifth of all profit to the crown—but huge sums dropped into the wrong pockets. Try as the viceroy might to stem the haemorrhage by tightening regulation of the markets, theft persisted all along the 12,000-mile line; that and flagrant corruption, with the result that Lisbon's prosperity enriched the international merchants swarming round the honey pot while the Portuguese as a whole remained poor. Except for the older African trade in slaves, gold and ivory, insufficient revenue reached the king's treasury to cover the ever-spiralling expense of policing the enormous endeavour, not to mention the loss of life entailed. By the time of his death in 1521 King Manuel, far from being the wealthiest monarch, was deep in debt to the foreign bankers.

A hundred years on, while Spain still stood crested in its proud authority, the life-blood of Portugal was draining into the oceans. Its African possessions could be retained only with the greatest difficulty against the rising challenge of a dynamic Dutch Republic, which secured formal possession of the Cape, fulcrum of the colonial structure though never fortified. The Dutch even seized bases in Angola and Brazil briefly—those two daughter-provinces that nourished the ageing and impoverished motherland, itself captive to Spain during the years 1580–1640. The collapse had been initiated by a catastrophic expedition to Morocco, where Portugal's greatness died in battle against the Muslims, its young King Sebastian being among the fallen.

In severing their bond with the Habsburgs, the Dutch introduced new realities. They superseded Portugal's trading monopoly in the East Indies so as to build the world's third greatest colonial empire there, after Great Britain and France. Miraculously, a moribund Spain clung to a slender portion of its transatlantic possessions until the end of the nineteenth century, finally losing Cuba and Puerto Rico, together with the Philippines, in 1898. What did Portugal have to show beyond Africa and Brazil for its striking adventurism born of the dreams of Henry the Navigator? The overseas missions, strangely anachronistic but bravely defiant, would recall how the mighty had fallen. The spread of its language and culture, flowing through Catholic evangelization, perpetuated the spirit of Portuguese endeavour.

Francis Xavier, Navarrese Jesuit and one of Loyola's original 'band of seven', had chosen Goa as his headquarters in 1542, whence he travelled the entire Orient bearing the message of Christ. He was among the first Europeans to reach Japan (Cipangu at last!). The earthly remains of St Francis Xavier now lie in that self-same Goa, beneath a tomb extravagantly encrusted with gems. What a monument for a man who throughout his life opted for the condition of penury! After his death the Portuguese established the Inquisition there. That holy office survived in Goa for nearly three centuries, ironic testimony to a Lusitanian resolution that transiently spread its pride across the globe.

Five hundred years have now elapsed since the events described in this survey carried the world over from medievalism to modernity. Much detail has been omitted in the interests of producing a universal picture. This account is but an extraction from a seamless continuity, in which the innovations of one century become the antiquities of the next.

To what degree can the narrative assist our comprehension of the present? We cannot even now truly answer the question: What is history? The gap separating actual happenings and their subsequent narration is occupied by the human factor, which can border on the metaphysical. Much therefore depends upon individual interpretation. Wherever the European has intruded upon other continents his culture introduced benefits, but till today native poverty exists in grotesque juxtaposition with colonist affluence. Some studies will be more precise, and contend that the poverty of one race is a function of the wealth of another. Humankind is divided largely by that same colour line created in the first confrontation of white men with those of a different pigmentation. Before 1492, when each civilization was physically compartmentalized, the rich fattened on the sweat of their own less fortunate cohabitants. Slavery was not a European invention though, shamefully, the Christians availed themselves of the system when their history might have shown them a better way.

As for the religious factor, touched upon in the foregoing pages as a crisis of trust in the Church edifice, a doctrine of brotherhood disappeared with schism, and the savage conflicts thus produced have been so difficult of solution as to threaten to become an eternal concomitant of politics.

Most significantly, the monarchs depicted here were largely allowed to conduct their affairs, involving matters of life, death and freedom, without domestic impediment. It was before those they ruled, both at home and overseas, had perceived the strength of their numbers. Revolt never grew into revolution. Nations had no identity except in the occupant of a throne.

Humanism, Renaissance and Reformation made the European arbiter of the global destiny, so much is self-evident. In 1492 he outmanoeuvred Islam in expansion, then defeated its expectation of controlling his continent. As a consequence Europe retained the initiative for these 500 years. But aren't we now observing the flame of that long epoch in decline? The hitherto anonymous, inarticulate millions—Africans, Arabs, Asians and the ethnic groups of the Americas—are in the process of clarifying their nationhood, and with the advantages of education have begun to narrow the gap.

Descendants of slaves in the Americas have discovered their muscle in forcing change upon the white mentality. Not a few of these have broken the psychological barrier to receive acceptance, even leadership, as public figures in politics, scholarship and the arts, while inter-racial marriage has ceased to be a rare phenomenon in North as well as South America. The Muslims, perennially discounted between the period of our study, when they represented an anti-European menace, until their political emancipation following the Second World War, have lately recharged their sense of pride. The achievement has revealed a nationalist dynamic previously unsuspected. With their transition from colonial servitude to independent statehood Muslim nations rightly demand that Islam be understood and respected by all. Previously, their religion had mostly attracted derision in the West; but it now wins converts in regions hitherto unattainable by the Koran.

In their turn, the disintegration of the Habsburg and other empires, capitalist and Communist, has released from subservience a host of different peoples who passionately cherished their roots against the tide of political uniformity. Still, where historic culture conditions patriotism it often brings racism into play, so that the winds of change blow exceedingly cold for 'alien' minorities. Questions related to territorial possession, when half-solved, continue to disturb the peace while they are half-alive.

The progress in store may conceal unexpectedly violent mishaps. We have observed evidence in the abrupt expulsion of Asians from the young East African states. Trouble is also prefigured in the renewal of still older animosities, such as between Armenians and neighbouring Muslims and in the discomfiture of Hungarians settled in Romania, not to mention the resentments gathering against Russian speakers in the Baltic countries. All these ethnic tensions bear the likelihood of persisting into the 21st century.

However, our preoccupations change with the decades. Arguments over survival in 1492 concerned the independence of a state, or a duchy, even a single city. They are now applied to the planet itself. The dangers inherent in over-population and over-consumption of resources have made ecology our major anxiety—that and its corollary, the poverty prevailing specifically where those old empires held sway. Indeed, they tempt us, mistakenly, to regard such historical dramas as portrayed in this book more like the stuff of classical fiction than the bedrock of brutal reality.

Why mistakenly? Because they are not detachable from our current situation except to the blind. The year 1492 was without doubt the first *universal* benchmark since the birth of the Christian era. That year changed direction for all the world's people, articulate and otherwise, and engendered the creation of a new America, a different Asia, an Africa revealed. We observe the profound consequences for Europe itself. This continent is at last reassessing its own political and social structures with a view to eradicating the chronic weaknesses of the last 500 years.

George Orwell leapt to a second benchmark with his celebrated novel *Nineteen Eighty-Four*. Published in 1949, the work spoke not a word on the subject of ecology, a theme barely even in scientific currency at that time. Orwell's satire envisioned a political condition at its socio-economic worst, humanity controlled to the nth degree. *Fourteen Ninety Two* employs the benefits of hindsight to reverse the process. The events it describes accompanied the beginning of our present stage of civilization, not its suppositional horrific climax. It seeks to reach down to the stirrings of modernism's miscalculations. We need such reminders if we are to be enabled to live with hope.

Ecology, Islamic terrorism, atomic holocaust !!!

2007

SELECT BIBLIOGRAPHY

General histories and reference

Cambridge Medieval History, Vol. VIII, The Close of the Middle Ages, 1932; New Cambridge Modern History, Vol. I, The Renaissance, 1957; New Cambridge Modern History, Vol. II, The Reformation, 1956; Cambridge Economic History of Europe, Vol. IV, 1967. New Catholic Encyclopaedia, 15 vols., Washington 1967.

BEAZLEY, C. RAYMOND, The Dawn of Modern Geography (3 vols.), Oxford 1897–1907.

BRAUDEL, FERNAND, The Mediterranean and the Mediterranean World in the Age of Philip II, 2 vols., London 1986–7.

CHAMBERLIN, E. R., Everyday Life in Renaissance Times, London 1969.

CIPOLLA, C. N., Guns and Sails in the Early Phase of European Expansion, London 1966.

COLLINDER, PER, A History of Marine Navigation (tr. M. Michael), London 1954.

COMMYNES, PHILIPPE DE, Mémoires (ed. J. Calonette and G. Durville), 3 vols., Paris 1924–5.

DICKENS, A. G., The Age of Humanism and Reformation, London 1977.

EHRENBERG, R., Capital and Finance in the Age of the Renaissance, (tr. H. M. Lucas), London 1928.

GREEN, V. H. H., Renaissance and Reformation, London 1975.

HALE, J. R., Renaissance Europe 1480–1520, London 1971.

HUIZINGA, J., The Waning of the Middle Ages (tr. F. Hopman), Harmondsworth 1955.

MATTINGLY, GARRETT, Renaissance Diplomacy, London 1955

ROUGH, C. N. R., They Saw It Happen in Europe, 1450–1600, Oxford 1972.

SELFRIDGE, H. G., The Romance of Commerce, London 1923.

TAWNEY, R. H., Religion and the Rise of Capitalism, London 1938.

Spain

BAER, YITZHAK, History of the Jews in Christian Spain, 2 vols, Philadelphia 1966, 1971.

DÍAZ, BERNAL, The Conquest of New Spain (tr. J. M. Cohen), London 1973

ELLIOTT, J. H., *Imperial Spain, 1469–1714*, London 1969.

HAMILTON, E. J., *American Treasure and the Price Revolution in Spain, 1501–1650*, Cambridge, Mass. 1934.

HEMMING, JOHN, *The Conquest of the Incas*, New York 1970.

HUME, M. A. S., *Spain: Its Greatness and Decay*, Cambridge 1913.

INNES, H., *The Conquistadors*, London 1969.

KAMEN, HENRY, *Spain 1469–1714: A Century of Conflict*, London 1983.

LAS CASAS, BARTHOLOMEW DE, *Brevissima Relación de la Destrucción de las Indias*. tr. by John Phillips as *The Tears of the Indians*, London 1656.

LEA, H. C., *History of the Inquisition in Spain*, 4 vols., New York 1906–7.

MATTINGLY GARRETT, *Catherine of Aragon*, London 1971.

MERRIMAN, R. B., *The Rise of the Spanish Empire in the Old World and the New*, 4 vols., New York 1962.

PARRY, J. H., *The Spanish Sea-borne Empire*, London 1973.

PRESCOTT, WILLIAM H., *History of the Reign of Ferdinand and Isabella; History of the Conquest of Mexico; History of the Conquest of Peru*, Collective Edition (ed. Wilfred H. Monroe), Philadelphia 1904.

RANKE, L. VON, *The Ottoman and Spanish Empires in the 16th and 17th Centuries*, London 1843.

SANTAMARIA, FERNANDEZ J., *The State, War and Peace: Spanish Political Thought in the Renaissance, 1516–1559*, Cambridge 1977.

Portugal

BEAZLEY, C. RAYMOND, *Prince Henry the Navigator*, London 1901.

BLAKE, JOHN W. (ED. AND TR.) *Europeans in West Africa 1450–1560*, Hakluyt Society 1942.

BOXER, C. R., *The Portuguese Sea-borne Empire, 1415–1673*, London 1973.

CAMOENS, LUIS DE, *The Lusiads* (tr. William C. Armstrong), Harmondsworth 1973.

FREENLEE, W. J. (ED.), *The Voyage of Pedro Alvarez Cabral to Brazil and India*, Oxford 1938.

JAYNE, R. G., *Vasco da Gama and his Successors*, London 1910.

LIVERMORE, H. V., *A New History of Portugal*, Cambridge 1976.

PRESTAGE, EDGAR, *The Portuguese Pioneers*, London 1933.

STANLEY, K. E. J. (ED.), *The Three Voyages of Vasco da Gama*, London 1869.

Italy

ADY, CECILIA M., *Lorenzo dei Medici and Renaissance Italy*, London 1955.

—*A History of Milan under the Sforza*, London 1907.

—*The Bentivoglio of Bologna*, Oxford 1937.

ANTAL, FRIEDRICH, *Florentine Painting and its Social Background*, London 1948.

BAYLEY, C. C., *War and Society in Renaissance Florence*, Toronto 1961.

BELLONI, M., *Lucrezia Borgia*, London 1948.

BUENO DE MESQUITA, DANIEL, *Ludovico Sforza and his Vassals*, London 1960.

BURCHARD, JOHN (JOHANN), *At the Court of the Borgia* (tr. and ed. Geoffrey Parker), London 1963.

✓ CELLINI, BENVENUTO, *Autobiography* (tr. George Bull), London 1956.

CLARK, KENNETH, *Leonardo da Vinci*, London 1958.

COLLISON-MORLEY, L., *History of the Borgias*, London 1932.

—*The Story of the Sforzas*, London 1933.

DEISS, JOSEPH J., *Captains of Fortune: Profiles of Six Italian Condottieri*, London 1966.

ETTINGER, L. D., *Complete Works of Leonardo da Vinci*, London 1968.

FISCHEL, OSCAR, *Raphael* (tr. Bernard Rockham), London 1948.

GAGE, JOHN, *Life in Italy at the Time of the Medici*, London 1968.

GARDNER, E. G., *The King of Court Poets: Ariosto*, London 1906.

GOLDSCHEIDER, LUDWIG, *Michelangelo*, London 1964.

GOLDTHWAITE, RICHARD A., *Private Wealth in Renaissance Florence*, Princeton 1968.

GUICCARDINI, FRANCESCO, *History of Italy* (ed. Sidney Alexander), New York 1969.

HIBBERT, CHRISTOPHER, *The Rise and Fall of the House of Medici*, London 1974.

HORSBURGH, E. L. S., *Girolamo Savonarola*, London 1911.

MAGUIRE, YVONNE, *The Women of the Medici*, London 1927.

—*The Private Life of Lorenzo the Magnificent*, London 1936.

MALLET, MICHAEL, *The Borgias: Rise and Fall of a Renaissance Dynasty*. London 1969.

POPE-HENNESSY, J., *Raphael*, London 1970.

PORTIGLIOTTI, G., *The Borgias, Alexander VI, Cesare and Lucrezia*, London 1912.

RIDOLFI, ROBERTO, *The Life of Girolamo Savonarola* (tr. C. Grayson), London 1959.

TOLNAY, CHARLES DE, *Michelangelo* (5 vols.), Princeton 1969–71.

TREASE, G., *The Condottieri*, London 1970.

VAUGHAN, HERBERT M., *The Medici Popes*, London 1908.

WADIA, BETTINA, *Botticelli*, London 1968.

WEINSTEIN, DONALD, *Savonarola and Florence*, Princeton 1970.

WOODWARD, W. H., *Cesare Borgia*, London 1913.

The Habsburgs and the Empire

BARRACLOUGH, GEOFFREY, *Origins of Modern Germany*, Oxford 1947.

BOYCE, JAMES, *The Holy Roman Empire*, London 1921.

BRANDI, KARL, *The Emperor Charles V* (tr. C. V. Wedgwood), London 1965.

✓ CRANKSHAW, EDWARD, *The Habsburgs*, London 1971.

RUPP, E. G., *Luther's Progress to the Diet of Worms*, London 1951.

SETON-WATSON, R. W., *Maximilian I, Holy Roman Emperor*, London 1902.

ZIMMER, H., *The Hansa Towns*, London 1889.

Christopher Columbus

BRADFORD, ERNLE, *Christopher Columbus*, London 1973.

COHEN, M. J., (ED. AND TR.), *The Four Voyages of Christopher Columbus*, Harmondsworth 1969.

KAYSERLING, M., *Christopher Columbus and the Participation of the Jews in the Spanish and Portuguese Discoveries* (tr. Charles Gross), New York 1968.

KEEN, BENJAMIN (ED. AND TR.), *The Life of the Admiral Christopher Columbus by his Son Ferdinand*, New Jersey 1959.

LANDSTRÖM, BJÖRN, *Columbus*, London 1967.

LAS CASAS, BARTOLOMÉ DE, *Historia de las Indias* (extracts), Madrid 1975–6.

MADARIAGA, SALVADOR DE, *Christopher Columbus*, London 1949.

MAJOR, R. H. (ED. AND TR.), *Letters of Christopher Columbus with other Original Documents relating to his Four Voyages to the New World*, London 1870.

MORRISON, S. E., *Admiral of the Ocean Sea* (2 vols.), Oxford 1940.

—*Christopher Columbus, Mariner*, London 1956.

VIGNAUD, HENRI, *Toscanelli and Columbus*, London 1902.

The Renaissance, General

ALLEN, J. W., *History of Political Thought in the Sixteenth Century*, London 1951.

ALLEN, P. S., *The Age of Erasmus*, Oxford 1914.

BOAS, MARIE, *The Scientific Renaissance*, London 1962.

✓ BURCKHARDT, JACOB, *The Civilization of the Renaissance in Italy* (tr. S.G.C. Middlemore), London 1944.

CARTELLIERI, OTTO, *The Court of Burgundy* (tr. M. Letts), London 1929.

✓ CASTIGLIONE, BALDASSARE, *The Book of the Courtier* (tr. Sir T. Hoby), London 1928.

CHABOD, FEDERICO, *Machiavelli and the Renaissance* (tr. David Moore), London 1958.

CHAMBERLIN, E. R., *The Bad Popes*, New York 1969.

✓ CLARK, KENNETH, *Civilization*, London 1971.

FROUDE, JAMES A., *Life and Letters of Erasmus*, London 1894.

HUIZINGA, J., *Erasmus of Rotterdam* (tr. F. Hopman), London 1952.

✓ MACHIAVELLI, NICCOLÒ, *The Chief Works* (tr. Allan Gilbert), Durham, N.C. 1965.

OSWALD, J. C., *A History of Printing*, London 1928.

✓ VASARI, GIORGIO, *The Lives of the Painters, Sculptors and Architects* (4 vols., tr. A. B. Hinds), London 1927.

WIND, E., *Pagan Mysteries of the Renaissance*, London 1958.

Eastern Europe

Cambridge History of Poland, Vol. 1, 1950.

DAVIES, NORMAN, *God's Playground: A History of Poland*, Vol. 1, Oxford 1981.

FENNELL, J. L. I., *Ivan the Great of Moscow*, London 1961.

SINOR, DENIS, *History of Hungary*, London 1959.

Islam

COLES, PAUL, *The Ottoman Impact on Europe*, London 1968.

INALCIK, H., *The Ottoman Empire: the Classical Age*, London 1973.

KIRK, G. E., *A Short History of the Middle East*, London 1948.

HITTI, P. K., *History of the Arabs*, London 1970.

MERRIMAN, R. B., *Suleiman the Magnificent*, Cambridge, Mass. 1944.

INDEX

Aachen, 73
Abrabanel, Isaac, 58–59
Adrian VI, Pope, 221, 223
Adrianople, falls to Turks, 3
Africa, Moorish, 23, 26, 27, 60, 66; Portuguese penetration there, 27–28, 29–30, 151–53, 231; and Cape route to India, 125, 126, 151, 152
Agincourt, battle of, 4, 107
Aguja, the, 188
Albania, 39
Albret, Charlotte d', 175, 181, 203
Albuquerque, Alfonso de, 246–47
Alcaçovas, Treaty of, 29, 120, 124
Alexander VI, Pope (Rodrigo Borgia), 7, 8, 40, 45, 56, 57, 133–34, 142, 161, 168, 172–82 passim, 218, 231; and Inquisition, 36–37; protects Jews, 59, 165; his election, 81, 98–101, 103; character, 97–101; progeny, 99–100, 101–102; and Catalan insurrection, 100; and Papal States, 101; and French designs on Italy, 102–103, 125; and King Ferdinand, 125–26; issues bull *Inter cetera*, 126; confers Catholic title on Spanish Monarchs, 129; and Charles VIII, 133–36, 137; his dynastic ambitions, 172–74; and Church reform, 174–75; and Columbus, 187; circumstances of death, 200–201
Alexandria, 26
Alfonso, Crown Prince of Portugal, 80, 124, 151–52, 162
Alfonso II, King of Naples, 133
Alfonso V, King of Portugal, 29, 42–43
Al-Idrisi, Abu al-Sharif, 8
Almagro, Diego de, 244
Almeida, Francisco de, destroys Egyptian fleet, 246
Amalfi, 26
Amboise, 72
Amboise, Georges d', Archbishop, 168, 175, 201–202, 208
Americas, the, their ethnic groups, 249
Amsterdam, usurps Antwerp's eminence, 228
Anghiera, Pietro Martire d', 142; as tutor to Spanish princesses, 162
Anne of Beaujeu, 54, 72, 139, 167; and Brittany, 75–76; her death, 76

Anne of Brittany (Queen of France), 75–76, 163, 167; Maximilian's proxy marriage to, 75; weds Charles VIII, 75–76; weds Louis XII, 167, 175
Anne of Hungary, as a Habsburg bride, 215
Antilia, mythic island, 106
Antilles, Greater, pacified, 235; Lesser, 141
Antwerp, its economic role, 67, 70, 72; and French aggression, 72–73; Jewish contribution in commerce, 79; loses place to Amsterdam, 228
Aquinas, St Thomas, 12; and Jews, 32–33
Arabs, *see under* Islam
Aragon, 15, 30; liberation from Moors, 23–25; religious persecution, 34–35; joint rule with Castile, 35, 36, 41–42, 44–45, 69; and Inquisition, 36–38, 43
Aragon, House of, *see under individuals*
Arawaks, their language group, 142; hostile in Jamaica, 142; genocide, 233
Arezzo, 86
Ariosto, Lodovico, 90
Aristotle, 8, 12, 157
Arthur, Prince of Wales, 163, 183–84
Artois, 75
Atahuallpa, Inca 'emperor', 243
Austria, conquered by Hungary, 17, 18, 19; freed from Hungary, 20; as Habsburg heritage, 73, 74; Ottoman attack upon, 80. *See also* Vienna
Avignon, as Papal seat, 11–12, 89, 90
Azores, the, 28, 116, 154
Aztecs, 239–42; their civilization, 240

Bacon, Roger, 8
Baglioni family, 137, 202
Bahamas, the, 109–10
Balearic Islands, 42, 204; and expulsion of Jews, 59
Barbary pirates, 151
Barcelona, 10, 121, 162; religious persecution there, 34, 37, 43–44; its Cortes, 205–206
Bartolommeo, Fra, 96, 101
Bastardy, no stigma, 171–72
Bay Islands (Honduras), 188–89
Bayezid II, Sultan of Turkey, 40, 133–34; and expulsion of Jews from Spain, 59; assault

Bayezid II (*cont.*)
upon Europe, 80–81; threatens Venice,
180; and Anatolian unrest, 199; and Per-
sia, 199
Bechalla, the, 30
Belém, 117, 120
Belgrade, 17, 80; captured by Turks, 224
Bentivoglio family, 90, 178, 202
Bermuda, the (*Santiago de Palos*, the), 187
Bible, the, 7, 12, 93; printing of, 32; Polyglot
Bible, 211
Bisceglie, Duke of, weds Lucrezia Borgia, 177;
murdered, 177, 180
Black Death, 5, 10–11, 66
Blanche, Queen of Navarre, 204
Boabdil, prince of Granada, 46–47; 52, 58;
terms for his surrender, 55–56, 60
Bobadilla, Beatriz de, 107
Bobadilla, Francisco de, 159, 169, 170, 186,
195; drowns, 188
Boccaccio, 12; his *Decameron*, 85, 101
Bohemia, 16, 17, 18, 19. *See also under* Hun-
gary
Bologna, 90, 133; and Bentivoglio family,
178, 202
Borgia, Alfonso, *see* Callixtus III, Pope
Borgia, Cesare (son of Rodrigo), 40, 56, 99,
134, 135, 172–74, 176–83, 200, 201; as
Archbishop of Valencia, 102; renounces
holy orders, 174–75; made Duke of Rom-
agna and Captain General, 175; as Duke
of Valentinois, 175–76; under arrest,
202–203; imprisoned in Spain, 203; dies
serving Navarre, 203
Borgia family, 24, 36–37, 97–100, 203
Borgia, Giovanni (son of Rodrigo), 100
Borgia, Jofrè (Prince of Squillace, son of Rod-
rigo), 102, 172, 177
Borgia, Juan (2nd Duke of Gandia, son of
Rodrigo), 125, 172, 177; his murder,
173–74; grandson canonized, 203
Borgia, Louise (daughter of Cesare), 203, 222
Borgia, Lucrezia (daughter of Rodrigo), 99,
172, 177, 181; weds and divorces Gio-
vanni Sforza, 102, 177; weds Duke of
Bisceglie, 177; weds Alfonso d'Este, 179;
as Duchess of Ferrara, 203
Borgia, Pedro Luis (1st Duke of Gandia, son
of Rodrigo), 101–102, 125, 173
Borgia, Rodrigo, Cardinal, *see* Alexander VI,
Pope
Bosnia, and its Bogomils, 18
Bosworth Field, battle of, 49
Botticelli, Sandro, 93, 96, 101; his 'Minerva
and the Centaur', 94
Bourbon, Duke de, Constable of France, 222–23
Bramante, Donato, 89–90, 93
Braudel, Fernand, 78
Brazil, 126, 232; commerce there, 79; coloni-
zation begun, 244, 247

Brindisi, occupied by Venice, 208; regained by
Ferdinand, 209
Brittany, contended for, 75, 102
Bruges, 67, 70, 218; and printing, 31; in
Longfellow, 67; economic role, 67, 70–
71, 72–73; and French aggression, 72–
73; holds Maximilian, 73–74; and Jews,
79
Brunelleschi, Filippo, 87
Brussels, 72
Buda, 17, 224, 228; Magyar puppet rule, 225
Buil, Friar, 146, 148, 149
Bulgaria, falls to Turks, 3
Burchard, Johannes, 201; quoted, 181–82
Burgos, 66; Laws of, on native rights, 233–34
Burgundy, extent of domain, 14
Byzantium, and Byzantine Empire, 2, 3, 7, 16,
19. *See also* Constantinople

Caballeria, Alfonso de la, 52
Caballeria family, 44
Caballeria, Pedro de la, 44, 52
Cabot, John and North Atlantic expedition,
155
Cabot, Sebastian, 155
Cabral, Pedro Alvarez, 232; at Calicut, 245–
46
Cadiz, preparations for 2nd voyage there, 139
Calais, 13, 76
Calderón, Pedro, 177
Calicut, 153, 157, 245–46
Callixtus III, Pope (Alfonso Borgia), 14–15,
36, 98, 173
Cambrai, League of, 208, 209
Camoens, Luis de, his *Lusiads*, 246
Canaries, the, 28, 29, 106–107, 108, 157;
and papal bull, 30, 120–21; as Castilian
possession, 124
Cannanore, 245
Canossa, 4
Caonabó, Carib chief, 143, 148; death, 150
Cap Haitien, 113
Cape of Good Hope, 54, 120
Cape St. Vincent, 27, 30
Cape Verde Islands, 28, 157
Capitalism, birth and growth, 65–66, 79; fol-
lows global expansion, 197; in Spain, 227
Capua, massacre there, 182
Carib tribes, 113, 141–44; infected by im-
ported diseases, 146; their genocide, 149–
50
Carlotta of Naples, 175
Caro, Joseph, 165
Carrillo, Alfonso, Archbishop, 44
Carvajal, Alonso de, 158
Casablanca, 28
Casiglione, Baldassare, his *The Courtier*, 91
Casimir, King of Poland-Lithuania, 18
Castile, liberation from Moors, 23–25; and
Hundred Years War, 24; and Portugal,

28–30, 35, 124; Sixtus IV's bull, 30, 37, 120–21, 125; action against heretics, 34–35; joint rule with Aragon, 35, 36, 41–42, 44–45, 69; and Inquisition, 36–38; and Columbus's 1st voyage, 77; Alexander VI's bull, 126

Catalonia, 15; religious persecution, 34; and Inquisition, 37

Catanei, Vanozza dei, 99, 101–102, 172, 174

Cateau-Cambrésis, Treaty of, 227

Catherine of Aragon (Queen of England), 136, 162–63, 167, 220; arrival at Plymouth, 183; weds 1) Prince Arthur, 2) Henry VIII, 183–84; meets sister Joanna in England, 205

Catherine, St, of Siena, 4

'Catholic Monarchs', the, *see separately under* Ferdinand of Aragon *and* Isabella of Castile

Cerdagne, 71, 76

Ceuta, 25, 26, 28

Chanca, Diego, surgeon on 2nd voyage, 140, 144

Charlemagne, 4, 7, 17, 132; and Moorish invasion, 22

Charles the Bold, Duke of Burgundy, 67–76 passim, 130, 218

Charles of Orleans, Duke, captured at Agincourt, 167

Charles of Valois, 42

Charles V, Emperor (Charles I, King of Spain; in minority, Charles of Ghent), 131, 184, 206, 207, 208, 211, 215–23 passim, 234, 241; birth, 205, 231; his titles, 220; weds Isabella of Portugal, 220; allocates governmental responsibilities within family, 221–22; victor of Pavia, 222–24; at odds with his time, 225–26; North African campaigns, 227; his abdication, 227–28; and Magellan, 236–37; agrees on division of Orient with Portugal, 238

Charles VII, King of France, 14

Charles VIII, King of France, 40, 54, 68, 70, 74, 176, 208; assumes crown, 72; marriage to Anne of Brittany, 75–76, 102; and intervention in Italy, 76, 98, 101, 102–103, 125, 131–38, 167; and Ottoman attack on Europe, 81; and Pope Alexander, 133–37 passim; death, 167

Chaucer, 12

China, and art of printing, 31; and European trade, 64–65

Chios, 3, 30

Cibao, 115; identified with biblical Ophir, 146

Cibo, Franceschetto (son of Pope Innocent VIII), 83–84, 88, 201

Cibo, Giambattisto, *see* Innocent VIII, Pope

Ciompi guild of Florence, 86

Cipangu, *see* Japan

Cisneros, Jiménez de, Archbishop, 60, 207, 211

Clement, VII, Pope, 165–66, 223

Cochin, 245

Colba (Cuba), 111

Colet, John, 93

Colombo, Domenico (father of Columbus), 30

Colombo, Susanna (mother of Columbus), 30

Colonna family, 91–92, 98, 133, 137, 182, 202

Columbus, Bartholomew (brother), 30–31, 48, 52–53, 57, 139, 156–59, 169–70, 185, 186; his missions for Christopher, 54; arrives in Indies, 148; establishes Santo Domingo, 157; on 4th voyage, 187–88, 190, 191–92, 193

Columbus (Colombo, Colón), Christopher, 8–10, 13, 15, 20, 27, 38, 61, 66, 92–93, 127–28, 153, 156–70 passim; 187–89, 197, 231–32, 235, 236; his miscalculation, 8–9; as mariner, 30–31, 40; weds Felipa Perestrello, 31; seeks patronage for project, 47–55; and Queen Isabella, 51, 57–58; prepares expedition, 57–58, 77–78, 79, 81, 97–98, 103; royal 'passport', 77

1st Voyage, (3 Aug. 1492), 105–26; land sighted, and landfall, 109–10; in search of treasure, 110–15; wreck of *Santa Maria*, 113–14; return voyage, 114–17; his report, 117, 120; audience with Portuguese king, 120–21; ennobled, 121; his discoveries, 124–25; and bull *Inter cetera*, 126; convinced of reaching Asia, 127

2nd Voyage (25 Sept. 1493), 129, 139–43; his signature, 140; his rule over Hispaniola, 143–51; explores Cuba, 146–47; nervous strain, 147–48; a new humility, 150

3rd Voyage (30 May 1498), authorised, 156; discovers Trinidad, 158; touches mainland, 158; 'Lord of Mosquitoes', 159; in disgrace, 169–70, 184–85; broken in health, 185, 190

4th Voyage (9 May 1502), authorized, 186–87; storm warning, 188; close to Pacific, 190; marooned in Jamaica, 191–93; and lunar eclipse, 192; arrives home, 194; fights for rights, 195; death, 195–96

Columbus, Diego (brother), 139, 157, 185; as Christopher's deputy, 146, 148, 169

Columbus, Diego (first son), 47, 48, 49, 121, 186; page to Prince Juan, 163; inherits dignities and title, 196, 235

Columbus, Ferdinand (second son), 51, 121, 159; his *Life* of his father, 105, 114, 148, 169–70, 194; page to Prince Juan, 163; on 4th Voyage, 187, 189

Columbus, Giannetto (cousin), 158

Commynes, Philippe de, 72, 90
Compostela, Santiago de, 51–52, 55
Constantine, last Byzantine emperor, 2, 88–89
Constantinople, 6, 15, 38, 79; falls to Turks, 2, 6, 10, 17, 39; its Santa Sophia Cathedral, 2; and Council of Florence, 87–88. *See also* Byzantium
Córdoba, 46–47, 50–51; as Moorish Emirate, 21, 22; recapture of, 23; as headquarters of Isabella and Ferdinand, 48, 51
Corsica, 10
Cortés, Hernando, 239–44; scuttles fleet, 240–41
Corvinus, John, 74
Cosa, Juan de la, cartographer, 127, 146, 160
Cosa, Juan de la, ship's master, 114
Costa Rica, 189
Coutinho, Fernando, Bishop, 165
Covadonga, 23
Covilham, Pero da, 153
Crescas, Abiathar, 44
Crete, 14, 39
Cromwell, Oliver, 59
Crusades, the, 3–4
Cuba, 238, 247; Columbus touches, 111–12; presumed to be Cathay, 142, 146–47; as location of Garden of Eden, 146–47; natives friendly there, 147
Cuneo, Michele de, diarist of 2nd Voyage, 140–42, 146
Cuzco, Inca capital, 244
Cyprus, 14, 39

Dante, 7, 10, 12, 13
Darien, a city abandoned, 236
Della Rovere, Card. Giuliano, 93, 102–103, 133, 179, 202; electoral contest, 98–99, as Pope Alexander's enemy, 101, 125. *See also* Julius II, Pope
Deza, Diego de, 52
Dias, Bartholomew, 120, 152; his expeditions, 53–54, 125
Díaz, Bernal, 242
Díaz, Rodrigo ('El Cid'), 23
Dijon, 67, 70
Diu (on Indian coast), 236
Dominica Island, 141
Dominican Order, 165, 233; in Mexico, 242
Dominican Republic, 113, 157
Donatello, 87
Doria, Andrea, 223
Dorset, Marquis of, 210
Dürer, Albrecht, 93, 131, 216
Dutch Republic, the, its rise, 247

Elba, 86
Elcano, Juan Sebastian de, 238
Eleanor (sister of Charles V), weds (1) Manuel of Portugal, (2) Francis I of France, 223
Elizabeth I, Queen of England, 227
England, 59, 71; and Hundred Years War, 13–14, 24; and Vatican, 36; its trading activities, 66; and designs on Brittany, 75, 76, 102; assault on Guyenne, 210
Enriquez, Maria, 125
Erasmus, Desiderius, 93, 221, 226; his *In Praise of Folly*, 202
Ercole, Duke of Ferrara, 90
Erikson, Leif, 9
Escobedo, Rodrigo de, 114, 142
Este, Alfonso d', weds Lucrezia Borgia, 179
Este, Beatrice d', 90; weds Ludovico Sforza, 89; her death, 95; pleads for Milan–Venice rapprochement, 136
Este family, 89
Este, Isabella d', 90, 137, 178, 179, 201, 203
Étaples, Treaty of, 76
Eugenius IV, Pope, 87
Eyck, Jan van, 70

Faenza, besieged, 178
Farnese, Alessandro, 103
Farnese, Giulia, 99–100, 133
Federigo, King of Naples, 175, 176, 179–80; exiled, 180, 182
Ferdinand, King of Aragon, 'the Catholic', 15, 35, 50, 51, 107, 121, 132, 135–37, 155–56, 161–72 passim, 176, 179, 182, 183, 202–203, 210, 211, 217, 231, 235; marriage to Isabella, 28–29, 38, 41–45, 52, 69, 100; papal bull *Aeterna regis*, 30, 37, 125; his lineage, 34; and Inquisition, 36–37; and Otranto expedition, 39; conquest of Granada, 46–47, 55–57, 75, 79; his undertaking to Moors, 56, 60; and Columbus, 48, 58, 117, 121, 124, 184–87, 195; edict of Jews' expulsion, 58–59; his aspirations for Spain, 66–67; his progeny, 69, 79–80; and Netherlands, 71, 102; relations with France, 76, 102, 103; ambivalent towards discoveries, 124–25, 129, 138; papal bull *Inter cetera*, 126; and dynastic union with Habsburgs, 136, 163–64, 194–95; unpopular in Castile, 152; and Neapolitan inheritance, 161, 168, 182–83, 202–203; seeks Mediterranean supremacy, 164; treats with Louis of France, 169, 179, 182, 204; and succession to Castile, 194–95, 204–206; weds Germaine de Foix, 204, 205; recalled as regent of Castile, 207; and anti-Venetian coalition, 207–208; joins Holy League, 209; invades Navarre, 210; and Laws of Burgos, 233–34
Ferdinand I, Emperor (Archduke of Austria, brother of Charles V), 206, 215, 220; named King of Hungary, 225; and truce

offer to Turks, 225; receives imperial title, 227

Fernando, King of Portugal, 24, 25

Ferrante, King of Naples, 90, 100–101, 102, 133; against Florence, 93–94; sponsors della Rovere as Pope, 98

Ferrantino, King of Naples, 133, 134–37, 175

Ferrara, 89, 90, 96, 179; Church conclave there, 87; and Lucrezia Borgia, 203

Ficino, Marsilio, 85, 95

Fieschi, Bartholomew, 187, 191, 192

Fiesole, 85

Flanders, *see under* Netherlands

Florence, 11, 12–13, 84, 95–96, 101; its bankers, 20, 86; Pazzi Palace, 83; Medici Palace, 85, 91, 97; San Marco monastery, 85; Palazzo Vecchio, 86; its *Signoria*, 86, 96, 98, 101; Medici influence, 85–87, 92, 95; and Renaissance, 86–88, 92, 93; Council of Florence, 87–88; Church of Holy Cross, 87; against Siena, 90; threatened by Naples, 93–94; Uffizi Gallery, 94; Savonarola's reforms, 96–98; surrenders to French, 98, 132; protected against Cesare Borgia, 177; 'broken reed', 179; Medici rule restored, 210

Foix, Gaston de, 209–10

Foix, Germaine de, 204, 205, 210, 222

Fonseca, Juan Rodríguez de, 139, 159–60

Forli, 178

Fornovo, battle of, 137–38

France, and intervention in Italy, 11, 14, 38–39, 76, 95, 98, 102–103, 125; and Hundred Years War, 13, 24; aspirations in Europe, 14, 66; Moorish advance there, 21–22; and Vatican, 36; and Netherlands, 49, 67–74, 80; and Brittany, 75–76; in Middle Ages, 86

Francesca, Piero della, 90, 91

Franche Comté, 68, 75, 76, 214

Francis, St, of Assisi, 4

Francis I, King of France, 216–18; captured at Pavia, 222–23; colludes with Turks, 223–24

Franciscan Order, 233; in Mexico, 242

Frankfurt, Diet meeting there, 73

Frederick, Archduke of Saxony, 221

Frederick III, Emperor, 17–20, 38, 73, 80, 129, 199, 200, 213, 214–15; liberates Maximilian from Bruges, 74; ignores Reichstag, 130; and Matthias Corvinus, 214–15

Fugger Bank, 10, 20, 63–64, 216, 219; as Maximilian's creditor, 72, 208; and Ottoman attack on Europe, 81

Funchal, 47

Gallega, the, 187, 190, 193

Gama, Vasco da, 152–57 passim, 169, 231, 245–46; his 2nd expedition to Orient, 186–87

Gandia, 1st Duke, *see* Borgia, Pedro Luis

Gandia, 2nd Duke, *see* Borgia, Juan

Garigliano, battle of, 182–83

Gaunt, John of, Duke of Lancaster, 24, 26, 68

Genoa, 20, 31, 34; its trading empire, 3, 10–11, 30, 132; as Columbus's birthplace, 9–10; naval action there, 133; its San Giorgio Bank, 10, 186

George III, King of England, 111

Germany, 16, 65, 69, 72, 73, 130, 131, 213–14; Teutonic Knights, 17; and Church, 36, 219–20; spread of Renaissance there, 219; Lutheran league of German princes, 222; and relief of Vienna, 229. *See also* Holy Roman Empire

Ghent, 68, 70–71; its Prinsenhof, 68; and van Eyck masterpiece, 70

Ghiberti, Lorenzo, 87

Ghirlandaio, Domenico, 85, 93

Gibraltar, 25, 30, 228

Giotto di Bondoni, 12, 87

Goa, 248

Golden Horde, *see under* Mongols

Golfo de las Flechas ('Arrow Gulf'), and first hostile natives, 115

Gomera Island, 106–107, 140, 141

Gonsalvo de Córdoba, 47, 52, 55, 180, 182–83; in Sicily, 135, 137, 142; viceroy in Naples, 202–203, 206

Gonzaga, Francesco, Duke of Mantua, 137, 179, 201, 203

Gracias á Dios, Cape, 189

Granada, as last kingdom of Moors, 23–25, 35, 38, 45–46, 48; surrender, 54–57, 60, 75, 79; Franco–Spanish treaty signed there, 169

Grand Turk Island, 110

'Great Khan', 2, 142

Great War, the (1914–18), 225

Greece, as possession of Turkey, 39

Gregory, St., 7

Guacanagari, Carib chief, 113, 143–44

Guadaloupe, Spain, 59, 140

Guadaloupe Island, 141

Guam, 237

Guanche cave-dwellers, 29, 107

Guaymi tribes, 189

Guelders, Duke of, 226

Guiccardini, Francesco, 99–100, 103

Guinea Coast, and Gulf, 28, 145; and Sudanese gold, 124, 152

Gulf Stream, discovered, 235

Gutenberg, Johann, 32

Gutiérrez, Pedro, 114, 142, 143

Habsburg, House of, *see under* individuals

Haiti, 113

Halevi, Rabbi Solomon, *see* Santa Maria, Pablo de
Hanseatic League, 70
Harana, Beatriz Enriquez de, 51, 78, 158
Harana, Diego de, 78, 109, 141, 142, 158; in command of Navidad, 114
Havana, 238, 241
Henry II, King of France, 227
Henry IV, Emperor, 4
Henry IV, King of Castile, 42–45
Henry IV, King of France, 204
Henry V, King of England, 4, 26
Henry VI, King of England, 13
Henry VII, King of England, 49, 74, 75, 136, 139, 155–56, 210; and battle for Brittany, 75, 76; his treaty with Ferdinand, 163
Henry VIII, King of England, 16, 184, 205, 209, 218, 223; and assault on Guyenne, 210; truce with France, 216
Henry, Prince of Portugal ('the Navigator'), 26–30 passim, 125, 152, 247
Hermandad organization, 58
Hindu traders, 154
Hinduism, and relations with Islam, 245
Hispaniola, 115, 139–50 passim; Columbus reaches, 113; native resistance there, 138–39, 148; its interior (Cibao), 144–45; first European women, 148; hurricane's devastation, 149; genocide of natives, 149–50, 233–34; importation of African slaves, 233
Höchstetter Bank, 63–64, 215
Hojeda, Alonso de, 148, 160, 243; leads expedition into Cibao, 146; names Venezuela, 160
Holland, *see* Netherlands
Holy League, against France, 209, 217
Holy Roman Empire, 16, 130, 166, 213–14, 225–26; its sovereign emperors, 7, 11, 19; its Electors, 16, 219, 220; its authority, 16–17; and Napoleon I, 17. *See also* Germany
Honduras, 236
Hundred Years War, the, 13–14, 24, 42, 66, 67
Hungary and Bohemia–Moravia, 18, 19, 214–16; and Holy Roman Empire, 16, 20; and crusade, 17; and Habsburgs, 74, 216; Ottoman attack upon, 80; crushed by Turks, 224–25; accepts Archduke Ferdinand as king, 225
Hunyadi, Janos, 17, 18
Hussite wars, 17

Ibn-Majid, Ahmad, 153
Iceland, 26
Imola, 178
Inca tribes, 242, 243–44
Indulgences, sale of, 32, 219

Innocent IV, Pope, 58
Innocent VIII, Pope (Giambattisto Cibo), 88, 201; and Inquisition, 37; corrupt practices, 83–85
Innocent X, Pope, 203
Inquisition, the, 35–38, 45, 48–49, 55, 56, 69, 204, 223; and Moors, 60; introduced in Portugal, 166; in Goa, 248
Isabella, beachhead in Hispaniola, 144, 148; slides to anarchy, 146
Isabella of Habsburg (sister of Charles V), weds King of Denmark, 220
Isabella, Infanta of Spain (eldest daughter of Isabella and Ferdinand), 79–80, 124; weds Prince Alfonso of Portugal, 151–52; widowhood, 162; weds Manuel of Portugal, 164–66; dies in childbirth, 166–67
Isabella, Queen of Castile, 'the Catholic', 15, 29, 30, 35, 66, 107, 140, 151–62 passim, 169, 171, 183, 184, 185, 205, 206, 207, 231; marriage to Ferdinand, 28–29, 41–45, 52, 100; rival claimant to throne, 43; and conquest of Granada, 46, 54, 75, 79; and Columbus's proposal, 50–58 passim, 77, 121; financing of project, 57–58; expulsion of Jews, 58–60; her progeny, 79–80; and Columbus's '*Letter to Santangel*', 117, 120; ennobles Discoverer, 121; proposals for second expedition, 124–25; and bull *Inter cetera*, 126; and enslavement of Indians, 145–46, 194; Discoverer's rights, 184–86; death and testament, 194, 200
Islam, 2–4, 5–6, 7, 24, 25, 33; Europe's wars against, 76–77; intimations of retreat, 128; penetrates India, 153, 245; enclosed, 198; Sunni-Shia struggle, 199; religious tolerance, 225; defeat in Europe, 228–29; present situation, 249–50. *See also under* Turkey
Italy, and claims for its possession, 11–12, 81, 97, 98, 161; its universities, 15; and printing, 32, 87; and Vatican, 36, 83–84; and interventions by France, 11, 14, 38–39, 76, 95, 98, 102–103, 125; resistance against Turks, 39–40; Ferdinand's designs on, 67; and Habsburgs, 73; Papal States, 88–91, 101; its fragmentation, 89; its *condottieri*, 89–91. *See also* Renaissance, *and under* France
Ivan III ('the Great'), Grand Prince of Moscow, 19, 49, 198–99

Jagiello dynasty, 19, 215, 216
Jamaica, 188, 191–93; discovered on 2nd Voyage, 147
Japan (Cipangu), 47, 248
Jativa, 24
Jeanne de France, 167; divorce from Louis XII, 175
Jem, Ottoman prince, as captive of Vatican,

40, 80, 88; in France, 133–34, 135, 180
Jerusalem, and its redemption, 25, 152–53, 164
Jesuits, 233, 248
Jews, 5, 46; as persecuted minority, 32–38, 60, 164–67; as New Christians and 'Marranos', 34–35, 49–50, 52, 58–59; and Inquisition, 37–38, 44, 49–50, 55, 58–59; and marriage of Ferdinand to Isabella, 43–44; expelled from Spain, 54–59, 78–79; in New World, 79; expelled from Portugal, 164–67; in Eastern Europe, 216; expelled from Naples, 222–23
Joan of Arc, 4, 14
Joanna ('the Mad'), Infanta of Spain, 69, 184, 200, 204, 207, 231; weds Philip of Burgundy, 163; inherits Castile, 194–95; meets sister Catherine in England, 205; her children, 206
John I, King of Portugal, 26
John II, King of Aragon (father of King Ferdinand), 35, 42–45, 71, 93; and Catalan insurrection, 100; as consort to Queen Blanche of Navarre, 204
John II, King of Castile (father of Queen Isabella), 35
John II, King of Portugal, 152, 153, 162, 171–72; and Columbus, 47–48, 52–54, 57, 120–21; his support for exploration, 124–25; and Treaty of Alcaçovas, 124; and bull *Inter cetera*, 126; avoids colonial rivalry, 151; his death, 151
Juan of Spain, Infante, 79, 121, 140; marriage to Margaret of Austria, 136, 163; death, 166
Julius II, Pope (Giuliano della Rovere), 202–203, 217, 218; and anti-Venetian coalition, 207–208; creates Holy League against France, 209; summons Fifth Lateran Council, 209; commissions tomb from Michelangelo, 210–11. *See also* Della Rovere, Giuliano

Kara Mustapha, Grand Vizier, 228–29
Khan, Genghis, 2
Khan, Kublai, 1–2, 27
Knights of St John (Hospitallers), 40; expelled from Rhodes, 224

La Gordas, the 170
La Guardia, and ritual murder charge there, 58
Ladislaus, King of Poland, 18
Las Casas, Bartholomew de, 108–109; his *Historia de las Indias*, 105; quoted, 149; and campaign for native rights, 234–35
Las Palmas, 106
League of Venice, against France, 136–37, 138, 163, 168
Lefèvre, Jacques, 93

Leghorn, 86, 133
Leo X, Pope (Giovanni de' Medici), 99, 172, 216–17, 218–19; created cardinal, 83, 85; and Luther, 221
León, absorbed in Castile, 23
Leonor, Queen of Portugal, 121
Lima, Peru, 244
Linz, 20
Lisbon, 24–31 passim, 47, 52–53; Columbus's landing there, 117, 120; its slave market, 28, 150, 154; commercial expansion, 165, 232
Lithuania, 18; joined to Poland, 198, 215
Livy, 8
Lorraine, Charles, Duke of, 229
Louis of Orleans, Duke, *see* Louix XII, King of France
Louis II, King of Hungary and Bohemia, betrothed as infant to Mary of Austria, 215; dies at Mohacs, 224
Louis XI, King of France, 42, 81, 167; and relations with Italy, 38, 94, 101; and Netherlands, 67–75 passim
Louis XII, King of France, 95, 167, 174–75, 176, 177, 182, 200, 203; his Italian claims, 167–68, 216; treats with Ferdinand, 168, 169, 179, 182 204; divorce and re-marriage, 174–75; his army defeated, 182–83; and anti-Venetian coalition, 207–209; defies pope, 209–10; 3rd marriage and death, 210
Louis XIV, King of France, 229
Low Countries, *see* Netherlands
Lucca, 94
Luther, Martin, 17, 83, 101, 129, 172, 216, 218, 219, 220; and Emperor Charles, 221; and peasants' revolt, 222
Luxembourg, 68
Lyons, 66

Machiavelli, Niccolò, 20, 86, 99, 102, 177, 179, 202
Madeira, 27
Madeiras, the, 29, 157
Magellan, Ferdinand, 127; his voyage, 236–38, 239
Magna Carta, 4
Magyars, *see under* Hungary
Maimonides, 12
Mainz, printing there, 31; as archdiocese, 219
Malacca, 236, 246
Malaga, siege of, 47, 52, 56
Malateste family, 178; Sigismondo, 90
Malay Peninsula, 246; wrongly identified by Columbus, 189
Malines, 71, 74
Manuel I, King of Portugal, 80, 152, 154, 167, 220, 232, 245–46, 247; claims widowed Infanta Isabella, 162, 164, 165; and expulsion of Jews, 164–65; weds Infanta

Manuel I (cont.)
  Maria, 187, 231; and Magellan, 237; agrees on division of Orient with Charles V, 238
Map making, 8
Marchena, Juan Perez de 49
Marco Polo, 27, 106, 110, 153, 232; The Travels of Marco Polo, 78
Margaret of Austria (daughter of Maximilian), later Duchess of Savoy, regent of Netherlands, 70–76 passim, 136–37, 208; weds Juan of Spain, 163; widowed, 166; second widowhood, 205
Margaret of York, 68, 70, 74, 76
Maria, Infanta of Spain (daughter of Isabella and Ferdinand), 80, 163–64, 167; weds Manuel of Portugal, 187, 231
Mariagalante, the (alternatively, Santa Maria), 140
Marignano, battle of, 217
Marina, Doña, and Cortés, 240
Marseilles, 13–14, 38
Martinez, Ferrand, 34
Martinique, 117; landfall on 4th Voyage, 188
Mary of Austria (daughter of Joanna and Philip), 215, 224; as Queen of Hungary, 220; as regent of Netherlands, 222
Mary of Burgundy (daughter of Charles the Bold, first wife of Maximilian), 72, 130, 152, 218; her marriage, 68–69, 73; death, 70
Mary I, Queen of England, 184, 227
Mary of England (sister of Henry VIII), 210, 216
Matthias, Corvinus, King of Hungary, 18, 19, 73, 74, 214–15
Maximilian I, Emperor, 19–20, 102, 103, 130–32, 161, 168–69, 199–200, 211, 213–20; and defence of Low Countries, 49, 70–76, 80; weds Mary of Burgundy, 68–70; relations with son Philip of Burgundy, 74, 200; as King of Romans, 73–74, 103; and Brittany, 75–76; battle against Ottomans, 80–81; invites French help, 103; character and aspirations, 129–30, 136–37, 178, 200, 213; conflicts with Reichstag, 131; weds Bianca Sforza, 132; and Fornovo, 137–38; and anti-Venetian coalition, 208–209; loses Trieste and Fiume, 208; never crowned emperor, 209–218; joins Holy League, 209; dies at Wels, 218
Maya civilization, 238–39, 242
Medici Bank, 13, 66, 72, 97, 160
Medici, Cosimo de', 32, 83, 85–88
Medici family, 12–13, 86, 92, 179; and Vatican, 84–85, 92; its decline, 95–96, 97
Medici, Giovanni de', see Leo X, Pope
Medici, Giuliano de', his assassination, 13, 84
Medici, Lorenzo de' ('the Magnificent'), 13, 14, 132, 197–98; and Pazzi conspiracy,
    13, 83, 100–101; and Vatican, 83–85; and Renaissance, 85–86, 88, 92–96; weds Clarisse Orsini, 91; and internal Italian conflicts, 93–94; last illness and death, 95–97, 101
Medici, Maddalena de', 83
Medici, Marie de', 204
Medici, Piero de', 97, 132, 177; dies in battle, 182–83
Medina del Campo, 66, 195
Medinaceli, Count de, 49–50, 57, 58
Memling, Hans, 70
Méndez, Diego, 191–93
Mercenaries, Swiss, 20, 46, 133, 135, 137, 176, 178, 217; German, 72, 214, 222, 223; Italian and Spanish, 178
Mers el-Kebir, captured for Spain, 207
Mesta, Spanish wool syndicate, 64, 66, 79
Michelangelo Buonarroti, 85, 87, 95; his 'Last Judgment', 93; his 'Hercules', 97; his lost 'Cupid', 178, 179; his "Pieta," 177–78, 181; his 'Moses', 211; and Sistine Ceiling, 93, 211
Michelis, Fiametta de', 181
Miguel, child prince of Portugal, birth and death, 166
Milo, Adriana de, 133
Milan (and Duchy), 11, 81, 85–86, 102, 132, 200, 217, 222; and Sforza influence, 89–90, 94, 95; and internal Italian rivalries, 98; joins League of Venice, 136; over-run by French, 168–69, 208; Sforza rule restored, 209–10
Milton, John, his Brief History of Muscovia, 19
Mina, trading post, 124
Ming dynasty, 65
Mohacs, battle of, 224
Moluccas, the (Spice Islands), 237, 238, 246
Mombasa, 152
Mona Passage, the, 188
Mongols, 27, 65; invasion of Europe, 1–2, 5; and Nestorian heresy, 5; Tatars, 17, 18
Monte Cassino, 12
Monte Christi peninsula, 115
Montefeltro family, 91
Montefeltro, Federigo da, of Urbino, 32, 94, 179; his library, 91
Montefeltro, Guidobaldi da, 179
Montezuma, Aztec 'emperor', 241
Montserrat island, 141
Moors (Muslims of North Africa and Iberia), their golden age, 21–22; their decline, 24, 55–56; religious differences and persecution, 33–34, 60–61, 166; and Inquisition, 37–38, 55; as 'Moriscos', 37, 60; and Granada as last enclave, 38, 45–47, 55–56; King Ferdinand's undertaking to, 55–56, 60; expelled from Spain, 60–61; their agricultural prowess, 66
Moravia, 18

More, Sir Thomas, 221; his *Utopia*, 93, 234

Morocco, 'Portuguese obsession', 237, 247

Moscow, Duchy of, 18–19

Mozambique, 152

Muhammad, the Prophet, 33

Muhammad II, Sultan of Turkey, 2, 39–40

Nancy, battle of, 67, 75

Naples, 15, 169; and 'Kingdom of Two Sicilies', 93–94; threatens Tuscany, 93–94; entered by French troops, 135–36

Narbonne, 22

Navarre, as disputed kingdom, 25, 71, 175–76; civil war there, 203–204; and Ferdinand of Aragon, 204, 207, 210

Navidad, 120, 121, 140–41; township established, 114; abandoned, 144

Navigational progress, 26, 47

Netherlands (Low Countries), 63–68, 70–71; ownership disputed, 49; as refuge for Jews, 59, 79; French and Spanish designs there, 67–76 passim, 102, 214; thriving economy, 69–70, 79; attitude to Maximilian, 69–72; its Estates General, 73; and Habsburg succession, 80; union with Castile, 194; dominates international trade, 226–27; portion as Dutch Republic, 247

'New World', as expression, 38

New York Public Library, 117

Newfoundland, 9

Nicaragua, 189, 236

Nicholas V, Pope, 31–32

Niña the, 77–78, 106–26 passim, 140, 146; brings Columbus home, 150

Norsemen, 155

Nuñez de Balboa, Vasco, 190, 243; discovers Pacific Ocean, 127, 236

Ojeda, Alonso de, *see* Hojeda

Oran, captured for Spain, 207

Orinoco river, 158

Orsini, Clarisse, weds Lorenzo de' Medici, 91

Orsini family, 91, 98, 133, 137, 202; deserts to French, 173, 174

Orwell, George, and his *Nineteen Eighty-Four*, 250

Otranto, beseiged by Turks, 39–40, 94, 138; Turkish withdrawal, 49, 91

Ottoman Empire (*see also under* Turkey), its military power, 1–4, 20; attacked by Hungary, 17; battle at Varna, 18; its control of Romanian coast, 49; as refuge for Jews, 59; assault upon Europe, 80–81

Ovando, Nicolás de, 186, 193, 195, 235; loses fleet in storm, 188

Oxford, Colet's lectures there, 93

Palaeologue, Sophia, 19

Palaeologus, John, Byzantine emperor, 87

Palermo, 93

Paloma of Toledo, 34

Palos (de la Frontera), 48–49, 77, 78, 98, 121

Panama, and Isthmus, 236, 243

Paolo, Giovanni di, 8

Paper-making, 24

Paria Peninsula, 158, 160

Paul IV, Pope, 227

Pavia, battle of, 101, 222, 223

Pazzi family, 92; and conspiracy, 13, 83, 84, 100; amnestied, 94

Pazzi, Giacomo de, 13

Pelayo, Don, 23

Perestrello, Felipa (wife of Columbus), 31, 47, 48

Perugia, 172; and Baglioni family, 137, 202

Perugino, Pietro Vanucci, 93

Pesaro, 102

Petrarch, 12

Philip the Good, Duke of Burgundy, 14

Philip, Duke of Burgundy (son of Maximilian), 74, 76, 130–31; his birth, 69, 70, 71; and Joanna of Spain, 136, 204–205, 208, 215, 231; relations with France, 168; wins Castile through Joanna, 194–95; terminates father's regency of Netherlands, 200; as Count of Flanders, 200; meeting with Henry VII of England, 205; dies at Burgos, 206

Philip II, King of Spain (son of Emperor Charles), 227–28

Philippines, the, 237, 238, 247

Pico della Mirandola, Giovanni, 95, 96

Pierre of Beaujeu, 76

Pinta the, 77–78, 106–109, 111, 112, 114–15; return voyage, 115–17, 124

Pinturicchio, Bernado il, 7, 100

Pinzón family, 140

Pinzón, Martin Alonso, 78, 108–109, 111, 112, 142, 161; as captain, 106; deserts Columbus, 111–12; rejoins Columbus, 115; return voyage, 114–17, 120–21, 124; death, 124

Pinzón, Vicento Yañez, 78, 109, 160–61; as captain, 106; return voyage, 114–17, 120

Pisa, 86, 133, 135, 172; its Archbishop, 13

Pistoia, 86

Pius II, Pope, 15, 90, 202

Pius III, Pope, 202

Pizarro, Francisco, 236, 242–43; his brothers, 242; establishes Lima as capital of Peru, 244

Poland, 17, 18–19, 215; joined to Lithuania, 198; Turkish pressure on, 228–29; and relief of Vienna, 229

Pole, Richard de la, 222

Poliziano (Angelo Ambrogini), 13, 85, 95

Pomerania, 19

Ponce de León, Juan, in Puerto Rico, 235; landfall on Florida, 235–36

Poor Clares, Order, 162, 164

Porras brothers, Diego and Francisco, 186, 187, 188, 190; their rebellion against Columbus, 192–94
Porto Santo, 31, 47
Portugal, and its empire, 22, 67, 231–33, 244–48; its explorers, 9, 27–28, 53–54, 125; liberation from Moors, 23–27; and Hundred Years War, 24; its developing empire, 27–29; and Castile, 29–30, 35, 124–25; bull *Aeterna regis*, 30, 37, 120–21, 125; and Inquisition, 38, 248; rejection of Columbus's project, 47–48; as refuge for Jews, 59; relations with Spain, 80; Columbus's return voyage, 116–17, 120–21; bull *Inter cetera*, 126; expulsion of Jews, 164–66; Oriental stations detailed, 246; impoverished motherland, 246–47; its Jesuit missions, 248
Prato, 86
Prescott, William Hickling, his *Conquest of Mexico*, 241
Prester John, the priest king, 27, 125, 153
Printing, 87; its beginnings, 31–32
Provence, integrated in French kingdom, 38, 161
Prussia, as Hohenzollern dukedom, 18–19
Ptolemy, 8–9, 53
Puerto Rico (Boriquen, St John the Baptist), 142, 247

Quetzalcoatl, god-king, 240

Rabida, La, Franciscan priory, 49
Racialism and racial purity, 22, 60–61; and religious attitudes, 32–38
Raphael, 211
Ravenna, battle there, 209–10
Reconquista, the, 23–24; completion of, 38, 45–47, 51, 55–56
Redonda Island, 141
Reformation, the, 17, 173, 174, 222, 249; and Counter-Reformation, 228
Reichstag, Imperial Diet, 130, 131, 138, 169, 214, 218
Renaissance, the, 6, 20, 89–90, 94–96, 99, 138; its rise, 12, 84–86; its spread from Italy, 15–16, 88, 93, 197–98, 249; and impact of printing, 32; status of Florence, 86–88; and Savonarola, 96, 98, 101
René, Duke of Anjou, 30
Rennes, 75
Reuchlin, Johann, 93
Rhodes, 40, 224
Riario, Girolamo, 92
Riario, Piero, Archbishop of Florence, 92
Richard III, King of England, 49
Rimini, 90; as Malateste power base, 178
Roger II, King of Sicily, 8
Roldán, Francisco, 157–59, 170; drowns, 188
Rome, 7, 102, 201; Ancient, 7, 11; St Peter's

Cathedral, 7, 177, 181, 210, 219; as refuge for Jews, 59; its rivalling clans, 91; embellishment of, 92–93; Castel Sant' Angelo, 93, 134, 178, 179, 180–81; and Savonarola, 96; French entry, 98; Palazzo Sforza–Cesarini, 99; Palazzo Venezia, 134; Church of Trinità dei Monti, 134; jubilee year, 181; under Pope Julius, 202; Church of San Pietro in Vincoli, 211; sacked, 101, 223. *See also under* Vatican
Rosselli, Cosimo, 93
Rousillon, 71, 76

Sabacz, captured by Turks, 224
St Ann's Bay, Jamaica, 147
St Christopher, 140
St Stephen of Hungary, 4
St Ursula, 141
Salamanca, 51, 52, 195; its university, 51, 166; its royal residence, 163, 166
Salonika, 79
Sanchez, Rodrigo, 77, 109
Sancia, Princess of Squillace, 175, 177
San Giorgio Bank, 10, 31
San Jorge Island, 141
Sanlúcar de Barrameda, end of 4th Voyage, 194
San Martin Island, 141
San Salvador (Guanahani, Watlings Island), 139; Columbus makes landfall there, 109–11; identified as Grand Turk Island, 110
San Sebastian, 66
Santa Anastasia Island, 141
Santa Cruz Island (St Croix), 141
Santa Fé, 55, 56, 57
Santa Maria (Azores), Columbus's reception there, 116
Santa Maria, the (flagship of 1st Voyage), 77–78, 106, 108, 112, 143; wrecked, 113–15
Santa Maria, Bishop Pablo de, 35
Santa Maria de la Concepción (Rum Cay) Island, 110
Santangel, Luis de, 46, 50, 54–55; and Columbus's project, 54–55, 57, 58; Columbus's report (his *Letter to Santangel*), 115, 117, 120
Santiago de Cuba, 239
Santo Domingo, third Hispaniola base, 157, 158–59, 186, 192, 236, 239; scene of catastrophes, 188
Saragossa, 22; and Inquisition, 37
Sardinia, 10, 15, 42, 67; and expulsion of Jews, 59
Sargasso Sea, 115
Savonarola, Girolamo, 85, 102, 132, 138; his assault on corruption, 88, 96, 97, 98; a French 'holy crusade', 98; his 'bonfire of the vanities', 101
Savoy, Duke Philibert of, 205

Scandinavia, 66
Second World War, 54
Segovia, 44, 195
Selim I, Sultan, 199
Senior, Abraham, 44, 55, 58; and expulsion of Jews, 59
Serbia, 17
Seville, 154; and Inquisition, 37; Columbus in retreat there, 154, 156, 195
Sforza, Ascanio, Cardinal, 142; electoral contest, 99
Sforza, Bianca Maria, 215; weds Maximilian, 132
Sforza, Caterina, 178–79
Sforza family, 89
Sforza, Francesco, 89, 168
Sforza, Giovanni, of Pesaro, 177, 178; weds Lucrezia Borgia, 102
Sforza, Jacopo, 89
Sforza, Ludovico ('the Moor'), of Milan, 89–90, 94, 95, 99, 102, 132, 136, 168, 176–79 passim; weds Beatrice d' Este, 94; captured by French, 95
Sicily, 6, 15, 37, 42, 67; and expulsion of Jews, 59; its commerce, 66; and Papal States, 89
Siena, 90, 94, 98; its *Palio*, 173
Sixtus IV, Pope, 13, 46, 69, 93, 100, 172; his bull *Aeterna regis*, 30, 37, 120–21, 125; and Inquisition, 36–37; his embellishment of Rome, 92; death, 84
Slaves, 23, 28, 60; transported to New World, 233; and Laws of Burgos, 233–34
Sobieski, John, King of Poland, 229
Spain, Moorish conquest of, 21–22; and racial purity, 22, 34, 61; Christian re-conquest, 23–24; religious differences and persecution, 33–35; conquest of Granada, 35, 55–56, 79; relations with Vatican, 35–36, 103; Inquisition, 36–38, 43, 48–49, 55; and Italy, 39, 95; as European power, 42–43, 45–46, 60–61; Columbus's proposal, 49–52, 57–58; expulsion of Jews, 54–60, 78–79, 125; expulsion of Moors, 60–61; its commerce, 65–66; and France, 71–72, 76; Columbus's 1st Voyage, 77; and Portugal, 28–80 passim; and bull *Inter cetera*, 126; as dwindling empire, 247–48. *See also* Aragon *and* Castile
Strasbourg, 31
Suleiman II ('the Magnificent'), Sultan of Turkey, 222; storms Balkans, 223–24; crushes Hungary, 224–25
Switzerland, and Holy Roman Empire, 16; its mercenaries, 20, 46, 135, 137, 217
Syphillis, 124, 142

Tabasco (Mexico), 240
Taino tribes, 110, 112, 113, 141, 147, 188; their language, 110

Talamanca tribes, 189–90
Talavera Commission, 52, 54
Talavera, Hernando de, 52, 60; arraigned, 56–57
Tangier, 28
Tatars, *see under* Mongols
Templars (Order of Christ), 27
Teneriffe, 107
Tenochtitlán, Aztec capital, 241–42
Terreros, Pedro de, 187, 188; dies in skirmish, 193
Teutonic Knights, 17, 18–19
Tobacco smoking, 112
Toledo, 44–45, 162; Moorish conquest, 21, 23, 34; religious conflict, 35
Tolfa, alum deposits there, 92
Tordesillas, Treaty of, 126, 149, 151, 155, 231, 237; Joanna's residence there, 206
Torquemada, Tomá de, 37, 50; his doctrine, 55
Torres, Antonio de, 140, 145, 148–49, 187, 188
Torres, Luis de, interpreter, 78, 111–12
Tortuga, 113
Toscanelli, Paolo, 47, 92–93, 106, 125
Tremouille, Louis de la, 203, 222
Triano, Rodrigo de, 109
Trinidad, 158
Tristán, Diego, 190
Turkey, and Turks (*see also* Ottoman Empire; *under* Islam), 128–29; its threats to Italy, 38–39; and Otranto, 39, 91, 94; succession to Sultanate, 39–40; Europe's wars against, 77; crushes Hungary, 216; ultimate extent, 228–29; defeated at Vienna, 229
Tuscany, 85. *See also under* Florence

Urbino, Montefeltro duchy, 91, 179

Valencia, 15, 23, 100
Valladolid, 44, 162, 195–96; Laws of, 35
Valois, House of, *see under individuals*
Varna, battle of, 18
Vasari, Giorgio, 95
Vatican (*see also under* Rome), 98; its library, 31–32; its influence in Europe, 35–36; Jem as captive, 80, 88; and corrupt practices, 81, 83–85, 91–92, 181–82; and Medicis, 83–85; Renaissance influence, 88; its territorial possessions, 88–89; College of Cardinals, 92, 125; and Sistine Chapel, 92–93; Raphael Rooms, 93; Borgia Apartments, 100; Curia, 101
Velasquez, Diego, governor of Cuba, 239, 241
Venezuela, 158, 160
Venice (Venetian Republic), 65, 130–33, 179–80, 198, 199, 202, 214; its trading posts, 3, 11; its influence, 14; as publishing capital, 32; wars against Turks, 38–

Venice (*cont.*)
39, 80–81, 180; and Habsburgs, 73, 103; League of Venice, 136; and sea route to India, 152; spice trade, 153; rivalry with Milan, 168, 176; anti-Venetian coalition, 207–209; joins France against Charles V, 216; in tribute to Porte, 224; finances Egyptian fleet, 246

Vera Cruz, 240–41

Veragua (Mosquito Gulf), 190, 196

Verrocchio, Andrea del, 94

Vespucci, Amerigo, outshines Columbus with fallacious claim, 160

Vienna, 73, 74, 199, 214; threatened by Turks, 199, 225, 228–29; its St Stephen's Cathedral, 215, 229

Vigo, 124

Villach, battle of, 81

Villon, François, 12

Vinci, Leonardo da, 89, 94–95, 97, 132, 168, 208; designs air-borne machine, 64; his greatness, 94–95; his 'Last Supper', 95, 177; his 'Mona Lisa', 95

Virgin Islands, 141

Visconti family, 14, 89, 92, 94, 132

Visconti, Giangaleazzo, Duke of Milan, 92

Viterbo, 133, 135

Vizcaína, the, 187, 190

Warbeck, Perkin, 74, 76, 156

Wars of the Roses, 13, 74

Windward Passage, 112

Wittenberg, its university, 218, 221

Wolsey, Thomas, Cardinal, 218

Xavier, St Francis, 248

Yucatan, and lands of Maya, 238–39, 240

Zacuto, Abraham, astronomer, 47, 51, 52, 125, 164, 165; expelled from Spain, 59